# JAZZ-FUSIO
## Blue Notes and Purpl

*Ken Trethewey*

*To Rick
With Best Wishes
Ken Trethewey*

*Jazz-Fusion Books*

First published December 2009
Second edition: January 2016

Jazz-Fusion Books
Gravesend Cottage
Torpoint
Cornwall PL11 2LX
United Kingdom

ISBN: 978-0-9926573-1-4

©2009, 2016 Ken Trethewey

All rights reserved. No part of this publication may be reproduced, stored in a retrieval system, or transmitted in any form, or by any means, electronic, mechanical, photocopying, recording or otherwise, without the prior permission of Jazz-Fusion Books.

For Chris, Joe and Helen, my musical family,
who love music as much as I do,
and
for James Brushwood,
who, in 2004, wanted to know more about jazz.
(Sorry it took so long, James.)

*Publications by Ken Trethewey in the Jazz-Fusion Series:*

*John McLaughlin: The Emerald Beyond (2008, 2013, 2016)*
*Pat Metheny: The Way Up is White (2008, 2012)*
*Jazz-Fusion: Blue Notes and Purple Haze (2009, 2016)*
*Herbie Hancock: Blue Chip Keyboardist (2010)*
*Miles Davis: Dark Prince (2011)*
*Weather Report: Electric Red (2012)*
*The Brecker Brothers: Funky Sea, Funky Blue (2014)*

*The Chick Corea Elektric Band performing at the Royal Festival Hall, London in 1991. Left to right: Eric Marienthal, Chick Corea, John Patitucci, Frank Gambale. (Photo: Ken Trethewey)*

## Contents

| | |
|---|---|
| JAZZ-FUSION: | 1 |
| Foreword | 9 |
| Foreword to the Second Edition | 16 |
| Jazz Roots | 17 |
| The Early Players | 24 |
| Swing, the Big Bands and Duke Ellington | 28 |
| Duke Ellington: Selected Discography | 31 |
| Gillespie, Parker and Bebop | 33 |
| Jazz Piano | 40 |
| Jazz Guitar | 43 |
| Free Jazz | 45 |
| References to Part 1 | 49 |
| Introduction: What is jazz-fusion? | 52 |
| Jazz-fusion: You either love it or hate it. | 58 |
| The Late-1940s and the Post-War Permissiveness | 59 |
| The Boost From Technology | 60 |
| The Mid-1950s: Elvis, Buddy and the Birth of Rock 'n' Roll | 61 |
| The Beat Movement | 62 |
| The Late 1950s: British Art Schools Take On The Music Business | 63 |
| 1960: Like No Others – The Beatles | 66 |
| 1962: British Rhythm & Blues, Alexis Korner, John Mayall and The Rolling Stones | 68 |
| 1963: John Mayall's Bluesbreakers | 70 |
| 1964: The Graham Bond Organisation | 72 |
| The mid-1960s | 74 |
| Rock Music and the Cult of the Guitar | 76 |
| 1966: Cream | 77 |
| 1966: Jimi Hendrix | 80 |
| 1966: Soft Machine | 82 |
| 1966: NYC, NY | 86 |
| 1966: Chicago IL | 89 |
| 1967: Blood Sweat & Tears | 91 |
| 1967: Chicago | 93 |
| 1968: Jon Hiseman's Colosseum | 94 |
| 1968: Jazz-Rock Fusion in Hindsight | 99 |
| 1969: Fusions Everywhere | 101 |
| 1969: Jazz In A Snapshot | 105 |
| 1969: Miles Davis Experiments | 108 |
| 1969: If | 111 |
| 1969: Dreams | 113 |
| So, Which Was The First Jazz-Rock Fusion Band? | 115 |

New Instruments: The Electric Piano ................................................................ 119
Keyboard Synthesisers ....................................................................................... 121
Drum Machines .................................................................................................. 121
Electrifying Music .............................................................................................. 122
Guitar Synthesisers ............................................................................................. 124
The Electronic Wind Instrument (EWI) ............................................................. 126
Bob Dylan and Folk-Rock Fusion ...................................................................... 127
Funk .................................................................................................................... 130
The Impact of Jazz on Popular Music: Pop-Jazz ............................................... 134
Acid Jazz and Smooth Jazz: Kinds of Jazz-Pop ................................................. 138
Jazz: The End of the Road? ................................................................................ 140
Concluding remarks ........................................................................................... 147
References to Part 2 ........................................................................................... 148
A Timeline of the Main Events in Jazz-Fusion .................................................. 153
Early jazz-fusion ................................................................................................. 157
Jazz-rock fusion .................................................................................................. 160
Miles Davis (1926-91) ....................................................................................... 162
Joe Zawinul (1932-2007), Wayne Shorter (b1933): Weather Report ................ 172
Herbie Hancock (b1940) .................................................................................... 181
John McLaughlin (b1942) .................................................................................. 187
Chick Corea (b1941) .......................................................................................... 193
Tony Williams (1945-1997) ............................................................................... 197
Billy Cobham (b1944) ........................................................................................ 199
Pat Metheny (b1954) .......................................................................................... 202
The Brecker Brothers: Randy (b1945) and Michael (1949-2007) ..................... 206
David Sanborn (b1945) ...................................................................................... 211
Jaco Pastorius (1951-1987) ................................................................................ 214
Stanley Clarke (b1951) ...................................................................................... 216
Marcus Miller (b1959) ....................................................................................... 219
Bill Evans (b1958) ............................................................................................. 221
Dave Weckl (b1960) .......................................................................................... 223
The Crusaders: Joe Sample (b1939), Wilton Felder (b1940), Nesbert 'Stix' Hooper (b1938), Wayne Henderson (b1939) .................................................... 224
Tom Scott (b1948) ............................................................................................. 228
Joni Mitchell (b1943) ......................................................................................... 229
Larry Carlton (b1948) ........................................................................................ 231
Yellowjackets ..................................................................................................... 232
References to Part 3 ........................................................................................... 238
Selected Albums and DVDs to Illustrate This Book ......................................... 239
Glossary ............................................................................................................. 244
Jazz-Fusion timeline: ......................................................................................... 250
Index ................................................................................................................... 257

# Foreword

This is the first book in a series. It started out as one book and became eight. There may yet be more. The series is about a form of jazz - a music hybrid - that I shall call jazz-fusion, something we might describe as a music *genre*. Jazz-fusion is not a new term; some people call it jazz-rock or just fusion. In truth there are many fusions of jazz: jazz with rock, folk, classical, Indian music, African music... to name just some. Perhaps *con*fusion might be a better word. I'll explain exactly what I mean by the names later. There's too much to write about jazz in one book, and in any case it's jazz-fusion I particularly want to cover.

Jazz-rock fusion evolved from about 1965 onwards and is still played today, although we don't really call it that any more, and there are other sub-styles of jazz that have emerged since then. Names we use today have been applied comparatively recently so were not used at the time the styles were created. A common element is that the music was intended to be 'progressive', and so to describe the music as prog-jazz could also be an accurate description.

I decided to write this book simply because it did not already exist. Why don't more people write books about music? Perhaps it's because it is not very easy to describe sounds. This is the sort of book I would buy instantly. I have very much enjoyed writing it and I sincerely hope you enjoy reading it. I have always found that the pleasure I get from listening to music increases greatly if I can read something about the music. I devour album sleeve notes, which have varied over the years from useless to wonderful. Recently, especially in jazz, they have improved enormously. In the 1970s it was unfashionable to provide information about an album. Many did not even list the musicians playing on it, something that still happens today in other genres, although not much in jazz. It is usually only 'compilation' albums that have useless sleeve notes. It should be against the law not to say who plays on an album. Facts matter very much, as does musical context. This book is intended to fill that gap in a broad musical genre.

Throughout my project I was inspired by Miles Davis's album *Aura* (1989) in which the titles of the tracks are assigned colours. Thus my book titles and descriptions also include colours. I think it's a nice correlation because description of music is often associated with painting and the word 'tone' has a certain commonality. It's also the case that the jazz-fusion I intend to focus on has characteristically rich sounds and it is easy to think of this kind of music as especially colourful: that is what originally attracted me to it. In Part 2, 'Technicolor' is a good description too because jazz-rock fusion was created as electronic instruments became available, so there has always been a technological element to jazz-fusion that is not a key element of 'pure' jazz.

The music fusion that occurred in the 1960s originated from combining the blue notes of jazz and the purple haze of rock. That revolution broke down musical barriers that had existed between different branches of music, and numerous fusions of jazz with other forms followed, such as the classical musics of Europe, Asia and Africa, American folk or country music and popular music too.

The careers of many top jazz musicians can be marked by their achievements in a particular genre and hence logically represented by a single colour. For example, as the *Dark Prince*, Miles Davis could only be represented by black, whereas Chick Corea's *Spanish Art* invokes a sense of hot, arid ochres and John McLaughlin's early mystic roots are associated with emerald green. Herbie Hancock is the *Blue Chip Keyboardist*, not only an icon of jazz piano but also a leading innovator with silicon technology encapsulated into synthesisers and computers. Red is the colour to be noticed, and the contributions to jazz made by Joe Zawinul and Wayne Shorter in Weather Report are as notable as any.

In *The Way Up Is White*, I describe how Pat Metheny's music is amongst the most diverse of all top jazz musicians. In the electromagnetic spectrum, white light is comprised of all of the familiar colours of the rainbow, so Pat is naturally represented by every shade and hue - hence white. In the author's view, the pinnacle of Pat's jazz-fusion was reached by the project entitled *The Way Up*, but the path at the start of a long series of innovative jazz-fusion albums essentially began with the album *Pat Metheny Group* (1977), which Pat has referred to as the 'White' album.

The musicians' discographies in the books are as complete as I can make them at the time of publishing each edition. The cataloguing of the recordings of musicians I write about is an on-going task. The dates given are generally the dates when the albums first appeared. Of course, albums are constantly being reissued, but that information is quite useless for an appreciation of the context in which the music resides. It is only of use if you need to acquire that particular edition of a disc.

As for the lists of albums at the back of the books, I would have liked to assign the correct name of every musician to every track. In reality, that would have been a gargantuan task. (It was pretty big anyway!) And in the end, some album notes did not provide enough detail. I hope that the compromise I have made does not spoil your enjoyment too much. There are lots of ways in which you can carry out crosschecking amongst the data I have given you. Again, it should provide you with extra fun and interest. I was always intrigued by Pete Frame's idea of "Rock Family Trees" that showed the relationships between rock musicians and the groups they played in. I tried to develop similar ones for this book but gave up because jazzers are so fluid in their work. The relationships are extraordinarily difficult to draw and the trees I came up with quickly developed into a hopeless tangle of meaningless lines! What came out of that exercise was the series of timeline charts that I have included in this book. I hope there is sufficient detail here to enable you to piece things together for yourself.

The results of my work have grown quite big as the project has progressed but I hope you will be able to dip into the material, rather than read it all at once. If you are unfamiliar with jazz, I do recommend that you approach this book in the order in which it is presented because it may not make sense otherwise. You may be tempted to look at the later sections first, which is fine if you are comfortable with the music already.

Having lived through the entire period of this book, I was surprised at how much I had lost the 'feeling' of the times when it came into being. I had to work hard to recreate it in my mind because it was essential to try to understand what happened, when and why, if I was to attempt to tell you about it. I hope I have succeeded in some small way. If you go out and buy some of the music I describe, and derive anything like the fun I have got from listening to it, I will have achieved my goal. Of course, tastes will differ widely and I accept the fact that you may spend money on something you later hate. I hope that I have provided sufficient information here so that it does not happen.

I accept full responsibilities for any errors of fact and apologise in advance if my personal opinions do not match yours: author's prerogative, as they say! If you write a better book than this, do let me know. I promise to buy it.

I want this book to reach as wide an audience as possible, so a lot of what I shall write is targeted at those who know little about jazz. I have therefore tried to explain musical terms and techniques, and I have included a glossary that may help to explain some of the terminology of music and musicians. I apologise in advance if that's a bit too simplistic for some readers.

I have also adopted a stylistic approach with which some readers may not feel comfortable. Opinionated authors can invoke bad reactions from their readers when they disagree. However, I have been encouraged by the likes of BBC film critic Mark Kermode who has led by example. Well-known for his vociferously expressed opinions about films, many in his audiences feel he is justified in doing so by his deep knowledge about his subject. Historians must be beyond reproach; they must be unbiased and as accurate in their reporting of facts as possible. (I am a jazz fan, not a historian.) However, the use of words to describe music is inevitably subjective. Therefore, music critics, unlike historians, express their opinions, although hopefully from an informed point of view. I have listened to this music for all of my adult life and hope I have a sound knowledge upon which to base my arguments. As a scientist and engineer, I have also tried hard to support my arguments by good, logical reasoning, but in the end, it remains just a viewpoint that many readers may disagree with. I am, however, independent with no axes to grind.

So what about jazz? Jazz is a peculiar word. What other words can you think of that use 'j' and 'z' no less than three times in just four letters? Scrabble players may love it, but I think this alone ensures that a lot of people never listen to it. They turn and run at the first sign of an encounter with this strange stuff. People who like jazz are regarded as eccentric. After all, it feels so much more natural to stay close to the likes and dislikes of our friends than it does to be different – to go out on our own...

Going out on your own: it's like being some kind of explorer. Attempts to commence a journey into the music, grouped by commercial interests into the idiom known as jazz, are rather like trying to find a path through the Amazon rainforest. The expedition might be one of the most wonderful things you do in your life, but a few poisonous snakes might also bite you along the way. Few people even attempt it, preferring to ride along the entirely unchallenging paved highway in their comfortable, mass-produced cars. After a while it becomes a habit. With their eyes directed towards their in-car entertainment, they don't even notice the scenery.

What about those of us who seek something extra in our lives? Is there more to music than banal, often aggressive chanting, or cloned boy-bands? As Dyer said, "Jazz is something that people arrive at when they become bored with the banality of pop music." [1] Well, perhaps. Music can be one of the greatest challenges to the human intellect, but it can also be the medium by which we are manipulated to feed 'the market' and make some people hideously rich. Some well-known modern TV shows are just the latest examples of that. The parlous state of the music industry seems to indicate that we have arrived at a point where it is more fun to scour the Internet looking for free downloads than it is to sit back in a good armchair and be carried off on a sonorous adventure.

So where do I start? Is there a *Lonely Planet* Guide to Good Music that will provide a map through the jungle, a sightseer's guide and a snake-spotter's primer? Yes, you've just found it. I make no apology for the fact that I am going to try to make you – not just like, but *love* jazz, for jazz is far more than just strange instrumental music. To paraphrase Miles Davis, good music is the best feeling you can have with your clothes on. I'm not going to cover rock or pop music in any depth, except where I need to explain where this jazz has come from. My inspiration for this project was obtained by the blank looks I get from people when I say I like jazz. They seem not to have the faintest idea what I mean. There are now so many ways of taking control of your own entertainment that young people can grow up without ever being exposed to this type of music. They don't hear it on the radio or TV channels they tune in to. They don't hear it at school or at work and their friends don't play it. If their parents play it then they take no notice or leave the room because it's not cool to like what your parents listen to. It's not surprising then that they have no idea what jazz is, or worse still, what they are missing.

These days we seem obsessed with the adoration of mediocrity: the triumph of celebrity over craft. Why do we so openly ignore something that very gifted people have spent their lives trying to make as exciting and beautiful as possible? Perhaps it's because the music industry doesn't profit enough from it and, after all, we generally buy what the industrialists, not the artists, want us to have. Broadly speaking, jazz is musicians' music, a highly developed art form for the discerning ear, although it hasn't always been that way. Don't be put off by the idea that you might actually need to think a little. Jazz can be appreciated at many levels, but, as with good food and fine wine, the experience will be much more pleasurable with a little education.

Like all good art forms, jazz communicates in such a way as to invite the listener to ask questions. It offers new ways of thinking, new kinds of experience – sometimes uncomfortable. If you're not careful it can even bite, but it also offers far greater levels of satisfaction to those willing to accept the challenge. Jazz, like other art forms, has had its ups and downs. Right now, it is at one of its lowest ebbs. So few people get to hear it, yet when they do, many are smitten by it. In fact, jazz-fusion has been so successful that jazz is now an intrinsic part of many of the musical forms being played today.

Jazz needs greater visibility right now. Thus I offer to be your guide through this musical jungle. Let me be clear from the outset that this book is intended to teach you what is good about jazz, not necessarily to decry certain music or musicians. My aim is to show you how wonderful you can feel listening to it, especially when armed with a small amount of extra information about the subject. But please expect to invest a little time listening because this is often not superficial music; I frequently listen to an album many times before I feel I understand it.

Over the course of this series of books I shall review many albums. Most of them you can still buy fairly easily, especially on the internet as I myself have done to fill in the gaps in my collection. I have adopted a familiar 'five star' system for my personal assessments. It roughly conforms to the sequence: (*) =

Forget the stars, this one's a turkey; (**) = Okay, but I wouldn't stay home from the pub to listen to it; (***) = Good enough to play when your friends come around; (****) = Save your beer money to buy this – it's healthier for you too; (*****) = Do anything – mortgage your wife or sell the car, to get a copy of this record. Please don't expect many five star awards: I jealously guard them.

As part of a commentary, it is sometimes necessary to be negatively critical about some of the music. I think you would expect that from me. I have been selective in what I intend to discuss – author's prerogative. Of course that does not mean that the things I leave out are, by definition, bad, merely that the choices are a result of listening to and loving jazz for some forty years and that even over that period of time I could not have listened to everything.

I also do not propose to discuss in detail anything prior to Charlie Parker, that is, earlier than the 1940s. For me, the early history of jazz is just that. The excitement really begins with Parker, who instigates a wild journey for the music fan to follow. The music takes in the hues and odours of all corners of the world and is today not restricted to the southern United States, but is truly international. Even so, my discussion of Parker and his peer group is in the context of the Miles Davis story, a topic about which a lot has been written. I have written quite a lot about this subject because I have my own views, which some of you may not agree with. That too is the author's prerogative.

There is a tendency to view a book such as this as an exercise in nostalgia. Whilst I accept that this may be true for some of you, I would prefer this not to be the case because I support the idea that, as Donald Fagen once said, nostalgia inhibits progress. I want to show you that jazz-fusion did not, as some say, end in 1978, but is alive and well, incorporated in much of modern music and as exciting now as it has always been. To achieve my goal I need to describe in detail the music that has brought us to where we are today and implicit in that description is the idea that the music has progressed.

We shall look closely at the process called 'fusion', whereby jazz has absorbed aspects from other forms of music from all over the world: people use the phrase 'world music' in this context. The word 'eclectic' is frequently used to describe the many styles of modern music. Mostly, the fusion involves the blending of jazz with elements of rock music. I shall begin by presenting a short history of jazz because everything needs context and we shall arrive at a greater understanding of why things are like they are if we do so. In Part 3 I shall focus on some significant musicians, and try to explain why their work is so valuable to the most important thing each of us possesses - our soul.

Sadly, it is a fact that there is great pressure on musicians to conform to ever-changing commercial demands. This results in the tendency to view jazz-fusion as old-fashioned, a trend that should be resisted at all costs. In these pages, I shall describe how some musicians have given in to such pressures. Others, most notably the Pat Metheny Group, Michael and Randy Brecker, and John McLaughlin, have met the pressure head-on and simply continued to make jazz-fusion music that just gets better and better. I intend to show that it is okay to indulge in nostalgia so as to enjoy the wonderful back-catalogue of jazz-fusion artists, but that we must not be prevented from encouraging the further progression and development of this great art form. With their continuing sequence of premier league albums, and especially the appropriately titled album *The Way Up* (2005), Pat Metheny's band has shown how. John McLaughlin has also been at the forefront of jazz-fusion and one book in this series is a narrative of his unparalleled contributions to jazz-fusion. In that book I nominate John as the Father of Jazz-Fusion. John continues to make stunning jazz-fusion albums such as *Industrial Zen* (2006), *Floating Point* (2008), *Five Peace Band* (2009), *To The One* (2010) and *Now Hear This* (2012).

## Foreword to the Second Edition

Since writing the first edition of this wide-ranging book, I have been made aware of a large part of the jazz-fusion story that took place in the UK, and was missing from my earlier work. I have therefore tried to rectify these omissions in this new, expanded volume. This enlightenment is due to many regular sessions in the company of my well-informed musical friends, Michael Adams, David Livingstone, and Philip Powell, to whom I express my sincere thanks.

In the ten years or so since this project began there have been a number of highly informative new books published about the musicians and the era, and my work has greatly benefitted from reading them. I have tried to give credit wherever it is due, but if I have missed anything I apologise and promise to make corrections in future editions.

I sincerely hope that readers will find this extended and updated coverage to be more balanced and informative.

Ken Trethewey, January 2016

# PART 1: Indigo Moods: A Brief History of Jazz

## Jazz Roots

Jazz derives from the southern states of the USA, in particular, Louisiana and the greater New Orleans area. Taken up as their own by oppressed black people, jazz has seen many evolutions. In its simplest form one man with a guitar sings the blues - making most of it up on the spot, an immediate expression of his emotions. Yet, after so many decades of intense development, jazz can also be one of the most sophisticated musical forms. Because of its roots amongst the illiterate population, jazz musicians have traditionally played with a very low dependence on written music and improvisation has played a large part in its performance. Furthermore, in most of its variations, the use of vocalists and lyrics has been towards the bottom, rather than the top of its popularity. More recently, the voice is often used without lyrics as just another musical instrument.

As an identifiable form of music (known as a genre), jazz is long-lived. It has been in existence for over a century. From our perspective today, we can identify many different forms of jazz (which are called sub-genres). Jazz has spread throughout the whole of western culture since just before World War I, when it was largely music that was indigenous to the wider New Orleans area. The first sub-genre to become popular was known as Dixieland or New Orleans Jazz (see the timeline chart at the end of this part) assisted by the fame of musicians like King Oliver and Louis Armstrong. Numerous other sub-genres of jazz have emerged, for example, Swing in the Big Band Era of the 1930s and 40s. In the late 1930s a revolutionary new form of jazz called Bebop emerged, from which another identifiable form called Hard Bop was created. In parallel with bebop was a slower, less frenetic style called Cool Jazz. Free Jazz emerged in 1959 and lasted even whilst the tumultuous effects of rock music were impacting upon jazz. Perhaps the most recent sub-genre is Smooth Jazz, a type of music that grew out of the commercial world of the North American radio stations. Of course, there were other genres of music too, three of which are Classical music, Ethnic (or Folk) music and rock 'n' roll, now embraced by the term Rock music. All of these genres have formed their own sub-genres and, together with Jazz, all have impacted upon each other. As Collier wrote, "Rock, Funk, Soul, show music, movie music, television music, and a good deal of modern concert music are filled with elements drawn from jazz. Jazz is the foundation upon which modern popular music has been built. There is, clearly, something terribly compelling about this remarkable music..." [2]

Articulating what jazz is all about is not easy and there are distinct differences between jazz, which has emerged from the American culture, and the music of the European tradition. The main differences can be summarised as follows.

First, the *timbre* is different. Timbre is a French word for which there is no good English equivalent so we adopt it as our own. It is a measure of the *quality of sound*. In the European style, the timbre of any given musical instrument is pretty much standard. Specialists of classical music instruments are expected to play their instruments in such a way as to produce a 'standard' sound. (Curiously, having done so, the very best soloists still develop slight variations in order to emphasise their own individuality.) Good timbre is something that is taught, and musicians aim to perfect their timbre to please their music teachers. In jazz, the timbre is highly personal. Indeed, jazz musicians make great efforts to have a unique timbre – it's what they call their 'sound'. It makes them more identifiable and, of course, attractive to record companies too because of their distinctiveness. The top jazz musicians have always made it an objective to explore different ways of playing their own instruments in order to create new sounds (timbres). The most obvious examples are, of course, the playing of guitars and saxophones.

The second difference is in *pitch*. European music is very much based upon two modes – technically called the major and minor diatonic scales. Some people might know this as the 'doh-re-me' scale. (Occasionally the pentatonic scale is important, for example, in Scottish and Irish folk music. This uses just five of the eight notes in the diatonic octave.) Pitch is the actual note played. Precisely, it is the number of vibrations per second made by the music-making device, which could be a vocal chord, a length of instrument string, or column of air. So-called, 'middle C' – the piano key in the centre of the keyboard is the note made when the string vibrates exactly 256 times per second. As a physical quantity, it is easy to measure and is absolute. When you press the key, you get middle C – nothing else. (Pedants will point out that you do actually get other harmonic overtones, but let's not be too picky.) Very little variation in pitch is allowed when musicians play in the European style.

In jazz, however, the pitch can be quite variable, so much so that to listeners unused to the styles of jazz it can sound out of tune. Modern keyboards have a tool – often a rotating device – that the players can turn to vary the pitch. When they press middle C with their right hand, they turn the wheel with their left hand and get anything from B to D, say. On electric guitars, some rock musicians use a lever called a tremolo arm that they pull with their right hand to stretch or slacken the strings, giving a similar effect. In the early days, it was used to give vibrato, literally a sound like a vibration, and which is associated with a 'better' sound in the European style. (Opera singers, for example, are well known for their voice vibrato.) In blues and jazz, guitarists generally use their left hand to bend the strings up and down, parallel with the fingerboard to give notes that are between the pitches of the notes they are fingering on the guitar neck. An essential characteristic of the blues is that it is based on its own 'scales' that are very different from the common European scale. These include some notes that are called 'the blue notes' and that, (musicologists argue) in their pure form, fall between the notes of the doh-re-me scale. [2, 3]

Finally, there are the differences in the beat or rhythm – clear and fixed in the European style, extremely varied in jazz. It is the rhythm of a piece that mostly defines the pattern by which music is described. The smallest unit of the pattern is the bar, within which there is a regular number of beats – usually two, three or four. Very often the melody line is divorced from the ground beat of the piece in jazz. Most non-musicians are aware of the musical characteristic known as the time signature – it's called the meter in American English. They are aware that most popular music is written with four beats to a bar (often called common time). Occasionally, music may have three beats to the bar, in which case the somewhat old-fashioned term 'waltz' might be applied. Soldiers march to music with two beats to the bar because (oddly enough) they have two legs. Rarely does ordinary, popular music step outside these bounds, because, it is generally believed, it does not sound natural. Why should this be so? Presumably it is purely a matter of what we are used to – the habit formed over decades of listening to four-in-a-bar music. Yet in the more modern forms of jazz, it is quite normal to use very different rhythmic structures. These provide a challenge to musicians needing to commit the music to paper, and listeners who are not experienced in listening to such music find it 'other worldly' or odd in ways they cannot explain.

One of the first to demonstrate the potential of unusual time signatures was Dave Brubeck (1920-2012) who, with his multi-million selling record, *Take Five* (1959), showed that a very good musical experience could be achieved with the unfamiliar feeling created by five beats in a bar. The phenomenal success he had with this record led Brubeck to make two entire albums, *Time Out* (1959) and *Time Further Out*, (1961), in which he successfully experimented with time signatures. Brubeck is reported to have regretted the diversion this caused in his career, for the public demanded reprises of these numbers for decades, long after Brubeck - great jazzer that he was - had been seeking to move on.

Meanwhile, many other jazz musicians have used experiments in rhythm to create wonderful feelings in their music that we rarely find outside jazz. One of the secrets of the most successful modern jazz bands is to use unusual (and, indeed, variable) time signatures in compositions, without making it obvious to the listener. Skilled musicians are able to read unusually structured music from charts and then, more importantly, to improvise within that framework in such a way as to make the experience interesting. At all times, the music sounds natural, if different. Pat Metheny is a master of this art, with many of his compositions not only featuring unusual time signatures, but so many other things that are interesting to listen to that the unusual rhythms are just one aspect of a truly novel and memorable experience. John McLaughlin's music is also filled with unusual meter, as is that of the Yellowjackets and the Brecker Brothers. Even competent musicians struggle to cope with some of the more esoteric rhythmic patterns.

Jazz also tends to have a significant social content. Jazz musicians like to play to a dancing audience, through which they gain feedback that helps them to play better. In this context, I shall use the word 'groove' a lot because it is a target for many jazz musicians - especially fusion players - to find a groove and inspire their audience to get up and dance. Musicians playing in the European style are under the total control of the written music and the conductor, and they should be entirely uninfluenced by sound or movement from the audience. Thus audiences at concerts of classical music are expected to sit still and in silence – applause at any point other than the end is frowned upon. Jazz audiences frequently applaud the musicians whilst they are playing, for example, after they have completed a particularly good solo.

Another characteristic feature of jazz musicians is their insatiable desire to 'jam', that is, to sit down together and play music with little or no previous planning or rehearsal. This, of course, is only sensibly possible with musicians having the capacity to improvise, because, unlike European classical-style musicians, they are generally unrestricted by written music and can invent music on the spot in any given key. British jazz musician and broadcaster Courtney Pine told a good story during his 2005 interview with Pat Metheny: "I don't know if you remember how we first met but you were recording a film score at CTS Studios in Wembley and we were like fifteen, sixteen and there were about four of us playing – stealing - some session time in one of the small studios, and we stood outside listening to you play for ages. Then at the end of your session you walked out and there we were standing there with Pat Metheny standing in front of us, and the first thing that you say to us was, 'Hi guys! Is there anywhere that we can go to jam?' And we all looked at each other and we all thought, your mum's house, your mum's house, and we couldn't think of anywhere..." [4]

Probably as a result of this considerable versatility that many jazz musicians have over others, we find that jazz bands are extremely unstable, with members joining and leaving on a very frequent basis. The idea of session musicians – guys who play for one or two tracks at a recording session – is very common for jazz records, but for bands too. Often musicians on tour in a band are different from those who played on the latest album. A good example of this was Miles Davis who was constantly changing the line-ups of his bands, depending on who was available and what type of sound he required. There are also many other examples where groups of musicians have remained together for comparatively long periods (though still short by the standards of rock groups) because they improvise better when they are more familiar with each other's styles and techniques. This great versatility of jazz musicians makes them excellent session musicians because they need little time to perform their duties at recordings. They arrive at a session with little or no knowledge of the job at hand. They do their stuff in as short a time as possible, and are out of the door straight afterwards, saving studio time and much project money in the process. Two of the greatest session men are Randy and Michael Brecker, and my book about them is dedicated to session musicians. [5]

Jazz is not African music. However, it was created by black people who were born (or had immediate ancestors) on the eastern side of the Atlantic. Yet, to some extent, white people also played a big part in creating it. Of course, there was an African tradition in the music, but it was an American phenomenon encouraged by the harsh, deprived conditions in which black people lived, first on the plantations, and later in the ghettos of the large cities. Collier chooses to call the original music of the descendants of the black slaves, "Black American Folk Music." He says that it was based on a culture that was essentially new, though it contained elements of African and European culture and music.

Jazz writers, Giddins and Devaux, phrase the creation of jazz especially well. "Jazz developed as a convergence of multiple cultures. The primary factor was the importation of African slaves to a world dominated by warring European colonists - particularly the French, Spanish and English. In striving to keep African musical traditions alive, the slaves eventually found ways to blend them with the abiding traditions of Europe, producing hybrid styles in North and South America, unlike anything in the Old World." [6] We see clearly, therefore, that – by definition - jazz was a *fusion* music.

Jazz developed gradually at first. In the southern USA, drums and loud horns were banned because the slave owners were afraid they could be subversive and encourage the people to make trouble for them. This led to greater use of quieter instruments such as the guitar and banjo. Over a long time the African musical heritage was coloured by European music that the black people heard in church. The main form of Black American Folk Music was a work song, encouraged by white people who felt their slaves were happy when they were singing. Christian Church music developed when freed black people inaugurated their own churches. Almost all of this was achieved without ever committing the music to paper. Attempts to reproduce old recordings on paper look clumsy because the music – often performed away from the main beat and using notes that were not quite of the pitch of those found on the piano (the blue notes) - defied translation onto paper. Examples in Collier's book show how rhythms in two and three beats were combined and used simultaneously. All look strange to musicians trained to read music in the European style. [2]

Collier has no clear answer to the source of the blues. He thinks it "probably began to develop from other black folk forms, especially the work song, in the 1880s and 90s." [2] There is no reference to the 'blues' as such in the nineteenth century, yet it was a developed musical form by about 1910. The notes used in the blues have been the subject of much controversy. The simplest explanation is to say that the European diatonic scale was changed by flattening (lowering in pitch) the third and seventh notes of the scale to produce two new notes, the so-called 'blue notes'. Musicologists claim that is not strictly correct for this can be played on the piano. On the contrary, they maintain, the blue notes are actually to be found in the *cracks* between the notes of the piano. It takes a good ear to pick this out.

Whilst we are unsure about the origins of the blues, there is no doubt that jazz originated in the vicinity of New Orleans. There are sufficient written accounts of the time to show that musicians of the north, east and west of America copied the playing of those in the south of Louisiana. Jazz 'emerged' during quite a short time period – 1900 to 1905. By the early 1920s, even the good *white* bands from New Orleans were playing better jazz than all but the very best black bands from elsewhere. New Orleans was a unique city where a blending of several cultures had occurred. It was founded in the Franco-Spanish tradition of the Caribbean, rather than the Anglo-Saxon culture of the northern USA. It was libertarian and determined to have fun. For over two hundred years it had developed a great emphasis on music and dancing. There were no less than three opera companies for a town of 50,000 inhabitants and it had a Negro Philharmonic Society in 1830. Much of the music that took place was performed with both black and white races mixed socially, unlike elsewhere.

There was also a sub-race of people called the Creoles – people of French or Spanish descent, born in the United States, who were either light- or dark-skinned, but who protested that they were not Negroes. They maintained their French cultural traditions, and the area in which they lived became known as the French Quarter of New Orleans, on one side of Canal Street; Negroes lived on the other side. The Creoles took music very seriously indeed, but it was based upon the European style. They could read music and did not improvise; they also looked down on the Negroes who played the blues and did. Creole musical functions tended to be elegant affairs, and, being generally Catholic, they were not exposed to the non-conformist church music of the Negroes. The black people of New Orleans developed their musical culture along the lines described above, and in parallel with the Creoles. Every day, musicians of all kinds played alongside each other in hundreds of musical events indoors and out, in bars, cabarets, honky-tonks, brothels and even funerals. Anyone who visits New Orleans today will know that this spirit lives on. It has also retained its reputation for sexual licentiousness.

A significant event in the development of jazz took place when people started to play the blues without singing, i.e. as an 'instrumental.' By 1900 this was a regular occurrence in the venues where the agenda had a stronger sexual focus. It may be that musicians began by imitating the sound of the human voice. Certainly the instrumental music that began to emerge was a great deal sexier than it was using vocalists. Of course, playing to imitate the voice required a great deal of skill outside the normal for a given instrument. The blue notes were possible on horns by breathing and lip control techniques, as well as other peculiarities of voice such as smooth or gruff tones, growls and shrieks. These styles of playing the saxophone, in particular, continue to form the mainstay of jazz technique on horns today.

Ragtime was another important development and had become very popular by the turn of the century, with Scott Joplin a famous exponent who made a good living from it. Music was much in demand and competition for bands was intense, but it was necessary to be able to play the ragtime tunes that the audiences liked. This was no problem for the music-reading Creole musicians, but most black musicians could not read. Thus one lead musician would learn the melodies by heart and the rest would improvise around him, trying to mimic the harmonies and rhythms of the style. The improvisations were not especially free, but rather as embellishments to try to blend in with what else were going on in the band. Since black and Creole musicians often found themselves playing alongside each other, the musical traditions quickly began to blend, and a fusion of styles was born. The main styles – march, ragtime, blues and popular songs – that had emerged from the African and European traditions, began to merge into one style under the title 'Jazz', though it was not called this until the 1910s. Many musicians said they were just playing 'Ragtime'.

A further event occurred that resulted in a spread of the new music to the wider USA during the period 1900-1905. The Spanish-American War ended in 1898 and resulted in the disbandment of large numbers of troops, especially bandsmen, from the lands bordering the Caribbean. This, in turn, resulted in a vast quantity of cheap musical instruments arriving onto the second-hand market around New Orleans, enabling the poor black musicians to acquire instruments and learn to play them as they never had before. The business and port activities of New Orleans were booming, which provided healthy business in the bars and brothels. This, in turn, provided lots of paid work for musicians. These effects proved to be the spark that caused the explosion of jazz music around the entire USA.

For a long time, jazz was simply music of a group, with no particular emphasis on one instrument rather than another. When a trumpet player called Louis Armstrong came onto the scene in the 1920s he made jazz a soloist's art. Now it became possible – even desirable – for individual members of a band to stand out in front of their group and take a leading role. Many players used this as an opportunity to show audiences (and other musicians too) how well they could improvise. This is an essential element of jazz performance today. [7]

One of the strongest developments when the fusion of music styles occurred concerned rhythm. Until then, most music was based upon two beats repeated, the most fundamental natural rhythm, because humans march and dance on two legs. Ragtime was based on two-beat music. Soon jazz musicians moved to four beats repeated – two groups of two played twice as fast. The famous pianist, Jelly Roll Morton, claimed to have invented jazz himself in 1902, based on this transition. The music, often required for outdoors, was generally played with marching band instruments, the saxophone not being included until somewhat later. When inside, bands could adopt the use of a piano or banjo, with the string bass replacing the tuba. The five essential elements of jazz were now in place. Syncopated rhythm reflected the ragtime style, variation of timbre provided colour and was a substitution of the human voice, blue notes represented the ethnic origins of the music and were used wherever appropriate, the melody lines were lifted off the ground beat of the songs, and vibrato was added to the ends of notes, an effect that became a hallmark of New Orleans jazz. "In sum," says Collier, "they were swinging." [2]

## The Early Players

It is said that Ferdinand Joseph LaMothe (aka Jelly Roll Morton 1890-1941) was the first person to commit jazz to a written form on paper, which he apparently did with his composition, *Jelly Roll Blues* in 1915. Perhaps more significantly, however, he claimed to have invented jazz in 1902, a fact that is still argued over by musicologists. Since Morton would have been only 12 years old at the time, it seems rather unlikely. One critic, Yanow, wrote: "One of the very first giants of jazz, Jelly Roll Morton did himself a lot of harm posthumously by exaggerating his worth, claiming to have invented jazz in 1902. Morton's accomplishments as an early innovator are so vast that he did not really need to stretch the truth." [8]

Certainly, his birth into a coloured Creole family and his outstanding proficiency on piano from an early age provided him with all the necessary qualifications. His early time was served providing musical entertainment in brothels, but it was his performances in touring vaudeville acts all across the southern USA from 1904 onwards that brought him fame and established a countrywide reputation as a player in, first, the "ragtime" and then the "stride" genres. Morton played a big part in exposing the American nation to the exotic new music of New Orleans by means of vaudeville minstrels' shows and other kinds of acts performed by black and coloured people. These shows were often known as *Uncle Tom and the Boys* routines, and were later seen as undesirable racist entertainment, despised by the enlightened seekers of racial equality. But in early 20th century America, musical entertainment (of which jazz was an essential element) became one of the most important tools for building bridges between the black and white communities.

Whilst Morton's impact on the wider world was immense, and unarguable, perhaps the most important character to bridge the black-white racial divide was Louis Armstrong (1901-71). Born and brought up in New Orleans, Armstrong faced racism every day of his life, but learned how to deal with it in the most effective ways imaginable. As a result, Armstrong's career spanned 50 years and was the most successful jazz has ever known. He died in 1971 as one of the most famous people in the world, with the help of several million-selling popular hits, such as *Hello Dolly* (1964) and *What A Wonderful World* (1967)

In the days of Armstrong's youth, "...Blues were everywhere, in the simple honky-tonks on the block where Armstrong lived, and in the casual singing of people he knew. Blues could be performed by ensemble, but it was primarily a solo idiom, a way for an individual to publicly identify himself or herself." [9]

As a young teenager Armstrong made friends with King Oliver who had very similar musical interests. Like Armstrong, "Oliver had dark skin, had been raised with church music and blues, and had no father in his life. Oliver noticed Armstrong's progress and invited him to his house for lessons at his kitchen table, teaching him the modern way of phrasing on the cornet." [10] Louis was the only student Oliver ever had.

Oliver had left New Orleans to join a band that had been taken to Chicago in 1915 by bass and banjo player Bill Johnson. Perhaps by stealth, Oliver gradually took over the inaccurately named Creole Jazz Band (none of the musicians were Creole by birth) that would soon lay down some of the earliest recordings by black New Orleans jazz musicians. Armstrong was invited to join Oliver's established residency at the Lincoln Gardens in Chicago, and left New Orleans in 1922. Thus, it was in the industrial north of America, in the heart of the new centre of jazz, that Armstrong launched his astonishing career. A fine collection of music is available on *King Oliver's Creole Jazz Band – The Complete Set*, a 2-CD publication by Retrieval, RTR 79007 (1996/2004). This contains the earliest recordings of their kind from 1923, whilst the band was playing in the Chicago area, and includes the young Louis Armstrong as second cornet to the leader, Joseph "King" Oliver (1881-1938). The perceptive writer, Brothers, points out that the irony is that these scarce, commercial recordings were merely a sideshow for jazz musicians, while for us they are the main events. [11] Recordings such as these are all we have left from these days when the creation of entirely new music was the be-all-and-end-all of a young black musician's life. (In fact, little has changed today when we survey the wider jazz scene in this set of books, especially with regard to musicians who are now dead.)

With the exception of a few female black singers, the recording of jazz played by bands comprised of black musicians was retarded compared to recordings of white musicians' jazz because of the perceived lack of market opportunity. Black people were poor and not able to afford phonographs on which to play the records. [12] Starting with his time in the King Oliver band, and continuing with his work in his own Hot Five (1925) and Hot Seven (1927) bands, Louis Armstrong was *the* primary influence and populariser of jazz from 1923 onwards, as he successfully bridged the racial divide with his positive, smiling attitude that went down well with so many audiences.

At the turn of the century, during the birth of jazz music, the perpetuation of harsh racial separatist traditions by white supremacists continued unabated more than a hundred years after the official ending of slavery. Brothers writes of the "…systematic subjugation of people of African descent… Yet most people, over the centuries, have intuitively sensed how music has occupied the thriving centre of that legacy. During the decades after emancipation, the African-American musical vernacular was bursting out of the plantations from which it spread through the Deep South and then eventually to the urban north, laying the groundwork for the spectacular success of ragtime, blues, jazz, gospel, and other African American idioms in the 20th century." [13]

Brothers interprets Louis Armstrong's influence as due to his intensification of the audible presence of his African heritage, and describes Armstrong as an "ordinary extraordinary man." According to Brothers, Armstrong was *ordinary* because "…he accepted, without hesitation, apology, or compromise, the social and musical values of the people he grew up with who were pegged as the lowest of the low." But he says Armstrong was *extraordinary* because "… not only was he a great trumpeter, but also a great singer and entertainer; further, he was a great melodist, who invented a melodic idiom of jazz solo playing…" that became tremendously influential. Brother defines the peak of Louis Armstrong's career as occurring in the decade after 1922. [14]

As to Armstrong's special playing technique, Brothers writes, "Part of the technique of playing cornets in those days was to make what was known as 'freak' music – the talking effects produced by growls, mutes, and timbral distortion. This complex musical culture thrived independently of musical notation; in fact, non-notatable features were emphasised. Most important was the format I referred to as fixed and variable, the musical model that is still ubiquitous in sub-Saharan Africa, from which enslaved people brought it to the New World. In this model one instrument or group of instruments plays a repeated rhythmic figure. This fixed level orients the listener or dancer, while the variable instrument (or group of instruments) brings the music to life by departing from the repeated figure in interesting ways …Music in this multi-layered format is easy to hear, but harder to talk about …The fixed and variable model became the key ingredients in Louis Armstrong's mature style. [15] It would be easy to argue that this formula has been used as a fundamental format ever since.

Brothers attributes two major paradigm shifts in music to Louis Armstrong. The first "… was created in the years 1926-28 and based on the fixed and variable model, was pitched primarily to the black community. Black people enjoyed his entertaining singing, but were also "in awe of his wonderful trumpet solos, which helped articulate the modern identity they were looking for …His compositional skills led him to craft solos of enduring melodic beauty." [11] Armstrong was driven to create a new melodic idiom, which made him different from almost everybody else.

His second change resulted from "…efforts to succeed in the mainstream market of white audiences. The key was radical paraphrase of familiar popular tunes." The idea was basically an old one whereby African American musicians spoke of 'ragging' the tune. "They meant creating their own stylised version of a known melody by adding embellishments and extensions. This technique was part of Armstrong's early musical training. In the early 1930s, with the assistance of the microphone, he invented a fresh approach to this old tradition, creating a song style that was part blues, part crooning, part fixed and variable model, plastic and mellow, the most modern thing around." [16] His recordings made him the best selling performer in the country in any genre or style, and his live performances were broadcast nationwide.

The jazz of the white musicians, bandleader Paul Whiteman and composer George Gershwin was very much written with the assistance of musical notation. "The jazz made by Armstrong was just as sophisticated as white jazz, but its terms of expression could not be transmitted through musical notation. This was the key to his success as a modernist who appealed as much to white people as to black in the late 1920s and early 1930s." [17]

A group of musicians from New Orleans came together early in 1916 for a period of employment at the famous venue, *Schiller's Café* in Chicago. The band took the name of Stein's Dixie Jass Band, after the drummer, Johnny Stein. During the rest of the year, the band's growing popularity led to new contract offers with good pay, and new groups of musicians playing under the name The Dixie Jass Band. At the start of 1917, the band had relocated to New York where, on 26 February, it recorded what are claimed to be the very first jazz recordings – *Livery Stable Blues* (1917) and *Dixie Jass Band One Step* (1917). These two sides of a 78-rpm record were issued on the Victor label and credited to the Original Dixieland Jass Band, in which 'Jass' was substituted by 'Jazz' later that year. Rarely, then, we have a simple statement of historical fact. There is, however, one nagging problem – the musicians were white. So it is with much regret to many observers that the incontrovertible fact that jazz was born from non-white cultures of New Orleans is subverted by these first recordings being made by white musicians – even though they were undoubtedly well qualified and emanated from New Orleans. Brothers cannot resist nominating the ODJB as the "white group that raked in financial rewards for ripping off black music." [18] Presumably, the popularity of the ODJB led to some collateral benefits to black jazz musicians?

## Swing, the Big Bands and Duke Ellington

A very popular version of jazz emerged in the period between the two World Wars, a time called the *Swing Era*. It was characterised by a host of 'Big' bands to satisfy the great demand for Saturday night dancing. The composition of these bands was fairly common. Besides a rhythm section, consisting of piano, string bass and drums, the brass section consisted of two or three trombones, three or four trumpets and four or five saxophones – a total of twelve to fifteen musicians. Naturally, they did not have the string section of the European orchestra. Occasionally other sounds were added. Saxophone players often doubled on clarinet or flute. Sometimes a banjo or guitar was added to the rhythm section, although amplified guitar was not in general use until much later. Finally, there was generally a singer, although only for some of the tunes because this was primarily instrumental music. However, some singers such as Frank Sinatra or Sammy Davis Junior were so outstanding that the public turned them into major stars in their own right. Then the Big Bands became the support to the singers (or crooners, as they were sometimes called), instead of the other way around.

Big bands are to be found today, although they are rare because paying the wages of lots of musicians makes them expensive to run. One of the best of modern times was the GRP All-Star Big Band, a group put together in the early 90s by Dave Grusin, co-founder of the GRP record label, to celebrate its tenth anniversary. As an example of just how much jazz has progressed, simply play any Big Band record from the forties or fifties and follow it with *GRP All-Star Big Band* (1992) or *GRP All-Star Big Band Live* (1993). The difference is stunning. Another example of a marvellous modern Big Band sound is to be found on Bob Mintzer's 1983 recording *Papa Lips* (2007) with his Horn Man Band. Mintzer – a major jazz star of jazz saxophone in his own right – has continued to lead this Big Band, releasing a solid sequence of entertaining albums. (In contrast, composers such as Michael Gibbs or Colin Towns, with respective albums such as *Tanglewood 63* (1971) or *The Orpheus Suite* (2004) have created an entirely original new sound for large groups of musicians, and jazz-fusion has had an influence on much of this music too.)

It was necessary to expend a lot of effort in writing sheet music for these bands and the bandleaders employed full-time musicians whose sole job it was to write out the arrangements. These were compiled into books – different for each musical instrument - and each piece was given a number. On finishing one piece of music, the leader would shout out the number of the next, and here we have the origin of the use of the word *number* applied to a musical piece.

Following the deprivations of War, the emphasis on having a good time gave jazz a strong focus in the dance halls of the 1930s. Musicians were plentiful (and cheap in a time of high unemployment) and many large bands dedicated to providing dance music were formed. Some names are well known even today: Duke Ellington (1899-1974), Count Basie (1904-84), Earl Hines (1903-83) (note the amusing fascination they had for English aristocratic titles), Jimmy Dorsey (1904-57), Benny Goodman (1909-86), Glen Miller (1904-44), as well as some lesser known names like Teddy Hill (1909-78) and Cab Calloway (1907-94). There's not enough space to describe them all, but one is very special.

Duke Ellington was a man of consummate musical vision and leadership who is rightly regarded as the finest jazz musician of his generation, yet strangely, he was quite a late starter. Born into a middle-class black family, he learned piano with only moderate interest, though he was a keen artist also. He began to play in bands as a means of making money. He arrived in jazz by the back door, so to speak, because he was influenced by some of the musicians around him, notably the trumpeters James "Bubber" Miley and Sidney Bechet. Duke's initial work in New York was at the *Cotton Club* in Harlem in 1927, a white club, thanks to the influence of Irving Mills who got Duke a contract at the Club, as well as his first recording contract. The band was required to accompany a variety of acts, dancers *etc*, and Duke started to write much of the music for these acts. Miley was responsible for putting a growl in his trumpet playing, and, when he left the band in 1929, Ellington ensured that his replacement, Cootie Williams, was able to do it also.

Two people became important to Duke's development. Will Vodry was a black promoter of black bands in white clubs. He taught Ellington a lot about the art of stage performance. The other was Will Marion Cook, who taught Duke musical composition. Duke's time at the Cotton Club was successful, and extremely important in the history of jazz. Ellington developed from a moderate musician into a polished leader of a well-known band, but in 1932 he became tired of the Club, and in 1933 left for London where he found that he was well known, both as a significant composer, and as a musician of standing in a new genre of music. He was impressed to discover that he was so highly thought of, and he began to work harder at improving himself as a serious composer.

The swing era began in 1935 with the sudden rise in popularity of the Benny Goodman Band. Goodman was white and his band played the pop music of the time. Ellington was never able to achieve the level of popularity that Goodman did, but was always close behind. Change also arrived in 1939 when Ellington's relationship with Mills was dissolved, but he was able to hire some of the best musicians, such as Ben Webster, a strong player of the tenor saxophone, and Jimmy Blanton, one of the best bassists. Blanton was to bass in 1939 what Pastorius would be to it in the late 1970s. Sadly, like Pastorius, Blanton's career was short, and he died in 1941 at the age of just 23, but his influence on the band and the future of bass playing was immense.

Throughout the 1940s Ellington and his band were at their peak with some of the best musicians in his employ (Johnny Hodges was the best alto saxophonist before Charlie Parker). One of the greatest jazz trumpeters, Dizzy Gillespie, played briefly in the Duke's band. In his autobiography, Gillespie wrote: "To play with the Duke, you have to forget everything you know. You can't use your own experiences because Duke has some new shit for you when you go in there. You don't rely on what you know from someplace else… Duke had his band set up and used it as an instrument to get certain musical effects, especially tonal colors. What he did for the instruments in the band – the sounds that came out of his band – was unprecedented in the history of jazz." [19]

By the late 1940s the Ellington band began to fragment as Duke reinforced his focus on long suites of music - some of it in the European tradition. Only in 1956, after a famous solo by tenor player, Paul Gonsalves at the Newport Jazz Festival, did Duke regain his fame with an appearance on the cover of *Time* magazine. His star musicians began to return slowly. As Collier writes, the band became "a band of old gentleman" with its stars, Ellington, Cootie Williams, Johnny Hodges, Russell Procope and Harry Carney mostly in their 60s. No longer at the forefront of jazz, the band did, however, continue to play music of substance and quality. Duke Ellington died in May 1974 and it is a great pleasure for me that I was able to see him lead his band in concert during his last UK tour.

As a painter himself, Ellington thought of his music in terms of paintings and his tones as their equivalents in colour. Collier attributes much of Ellington's genius as a creator of new music to this ability to see sound in colour and uses the piece *Mood Indigo* (1930) as a prime example. Here the music exhibits a quality of sound split between trumpet, trombone and clarinet that was quite unique at the time. He also credits Ellington as having an "extraordinary command of dissonance". Intervals that might have sounded ghastly in the hands of other musicians are made to sound agreeable and exciting - even luscious at times. Ellington was also the master of melody and is credited with some of the most memorable and popular themes to come out of jazz. Finally, he was able to break free from the constraints of the 8, 16 and 32 bar formats used for most pieces. Thus, *East St Louis Toodle-oo* contains 18-bar segments as well as 8- and 16-bar ones.

The Swing Era of the Big Bands entered serious decline after WWII because of the increasing costs of employing large groups of musicians. Only the most successful Big Bands could survive, such as those led by Duke Ellington, Count Basie, Woody Herman and Artie Shaw. Their livelihoods under threat, the crooners that fronted them up made their exits to Hollywood where the vehicle of the movies was ideal for the promotion of their careers in a new kind of popular music. The musicians they left behind sought work wherever they could get it, often in smaller bands that played bebop and other forms of jazz.

## Duke Ellington: Selected Discography

Ellington was one of the first masters of jazz composition, and made the writing of jazz music as important a strand of his career as his band leadership. In an age before the Long-Playing record (or album), when the three-minute 78-rpm disc was the primary focus for recordings, Ellington's music was characterised by some of the finest jazz music of the era, encapsulating for many, in retrospect, better than any other jazz composer the essence of this quintessential American genre of music. His writing was boosted from 1941 onwards when he collaborated extensively with Billy Strayhorn with whom he worked on more substantial themed suites of jazz. A list of some of his most famous compositions follows:

*East St Louis Toodle-oo* (1926)
*Creole Love Call* (1927)

*Mood Indigo* (1930)
*Creole Rhapsody* (1931)
*It Don't Mean A Thing (If It Ain't Got That Swing)* (1932)
*Sophisticated Lady* (1933)
*Solitude* (1934)
*In A Sentimental Mood* (1935)
*Caravan* (1937)
*Prelude to a Kiss* (1938)
*Cotton Tail* (1940)
*Don't Get Around Much Any More* (1940)
*Do Nothing Till You Hear From Me* (1940)
*Take The A Train* (1941)

Examples of all of these Ellington compositions, as well as some other tunes he made famous but did not write, such as *Perdido*, can be found on the 2CD set, *The Essential Duke Ellington* (2009) Not Now Music. Cover versions of all of these great Ellington tunes can be found liberally sprinkled across the great range of records, not just in jazz, but in popular music generally, as they achieved what is called 'standard' status.

His band achieved enormous success in the 1930s when concentrating on the more popular dance band format of jazz tunes, but in the 1940s, as he worked with Strayhorn on more cerebral, longer groups of compositions, themed in suites along the lines of the traditional European classical music, Ellington works were received with some indifference. Often with strong racial themes, a succession of major jazz works followed from his authorship. *Jump For Joy* (1941) celebrated the African-American Identity and ran in different forms with modest success for a number of years. The suite such as *Black, Brown and Beige* (1943) was an early jazz musical journey that told the story of African-Americans, their enslavement and their salvation in the church. *Beggar's Holiday* (1946) was a full musical. By the 1950s Ellington was regarded by many as being old-fashioned, as the Big Band era had given way to the small group bebop era, and suites such as *Harlem* (1950) did not achieve the success that deserved.

Ellington's career was revitalised in 1956 at the Newport Jazz Festival, where a sparkling show by his band was recorded and offered to a thankful audience on an early LP album, *Ellington At Newport*. The Columbia-released album became Duke's best-seller from his long career. Today, *Ellington Complete At Newport* (1956) on CD is a must-have part of any jazz collection. After this stroke of good fortune, Ellington collaborated on more suites with Strayhorn, and produced two masterpieces - *Such Sweet Thunder* (1957) and *The Far East Suite* (1967).

## Gillespie, Parker and Bebop

From the mid-1930s, some young musicians began playing in a way that was sufficiently different from the standard approach to jazz that made other musicians sit up and take notice. It led to a musical revolution. Bebop was a milestone that marked the beginning of a period known as *Modern Jazz*, rather than the period of *Traditional (Dixieland) Jazz* that preceded it. Just as the cosmic background radiation is an echo of the Big Bang that marked the creation of the Universe, bebop permeates a significant amount of the jazz we hear today. The first musicians to become involved were John 'Dizzy' Gillespie (trumpet), Charlie Parker, known as 'Yardbird' or just 'Bird,' (alto saxophone), Kenny Clarke (drums) and Thelonius Monk (piano). Between them, Gillespie, Monk, Parker and Clarke changed the face of jazz.

In 1936, Gillespie was hired to replace his hero, the great Roy Eldridge, in a New York-based Big Band led by Teddy Hill. It was his first experience of life in a Big Band. The band's drummer was Kenny Clarke and Gillespie knew right away that he was a different kind of player. Gillespie recalls how Clarke got the nickname 'klook-mop' because of the way he accented rhythm. "Kenny was modifying the concept of rhythm in jazz, making it a much more fluid thing and changing the entire role of the drummer, from just a man who kept time for dancers to a true accompanist, who provided accents for soloists and constant inspiration to the jazz band as a whole. Kenny's style of drumming with 'bombs' and 'klook-mops' in the bass drum and regular rhythm in the cymbals was just right for me. It furnished just the right amount of support, push or embellishment I needed... Kenny initiated a new language into the mainstream of jazz drumming. You know, like you 'infuse'. He infused a new conception, a new language, into the dialogue of the drum, which is now THE dialogue... The trumpet and the drums are cousins. That's why you find a lot of trumpet players can play drums. You find quite a number because it's a closeness there with the brass. [20] ...Kenny Clarke set the stage for the rhythmic content of our music. He was the first one to make accents on the bass drum at specific points in the music. He'd play 4/4 very softly, but the breaks, and the accents on the bass drum, you could hear, like, we called them, dropping bombs." [21]

Clarke was similarly attracted to Dizzy's style. "I noticed something unique about Dizzy's playing, that's why I was hanging out with him. His approach to modern harmonies, but rhythms mostly. He could take care of all that harmony, but his rhythms interested me real profoundly and I just had to find out about that gift he had hidden in him, the gift of rhythm... It was the idea of cymbals that blended with the trumpet. It was a certain way to play the cymbals that Dizzy liked very well and I just happened to be playing like that at the time. The cymbals and the trumpet have something in common they're both brass. It's a perfect blend and when the cymbals are played according to what the soloist is playing, something that corresponds, it's really beautiful. That's where the whole thing happens, right there." [22] The other players in the band didn't like Clarke's playing because he was different from what they were used to. According to Gillespie, they told Teddy they couldn't use Klook because he broke up the time too much [22]

At first, Gillespie modelled his playing on Roy Eldridge, who many saw as the greatest trumpeter of the time, but Gillespie soon realised that if he was going to be successful he couldn't simply copy another player – he needed to develop his own style. If there was one thing that began to pull Dizzy away from sounding like Roy Eldridge it was Dizzy's use of the flatted fifth, shown to him by Rudy Powell. [23] Dizzy adopted and developed this use of a new chord in such a way that it became a pivotal part of his role in the creation of bebop. It was 1939. Lionel Hampton (1908-2002) recognised Gillespie's recording of *Hot Mallets* for him that year as the first time he heard the new bebop style. [24] Hampton: "That first day he played on 'Hot Mallets' he amazed me because that's about as fast as I've heard a trumpet played. I had never heard a trumpet played that fast before. The first time I heard bebop played on a trumpet – I mean that style later called bebop – was when Dizzy played 'Hot Mallets' with me." [25]

Other players present also noticed it as special. Milton Hinton (bass): "I won't call that session the beginning of bebop. It was one of the most progressive sessions. He had all of the giants there; I think Hamp really planned it that way. That's the one with all the saxophones on it, with Ben (Webster) and Coleman (Hawkins), and Clyde Hart on piano. Charlie Christian was on guitar. It was one of the first sessions I'd ever been on with all of the guys together, the real biggies. And I thought it was one of the most progressive as far as the 'giant steps' sessions were concerned. We weren't even using the word 'bebop' then, you know. And then when Dizzy walked in with this new innovation it really tied in with everything that we had there because we had all of the soloists." [25]

Another, more independent contributor to the process of change was Charlie Christian. Though he was not the first to amplify a guitar, he was the first to bring it to the attention of American musicians and the public in 1939. Such was the impression he made that soon he was playing with the famous bandleader and clarinettist, Benny Goodman with whom he had made successful records. By 1940 his music was popular with the other jazz musicians too, for here was a guitar that could be as loud as you needed it to be – as loud as a horn! But it was the music he was playing that stunned people, not so much for its technical difficulty, for today it sounds very modest. It was all about the changes to the rhythm and harmony that he made in his playing. When we listen to his music today, we must remember how new it sounded to his contemporaries. Such a fresh approach proved to be extremely influential, but sadly, weakened by tuberculosis, he died in 1942 aged only 25.

Gillespie was always ready to give others credit where it was due. "Charlie Christian was baaad! He knew the blues and he knew how to do the swing. He had a great sense of harmony, and he lifted the guitar up to a solo voice in jazz. [26] ...Within the next few years I would exchange ideas with Monk in jam sessions at Minton's and learn about Monk's use of chromaticism. I learned rhythm patterns from Charlie Parker and Benny Carter, the drummer. I learned a lot about harmony from Benny Carter (the saxophonist), Art Tatum and Clyde Hart. But Monk is the most unique musician of our crowd. He was the one least affected by any other musician...When I heard him play he was playing like Monk, like nobody else [27]...And Roy (Eldridge) used to come by *Minton's*. Roy is the most competitive musician. Roy used to just shower trumpet players with chops (high notes) and speed. 'Look, you're supposed to be the greatest trumpet player in the world,' Monk would tell him, 'but that's the best' and he'd point to me." [27]

Gillespie's boss, Teddy Hill, didn't like the new style that was emerging in his band, almost outside of his control. He wanted to fire Dizzy, but Gillespie argued with him. Eventually, Hill got a gig at the World's Fair but then lost it as a result of a Union dispute. With no work and no income, Hill lost his band, but fortunately got a job as manager at *Minton's* where, ironically, he hired his old musicians, including Clarke and Gillespie and in so doing helped promote their new music.

Dizzy next played in a band led by Edgar Hayes with Clarke, once again, as drummer. This was followed by a very important spell in Cab Calloway's band from 1939-41. It was one of the best bands in the USA and he soon got used to playing with the biggest names in jazz. He also met some less famous ones... Gillespie: "We used to play at a theatre in Kansas City. I had a friend - a trumpet player in Kansas City - named Buddy Anderson. We'd talk between sets and exchange ideas, and he told me once (in 1940), 'I got somebody I want you to hear, a saxophone player. You've got to hear this saxophone player I know, an alto'. I'd known all these guys, great saxophonists, you know, and I said I wasn't too interested. 'Well, look,' Buddy said, 'I'm going to bring him by the hotel anyway.' And I was astounded by what the guy could do. These other guys that I had been playing with weren't my colleagues really. But the moment I heard Charlie Parker, I said, there is my colleague. Buddy and I and Charlie Parker went up into this hotel room and locked up. We locked up in that room and Charlie Parker played. I never heard anything like that before. The way that he assembled notes together. That was one of the greatest thrills because I had been a Roy Eldridge fan up until then but I was definitely moving on into myself. Charlie Parker and I were moving in practically the same direction too, but neither of us knew it. Later on, about 1942, Charlie came to New York with Jay McShann, and we became friends." [28]

Buddy Anderson: "It wasn't a hotel room, it was at the Musician's local where there was a piano, and Dizzy sat at the piano and played piano for Charlie and myself to play. He didn't play trumpet, he just played piano ... But Dizzy was far more advanced, musically, than I was. But Bird was highly advanced theoretically too. But Dizzy was then and always has been out front, theoretically, of most of the cats. Diz is something else. I mean Diz is a terrible (i.e. brilliant!) rhythm man. Max Roach made a point of saying that ... Diz and Bird seemed to me like two different things altogether. Diz, as one cat expressed it, made it up through hard work, and Bird's was a more 'natural' thing. And he was highly collective Bird was. Bird paid strict attention to what people did, and if he found anything that they did that struck him, he brought that into his thing ... But Diz is damn near all Diz, and it's a little bit studied but nobody could do it but Diz. They couldn't copy Diz. They copied Charlie, but couldn't nobody copy Diz ... They could copy Miles and cats like that, but they couldn't copy Dizzy. A lot of them started to try back then, but them cats couldn't make it because they didn't have the technique to do it with." [29]

Clarke: "Bird was playing stuff we'd never heard before. He was into figures I thought I'd invented for drums. He was twice as fast as Lester Young and into harmony Lester hadn't touched. Bird was running the same way we were, but he was way ahead of us. I don't think he was aware of the changes he had created."

In 1942 Cab Calloway fired Gillespie – a well-known practical joker - after a trick played by someone else back-fired. Dizzy took the hit and left. After Cab Calloway, Diz spent a lot of time playing at *Minton's* with Monk and others. Unfortunately, a dispute arose between the musician's union and the record companies. No records were made from 1942 to 1945, a key time in the development of bebop. The Union was a powerful force behind the scenes in New York at this time. Musicians were not allowed to play without a contract and there were big fines ($100-500) for any musicians caught playing in jam sessions. They were forbidden because it undermined all the work done by the Union to establish standard rates of pay for musicians. Union officials walked the streets of New York looking for musicians playing in jam sessions, but constant playing was so important to the young jazzers that they ignored the rules whenever they could. [30] Diz was one of them: he said that he never actually worked at *Minton's*, he only jammed. It was a big risk to take.

In 1946 Gillespie put together a Big Band at the New York club called the *Spotlite* that was owned by an impresario named Billy Shaw. This was to be a seminal event in jazz. It got the band together, and allowed them to get tight with a set of wholly new arrangements and compositions. Big bands inevitably created lots of work by their need for written sheet music. Gillespie's band was no exception, especially as his arrangements were so new. He hired Gil Fuller as arranger. Then, from 1946-50, Dizzy went on the road with his big band, promoting bebop as the new thing in jazz. [31] Fuller: "As a musician, Dizzy didn't have the tone that everybody else had. He concentrated more on technique than he concentrated on tone and the kind of sound he got. His sound and tone wasn't as big as, say, Freddie Webster's. Or you could say that his tone wasn't like Miles, because Miles tried to sound like Freddie Webster when he started out. And Miles had a softer tone. When you look at Miles as a whole, he didn't have the technical facility for getting over the horn like Dizzy had... Dizzy specialised in technique. Other fellas specialised in tones. He had fully developed harmonically. He had totally developed technically... but when it came to tone he didn't place much importance on it at the time. Well, he never held a note for that long. [32] Guys like Dizzy spoiled me because you could write an arrangement and give it to him and he could read it down the first time flawlessly." [33]

Elmon Wright: "Like Diz was to trumpet players what Charlie Parker was to saxophonists. Overnight it changed. When you heard Diz - Boom! It just changed overnight. Just about every modern trumpet player, Diz played a part in your life as far as trumpet playing goes. In his upper register he can do things that I haven't heard any other trumpet player do. You hear him do these things and you say, "That's impossible, man! How the heck can a guy do that? He ain't got but three valves. Diz used to get mad at saxophone players. He'd say, 'Man, you guys got a key for every note, man. Say, we ain't got but three valves.'" [34]

The rhythm section of Gillespie's big band evolved into a famous jazz group called the Modern Jazz Quartet. It was comprised of Percy Heath (bass), Milt Jackson (vibraphone), Kenny Clarke (drums) and John Lewis (piano). The big band promoted bebop on all its tours over the US, as well as in Europe, where the music was well received. In many parts of the USA, however, people simply could not comprehend it. They got angry when they couldn't dance and there was no singer. John Lewis: "Before (the war) it was functional music, for dancing, principally for dancing, and also for shows, some stage appearances and a few concerts, very few. Duke Ellington was the principal concert artist that we had. He was the best one as far as I'm concerned. But then that changed with what Dizzy was doing. That was something really completely different. [35]

It took a long time for bebop to be accepted. Dizzy names a concert at *Carnegie*

*Hall* on 29 September 1947 as a turning point for the music and its acceptance in the USA. "After that *Carnegie Hall* concert everybody started paying attention to the music." [36] Until then, the press had been largely against the new music, but now began to write more favourably. Awards followed. *Metronome* magazine named Gillespie as the best trumpeter in each year from 1947 to 1950. His band was "Band of the Year" in 1948. Barry Ulanov of *Metronome* wrote "A new era in jazz began in 1947, that modern jazz had come to stay." [37]

Another, almost inconsequential innovation was made by Gillespie in 1947 when he introduced Chano Pozo, a Cuban conga player, to his band. Between them they created *Monteca*, which became a big hit. This was the first use of Latin percussion in American jazz music. Gillespie had got the idea to use Latin drums from his friend Cuban trumpeter Mario Bauza. [38] Mario Bauza: "In those days those American musicians didn't have the slightest idea about Latin music. The rhythms were too complicated for them." [39]

Soon afterwards, Dizzy collaborated with composer George Russell on another song that was to become famous, *Bubana Be, Cubana Bop*. Russell says that the introduction he wrote for it was modal and ten years ahead of its time. It wasn't until the late '50s when Miles Davis (1926-91) began to popularise the modal style of playing, again influenced by Russell. [40] "Diz had a very unique sense of putting chord progressions together, you know, and his theme *Cubana* was really fabulous, amazing for that time. So really imaginative in a harmonic sense." [40]

Slowly, bebop was transforming jazz from a medium of dancing to one of listening. It was a permanent and major shift in social culture. Many hated the move away from dancing, but Gillespie thought it was for the better. Billy Eckstine led a band in 1944 with Gillespie and Parker as members and Sarah Vaughan as vocalist. Eckstine: "We didn't have it easy; our type of music was more or less a concert style of jazz. People would start to dance and then they would turn around and listen. Sometimes our tempos were not danceable either." [41]

The change did not take place overnight, however, but took a number of years over which it evolved. Gillespie recalled how the term 'bebop' finally came into use whilst he played at the *Onyx Club* on 52$^{nd}$ Street in 1944: "In the *Onyx Club*, we played a lot of original tunes that didn't have titles. We just wrote an introduction and a first chorus. I'd say, 'Dee-da-pa-da-n-de-bop…' and we'd go into it. People, when they wanna ask for one of those numbers and didn't know the name, would ask for bebop. And the press picked it up and started calling it bebop. The first time the term bebop appeared in print was while we played at the *Onyx Club*" [42]

By 1950 Gillespie's big band period was over. Gillespie: "Suddenly ...we were struck with the old bebop dilemma, whether jazz is primarily a music for dancing or listening... Dancers had to hear those four solid beats... they didn't care whether we played a flatted fifth or a ruptured 129th! I had to abandon my big band, which all of us who loved modern jazz knew was a great artistic success. The fad was finished, but the style stood firmly. It was there to stay." [43]

Parker is probably given more than his fair share of credit for the bebop revolution when Gillespie is seen now to have been more methodical and deliberate about it. One thing is for sure: both men were virtuosos on their instruments. One factor that always enters into the equation is that reputations are changed – often enhanced, sometimes destroyed – when someone dies. In Parker's case, death turned him into a legend. Gillespie, on the other hand, lived to a ripe old age, playing almost right up to his death in 1993. However, because he was always available for comment and consultation, or, to put it crudely – *because he was alive* – he was not elevated to the mystical level accorded to Parker. In any case, some view the saxophone as the sexier of the two instruments, others that sax is simply the premier instrument of jazz. It may also be true that Parker was much farther ahead of his contemporary sax players than Gillespie was ahead of his. Biased judgements are always somewhat inevitable. Perhaps the fairest conclusion is that both should receive equal credit.

The essence of the bebop revolution was a drive for the acceptance of a wider range of harmonies. Parker explained his contribution as a feeling of boredom with what he had been playing up to that point. He had been looking for a more exciting way of playing, and it finally occurred to him one day during a performance of the number *Cherokee* in December 1939. Another feature of bebop was the use of different chords in certain numbers of the musical repertoire. Although this in itself was not new, the bebop players made it standard practice. The final important change they introduced was the extremely rapid playing of notes. Gillespie had already modelled his playing on Roy Eldridge, who had deliberately set out to become the fastest trumpet player. Parker, too, became machine-gun fast with his delivery. They played at speeds other jazz musicians couldn't even approach. Even when they played ballads, they introduced extremely fast groups of notes into the melodies. Dizzy Gillespie said that, "playing bebop was like someone put a bomb in your mouth and light it!" [44]

As the new music developed, new characteristics appeared. Melodies that had traditionally been constructed with gentle inflections and modest ascents and descents of the scales were soon delivered with a much sharper edge. They would rise and fall dramatically often many times in each phrase, and were delivered at break-neck speed. The name of the music is bebop, a name that is onomatopoeic; if you say the syllables 'be bop' fast, you get a rough idea of the music's main characteristic. This way of playing became the stock-in-trade of 'Bird and Diz', as they were known, and only the very best musicians had the technical skill necessary to play jazz in this way.

I shall argue later that Miles Davis, who by the mid-1940s was hanging out with them on a regular basis, was required to perform beyond the limit of his technical ability and was thus never entirely comfortable with bebop music. This would explain why, in the late 1940s, he left bebop behind and became a founder member of a style of music that oriented itself in the opposite direction and called itself 'Cool'. Dyer looks at it in a positive way: "Miles's lonely, chillingly beautiful sound came about as a result of his inability to sustain the high register leaps that were Dizzy's trademark." Dizzy too had been trying to play like Roy Eldridge early on, and when he found out he couldn't he "tried something else." [45]

Diz: "It was the same music (as bebop), only cooler. I liked to fill up a bar myself - the Charlie Parker school - to take good advantage of every space that's there instead of just leaving it to go over into the next bar. Miles had wide-open spaces, and the guys that followed him didn't take full advantage of the whole space in a bar. Sometimes they would let a whole two bars go by and play one note. [46] ... Sometime later people were talking about third stream ... Apparently they meant that there was one stream that dealt with European classical music, another stream - the second stream - flowed from jazz; and then they tried to create a new stream, called third stream. 'Coolness' was supposed to be characteristic of it too. [44] ... In contrast to the cool school, another movement arose that was tagged 'hard bop' because it reasserted the primacy of rhythm and the blues in our music and made you get funky with sweat to play it. Max Roach, Fats Navarro, Art Blakey, Horace Silver, and, later, Cannonball Adderley became major exponents of it. Hard bop with its more earthy, churchy sound drew a lot of new black fans to our music, so both movements, it and the cool, extended the scope and popularity of modern jazz." [47]

Gillespie viewed the bebop that he created as the beginning of the modern jazz movement. All subsequent styles, he felt, were derivative - except for free-form jazz, of which the leading exponent was Ornette Coleman.

## Jazz Piano

Once the reign of the leaders of the big swing bands entered decline, mostly for reasons of cost, jazz became a genre more common in small groups of musicians, and has remained so more or less ever since. Besides the main characters we have met so far, jazz was strongly shaped by a number of pianists and I will devote a few paragraphs to this subject.

Art Tatum, Bud Powell and Thelonius Monk are regarded as defining the way jazz piano would be played at the time of the bebop revolution. In contrast, George Shearing, Oscar Peterson and Errol Garner, were in their own right great jazz pianists who, whilst capable of playing the new bebop style (and, indeed, contributing to it), chose to build their careers more on the traditional swing styles. As a result they – arguably - gained more success by attracting a bigger share of the popular audience than Tatum, Monk and Powell. But, in so doing, they sacrificed the ability to generate the great variety of innovative and creative jazz in favour of the more repetitive and derivative lines.

Art Tatum (1909-56) was born in Toledo, Ohio, with cataracts on both eyes that made him virtually blind. He took to the piano at the earliest possible age and developed an ability that other piano players found astonishing - even intimidating. Many refused to play when they knew he was present. Even some of the great classical concert pianists were amazed at his skills. Though he did work with bands and other musicians, he mostly played solo. Despite his immense talent, his career waxed and waned over the 1930s and 1940s and he made relatively few recordings. It wasn't until the early 1950s when he recorded over one hundred pieces for the impresario Norman Granz. These were released in a set of eleven LPs. By this time, however, he was seriously ill and he died in November 1956.

Tatum began as a pianist in the 'stride' style, but gradually developed his own distinctive style that was of interest to the musicians playing bebop. His style, at first built around rapid runs up and down the keyboard with arpeggios and flourishes, slowly took on a new style in which he made unusual steps into new keys. These brief modulations, lasting only a few bars, were considered to add significant new colour to the music, and this was an original aspect to piano jazz in these times when Parker and Gillespie were still working up their revolutionary bebop styles. Collier puts it succinctly: "Tatum was not merely improvising against chords as horn players - and other piano players - were doing; he was reshaping the whole harmonic structure of the song itself. His ability to improvise whole sequences of chords that could be set in place of the standard changes without disturbing the flow of the tune astonished fellow musicians. By 1933, when he made his first records, he clearly had a better grasp of harmonic possibilities than anybody in jazz at that time."

But as well as his immense harmonic capabilities, Tatum was one of the fastest piano players the world had ever seen, sometimes playing at a rate of a thousand notes a minute. Soloists frequently lose the discipline of playing in bands with other musicians, but Tatum's sense of time was superb and he was always an excellent band musician.

In the late 1940s and early 50s the pianist having the greatest influence in jazz was Earl 'Bud' Powell (1924-66), born in New York into a musical family. He studied piano from the age of six and became proficient in European classical music. He left school at the age of 15 for a career as a musician. He gravitated to *Minton's Jazz Club* in New York where most of the action was at the time and where he gained the support of Thelonius Monk. He soon became accepted into the inner circle of bebop musicians, most of them a few years older than he was. Though he was clearly influenced by Earl Hines and Art Tatum, his greatest influence was not a pianist but a saxophone player - Charlie Parker. This led Dizzy Gillespie to say: "Bud Powell didn't play the piano like a piano player; he played like a saxophonist..." [48] Powell developed his single-note style of soloing with the right hand to an amazing degree, and whilst his right hand was pushing out rapid strings of bebop solo lines his left hand was playing a new kind of accompaniment specifically designed to help the other soloists. Rather than playing the normal full chords he injected occasional bare combinations of notes - place markers and rhythmic accents, according to Collier. These allowed the horn players the freedom to explore the new harmonies without the restraint of the standard piano accompaniment. For these reasons, Powell became the pianist of choice for many of these musicians.

In 1945, whilst still only 21 and working for trumpeter Cootie Williams, Powell was arrested in a drugs bust. It is said that he was beaten about the head, and from this point onwards he suffered from extended periods of mental disorder, which kept him out of the musical scene. He is reported to have been at the peak of his powers around 1949 to 1951 when he made two series of recordings for Blue Note [47a] and Norman Granz's Verve labels. In between these dates he spent eighteen months in a sanatorium. Powell established his reputation amongst the wider jazz public with the records that emerged from these sessions. Though he did not pass away until 1966, he suffered bouts of mental illness for a period of around twenty years.

We say almost every day now that "Hindsight is a wonderful thing." The big problem with hindsight is that when you eventually get around to listening to a truly great musician, it is hard to understand what all the fuss is about. Of Powell, Dyer wrote: "Bud Powell sounds like any other pianist." He was alluding to the fact that Powell was so influential that what we should say is that *every other pianist sounds like Bud Powell*. [49]

Thelonius Monk (1917-82) was born in Rocky Mount, North Carolina, though he was taken to New York while still an infant. He was clearly influenced by Art Tatum, yet the style he developed became almost the exact opposite of Tatum's. From the start of his career, Monk was playing with Gillespie, Parker and Clarke and so is considered to have been one of the creators of the bebop style. However, Collier points out that bebop is not an accurate description of his style, which was too distinctive and individualistic. Monk was not chosen to play on the early bebop records because of it - Bud Powell was often considered a better choice.

Like Miles Davis, Monk was never really at home playing at the enormous speeds typical of bebop and his phrasing too was different. His use of unusual harmonies differed significantly from the beboppers, for whereas they would adopt the bebop harmonies throughout the pieces, Monk used them sporadically and his music was heterogeneous rather than their homogeneous. Some audiences found this aspect of his style annoying, but it became an important aspect of Monk's brand. This resulted in him being very much out on a limb and isolated from the rest. He struggled to find work and made few records, but stubbornly refused to change his style. Though he did make a series of recordings for Alfred Lion's *Blue Note* label (which are now considered to be jazz masterpieces), he was found in a car in which there were drugs (apparently they were not his) and his cabaret license was revoked. He was then out of work for six years from 1951 to 1957. During these years he was able to record and made records for the Prestige label. Once he was able to work in public again he was fortunate to get a gig in New York at which he hired the unknown John Coltrane. So successful were the resulting gigs that the careers of the two men were solidified thereafter in the most significant chapters of jazz history.

## Jazz Guitar

Although the origin of the guitar lies deep in the ancient cultures of Asia and India, the modern guitar is descended from an instrument called a cithara, brought by the Romans to Hispania – what is now Spain - around 40 AD. Therefore, the most recent lineage of guitars emanates from Spain and the Spanish/Moorish cultures. Throughout most of the $20^{th}$ century, students of guitar have started with the gut/nylon stringed Spanish acoustic guitar and progressed their studies in the genre of European classical music under the leadership of the maestro, Andres Segovia (1893-1987). John Williams (b1941) is one such guitarist, a student of Segovia who was later hailed as a maestro of classical guitar in his own right. However, Williams took the very unusual step of broadening his scope into the popular music arena, and through a number of albums released in the 1970s, some under the name of his band, Sky, is regarded as a jazz-fusion musician. In Europe, jazz and blues (but not swing) were very much a minority interest until the arrival of rock 'n' roll culture turned everything upside down in the 1950s, so the guitar was not as significant as perhaps other instruments, especially the piano.

In the early 20$^{th}$ century in the USA, the guitar was not a significant instrument in jazz either, because that genre of music had grown up around more traditional marching band instruments. Although the Gibson Company existed from the early 1900s, it was to make mostly mandolins and did not focus its efforts on guitars until much later. In fact, the manufacture of most acoustic (non-Spanish) guitars was, from the 1890s, by a company called Martin, and it was based upon the designs of this company that most modern acoustic guitars are still based. Where the guitar was used, along with the banjo or mandolin, it was mostly for rhythm when a piano was not available.

For a long time, the use of the guitar was restricted to Spanish, Moorish or Romany cultures and it was from the last of these that a great Belgian-born musician called Django Rheinhardt (1910-53) came to the fore playing jazz on an acoustic guitar at the *Hot Club de France* in Paris in the 1930s. In the USA, the growth of guitar use tended to be for solo or small group work such as in Country and Western, and blues music. It was not until the late 1930s that Charlie Christian (1916-42) began to show people how the (acoustic) guitar could be amplified through electrification that the guitar started to appear in larger bands playing the popular swing music. Thus, in 1939, when he began to play alongside the likes of Lionel Hampton, Dizzy Gillespie, Benny Carter (1907-2003), Coleman Hawkins (1904-1969) and Ben Webster (1909-73), and when he was hired by Benny Goodman the same year, the moment of the electric guitar in jazz had really arrived. This provided a stimulus for companies such as Gibson to focus their attentions on the manufacture of purpose-built electric guitars such as the Gibson 150 and later the Gibson ES 335, the world's first commercial semi-hollow-bodied electric guitar.

As a jazz solo instrument, the guitar was almost unknown until the 1940s when, in its electrified form, it was played by the likes of Barney Kessel (1923-2004), Wes Montgomery (1925-68) and Jim Hall (1930-2013). Solid bodied guitars were still some way into the future, and the jazz legacy of electric guitar created by these musicians was the use of a hollow-bodied instrument with steel strings amplified by externally mounted pick-ups. Apart from a volume control and a simple tone adjustment, there was little scope to experiment with the sound of the guitar, and so the basic guitar sound of all of these players was very similar, with a warm, rounded tone and a percussive attack as the strings were plucked by hard picks that were less pliable than the soft flesh of fingers. In contrast to the full use of fingers of the right hand for plucking the strings (later known as the finger-picking style) adopted by all classical guitarists, jazz musicians almost exclusively chose to use the pick or plectrum – a small rounded piece of plastic held between thumb and forefinger - as the means of creating sound. This led to significant differences in both sound and style.

Despite the growing popularity of players like Montgomery and Hall, jazz guitar was still not entirely in the mainstream of 1960s jazz. A brief burst of popularity for guitar occurred during the bossa nova period of 1963-68 when the likes of Charlie Byrd (1925-99) and Joao Gilberto (b1931) came to prominence, yet, because this was Latin music, they both played unamplified 'Spanish' guitars with their fingers. The leading jazz groups of the time, led by the likes of Miles Davis and Art Blakey (1919-90), almost never used electric guitar, preferring the piano as the 'chording' instrument. We almost need to pinch ourselves to realise just how strange it was for audiences to find electric guitar players such as George Benson, Joe Beck and John McLaughlin sharing the floor with Miles Davis. Thus, only after the irresistible effects of rock music on popular audiences finally impacted on jazz with the creation of jazz-fusion, was the guitar finally accepted as a normal instrument to find in jazz groups. And when the guitar itself became the focus of the jazz group, as it was in John McLaughlin's Mahavishnu Orchestra, then the music was a true jazz-rock fusion.

## Free Jazz

In the late 1950s, post-war society became obsessed with change, in ways that I shall describe in detail later. The overturning of long-established practices in music became all-consuming and the inevitable result was the abandonment of all rules and the creation of a new genre of jazz that was called *avant-garde* or 'free' jazz. As a movement with roots in experimentation, free jazz had a number of sites of creation, but several recordings are regarded as marking out the territory. Musicians to make early explorations were Ornette Coleman (b1930) and Cecil Taylor (b1929), but soon afterwards, the musical style of free playing became associated with musicians such as John Coltrane (1926-67), Charles Mingus (1922-79), Eric Dolphy (1928-64), Sun Ra (1914-93), Albert Ayler (1936-70) and Archie Shepp (b1937).

Starting with Ornette Coleman's album, *The Shape of Jazz to Come* (1959) and followed by his *Free Jazz* (1961), it had become clear that the paper specifications that defined the jazz genre had been shredded. Why should American jazzers be interested in those irritating backbeat-driven sounds from Merseyside in a small, insignificant country across the Atlantic? British trumpeter Guy Barker once asked Coleman what he was thinking at this time. Coleman replied that, until then, "all the music I had been playing seemed to follow the same route, harmonic progressions like II-IV-I. All I did was throw away the map. [50] It was a remarkably simple formula for something that was to prove so revolutionary.

Up to that point, jazz had been a clearly identifiable music form, with all the characteristics of melody, harmony, timbre, rhythm and form that I discussed earlier. Almost at a stroke (or perhaps it should be at a puff) Coleman presented the world with a musical revolution. Perhaps the most remarkable thing was that, although he was widely hated for it, the music took a hold like a spark to a pool of petrol. It may have been a valid experiment with a new art form, but in retrospect it was a serious red herring for the music industry. Free jazz has never been popular. It is my opinion that a lot of the early jazz-fusion music went off in the wrong direction because of the distraction caused by free jazz. Miles Davis - one of the leading experimenters - became too pre-occupied with the dissolution of rules, at the same time that he was also contemplating the absorption of elements of rock into jazz. Consequently, I believe he drove his own bandwagon up a dead end and by 1976 had retired exhausted. Similarly, the early experiments by Davis's disciples - Corea, Zawinul, Shorter and Hancock - all absorbed valuable time investigating the area of free jazz when they could have been generating a more successful style of jazz-fusion. Thus, they took longer to become established in the new jazz-fusion genre than might otherwise have been the case.

The full story of free-jazz is too long to tell in detail here, but the scene was set for jazz musicians throughout the 1960s to become pre-occupied with experimentation in the *free thing*, as it became called. Jost wrote: "The break from a traditional system of rules led to a precarious situation full of contradictions and insecurity, for with the liberation from old norms the question arose what this liberation should be for... A common harmonic and rhythmic language and a fundamental beat did not mean that all this was now and forever forbidden, but that it was not automatically required." In his excellent, concise analysis, Jost listed the main points in the new philosophy. [51]

(1) The questioning, not the abolition, of rules;
(2) The growing importance of spontaneous interaction among players;
(3) The growing tendency towards collective rather than solo improvisation;
(4) The emancipation of sound colour, to include scope for amelodic improvisation;
(5) The importance of energy and intensity as communicative elements and sources for collective ecstasy;
(6) A turn towards musical cultures of the Third World and thereby the integration of diverse exotic elements into jazz;
(7) A growing consciousness of social, political and economic problems among musicians and the consequent development of a new form of understanding.

Presented in such clear and unequivocal terms, this manifesto offered so many opportunities for musical exploration that in 1960 few jazz musicians could even appreciate them, let alone try to play them. It fell to those in the jazz *avant-garde* to present these new ideas in a thousand different ways and invite the reaction of audiences. Unsurprisingly, it took time for the ramifications to reach deep into the jazz highways and byways where, in the meantime, people were starting to wake-up to the additional opportunities offered by the fusion of elements of rock into jazz - a small task in comparison. As we shall find out in this book, the effects were very varied amongst the different musicians.

The investigation of spontaneous interaction was a big part of what Herbie Hancock, Ron Carter and Tony Williams were trying to achieve in their quartets and quintets of the mid-1960s. Hancock then expanded on what he had begun in his Mwandishi period (1970-73), whilst the early albums of Weather Report (1971-73) had similar stated aims.

A proportion of the music I describe is played in a way that focuses on the band as a whole, rather than on a given soloist. It was very much the theme for Miles Davis bands during his first jazz-fusion period (1969-76). At the same time he began the process of absorption of elements of Third World music. Many American black musicians such as Davis and Hancock, naturally inclined towards Africa in celebration of their own racial heritage, whilst others like Joe Zawinul, John McLaughlin and latterly Pat Metheny brought in European and Asian elements. Jost's phrase 'the emancipation of colour' is especially appropriate. I propose in these books that the creation of a wealth of new colours into jazz was one of the greatest gifts offered by jazz-fusion, for example, the blending of groups of instruments that were the norm in soul and funk music. In their simplest terms, energy and intensity became the focus for bands such as The Tony Williams Lifetime, Mahavishnu Orchestra, Return to Forever and Billy Cobham's groups. More recently, new methods for creating energy and intensity within jazz have been invented by such musicians as Pat Metheny and Marcus Miller.

Inevitably, the profound changes taking place in American society in the 1960s impacted strongly on jazz. Musicians are, like the rest of us, not usually political activists, but figures like Charles Mingus and Miles Davis were especially influential in the problems of black people in the USA. Davis spent much time in the 1970s wondering how he could relate his music to young black people. Ornette Coleman's colleague in his early free-jazz music, Charlie Haden, for example, became known for music formulated around overt political statements in his work for the Liberation Jazz Orchestra. Last, but by no means least, almost all of them tried amelodic improvisations and non-traditional harmonies at some point in their careers, with varying degrees of popularity. Those who persisted were, in general, less financially successful than those who retained an observance of at least some of the rules.

With so much change going on, it resulted in exponential growth in the width of jazz music on offer to the general public and increased greatly our cultural heritage. However, it must be admitted that a significant proportion of the experimentation passed over the heads of an even more significant proportion of the music-listening population. Audiences liked some changes to the rules of music, but hated others. To many people it seemed that jazz was being driven further towards the margins of high art that could be enjoyed only by a small number of music intellectuals. The situation has not changed much today from what it was when free jazz emerged. Thanks to the wonderful efficiency of Internet retailers such as Amazon, there has never been a better opportunity to obtain the music from the free jazz experimentations of the 1960s, yet it is no more listened to now than it was then. Audiences have voted with their wallets, and the results of the poll are clear. Whether the custodians of our cultural and artistic heritage like it or not, audiences do not like music that abandons too many rules, and musicians who insist on pursuing these art forms are destined to live in poverty and obscurity. Jazz-fusion, on the contrary, has been an overwhelming success, to such a degree that it has been a completed process now for more than a decade. It is possible to identify examples of overt jazz-fusion music being recorded and played today, but on the whole there are significant amounts of modern music, presented in so many aspects of everyday life, in which there is very little differentiation between what used to be called rock and jazz. This particular part of the experiment was a resounding success.

There was also a strong social aspect to the music. "Bellevue (the oldest public hospital in New York City) has an almost equal claim to *Birdland* as being the home of modern jazz", wrote Dyer, commenting on how the list of non-addicted jazzers is far less impressive than the list of those who were. Jazz stars were mostly addicted to drugs or alcohol and many ended up having mental breakdowns. [52] The writer was struck by comparisons of the lives of jazz musicians and those of other doomed artists such as Shelley, Keats and Schubert. These men were "fulfilling the doomed caveat of the Romantic agony", a talent that that consumes itself even as it flourishes and in which "premature death is a condition of creativity." [52] This has continued into the era of modern pop music, as in the tragic lives of, for example Kurt Cobain (1967-94) or Sid Vicious (1957-79). What might Clifford Brown (died aged 25) or Jimmy Blanton (died aged 23) have achieved if they had lived? On the other hand, Dyer speculates, "imagine what would have been lost had Miles not lived past thirty?" [52] Jazz was an art form that allowed black people a means of expression like no other, elevating a significant number of them to the rank of genius. Without jazz, most of these men would have led insignificant lives. [53]

The story of jazz is, of course, very long and detailed and I have given you but the briefest outline here, but I have tried to make it as comprehensive as space allows, and you have now met most of the main characters who shaped it up to the mid-1960s. So, the first lesson is now over and the scene is set for us to embark on a journey of discovery, through the dark forests of jazz-fusion.

## References to Part 1

Lewis Porter's book, *John Coltrane: His Life and Music* is published by University of Michigan, 1998. This is a scholarly work and essential for the serious enthusiast. Its only disappointment is its lack of a discography.

Geoff Dyer's book *But Beautiful: A Book about Jazz*, North Point Press, New York (1996) is just that – beautiful! It's one of the loveliest descriptions of jazz music that you are ever likely to read. Everyone should have a copy.

Dizzy Gillespie's autobiography *To Be or Not to Bop*, written by Al Fraser, Quartet Books (1979) is filled with excellent anecdotes and first-hand quotations from a large number of his contemporaries. The book is an excellent source of comment and opinion about the birth of bebop. Sadly, it lacks hard historical fact, but does contain some useful data in its appendices and also some rare musical explanations of Gillespie's approach to playing bebop. Diz was a great entertainer throughout his long lifetime and this book is as much fun as his live shows. Thanks Diz!

The most authoritative history of Louis Armstrong and the early years of jazz in New Orleans is surely provided by Thomas Brothers, whose two books are essential reading for all those interested in this period. The books are: Thomas Brothers: *Louis Armstrong's New Orleans*, W. W. Norton & Company; 1st Edition (25 May 2007), 978-0393330014, and Thomas Brothers: *Louis Armstrong, Master of Modernism*, W. W. Norton & Company; 1st Edition (28 Mar 2014), 978-0393065824.

Many relevant references can be discovered in the recently published luxurious history of Blue Note Records, written by Richard Havers and titled *Uncompromising Expression*, Thames & Hudson, London (2014). A somewhat expensive volume, this book is nevertheless essential for all good collections of jazz books.

Specific References:

1. Dyer, p205.
2. James Lincoln Collier, *The Making of Jazz*, MacMillan (1978). I have drawn on Collier's summary of the development of jazz for my work in this chapter, for which I am grateful. He draws a nice balance between the history and the explanation of the music.
3. Wikipedia: Blues scale
4. Courtney Pine, *Jazz Crusade*, BBC Radio 2, Interview with Pat Metheny (14 February 2005).
5. Ken Trethewey, *The Brecker Brothers: Funky Sea, Funky Blue*, Jazz-Fusion Books (2014).
6. Gary Giddins and Scott DeVeaux, *Jazz* (2009), Norton, p43.
7. Dyer, p208.
8. Scott Yanow, allmusic.com
9. Thomas Brothers, *Louis Armstrong: Master of Modernism*, (2014) Norton, p4
10. Brothers, p5
11. Brothers, p8
12. Laurie Wright: *King Oliver*, pub. by L. D. Wright, Storyville Publications (1987)
13. Brothers, p3-4
14. Brothers, p7
15. Brothers, p6
16. Brothers, p9
17. Brothers, p10
18. Brothers, p23-4
19. Gillespie, p184.
20. Gillespie, p98.
21. Gillespie, p137.
22. Gillespie, p99-100.
23. Gillespie, p103.
24. Gillespie, p104.
25. Gillespie, p105.
26. Gillespie, p137.
27. Gillespie, p136.
28. Gillespie, p116-7.
29. Gillespie, p118-9.
30. Gillespie, p139.
31. Gillespie, p250.
32. Gillespie, p259.
33. Gillespie, p260.
34. Gillespie, p264.
35. Gillespie, p266.
36. Gillespie, p312.
37. Gillespie, p314.
38. Gillespie, p115.
39. Gillespie, p116.
40. Gillespie, p324.
41. Gillespie, p190.
42. Gillespie, p208.
43. Gillespie, p356.
44. Gillespie, p360.
45. Dyer, p188.
46. Gillespie, p359.
47. Gillespie, p369.
48. Gillespie, p138.
49. Dyer, p214.
50. *Jazzwise*, Issue 115 (Dec 07 / Jan 08), Guy Barker talking to Stuart Nicholson, p30.
51. Ekkehard Jost, Da Capo Press (1994).
52. Dyer, p196.
53. Dyer, p192-3.

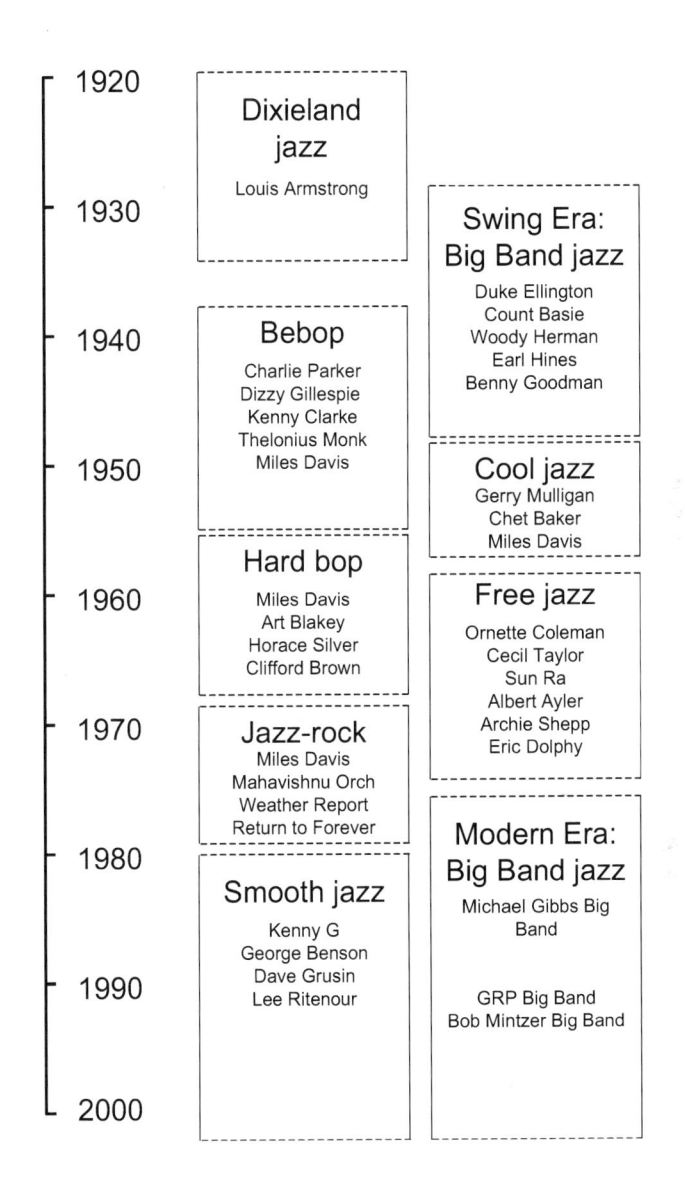

```
1920 ┬
     │   ┌─────────────────┐
     │   │   Dixieland     │
     │   │     jazz        │
     │   │                 │
     │   │ Louis Armstrong │
1930 ┤   │                 │   ┌─────────────────┐
     │   │                 │   │   Swing Era:    │
     │   │                 │   │  Big Band jazz  │
     │   └─────────────────┘   │                 │
     │                         │  Duke Ellington │
     │                         │   Count Basie   │
1940 ┤   ┌─────────────────┐   │  Woody Herman   │
     │   │     Bebop       │   │   Earl Hines    │
     │   │                 │   │  Benny Goodman  │
     │   │  Charlie Parker │   │                 │
     │   │ Dizzy Gillespie │   └─────────────────┘
     │   │  Kenny Clarke   │
     │   │ Thelonius Monk  │   ┌─────────────────┐
1950 ┤   │   Miles Davis   │   │   Cool jazz     │
     │   │                 │   │                 │
     │   │                 │   │ Gerry Mulligan  │
     │   └─────────────────┘   │   Chet Baker    │
     │                         │   Miles Davis   │
     │   ┌─────────────────┐   └─────────────────┘
     │   │    Hard bop     │
     │   │                 │   ┌─────────────────┐
1960 ┤   │   Miles Davis   │   │    Free jazz    │
     │   │    Art Blakey   │   │                 │
     │   │  Horace Silver  │   │ Ornette Coleman │
     │   │ Clifford Brown  │   │   Cecil Taylor  │
     │   │                 │   │     Sun Ra      │
     │   └─────────────────┘   │   Albert Ayler  │
1970 ┤   ┌─────────────────┐   │  Archie Shepp   │
     │   │    Jazz-rock    │   │   Eric Dolphy   │
     │   │   Miles Davis   │   │                 │
     │   │ Mahavishnu Orch │   └─────────────────┘
     │   │ Weather Report  │
     │   │ Return to Forever│  ┌─────────────────┐
1980 ┤   └─────────────────┘   │   Modern Era:   │
     │                         │  Big Band jazz  │
     │   ┌─────────────────┐   │                 │
     │   │   Smooth jazz   │   │Michael Gibbs Big│
     │   │                 │   │      Band       │
     │   │     Kenny G     │   │                 │
     │   │  George Benson  │   │                 │
     │   │   Dave Grusin   │   │  GRP Big Band   │
1990 ┤   │  Lee Ritenour   │   │Bob Mintzer Big Band│
     │   │                 │   │                 │
     │   │                 │   │                 │
     │   │                 │   │                 │
     │   │                 │   │                 │
     │   │                 │   │                 │
2000 ┴   └─────────────────┘   └─────────────────┘
```

*Figure 1: A Timeline for some of the sub-genres of jazz.*

# PART 2: The Technicolour Music of Jazz-Fusion

## Introduction: What is jazz-fusion?

In this second part of my book I shall describe the processes in which different musical forms became fused. Naturally, I wish to focus on *jazz-fusion*, the term that best describes the kind of music in this series of books. Fusion is not new; fusion has occurred since music was first played. Musicians are *listening* people. As they develop their own craft, they listen to other musicians and are influenced by them. It is inevitable that some aspects of music that appeals to them will be incorporated into their own work. When such influences cause the musicians to play slightly differently, their musical style develops. However, fusion is the blending of *different* musical styles, cultures, or *genres*. Thus, in the past, when distinct musical styles became established (usually associated with the peoples and cultures of the world), *fusion* was the cross-fertilisation of music from one culture into another. Sometimes, it may be a two-way process.

Musical fusions ought to be a cause for celebration. They revitalise some genres and cross-fertilise others. They bring together people from diverse musical backgrounds, helping them to enjoy a wider musical spectrum than they might otherwise have done. Multiculturalism is not, however, universally popular, and those with some kind of agenda or vested interest have often denigrated fusions as diluting or dumbing down music. The arguments used are just another version of the classic controversy that occurs in so many walks of life: is it better to study in depth or in breadth? The answer that so many people find hard to discover is that *both* are equally purposeful, providing a positive, progressive evolution of music. The fusions we are dealing with in this book relate to the many ways that *jazz* influenced other genres. We have already studied the early developments of jazz into a defined genre. The remainder of this book is about a particular period in the history of jazz when the music had become so influential that cross-fertilisation of jazz by other genres took place, i.e. from 1945 to the present day.

It's always difficult to be accurate about descriptions because people disagree. I see jazz-fusion as a hybridisation process by which some or all of the characteristics of a genre called jazz are blended with some or all of the characteristics of another type of music such as classical, ethnic/folk and rock. (Notice how I like to include a hyphen between the words: it's a joining symbol in English, so it is both sensible and consistent.)

At the time of writing, the most fluid reference source containing (hopefully) the version with the most highly distilled wisdom is (whether you like it, or not) Wikipedia, from which the following is obtained:

"Jazz fusion is a musical fusion genre that developed from mixing funk and rhythm and blues rhythms and the amplification and electronic effects of rock music, complex time signatures derived from non-Western music and extended, typically instrumental compositions with a jazz approach to lengthy group improvisations, often using wind and brass and displaying a high level of instrumental technique. It was created around the late 1960s. The term 'jazz-rock' is often used as a synonym for 'jazz fusion' as well as for music performed by late 1960s and 1970s-era rock bands that added jazz elements to their music." [1]

First, let us be clear that the sensible use of the word 'fusion' is the incorporation of influences from (or elements of) another genre. Hence, the term 'jazz-fusion' can only have one sensible interpretation, that is, the fusion of jazz with other identifiable genres or sub-genres. Figure 2 provides a visual representation of the idea of jazz-rock fusion. Unfortunately, this idea is not conveyed by the definition of 'jazz fusion' cited in Wikipedia. The situation is not helped by the assertion that 'jazz-rock' is often used as a synonym for 'jazz fusion.' However, we must accept that *this is so*, in common parlance.

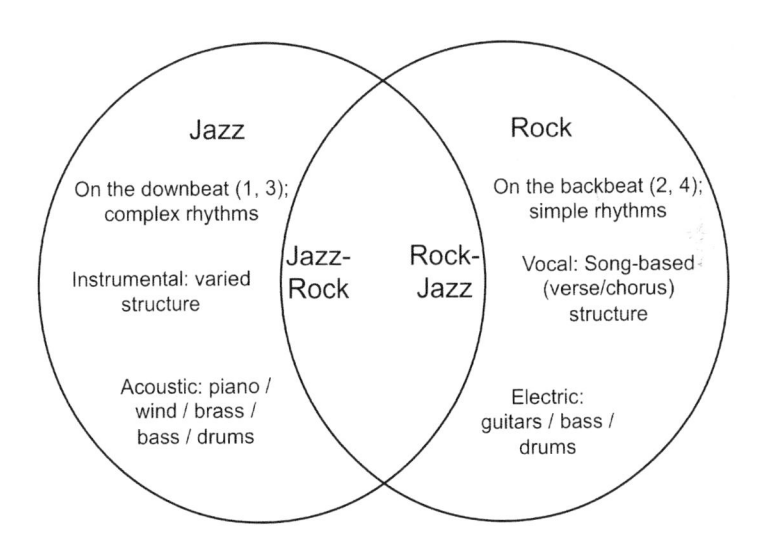

*Figure 2: A Venn diagram showing the characteristics of jazz and rock in the 1960s, and a representation of jazz-rock fusion.*

In this author's opinion, 'jazz-rock' is better used for the fusion of jazz (as the primary component) with rock (as the secondary component), and it is perfectly logical to use the term 'rock-jazz' to mean the opposite. It seems that the reason for much of the argument that has raged over decades is because of the failure to appreciate the difference between these two terms, which I shall now explore.

The best definition we have for rock music, fortunately, makes more sense:

"Rock music is a genre of popular music that originated as 'rock and roll' in the United States in the 1950s, and developed into a range of different styles in the 1960s and later, particularly in the United Kingdom and the United States. It has its roots in 1940s' and 1950s' rock and roll, itself heavily influenced by rhythm and blues and country music. Rock music also drew strongly on a number of other genres such as blues and folk, and incorporated influences from jazz, classical and other musical sources. Musically, rock has centered on the electric guitar, usually as part of a rock group with electric bass guitar and drums. Typically, rock is song-based music usually with a 4/4 time signature using a verse-chorus form, but the genre has become extremely diverse." [2]

It is important to notice that this definition includes the structure of the band, as well as the typical influences contained in it. The visual approach I adopted in Figure 2 is called a Venn diagram. The idea is to use a number of overlapping ellipses that represent distinct music genres. I am going to use four ellipses and name them after four musical genres, namely jazz, rock, classical and ethnic/folk music. See how the spaces overlap. In Figure 3, as in Figure 2, the ellipse of rock overlaps the ellipse for jazz, and those parts of the jazz and rock ellipses that are shared represent the kind of music that many have called jazz-rock. Just as the hyphen clearly indicates the joining of the two words, so it is consistent with the fusion of the two genres. Similarly, those parts of the jazz and classical ellipses that overlap represent the music of jazz-classical, and so on... Later, I am going to suggest which parts of these spaces different musicians occupy.

Let's now use a direct analogy with the spaces we actually do occupy from day to day. For example, I could say that I live in London. Clearly, I don't live everywhere in London – just in a very small part of it with my house at the focal point. If I include all of the places I visit, for work, for shopping, or recreation, it will still be only a small part of this very large city. Another person occupies a different part of the same city. It may be entirely different and we may never meet, but it is possible we both live on the same street and visit the same shops. I hope the analogy is starting to make sense. Let's think of jazz music as being like a city. Miles Davis, for example, could be found in a number of different parts of the city of Jazztown, such as the angular Bebop Street or the more highly architectured Hard Bop Avenue, but rarely in the lush Big Band Park or the popular suburbs of Swing-time. Some musicians buy houses in a certain part of a town and go and live there. Other musicians buy a plot of land in an uninhabited area and build their own house there. Charlie Parker, for example built a house in the uninhabited part of town that later became Bebop Street. By making it look good and giving it a certain kind of style they may well attract others to go and live nearby. Many of the musicians I describe in these books are house-builders.

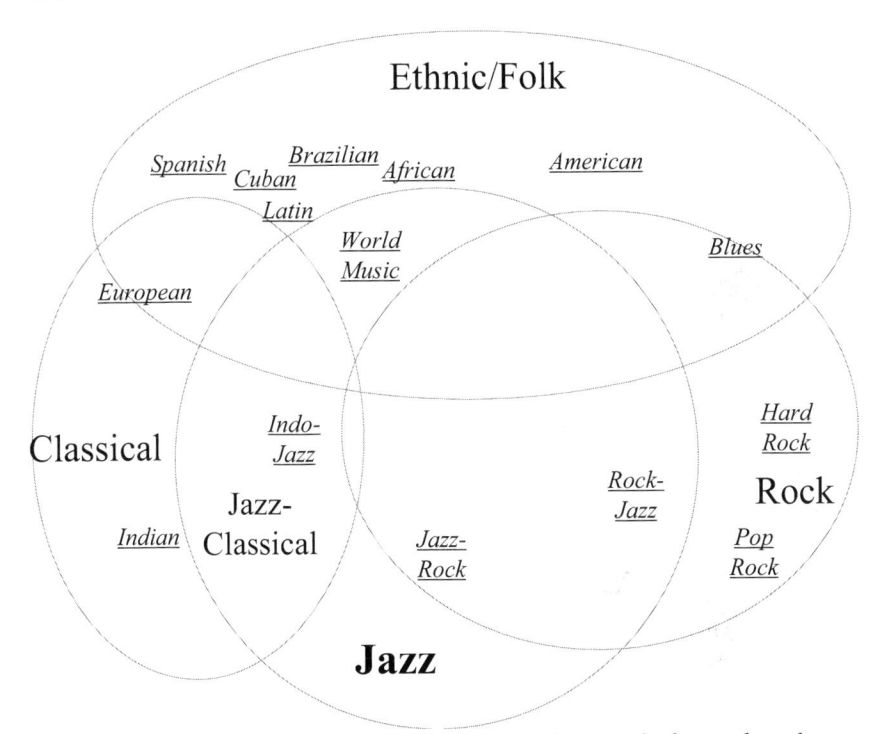

*Figure 3: A Venn diagram showing fusions of jazz with classical, rock and ethnic/folk genres of music*

Now, close to Jazztown there is another rapidly expanding city called Rockville. I'm sure you can see that there are a greater number of musicians who occupied space in Rockville. Elvis Presley built his own house before anyone else lived there, and now there are many inhabitants. The town has grown very large (and prosperous) compared to Jazztown, so much so that parts of Rockville overlap parts of Jazztown. (They'll have to fight it out over the precise location of the city boundary!) I think by now it's pretty clear that the region of overlap represents the fusion of jazz with rock, in other words, jazz-rock (or rock-jazz, if you prefer). This is just one possible jazz-fusion.

I think it is also clear that there are some parts in the region of overlap that are very close to Jazztown and other parts that are very close to Rockville. People with houses in Jazztown might visit clubs and bars in Rockville, and vice versa. Hence we could come up with titles for two new sub-genres called jazz-rock (closer to Jazztown) and rock-jazz (closer to Rockville). My own analysis places bands like Chick Corea's Elektric Band in the jazz-rock part of town, whilst Tony Williams' Lifetime is quite a few blocks away in rock-jazz.

Another fusion is the one with jazz and (European) classical music, often called Third Stream; the one with jazz and ethnic/folk could be jazz-ethnic or jazz-folk, perhaps more generally known now as world music. (Some of these terms are uncommon and it's arguable whether the term 'world music' includes jazz or whether it is used as a collective term just to describe the different types of ethnic music.) There is no true scientific way to determine where the musicians live: unfortunately, there is no musical GPS. So what we have here is the result of my deliberations. Some of you may not agree with my placements, but you can have fun looking at the charts, listening to the music and working out your own maps. (Some of the musicians have more than one home anyway.) My objective here is simply to try to describe jazz-fusion music to those readers who are unfamiliar with this wonderful musical legacy.

So, my Venn diagram in Figure 3 shows the way I have chosen to draw the overlap of spaces representing jazz, rock, classical and ethnic/folk genres. Let's be clear. The Venn diagram shows lots of fusions: wherever two or more ellipses overlap is a fusion. So, by my definition, anywhere that the jazz ellipse overlaps an ellipse for another genre is a jazz-fusion. I must stress that there is no absolute way to do this, and it is possible to see other ways of doing it. For example, it could be argued, as I did in Part 1, that jazz is actually already a hybrid of spaces, having grown out of earlier forms of music created by black and Creole people in Louisiana. To do so, however, does not help my argument. If I were writing a different book it might make more sense to do so. I have chosen to represent jazz as a genre in its own right and to identify the purer forms of ethnic music under a separate genre. I then indicate sub-genres of ethnic music based upon their geographical source, such as Spanish, Brazilian, Latin (Cuban), and American. I have indicated blues as growing out of ethnic American music. I have also tried to place ethnic American music close to ethnic African music, for some of the former grew out of the latter. Similarly, what we now think of as Spanish music grew out of the music of North Africa, but also out of European influences too.

Of course, since this book is a description of jazz-fusion, my primary interest is the regions of overlap between jazz and the other three genres. The overlap between jazz and the European flavour of classical music is often referred to as the Third Stream. There are some notable examples of this type of fusion that I shall describe shortly. However, we need to realise that the Indian sub-continent also has its own classical music; so does China. From the late 1950s there was a strong interest from European and American musicians in Indian music and many were content to immerse themselves in the pure forms of Indian classical music. Others made many successful attempts at what became known as Indo-Jazz fusion. From our point of view, the most significant musician by far is John McLaughlin, but it would be naïve to think that this immensely important guitarist only played Indo-Jazz. McLaughlin was also one of the most important musicians to establish a presence in what became a new suburb of Jazztown: the community of jazz-rock fusion. There he built his own house where there were very few people in sight. He still lives there; a lot of musicians who used to have properties there have moved out. (But John McLaughlin's house is still one of the best in town!)

The descriptions of music in the Venn diagram ellipses are not complete; only those sub-genres relevant to my discussions are included. For example, besides blues, which is very important to my discussion, there are many other sub-genres of American ethnic music: country and western, bluegrass, gospel, soul - the list goes on. As well as blues, we could have rock music as a sub-genre of ethnic music, but because of its importance I have made it a genre in its own right. I could argue the same for the others I just listed. Thus, you can see how different people could draw different diagrams, depending upon what they wish to illustrate. The purpose of this diagram is to help you pinpoint the very different musical styles of the musicians I am writing about. The same is true for the other genres. For example, I have not tried to indicate any of the sub genres of jazz on the Venn diagram: it would simply become too complicated.

To sum up, then, my use of the term jazz-fusion describes any music that results from the influence of jazz on another musical genre. In common parlance, as defined in Wikipedia, the term *jazz-rock* is sometimes associated with the same music as is embraced by the definition, *jazz-fusion*. However, I believe that this is an inadequate definition and that my approach is an improvement and an aid to better understanding. For example, 'jazz-rock' or 'jazz-fusion' could also include a whole swathe of music that might be described as *progressive rock* (*prog-rock*), examples of which might be the music of Soft Machine, Yes, King Crimson or Emerson Lake and Palmer, but prog-rock was clearly influenced by jazz. Therefore, I intend to use the phrase *rock-jazz* to describe music that is more rock than jazz, and jazz-rock to mean the opposite. I shall try to use the term 'jazz-fusion' in its most logical context, i.e. the one I have defined above.

## Jazz-fusion: You either love it or hate it.

From time to time, throughout this series of books, I shall write some things that are controversial. From the start, when jazz began to absorb elements of other musical genres, some listeners hated the results. This was because jazz was a way of escape for those people who liked to think they were intellectually superior. They wanted to preserve jazz for their own cliquish principles and the thought that large audiences could enjoy jazz was anathema to them. Others were simply jazz purists who wished to preserve the form unsullied by popular idioms. It is natural for people to dislike change, especially when it threatens something they hold dear. Jazz writer Bill Milkowski wrote: "Fusion was a generational thing – younger people tended to love it; older jazz fans hated it. It ambitiously melded instrumental virtuosity on the level of Charlie Parker or Dizzy Gillespie with the sheer decibels of The Who." [3]

Some called it *con-fusion*. That was one of the more polite insults. Later, as jazz-fusion-inspired music became absorbed into everyday life (because, heaven forbid, people liked it!) another derogatory term *fuzak* was invented. The establishment of radio channels devoted to what was called *smooth jazz* made matters worse, for jazz channels had always struggled to attract audiences large enough to make them commercially viable. However, even smooth jazz struggled, especially under a tirade of abuse. Thus, for example, in 2008, the UK digital radio channel *theJazz* closed down after barely two years of operation, despite growing audiences. Other jazz radio stations have come and gone since then, run on small budgets and large amounts of goodwill by a few dedicated people.

People have always argued that taking elements of two things and mixing them results in a dilution of their individual quality. They conclude that you fall between two stools, whereas I maintain that you actually build a taller structure out of them. Writing about Wayne Shorter's retrospective album, *Footprints* (2005), jazz critic, Nick Coleman wrote that Shorter's early years with Miles Davis and Weather Report were "brilliant", but that "later solo fusioneering and activities as sideman to Joni Mitchell and Steely Dan were not so much a by-way as a suburban cul-de-sac: nice, tidy, unthreatening and not going anywhere." [4] And that was from someone who likes Weather Report! Coleman describes Shorter as a "visionary-architect, composer of strange new buildings" that he, Coleman, prefers. I can sympathise with the desire for innovation, but not to the extent that it is necessary to denounce as pointless his contributions to the music of Joni Mitchell and Steely Dan. In fact, the music of Joni Mitchell and Steely Dan is as important to the development of jazz-fusion as anything else that this particular critic might prefer, and probably a lot more palatable when you're not as deep into jazz as Coleman obviously is.

## The Late-1940s and the Post-War Permissiveness

From our vantage point in the 21$^{st}$ century, it is clear to anyone who looks back at history that the twentieth century was the most eventful in human history. A large number of factors that had been developing throughout the 18$^{th}$ and 19$^{th}$ centuries finally came together to generate cataclysmic events, mostly in the form of two World Wars and the terrible possibility of a Third. Entire countries were created and destroyed, as they never had been before, so it is hardly surprising that Western culture was also subjected to major changes. In the almost total absence of mass media, the First World War had a smaller effect on the well-insulated USA than it did on Europe. The fledgling jazz music continued its development in the musical bubbles of New Orleans, Chicago and New York as the brave soldiers went over the top to their deaths in the mud baths of France, Belgium and Holland. The effects of the War were, however, much more visible through the 1920s and 30s in the USA as the financial crisis caused by bankrupt European countries reached Wall Street. The First World War had certainly changed Western Society, but even bigger change was to come.

The end of the Second World War in 1945 heralded profound changes for Western civilisation as the rapidly developing mass media helped people to realise the enormity of the events they had survived. Then, over a period of ten years or so, they began to celebrate their hard-won freedoms. In some ways, the celebration of freedom was manifest in an abandonment of rules. The nineteenth and early twentieth centuries had been about the establishment of rules and the oppressive regimes of Stalin, Hitler and Franco. Even in the home of democracy, the British people today associate the adjective 'Victorian' with a social hierarchy that conformed to strict rules of behaviour and in which Conservatism became the creed by which the ruling classes could preserve the status-quo. Governments insisted that rules were essential to the maintenance of order, none more so than the various Communist regimes that had been established. From 1945 all that began to change in the West so that by the 1960s it had become an unstoppable tide.

The performing arts, in particular, were shaken to the core by a barrage of change brought about by the artists themselves who now refused to accept the rules of their art that had evolved over many centuries. The desire for a fresh start caused everything to be thrown into the melting pot. Music that had been so formally and neatly categorised was now less easily classified and musicians experimented with mixtures of classical, folk, jazz and popular music in the search for new forms of expression. This was the process of fusion, which was unrecognised as such before the Second World War.

Art and music were also subject to other influences stemming from changes occurring in the wider world. In particular, the process of making music, which had been constrained by the availability of traditional instruments over centuries, was suddenly transformed by developments in science that gave rise to astonishing new electronic instruments. Computers changed everything from the recording of thoughts during composition to the storing of musical activity in the studio and, nowadays, the dissemination of it. Suddenly, the possibilities for new art seemed limitless. That revolution continues to this day with the transition to digital musical activities in the clouds, and the demise of traditional physical media such as vinyl, magnetic tape and CD.

## The Boost From Technology

The war years had imposed so much discipline on everyone that parents of the 1950s were determined not to be so strict with their own children. This was the beginning of what became known as *the Permissive Society*. At first, forms of entertainment were very limited, and in the UK most people looked to television and the single channel offered by the BBC for their relaxation. Young people, however, soon decided that they did not want the normal fare being served up for them by old men in suits at the BBC. Everything was changing: music, theatre, art, film and fashion too, but at this point, it was probably music that was affected most, and not only changed itself but induced change in the other art forms too. The guitar took over from the saxophone as the sexiest instrument, just as in the previous decade the saxophone had taken over from the trumpet. By 1950, catalysed by music, people began to enjoy life once again. Two things played a large part. The first was the development of new, simple but commercially effective recording media and formats; the second was a new craze to record onto them: rock 'n' roll.

Until the late 1940s, music recordings had been made available as 'sides' of black Bakelite plastic that were played on rotating 'record decks' at 78-rpm. Unlike the later discs made from flexible vinyl, Bakelite was inflexible and brittle: sudden impact would result in the disc shattering into hundreds of sharp shards. But most importantly, the music recorded onto 78s was conceptualised as stand-alone songs, with an existence that was largely independent of other recordings. True, there was perhaps a weak relationship with the song on the other side of the disc, but by-and-large, the concept of an 'album' was unknown. Each song was a maximum of 3 minutes in length and the recording was made by cutting a very fine groove into the plastic with a diamond that vibrated in resonance to the music. The reverse process – in which the diamond pulled along the zig-zag groove as the record revolved beneath it, caused a resonance that could be converted into electricity, and then became music when the signal was applied to coils wound around magnets inside speaker cabinets.

The LP-record played at 33.3 revolutions per minute (rpm) and was introduced in 1948. At first it was 10 inches (25 cm) in diameter, but later increased to 12 inches (30 cm) and could hold just over 50 minutes of music. The idea of collections of music known as 'albums' was quite new at this time. The concept is attributed to a German company called *Odeon* who in 1909 issued a collection of plastic 78-rpm records of Tchaikovsky's *Nutcracker Suite*. In the 1920s bound collections of empty record sleeves were sold as albums in the same way as books designed to hold photographs. It was not really until the 1930s that collections of music by one particular artist or on a given topic began to be known as albums.

The new, versatile, 45-rpm, seven-inch vinyl disc that took over from the 78-rpm disc was introduced by RCA in 1949. Like the 78, it could contain only a short piece of music, about three minutes in this case, but it was cheap and young people took to the new format very favourably: it was one of the first significant artefacts they could buy that could distinguish them from their parents. Owning a record player and some records was something their parents simply did not do! The 45 'single' record medium concentrated popular musical statements into around three minutes or less. Most of the music was sung, but with a short (generally eight bars) section of instrumental playing. Rock 'n' roll music was perfect for the time, certainly for listening, but also for dancing. Of course, it was immediately exploited by the music business and purveyed extremely effectively across the rapidly expanding mass media. The first person to benefit significantly from this new technology was Elvis Presley.

## The Mid-1950s: Elvis, Buddy and the Birth of Rock 'n' Roll

Elvis Presley was remarkable for several reasons. Not only is he unquestionably responsible for the biggest revolution in popular music, but he was a *white* southerner singing *blues* tinged with *country* and *gospel*. He fused these types of music that had until then been very much divided along racial lines. But here was a key difference from everything that had gone before: *Elvis was about more than just music.* He changed the direction of youth culture in many ways, for example, by adding that powerful ingredient, sex! His sexy leg and hip movements alone (he acquired the nickname, Elvis the pelvis) made him an idol for most teenagers and a role model for generations of young rebels. And when he was seen clutching a guitar, that too became a symbol of youth expression in its own right.

Elvis was born in Tupelo, Mississippi on January 8, 1935 and his parents bought him his first guitar in 1946. His family moved to Memphis in 1948, where Elvis spent much time imbibing the blues music of the famous Beale Street played by such musicians as B. B. King and Furry Lewis. Throughout his time in High School, he played music and grew used to performing to audiences. One day Elvis decided to make a simple acetate recording for his mother's birthday present. He visited the Sun Record Studios in Memphis where a recording service was available for a few dollars. There he met the owner, Sam Phillips, who recognised Elvis's talent. During the early part of 1954 when Elvis was 19, Sam made a number of recordings from which the first records were made and sold on Phillips' *Sun* label. In the latter part of 1954, Elvis started to play gigs in the local area and, as his fame grew, soon he was touring the southern states, wowing audiences with his totally original singing style. In 1955, his career blossomed under the direction of his new manager, Colonel Parker. His first major hit was with *Heartbreak Hotel* (1956). After this, nothing would be the same, and Elvis was a major star. The new music became known as *rock 'n' roll*, probably derived from another form of music that was known as *Rockabilly*. One of the earliest songs was *Rock Around the Clock*, copyrighted as early as March 1953 and made famous by Bill Haley and the Comets. Rock 'n' roll was a blend of black peoples' ethnic/folk music (rhythm-and-blues) with white peoples' ethnic/folk music (country-and-western).

Another highly popular contemporary of Elvis was Buddy Holly, born in Lubbock Texas in 1936. At the age of 11, he began to play piano, but despite showing early promise he quit in order to take up the guitar. Having performed as a warm-up act at an Elvis Presley gig in 1955, he decided he wanted a career in the new music. He formed a band called the Crickets that topped the charts with their first record, *That'll be the Day* (1957). A string of hits followed, both with and without his band until Holly was killed in an air-crash in February 1959.

## The Beat Movement

It was writer Jack Kerouac who, as much as anybody, helped to create a new way of thinking. In the late 1940s, his circle of friends in New York was affected by a way of life characterised by anti-conformist behaviour, and in 1948 Kerouac used the phrase "The Beat Generation" to describe them. Memories of the war were still very fresh, and Kerouac, along with poet Allen Ginsberg, saw capitalism, sexual repression and conformity as destructive forces. According to Kerouac, the word "Beat" was unrelated to music, but instead came from underworld slang, a world of hustlers, drug addicts and petty thieves, where he and Ginsberg sought inspiration. "Beat" was slang for "beaten down" or downtrodden, but it also had a spiritual connotation as in "beatitude". A third writer, William S. Burroughs, was also prominent in promotion of the post war counterculture. Born into a wealthy family from St. Louis, Burroughs had the luxury of great personal freedom, which he used with mixed results. A period of heroin addiction somehow led to a series of autobiographical novels that later became accepted as examples of fine American literature. With Kerouac and Ginsberg, this triumvirate became a potent part of the cocktail of postmodern influences with many consequences for the 1960s culture on both sides of the Atlantic Ocean. It was a journalist, Herb Caen from San Francisco, who, inspired by the launch of the sputnik, first attached a suffix to conveniently describe members of the Beat generation. From that time, a beatnik became a prolific word used for a young person who was part of a social group in the 1950s and early 1960s. Beatniks rejected the traditional rules of society and encouraged people to express themselves through art. More stereotypically, being a beatnik involved growing long hair, dressing unconventionally, smoking pot, and listening to jazz. So, for a short, beautiful period before rock 'n' roll took off, jazz was 'in'.

And with jazz went poetry, driven in the UK by Michael Horovitz who, in 1959, founded the New Departures group to promote the fashionable authors of the new literature. Gradually, an alignment of jazz and poetry occurred, as, from 1960, Horovitz was joined by another poet, Pete Brown, and saxophonist Dick Heckstall-Smith, and they arranged trendy performances that fused art, literature and music. Later, Brown's poetry was matched with John McLaughlin's amazing guitar performances in a group called The First Real Poetry Band.

Christopher David Allen (b1938, Australia) became that stereotypical beatnik. He also changed his name to Dævid. Thanks to a job in a Melbourne bookshop, he became interested in the Beat Generation writers, and travelled to Paris where the cult had developed a strong following. He tried to find work as a musician, and soon moved to Kent where in 1963 he was playing in his own trio with 16-year-old Robert Wyatt (drums) and Hugh Hopper (bass). This seemingly innocuous event turned out to be an important milestone in the story of the development of modern music.

## The Late 1950s: British Art Schools Take On The Music Business

Elvis and Buddy were, of course, extremely popular in the UK, but the Brits soon got involved on their own accounts. For example, Lonnie Donnegan invented skiffle, an early music craze in the UK and probably the first true 'garage' music because it involved the use of cheap, simple instruments. Donnegan's record *Rock Island Line* (1954) was a big hit, and consequently Lonnie, a guitarist, had a big role in the growth in popularity of the guitar in the UK. Until Donnegan, the playing of the guitar in the UK was uncommon; there were few teachers. Skiffle was street-corner busking. It encouraged ordinary people to play by making music more accessible. John Lennon's first attempts in music were playing guitar with a skiffle group called the Quarrymen. The music industry began to take notice of the skiffle movement, but the BBC resisted it, so young people had to look to European stations like Radio Luxembourg for popular broadcasting. Finally, the BBC realised that it needed to move with the times and commissioned the first teenage all-music programme *Oh Boy!* in 1958.

With skiffle, for a short time at least, music was in the hands of ordinary people, but as businessmen began to spot moneymaking potential the pendulum gradually swung towards the side of the manipulators. Tommy Steele was the first popular UK singing star to become famous for his charisma rather than his musical skills. Following the template established in the USA, Steele was drawn into mainstream entertainment, leaving pop music behind. Meanwhile, other music acts were manufactured by men such as Larry Parnes who was responsible for the likes of Vince Eager and Billy Fury. For the first time, Parnes' acts created hysteria amongst young girls, an effect that was equivalent to the effect of later "boy bands". Cliff Richard began as a similar act, targeted at young girls by his persuasive management, and (according to Bruce Welch, Cliff's friend in his backing band, the Shadows) he soon became manipulated by older men from the showbiz industry, instead of from the music business. It was inconceivable that pop and rock 'n' roll music could ever appeal to anyone older than 25. (How wrong that turned out to be!) Conventional wisdom had it that rock 'n' roll stars were "here today, gone tomorrow" and that longevity as an artist was to be achieved in the wider sphere of entertainment. Nevertheless, Cliff Richard was one artist who bucked the trend by remaining true to his musical commitments and retaining his credentials as a rock 'n' roll singer. Until the Beatles arrived, Cliff was the biggest pop act on the British scene. Unlike some of the fly-by-night acts, Cliff Richard had true talent, sadly never recognised in the USA.

For many British youngsters, however, Cliff and his pals were not the answer; they wanted authentic American music. What's more, they also wanted a slice of the American culture they were beginning to discover in films and on TV. At first, they were happy with Elvis and Buddy Holly, but Elvis was unable to maintain the pace he had set. A combination of being drafted into the Army for two years and a concurrent running out of musical inspiration caused him to be distracted by the lure of Hollywood. His musical direction was diverted from the innovative material for which he had already become legendary to the schmaltzy content of '60s chick-flicks.

By the end of the decade, things were starting to stagnate in the music world, at least on the western side of the Atlantic. Bob Dylan noted that, "Things were pretty sleepy on the American music scene in the late '50s and early '60s.

**1950s Influences from the USA**
*The Beat Culture - Literature*: Kerouac, Burroughs, Ginsberg; *Films*: James Dean; *Art*: Pollock, Warhol; *Rock 'n' Roll*: Elvis, Buddy Holly, Chuck Berry; *Blues*: Muddy Waters, Howlin' Wolf, John Lee Hooker, Sonny Boy Williamson; *Jazz*: Charlie Parker, Dizzy Gillespie, Miles Davis, Ornette Coleman, Cecil Taylor, Charles Mingus

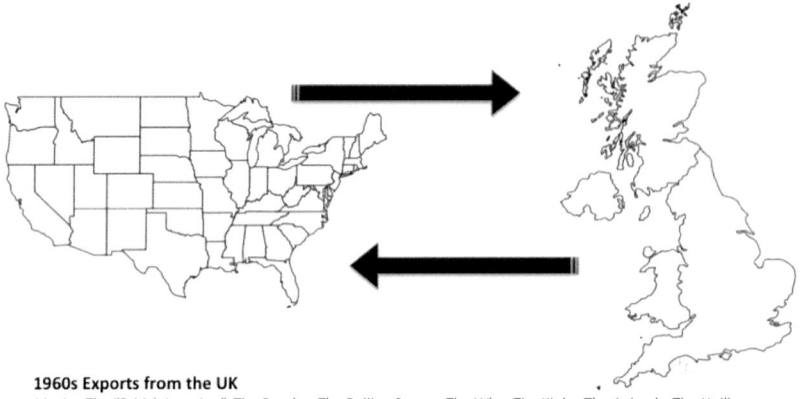

**1960s Exports from the UK**
*Music - The "British Invasion"*: The Beatles, The Rolling Stones, The Who, The Kinks, The Animals, The Hollies; *Jazz-Rock-R&B*: Cream, Led Zeppelin, Soft Machine, Colosseum, John Mayall, David Bowie, Yes, King Crimson; *The Mod Culture - Fashion – "Swinging London"*: Mary Quant, Twiggy, Jean Shrimpton; *Films*: James Bond, The Beatles, Julie Andrews, Peter O'Toole, Michael Caine

*Figure 4: Transatlantic Cultural Influences*

Popular radio was sort of at a standstill and filled with empty pleasantries." [5] This was probably a viewpoint from one side of the racial divide - the white community. In the segregationist society of '50s and '60s America, the dominant white culture was uninterested in music made by African Americans. The exact opposite was the case in British Art Schools of the period, where all aspects of American culture were being absorbed and mixed into cocktails that intoxicated minds with the possibilities of social revolution. So the spark of real change came in British student campuses where, importantly, there was no such racial segregation. (In the late 1950s, they were packed with modern jazz musicians – very few of whom were studying music formally! The British club scene too was vibrant with jazz. Players like Humphrey Lyttelton, Tubby Hayes, Joe Harriott, Ian Carr and Don Rendell showed that the best British musicians could do more than just keep up with the Americans. Bandleaders like John Dankworth and Ted Heath acted as focal points for the best of British musicians.) This mix of modern jazz, Beat culture and black American music crystallised into a new British counterculture that was powerful enough to impact upon, and slowly overturn, the prevailing culture of staunchly conservative, Conservative Britain (repetition intended).

An excellent analysis of the Influence of British Art School culture is given by

MacDonald in his incomparable book about the Beatles' music. [6] The British Art School of the 1960s with its "... anarchic individualistic art school ethos..." offered unparalleled artistic license to fertile young minds. They became "... a home-from-home to the gifted but wayward, and often (frankly) eccentric people with which English life used to overflow ... John Lennon was a classic case of the art school type: an academic misfit who could more or less draw and was otherwise consumed with a chaotic creativity in need of channelling." The key to this unique circumstance was that it "...was founded on talents rather than on official qualifications. In such an environment, one might interact with a wide spectrum of people, regardless of class or education, and draw from a multitude of activities often taking place in the same hall... In addition to this, the quarterly dances – supplemented by more frequent one-nighters as the arts schools became incorporated into the UK gig circuit – during the 1960s provided opportunities for students to hear the top British R&B and jazz-blues groups, as well as visiting bluesmen from America. Already a crucible for creative fusion, art school, as a result, became the secret ingredient in the most imaginative English pop rock." [7]

## 1960: Like No Others – The Beatles

With the aim of simplicity, but at the risk of being simplistic, I have included the graphic, Figure 4, to describe in the broadest terms, the trans-Atlantic musical influences that took place in these dramatic years. Having listened to what was transmitted from the USA in the 1950s, British musicians were now in a position to make their own marks on music. From March 1960, a new music rocket was constructed on the launch pad in Liverpool, warheaded by the Beatles. Until their break-up on 10 April 1970, when Paul McCartney announced that the Beatles no longer existed [8], they transformed the face of popular music based on the guitar-group and its associated rebellious, confrontational culture. They also used purpose-made electric guitars and basses instead of amplified acoustic instruments. Thanks to their manager, Brian Epstein, the Beatles won a contract with *Parlophone* and producer George Martin, whose experience up to that point was only in the making of comedy records! However, Martin possessed the vision and the skills to perceive the potential of the Beatles, and to bring about one of the most stunning changes that the music world had known. Now in place were all the pieces of the jigsaw necessary to turn the Beatles into the biggest-earning music machine the world had ever seen. *Love Me Do* (1962) was the first significant record by the Beatles that appeared at the head of a great stream of new-sounding records emanating from the clubs of Liverpool. The song was a knockout for almost all who heard it. As a spotty twelve-year-old myself, I recall perfectly the amazement I felt when I first heard the Beatles; I was permanently converted from that point on.

Paul Stump has written a particularly successful analysis of the societal changes taking place in the late 1950s and early '60s. [9] He places emphasis on the role of the Beatles and the essential Englishness that was part of their music. The Lennon and McCartney approach was built upon the prevailing art college culture of the time, which was based around a revolutionary mix of Kerouac, Ginsburg and jazz. The beatnik culture was heavily infused with experimental poetry, extravagant art by the likes of Jackson Pollock, and the *avant-garde*, all of which encouraged the abandonment of rules in the accepted forms, and the adoption of experimentation at all costs. However, the Beatles had set out on a course away from the pre-existing one. Apparently, John Lennon told the Music Club of Liverpool College of Art, "What a lot of fucking shit you play. Why don't you play something proper – like Chuck Berry?" [10] Stump continued: "Not only did the Beatles change music beyond recognition in the 1960s, they also changed society; or, at the very least, the changes that took place in the 1960s Britain would have been unthinkable without them." In particular, Stump made the point that progressive rock of the 1970s "...could not have been created without those aspects of the 1960s that might never have reached mainstream cultural awareness had the Beatles not existed." [11]

By 1961 there were 273 garage bands playing in the Liverpool area alone – according to Nicholson, it was "a basic umbrella style rooted in R&B." [12] The result was that, for a few years, British musicians, led by the Beatles, were the most influential in the world. The world's most famous musicians rushed to record Beatles' tunes. Jazz was no different: Ellington, Basie and the Crusaders all did. But it wasn't just in music, for the music of the Beatles was embedded into an entire form of culture and if you wanted one, you got the other too.

Though the Beatles gave their respect to what Elvis had started, it was their music now, and the new rock musicians totally rejected the kind of sentimental material that Elvis had eschewed in his movies. Suddenly a new effect appeared as, according to Nicholson: "the young generation created a gap between themselves and their parents for the first time. Young fans of the Beatles wanted their parents to like them too; young fans of the Rolling Stones didn't." [13] As 'grown-ups' learned to accept the new music, albeit with some reluctance, teenagers went further. The more rebellious minds rejected their traditional upbringing entirely, and struck out on their own, encouraged by commercial interests who could see the emergence of profitable new businesses. Soon, even the Beatles looked too homely, as they performed for the Queen and an audience of aristocrats. (Instead of asking them to sing-along, Lennon, with characteristically dry humour, invited them to "… rattle your jewellery!") But now it became fashionable to create music that was farther and farther 'out'. Until now, there had always been a 'right' and a 'wrong' way to do things. Now, wrong became right. Prose appeared without capitals; words and names were 'groovy' when written backwards. Thus, for example, a Miles Davis album was entitled *Live Evil* (1971) on which were tracks called *Selim* and *Sivad*. Prose and poetry became nonsensical. Then, music too became anarchical as young people set off in new directions with the deliberate aim of inventing forms of music that their parents did *not* like, and in large measure, this philosophy became the norm for most of the following decades.

## 1962: British Rhythm & Blues, Alexis Korner, John Mayall and The Rolling Stones

The kind of early rock 'n' roll provided by the music industry had pitched be-suited guys with slicked-back hair incongruously jigging around with girls wearing ponytails, frilly dresses and bobby socks. Now a new music came to the foreground to counter the kitsch brand of British pop music with which the youth culture had become associated. For a number of years, it smothered the life out of jazz in Britain. Once the non-conformist pop culture had become accepted as conformist, young rebels had to come up with something even farther out. The new music was a British form of Rhythm and Blues and it had buckets full of attitude. It brought subscribers flocking to the London underground scene, since it represented a direct opposition to the overt commercialism of pop music. As music industrialists started to capitalise on the popularity of music issued on singles, so there was a large number of opponents who wanted to overturn the traditional establishment rules in favour of the counterculture represented by the burgeoning British R&B scene. Thus, as The Beatles came increasingly to represent the modern culture, as seen from the establishment point-of-view, The Rolling Stones found themselves in the vanguard of the 'Progressives'. But although they became the most popular, they were by no means the first on the R&B scene.

It is not clear whether it was John Mayall or Alexis Korner who first delivered blues to the British audience so let's allow them both equal credit. Though both men played the blues in public from the mid-1950s - Mayall centred on the northwest of England, Korner in London - this process was in full flow by early 1963. Some readers might feel that Korner was more in the heart of things from his London hub. In the USA, Paul Butterfield was performing a similar service. His album *Paul Butterfield's Blues Band* (1965) introduced the blues to American white people who had up to now been indifferent to what was going on in their own country.

The Beatles, as we know, started an explosion of activity in the *Cavern Club* in Liverpool. Both it and the *Marquee* in London had been playing jazz up to the late 1950s, but now gave up jazz in favour of the new 'Beat music' and British R&B. Jazz trappings were recognised as a hindrance to success in an environment that demanded R&B. The London club, *Flamingo*, tried to continue for a while with both jazz and R&B, whilst another club called the *Little Theatre Club* retained its jazz-only format. Through the dedication of drummer John Stephens and his formation of the Spontaneous Music Ensemble, it became the focus for *avant-garde* jazz, which at the time was strongly focussed on free jazz. Those jazz musicians who wanted to remain loyal to the purist cause used either this venue or *Ronnie Scott's* club as their hub.

The years from 1962 to 1965 were a time of explosive change in London's cultural scene, of which music was the pre-eminent influence. Before 1963/4, British ears were focussed on American Culture, but from around that time, the period known as the 'Swinging 60s', introduced a new time when the British were clearly aware that a new vibrant strand of culture had arrived in Britain. With the Beatles having detonated the charges, the avalanche was promoted by bands such as the Kinks and the Who, and was embraced by the new 'mod' culture.

In 1962, John McLaughlin was working by day as a guitar salesman at Selmer's in London, but he was well known by guitarists and *cognoscenti* as one of the best guitarists. Through incessant nocturnal activities, he performed at all the top venues and brought his strong jazz background to the rapidly developing R&B scene.

The *Flamingo* club was one of the most important establishments - funkier and jazzier than the *Marquee*, according to John Paul Jones. [14] Here John McLaughlin would play with many other jazz-influenced, progressive musicians such as Brian Auger (who was a jazz keyboard player), Red Reece (drums) and Mick Eve (saxophone). Harper is in no doubt that Brian Auger first started playing jazz-rock with his new Hammond L100 organ when he formed his trio Trinity in early 1965, but long before that John McLaughlin sat in on gigs, where he acquired early first-hand experience of the new jazz-fusion experiments. [15] Through the very early 60s, the *Flamingo* was very often packed with US servicemen who got paid every other week and loved to spend their money in what they perceived was the best club in town. In this open, relaxed and vibrant atmosphere, the GIs constantly fed American influences to the bands that would learn new material accordingly. By September 1962, Georgie Fame and the Blue Flames were playing at the *Flamingo* on Monday, Thursday, Friday and Saturday, with the last two nights' extremely popular shows running from midnight to 5 am. In November 1962, Georgie Fame was given a Hammond organ, paid for by the club owner. He never looked back. [15] These times were a period of frantic musical activity of which little remains apart from those distant echoes of influence. There are no known recordings in existence.

At this time too, three young men, Mick Jagger, Keith Richard and Brian Jones, made frequent visits to the *Marquee* Club. There, a blues player called Alexis Korner had made a name for himself playing regular gigs with a harmonica player called Cyril Davies in a band called Blues Incorporated. In these relaxed environments, jamming was a perfectly normal activity so they often sat in with the band whose drummer was Charlie Watts. The first Alexis Korner Blues Incorporated album was the live *R&B from the Marquee* (1962). It was the first full-length R&B album by any British band.

Jagger and Co. were so eager to play R&B that on 12 July 1962 they formed a band of their own and played their first formal gig at the *Marquee*, billed as The Rollin' Stones. The line-up was Mick Jagger, Keith Richards, Brian Jones, Ian Stewart on piano, Dick Taylor on bass and Tony Chapman on drums. Bill Wyman replaced Taylor in December and drummer Charlie Watts, needing persuasion to divorce him from Blues Incorporated, joined the following January. Sadly, as the Rolling Stones rocketed to fame over the coming year, Korner did not adapt to the rapidly changing face of R&B, preferring not to dilute his purer descriptions of the blues in the name of commercial success. As a result, Korner and his work were left largely unrecognised, except by blues *aficionados*, until much later, by which time it was too late for him to get rich.

Alexis Korner's Blues Incorporated evolved slowly. Shortly after Watts left for the Stones, they were playing at London's *Ealing Club*. Besides the leader, this band now included Ginger Baker (drums), Jack Bruce (bass), Dick Heckstall-Smith (sax), Johnny Parker (piano) and Cyril Davies. Baker, Bruce and Heckstall-Smith were all experienced jazz musicians, but Baker and Bruce had recognised the money-earning potential and decided to make their music in R&B. Their future, too, would be rosy – but without Korner. Between them, Alexis Korner and John Mayall inspired a craze for Rhythm and Blues in the UK that was in full swing by early 1963. Within a year, the Rolling Stones had become the first enormously successful British R&B band, followed closely by Manfred Mann. The same year, Eric Clapton started in a blues band called The Roosters, where he spent only 6 months before leaving to join the Yardbirds.

## 1963: John Mayall's Bluesbreakers

John Mayall (b1933) was born in Cheshire, and spent his early years in the Manchester area. After completing three years of National Service he attended Manchester Art College where, from around 1956, he began playing blues guitar seriously – one of the first in the UK to do so. He formed his Bluesbreakers in 1963 with Roger Dean (guitar), Hughie Flint (drums) and John McVie (bass) and the band began to play gigs around the Manchester area. Then, after advice from Alexis Korner, who was by now a great friend, Mayall decided to turn professional and moved to London where he immediately found success in clubs such as the *Flamingo* and the *Marquee*.

Mayall's first album was *John Mayall plays John Mayall* (1965), and featured himself with Dean, Flint and McVie. Interestingly, some numbers featured the unknown Nigel Stanger on saxophone. At the same time, Mayall had been attracted by Clapton's magnificent blues guitar playing on *Got To Hurry*, the B-side of the Yardbirds' single *For Your Love* (1965). He decided it was exactly what his band needed so he fired Roger Dean to make way for Clapton. (The Yardbirds hired Jeff Beck to replace Clapton. Later, Jimmy Page joined as well, and the rivalry between them proved too much for Beck who left.) The album that ensued (Mayall's second) was *John Mayall's Bluesbreakers with Eric Clapton* (1966), lovingly referred to as the *Beano* album after the name of the well-known British comic paper that Clapton is seen to be reading in the album's artwork. It was a big hit and solidified the reputations of both men, Clapton's perhaps rather more, for he became an even bigger star. (Most of us who were alive at the time remember seeing the slogan "Clapton is God" appearing on walls everywhere!)

The presence of Mick Taylor in the Bluesbreakers led to a rise in the band's jazz content, and their producer, Mike Vernon, regards the *Bare Wires* (1968) album as a forerunner of the jazz-rock movement. [16] This is an exaggerated claim, although the album was certainly influential in the UK, reaching No 3 in the album charts. With Henry Lowther (trumpet), Chris Mercer and Dick Heckstall-Smith (saxes), Jon Hiseman (drums) and Tony Reeves (bass) the band was certainly heavily loaded in favour of jazz musicians. Whatever its effect, thoughts of fusion (he didn't call it that, anyway) did not last long with Mayall. His newly discovered wind section was fired a few months later.

In 1969, Mayall emigrated to the USA and re-formed the band with the aim of producing a new sound. *The Turning Point* (1969) was a change to a more acoustic sound, but always firmly planted in blues, rather than jazz. Baker concurred with this theory when he said recently that they deliberately avoided jazz in the early days of the Bluesbreakers in order to make money. [16] Consequently, it would be disingenuous of anyone to claim that the Bluesbreakers were *the* first, or even an early, fusion band. It *is*, however, true to say that the Bluesbreakers' prominent guitarists, Clapton and Green, as well as the likes of Jimmy Page (Led Zeppelin) and Jeff Beck (Yardbirds), were so enormously influential that *the way jazz guitarists played from then on was radically different*. This is without doubt one of the great driving forces in the creation of jazz-fusion, even though these guitarists were themselves not jazzers. Later, in the USA, Mayall built a home in Laurel Canyon adjacent to Frank

Zappa and Joni Mitchell, but was devastated after it burnt to the ground with all his possessions. His career began to founder and, despite a new album that was explicitly entitled *Jazz-Blues Fusion* (1972) it did not achieve success, supposedly because of the new 1970s craze for disco music. However, Mayall did not give up and gradually rebuilt his band, his career and his life after a spell of personal problems and years of heavy drinking.

Over a career spanning some fifty years, Mayall has become famous for nurturing some of the best British rock and blues musicians. For example, Mick Fleetwood, John McVie and Peter Green formed Fleetwood Mac in 1967 after playing with Mayall. The first album was *Peter Green's Fleetwood Mac* (1968), reflecting just how much of a name Green had already made for himself. Other Bluesbreakers members of note were Aynsley Dunbar (1964-67), Mick Taylor (1964-69) and Hugh Flint (1964-66), but the most famous of all was Eric Clapton. Despite the short professional relationship between Clapton and Mayall, it has attracted much attention ever since the split, more than forty years ago. Mayall celebrated his 70th birthday in 2003 with a reunion concert with some of the members of the old band, including Clapton and any rift that once may have separated the two men has been long forgotten. John Mayall continues to perform with his band today

## 1964: The Graham Bond Organisation

Alexis Korner began to adapt the style of Blues Incorporated by adding horns, but harmonica-player and vocalist Cyril Davies, who had co-founded the band with him, disagreed with Korner's plan. Davies left, and his place was taken by the eccentric Graham Bond, a saxophone-playing organist. Bond had started out playing alto sax with Don Rendell's jazz quintet, only the second British band to record for an American jazz label – the first being Joe Harriot's band. Material on the album contained jazz with lashings of blues. In September 1962, Dick Heckstall-Smith's tenor sax was added to the band's line-up that already had Rendell on soprano and Bond on alto. But by the end of the year Bond recognised his poor prospects in jazz and left Rendell to join Korner, with Ronnie Jones (vocals), Johnny Parker, Jack Bruce and Ginger Baker.

But Bond, restless in Korner's band, was a leader-in-waiting. He began to engineer the formation of his own band. At first he began to play separately in a Hammond organ trio with Bruce and Baker, whilst working in parallel with Blues Incorporated, and, to keep as many options open as possible, Bond even worked simultaneously in another band, the Johnny Burch Octet. As doors began to open for him, Bond left Korner completely and took Baker and Bruce with him. His group was now Graham's main source of income, but he still contributed to the Burch Octet and was also occasionally involved with Live

New Departures, a jazz and poetry unit that included poet and lyricist Pete Brown. That band had been performing sporadically at the St. Pancras Town Hall since 1961.

Bond's approach to music was unconventional as he freely mixed elements of jazz into his brand of R&B. According to recent research by Harper, [17] Bond overtly described the music as jazz, but the band's management described it as R&B for commercial purposes. Part of the motivation of forming the band was to break away from Blues Incorporated, which was being closely associated with the nascent Rolling Stones whom Bond, Bruce and Baker all disliked. They saw no good musicianship in the Stones and they did not like Jagger. For the time being at least, Dick Heckstall-Smith stayed on with Korner. Bond told *Melody Maker* that there was a tremendous parallel between the blues and free-form jazz. "We are playing the blues of today and I can get away with playing practically anything. There is no reason at all why you can't take the blues and put the technique of modern jazz on it." [18]

From February to April 1963 the Graham Bond Trio became a Quartet with the addition of virtuoso guitarist John McLaughlin to the line-up. McLaughlin was well known around the British scene and had recently been a member of the Blue Flames that had first backed Billy Fury and then Georgie Fame. The Graham Bond Quartet began to play gigs at the *Marquee Club*, taking gigs away from Korner.

Heckstall-Smith remembers McLaughlin as simply the best. "Well, I mean, the kid was 18. And I'm coming down the stairs into this venue, which was absolutely packed with black American servicemen. You wouldn't find a white (person) there. They were there because of what the music was - Georgie and the Blue Flames. And one part of the Blue Flames was the guitar player ... he was absolutely lifted by the boots and it would turn you into another creature straight away. For me, that happened every time from that second. First time I heard him onwards, I new John was the best guitar player in the world." [19]

With such credentials, it is difficult to argue that the Graham Bond Quartet was not a jazz-fusion band, even though the term had not then been invented. If so, they must be regarded as the first of a kind. The band signed a contract with EMI and in the summer released their first record. But all was not well in the band: McLaughlin was chalk to their cheese. He liked foreign cultures, philosophy and religion, and in their company he was a square peg in a round hole. Baker had taken over as leader. He fired McLaughlin on the grounds that "he was a moaner", but in truth there was really nothing in common between them that might act as band glue. McLaughlin was replaced with the more amenable tenor sax player, Dick Heckstall-Smith.

It was April 1964. The Graham Bond Quartet evolved once more into the Graham Bond Organisation, a name for which they are best known. Indeed, Bond was keen to move away from the jazz alto saxophone (on which he was a very good player) to the more versatile keyboard (on which he was also very competent) that was a better symbol of the developing genre in which he wanted to be seen. He promoted his band as an 'ORGANisation'. A pivotal point in the history of jazz-fusion had been reached. The GBO went from strength to strength, backing Marvin Gay during his first visit to the UK and appearing on the bill with Chuck Berry during his British tour of January 1965. In July 1965, the band appeared on ITV's weekend show, *Ready Steady Go!* Bond used the opportunity to demonstrate a new keyboard, the Mellotron, which resembled an organ but was able to simulate strings, brass and woodwind, giving Bond the power of a small orchestra. Later, a Mellotron was used for the memorable opening chords to the Beatles' *Strawberry Fields Forever* (1967). Bond told *Melody Maker*: "The Mellotron uses pre-recorded tapes of other instruments. For example, every note in the register of the trumpet is recorded - and I can play it on the organ keyboard getting the real sound." But there were disadvantages in the use of such trail-blazing instruments. As Dick Heckstall-Smith remembers: "The Mellotron was only used in a studio context because it went out of tune the whole bloody time. It was also very big." [20]

Even with McLaughlin gone there was discord. Intense rivalry then broke out between Baker and Bruce. What started as a normal jazz competitiveness in their playing, developed into something more personal and resulted in Bruce being fired by Baker - with some threat of violence involved! Bruce joined Mayall for three months and then Manfred Mann, where his exceptional skill on bass made him far too good for the rest of the band. He didn't stay there either. GBO released two albums with Bond, Baker, Bruce and Heckstall-Smith in the line-up: *The Sound of '65* (1965) and *There's a Bond Between Us* (1965). Both included Bond on Mellotron – probably a Mark II model. In the context of the development of electronic keyboard instruments, this was remarkable. Bond is thought to have been the first British musician to use this instrument and, in terms of a band consisting mostly of jazz musicians, this is surely an indicator of very early jazz-rock fusion.

## The mid-1960s

By the mid-1960s, the scene was set for further changes to occur in music. The landscape of rock 'n' roll territory had largely been mapped out into new districts, most as yet unnamed, and the trails ripe for exploration had largely been identified. The supplies for the expeditions had been requisitioned and the gold rush began. Less innovative rock 'n' rollers went about their business satisfying the exploding commercial market most of us would associate with 'pop' music. Other musicians who thrived on innovation developed the music that is better associated with the term 'rock'. Some routes led into the numerous paths of fusion that I have begun to identify. As the explorers set out on their journeys, the influence of mind-altering drugs hung heavy in the air around their chuck waggons, and became the engine for much of the 'psychedelic rock', of which Pink Floyd became leading exponents in the UK. That these explorations had started from the new underground Beat culture and were a yardstick for the advancement of music led to the labelling of a swathe of new musical territory as 'progressive' or 'prog-rock'.

*Rahsaan Roland Kirk and his band performing to a psychedelic light show at Lanchester Polytechnic, Coventry UK in January 1972. (Photo: Ken Trethewey)*

Jazz was never far away in the output of prog bands, although the scales of balance between the two extremes could swing quickly across the wide range of genre-mixing that was available to suitably open minds. Where present, the influence of jazz was strongest because of the fashionable ideas currently being explored by the avant-gardists such as Ornette Coleman, Cecil Taylor and John Coltrane, so many of these early jazz-rock fusions were laced with large quantities of spontaneity and abstract ideas, rather than structured compositions and conventional sounds. Musical experimentalists bandied about names like Archie Shepp, John Cage and Karlheinz Stockhausen with a zeal that varied from hushed reverence to evangelical energy. The more extreme the idea, the more acceptable it became to audiences eager to sample very latest inventions like slavering newshounds. Somehow, it became desirable to spend an hour listening to a pianist playing with bandages covering his hands.

The inclusion of electronics became fundamental to the entire enterprise, and was taken up by all of those bands that were interested in heading deeper into the unknown. There was also a strong, deliberate association with the arts, assisted by the inclusion of psychedelic elements to the stage performances – notably, abstract light shows and other theatrical effects. All this helped to delineate between the lowbrow output aimed at the mass-market, and the highbrow productions that, to avoid opprobrium, needed to be artistic rather than commercial. These trappings appealed to the *avant-garde* jazz musicians like Roland Kirk, whose gig I attended at a University venue in the early 1970s, and was laced with extrovert stage acts and giant projections of abstract art. Fortunately, Kirk played without bandages, but his stage antics were almost as outrageous, compared to the 'norms' expected of mainstream jazz artists.

The anarchical philosophy of 'anything is all right' manifested itself not only in abstractions of sound, but as whimsical, nonsensical lyrics. Started, again by the Beatles, who invented titles such as *Lucy In The Sky With Diamonds*, and the incomparable *Sergeant Pepper's Lonely Hearts Club Band*, this artistic force spread widely into many spheres. The creation of TV shows like the riotous, irreverent, even surreal, *Monty Python's Flying Circus* is a good example. Its title alone is an illustration of how the fashion of the art had made it compulsory to combine colourful nouns and adjectives into amusing titles and lines that conveyed a sense of the intellectual, but meant nothing at all. Such menus could be interpreted as comic. However, to those left bemused by the attractions of the underground, it appeared quite the opposite - unfunny, worthless and, to say the least, irritating. To these poor folks, 'progressive' art was an unturnable tide.

## Rock Music and the Cult of the Guitar

Rock music is very much about the guitar, a truly unique musical instrument. Once in the hands of the rock 'n' rollers, guitars were musical dynamite and the shock wave from its explosion of popularity rapidly penetrated the jazz world. David Schiller wrote: "There has never been another musical instrument like the guitar. There's never been an instrument as versatile: it plays rhythm, it plays melody... and it is as sophisticated harmonically as a piano. In the hands of a highly skilled player, in fact, it can perform all of these roles simultaneously. It is arguably the world's most pleasing solo instrument." [21]

The popular fashion for playing the guitar began with Elvis and Buddy Holly in the USA and Hank Marvin in the UK. (Curiously, it was Bert Weedon's primer for the guitar that all British students turned to for their first lessons. For years, Weedon had been one of the very few popular exponents of electric guitar in

Britain.) Elvis was at first seen playing an acoustic guitar, but in the late 1950s Hank Marvin of the Shadows played the first solid-bodied electric Fender Stratocaster to be imported into the UK (by Cliff Richard), and was extremely influential in moulding that early image of the solid-bodied guitar player. By the mid-1960s, the solid-bodied guitar had become a cult because of people like Eric Clapton and Jimi Hendrix. As such, it became about more than just playing an instrument. Sometimes, it was even about smashing it. Bands such as The Who and Janis Joplin's Big Brother and the Holding Company set the lead in extreme behaviour off-stage as well as on it.

By around 1964, it was clear that the rock 'n' roll format had changed so much that it was appropriate to adopt a new description for modern, electric guitar-based music. Now, the term 'rock' was used in common parlance, and represented the music played by the typical line-up of lead guitar, rhythm guitar, bass guitar, and drums. This was a format adopted from the first days of change in Liverpool UK, and very much defined by the Beatles. Thus, the morphing of rock 'n' roll into rock took place at around the time of the British Invasion of America (starting with the Beatles first tour in February 1964). Even so, the Beatles were always considered too innovative and wide-ranging to be restrained by the application of the narrow label of 'rock'. Arguments about the identity of the first 'true' rock band will probably never be satisfactorily resolved, although there are some clear candidates.

## 1966: Cream

Splits in the seams of the rock 'n' roll culture were already well developed when Eric Clapton, tired of much of what he saw in the mainstream, joined Jack Bruce and Ginger Baker to form Cream. For a short period from about October 1966 to their last concert in London in November 1968 the band established themselves as the 'band of bands' – essentially the world's first 'supergroup'.

By 1966, the Graham Bond Organisation had started to fail because of Bond's drug addiction. Ginger Baker decided that another band was needed and asked Clapton to join him in a band that would be the cream of the country's musicians. They discussed bass players and decided that there was none better than Bruce, with whom Baker had previously fallen out. Baker realised the potential of such a band and the two men settled their differences. Cream was formed in 1966. Clapton had been with Mayall for little more than a year (1965-6) before accepting Baker's invitation to join Cream. Clapton says that he and Mayall fell out over a woman and that Mayall fired him [16], though the diplomatic Mayall is vague about it. Subsequently, having fired Clapton, Mayall also fired Flint because of his grumbling about the loss of Clapton. Then he fired McVie because of his heavy drinking. Despite everything, Mayall was always respected as 'the boss' and retained the respect of his men, even to this day. Mayall's reasoning was that the good of the band always came above personal relationships.

The brilliant young drummer, Jon Hiseman, was tempted to turn professional by accepting Baker's place in the GBO. For a long time afterwards, Bond was mortified by the treachery of Baker and Bruce in leaving him to find success elsewhere. However, Bond recovered himself for a time to lead a successful, if extremely chequered career, until 1974 when, suffering from depression and mental illness, it is said, he jumped in front of a London Underground train.

Needless to say, Mayall was not impressed to lose Clapton to Cream so soon after he had won him, despite the fact that he had himself used similar tactics to hire Clapton in the first place. Cream was an instant success and began to tour, taking over all the gigs that had previously belonged to the Graham Bond Organisation. The music Cream created in the years 1966-68 was very much based around extended improvisations that form a major part of the jazz genre and they must be regarded as one of the first rock-fusion (rock-jazz) bands.

Cream smashed down a number of barriers, including the accepted idea of musical form. Alexis Petridis wrote: "Their star-heavy line up of Clapton, drummer Ginger Baker and bassist Jack Bruce gave birth to the notion of the supergroup, in which already-famous rock musicians struggle to squeeze their collective egos into a confined space, usually with artistically disastrous results. Their massive-grossing US tours gave rise to the concept of stadium rock as we know it today." [22] In fact, the Beatles began the stadium rock concept in August 1965 with their performance at *Shea Stadium*, New York, but the point is made.

Baker's drumming skills illustrate perfectly one of the distinguishing features of jazz-rock. Most rock music, having a time signature of 4/4 (four beats in a bar), is punctuated by a solid, unchanging four beat pattern on the drums with an emphasis on beats two and four (called the *backbeat*); this could be called *monorhythmic*. A novice drummer could become a competent member of a rock band in a very short time – weeks or months of practice were often sufficient. The same was not true of jazz drummers. From the time of bebop (exemplified by Kenny Clarke) onwards, jazz drummers became ever more creative with the accompanying rhythms they used, but emphasis was mostly on beats one and three, known as the *downbeat*. This extraordinary versatility is known as *polyrhythmic* drumming. The degree of skill required to become a good jazz drummer was orders of magnitude greater than for drummers playing pop and rock music and took much longer to achieve, unless you were a musical prodigy. Ginger Baker was an extraordinary drummer. He was one of the first great polyrhythmic drummers – in the USA Tony Williams is accorded similar status. In Cream, Baker was playing in a rock context and his work for the band is a very good indicator of the fusion of jazz with rock.

Bruce and Baker were quite clear about the importance of jazz in Cream's music. Jack Bruce says: "What it meant was that I could play jazz in front of vast audiences and get paid for it, 'cos that's basically what Cream was – a free jazz trio with Eric playing the Ornette Coleman part without knowing it!" These words indicate that Bruce, for one, believed Cream to be one of the very first rock-jazz bands. John McLaughlin agreed: "When I heard the records – they were jamming, they were really playing. I mean, what a rhythm section! Jack Bruce and Ginger Baker – you play or you go with Jack and Ginger." [23]

In rock music, volume played a big part in determining a band's street cred amongst the fans. At the time, the Who were known as the world's loudest rock band, until, at Windsor race-course where the 6$^{th}$ National Blues and Jazz Festival was taking place on 31 July 1966, Cream closed the show after the Who. According to Clapton, "The music press went crazy, describing us as the first supergroup." [24] Cream's first album was *Fresh Cream* (1966), released in December with the single *I Feel Free*. From the beginning, jamming was a big part of the act, and Jimi Hendrix sat in on an early gig on 1 October at the Central London Polytechnic, in Regent Street, London. Later, when Clapton was on his first trip to the USA, he would spend time similarly sitting in on Hendrix's sessions in New York City.

As time passed, extended improvisations became increasingly important to Cream's performances. This was especially true from around the time of the band's first gig at Fillmore West, encouraged by the burgeoning drug culture in San Francisco, as well as by promoter Bill Graham, who allowed Cream to play what they liked, for as long as they liked. [25] Yet, just as Clapton was establishing his own credentials as a rock-jazz guitarist, he was on the point of pulling his own plug in favour of a simpler form of blues music, a genre with which he had always felt more comfortable. Extreme demands were placed upon them to tour incessantly and by 1968 the band was so tired that they could not go on any longer. Baker, a jazzer at heart, was even beginning to dislike the music. For one thing, he said it was too loud! They split at the end of 1968 after a gig on 26th November at London's *Albert Hall*. (Interestingly, the Yardbirds suffered an almost exactly similar fate, splitting in the same year during an exhausting US tour, with Jimmy Page moving on to form Led Zeppelin.)

From Cream came a new band, Blind Faith, with Clapton, Baker, Ric Crech and Stevie Winwood from Traffic. Their ambition was to become even bigger than Cream, but Eric Clapton's interest soon waned. He drifted towards a band called

Delaney and Bonnie and thence to his own Derek and the Dominoes from where he reverted back to a career in the blues where felt he belonged. Baker was upset at Clapton's unannounced defection from Blind Faith and went on to form Air Force with Graham Bond, Chris Wood, Stevie Winwood, Ric Crech and Denny Laine. This band too was ill-fated and lasted for only one year.

At a time when musicianship was as much about technical ability as interpretation, guitarists, in particular, knew where they stood in the pecking order. Clapton recognised his own limitations in that regard: "As for technique, there were hundreds of guitar players who were better than me." [25a] Clapton thought that Memphis session player Reggie Young was the best blues guitarist he'd seen, whilst in England, he concluded that the best players were Bernie Watson and Albert Lee, who played in Screaming Lord Sutch's band, the Savages. (Today, amazingly, Pat Metheny has quite a low opinion of himself as a guitarist. My own assessment, for which there is plenty of support, is that all this mill-grist was irrelevant to John McLaughlin who *knew* he – McLaughlin - was the world's greatest guitarist!) To Clapton, Jeff Beck and Jimmy Page were probably not viewed as competitors since he subconsciously entered himself into the contest for blues guitarists and they were playing in a different style. Hendrix was the only black musician in this group of super-guitarists. Similarly, Peter Green, who had taken Clapton's place in Mayall's band while Eric went on an unauthorised sabbatical to Europe, was a "phenomenal guitarist." Of course, the record-buying public viewed things differently: Clapton *was* God.

## 1966: Jimi Hendrix

The short, unbelievable era of Jimi Hendrix began barely ten years after Elvis became famous. Hendrix was born Johnny Allen Hendrix on 27 November 1942 in Seattle. Encouraged by his father, he took to guitar playing from the age of five and was soon playing songs from the radio. After a year in the US Army, he began his career playing for Little Richard, Sam Cooke and the Isley Brothers. Whilst playing in Greenwich Village, he was noticed by Chas Chandler, former bass player for the UK band the Animals. With Chandler as his manager, Hendrix changed his name, moved to London and formed the Jimi Hendrix Experience with Noel Redding (bass) and Mitch Mitchell (drums). The band was a knock-out from the moment their first single *Hey Joe* (1966) was released. The success was followed up by the hits *Wind Cries Mary* (1967) and *Purple Haze* (1967). It is ironic, therefore, that we might consider the inclusion of Jimi Hendrix in the package that the British exported to America in the 1960s.

I distinctly remember how unusual it was to have a band comprised of only three musicians. Bands always had four or more members. Surely a trio would sound thin? (Sting decided to make the trio format a positive aspect of the style of the

Police – the "less is more" philosophy. In Cream, Eric Clapton, on the other hand, was not always comfortable with the responsibility of playing lead guitar with just bass and drums in support. [26] He got over it!) Well, as soon as I heard the Jimi Hendrix Experience, I knew how. Hendrix had a stage presence larger than anything that had been seen before. I saw that, just as Schiller said above, Hendrix was such an amazing guitarist that he could play both rhythm and lead parts at the same time, something Jaco Pastorius did later on the bass! It was as if he was a band all by himself. Hendrix's music was permeated with spontaneous, even ferocious improvisations on guitar, yet the music always remained firmly rooted in rock. Although Hendrix was closely associated with jazz musicians - he became a friend of Miles Davis, and jammed with Rahsaan Roland Kirk at *Ronnie Scott's* jazz club in London in early 1967 - he never considered himself a jazz guitarist. Nevertheless, his playing, focussed on improvisation, had an enormous influence on a generation of jazz guitarists, to name but one small group of people.

Interestingly, it was the teaming up of Hendrix with two *white* English musicians – Noel Redding (bass) and Mitch Mitchell (drums) - as the Jimi Hendrix Experience that enabled Hendrix to explode onto the scene with the single *Hey Joe* (1966) and the follow-up album *Are You Experienced* (1967). Yet it was in a different combination called the Band of Gypsys with two *black* musicians - Buddy Miles (drums) and an old army pal, Billy Cox (bass) - that Hendrix was to get as close to jazz as he was ever going to. The music on *Band of Gypsys* (1969) was mostly vamps – long sections of music based all on one chord with almost complete improvisation going on. One of the most famous pieces is *Machine Gun*, the track that became the favourite of Miles Davis. From this point on, Miles adopted the same kind of format for his own form of jazz-fusion. Described by musicians today as both "primitive" and "an epiphany" [27] Hendrix's music, though not especially attractive to black people at the time, became more so in this format. (That was a crucial thing for Miles Davis.) The change from white to black sidemen transformed Hendrix's appeal to black audiences and the music of the Band of Gypsys was seen as prophetic for the future of black music which, up until then, had been much in the shadow of white men's rock. BOG survived for just one album, a project created to meet a commercial obligation for another record company (Capitol Records). Once the album had been recorded, the JH Experience was re-formed in a different guise. Jimi's recording engineer, Eddie Kramer, saw the Band of Gypsys as a transitional stage to enable Hendrix to move on once the first incarnation of the Jimi Hendrix Experience had become stale. For Kramer, BOG was a rock-funk fusion band.

Once again, virtuosity was a key element of Jimi's success. He wasn't just a great guitarist: he completely changed the way the electric guitar was played and it became a totally new instrument in his hands. His extraordinary playing, unparalleled technique and outrageous on-stage antics (which had become *de rigeur* for rock musicians) caused Jimi to be regarded by many as the messiah of the electric guitar. Superlatives are rarely adequate to describe his impact on contemporary music. The world was understandably shocked when Hendrix died accidentally in London in 1970, although by that time sudden death amongst rock musicians was becoming the rule, rather than the exception. Hendrix's last gig was a jam session at *Ronnie Scott's* London jazz club. Another irony...

## 1966: Soft Machine

From the field of experimental rock-jazz, possibly the best-known British band was Soft Machine, formed in 1966 and named after a book by the influential writer who occupied a focal point for the culture of the Beat generation, William S. Burroughs. This bald fact, important though it is, does not convey anything of the extensive groundwork put in by many musicians to arrive at the seminal band's formation.

One of the names most often associated with the band is Robert Wyatt (b1945, Bristol), a somewhat stereotypical 1960s musician whose extreme indulgences took him close to death. You could call him one of the lucky ones. A serious abuser of alcohol, on one occasion in 1973 (after he had left Soft Machine), whilst under its influence, he fell out of a fourth floor hotel window. Wyatt lived, but was paralysed from the waist down, and since then has conducted a modestly successful career in his own style of jazz-fusion from the confines of a wheelchair. The life expectancy of a rock musician in the 1960s was not great, so in that sense Wyatt was lucky.

A misfit at school, Wyatt came from a well-off family and was brought up in the regions of Dover and Canterbury on a broad diet of music, with jazz featuring highly in his mix of interests. He learned several instruments, but focussed on drums. In the early 1960s, a loose collection of Bohemian friends, experimenting mostly at Wyatt's large home in Canterbury, developed a music style that became known as "The Canterbury Scene". This term is "largely defined by a set of musicians and bands with intertwined members. These are not tied by strong musical similarities, but a certain whimsicality, touches of psychedelia, abstruse lyrics, and a use of improvisation derived from jazz are common elements in their work. The real essence of 'Canterbury Sound' is the tension between complicated harmonies, extended improvisations, and the sincere desire to write catchy pop songs. In the very best Canterbury music...the musically silly and the musically serious are juxtaposed in an amusing and endearing way." [28]

The beatnik environment was as much a lifestyle school as it was intended for music-making, with the usual gurus of contemporary art and literature at the centre of attention. Besides Wyatt, there were the Hopper brothers - Hugh (1945-2009) and Brian (b1943), both born in Canterbury, as also was Richard Sinclair (b1948). Mike Ratledge (b1943, Maidstone) and Kevin Ayers (1944-2013) were also Kentish men. The intellectual circle was squared with strong appreciation for the modern jazz of Charlie Parker and Miles Davis, but especially the deprecation of rules and espousal of improvisation. In such environments, the idea to create music that was spontaneous and beyond the current boundaries of jazz and rock was entirely natural, indeed, encouraged by a dependency on alcohol and mind-altering substances.

Hugh Hopper's significant presence on the Canterbury Scene started in 1963 as bassist with The Dævid Allen Trio, alongside drummer Robert Wyatt. His proclivities alternated between free jazz and rhythm and blues. In June 1963 with his brother, Brian Hopper, Robert Wyatt, Kevin Ayers and Richard Sinclair, he formed a band called The Wilde Flowers, now acknowledged as the founders of the Canterbury Scene, and spawned its two most important offspring, Soft Machine and Caravan. Although The Wilde Flowers never released any records during their existence, they did make recordings and an eponymous compilation was released some 30 years later. The CD contains 22 tracks with a variety of participants including Hugh Hopper (bass), Robert Wyatt (drums, vocals), Kevin Ayers (vocals), Graham Flight (vocals), Richard Sinclair (rhythm guitar, vocals), Pye Hastings (guitar, vocals), David Sinclair (keyboards), Richard Coughlan (drums) and Brian Hopper (lead guitar, alto saxophone, vocals). It is clear from this music that the compositions were raw, and the performances exhibit only a limited degree of musicianship. There is virtually no sign of jazz amongst the many tracks, which mostly try to imitate the R&B style of those more accomplished bands that had already found success. No self-respecting A&R man would have given these guys a contract on the basis of these tapes.

Clearly, the membership of The Wilde Flowers had been variable, and, like the musicians, band names came and went. Eventually, a new line-up featuring Kevin Ayers (bass), Robert Wyatt (drums, vocals), Mike Ratledge (keyboards) and Dævid Allen (guitar) settled on the name Soft Machine. Long, improvisations were sometimes incorporated, jazz-like, into their performances.

In September 1966, after a brief appearance in Hamburg, like the Beatles, the new band quickly moved to high profile gigs at London venues where, as an example of the new psychedelic music, they became very popular with the hip, underground scene. It was important to remain part of the underground in order to maintain credibility, and to that end commerciality was shunned. According to Stump, Soft Machine were offered a lucrative contract from pop entrepreneur, Mickie Most in 1966, which they refused, [29] but by the end of 1966 Soft Machine and Pink Floyd were the most talked about bands in London.

One of Soft Machine's founding members was Mike Ratledge. A classically trained pianist, as a teenager he soon befriended multi-instrumentalist, Brian Hopper. Thanks to Brian's younger brother Hugh, and other friends Robert Wyatt and Dævid Allen, Ratledge became part of Allen's Trio in 1963. His Canterbury friends converted him to free jazz and the anarchic playing of Cecil Taylor, which seemingly offered him the inspiration to develop a unique style, and thus to redefine Soft Machine's credentials from psychedelic rock to jazz-fusion. As Soft Machine's longest-lasting member, today, Ratledge is regarded as a seminal figure on the Canterbury music scene.

Soft Machine recorded a single in February 1967, and by the end of the month, *Love Makes Sweet Music*, with *Feelin', Reelin', Squeezin'* on the B-side was getting airplay on John Peel's popular radio shows. The sudden surge in popularity was a propellant into a wider circle of activities. Despite a rather unsuccessful summer in the South of France, the band returned to the UK, but without Allen, an Australian who was refused entry for visa reasons. Allen was forced to settle in France where he formed the band Gong. Soft Machine continued as a trio, and it was in this format that Wyatt, Ratledge and Ayers performed at all major venues alongside acts such as Pink Floyd and the Jimi Hendrix Experience. It was thanks to a bond formed with Chas Chandler of the Animals (who became the driving force behind the original Hendrix trio) that Soft Machine recorded their first album *The Soft Machine* in April 1968 with Chandler as producer.

On the original album, Arnold Shaw wrote of the music: "It's a Now sound, swings like jazz, rocks like rhythm-and-blues, hairy with fuzz-box distortion, of-the-keyboard with electronic atonalities - the sound of music updated by the music of sound." [30] Mark Powell later wrote, "The music written and performed by Soft Machine [on their first album] is arguably some of the finest produced during the latter days of psychedelia and the first throws of what would later be described as progressive rock. Compositions recorded had all been tried and tested in concert, and on record Soft Machine revealed the extent of their considerable musicianship and creativity. The experimental editing techniques used in the recording process would serve as an inspiration for legions of aspiring musicians over the following decades and resulted in a seamless and perfect work." [31]

With the debut album in the can, the band extensively toured the USA alongside Jimi Hendrix when the musicians were able to take their brand of experimental rock-jazz to a wide audience. Hendrix himself generously accepted their unique style. Wyatt said, "Hendrix wasn't a jazz fan, but he had the heart of taking risks all the time." [32] 1968 was a year in which the level of drug and alcohol abuse amongst rock musicians was growing fast. Soft Machine was reported to have toured widely across the USA "with no sleep at all" [32] – a feat accomplished by means of the heavy use of amphetamines. Kevin Ayers (1944-2013) found life on the road with Hendrix particularly hard. In addition, he began to disagree with his band mates, who wanted to take the music farther into jazz with less vocal music. Ayers dropped out of Soft Machine to pursue a softer, mostly solo career with albums such as *Joy Of A Toy* (1969), and *Shooting At The Moon* (1970).

Soft Machine's second album, *Volume Two* (1969), was recorded in trio format again, but now with Hugh Hopper on bass instead of Ayers. Ostensibly, the album contained two long suites called *Rivmic Melodies* and *Ester's Nose Job*, each consisting of a medley of pieces of differing lengths. A BBC reviewer wrote: "It was Hugh's vastly developed sense of melody, combined with the aforementioned love of jazz that saw the band enter Olympic Studios ... and record this masterpiece." [33] On tour in May 1969, the band now included Hugh's brother Brian on saxophone.

There is clearly dangerous quicksand ahead for those daring to question the long-term value of this music. Reviewer Chris Jones wrote, "Volume Two's first side begins with Wyatt reciting the alphabet, ending the side's suite of songs by doing the same, backwards. This mixture of the absurd and the serious that was to eventually tip in the direction of the latter (forcing out the more whimsical Wyatt, in 1971 after the *Fourth* album) provides a wonderful tension that no other band has ever really replicated. Fearsome chord progressions (*Dedicated To You But You Weren't Listening*), free noise (*Fire Engine Passing With Bells Clanging*) and even scatting in Spanish (*Dada Was Here*): this was no ordinary college band." [36] It was certainly a time when anything was possible in music, and listeners had no choice but to accept it, or at best be labelled "square".

Meanwhile Soft Machine moved further into jazz-fusion with the inclusion of horn players, notably Elton Dean (1945-2006). By the mid-1960s, Dean had started playing in London pubs, and had become a professional musician. In 1966-67, he played alongside trumpet player Mark Charig (b1944) in Long John Baldry's band Bluesology (whose piano player borrowed his and Baldry's first names to start a career as pop singer under the name Elton John). Late in 1967, Dean and Charig met jazz pianist Keith Tippett (b1947) and trombone player Nick Evans, and this resulted in the formation of the Keith Tippett Sextet, which played in various clubs in 1968-69, and recorded two albums for the Vertigo label.

In the autumn of 1969, Tippett's brass section of Dean, Evans and Charig was absorbed into Soft Machine. While Evans and Charig left after only a couple of months, Dean stayed on, and for two years was part of the band's best remembered line-up, alongside Robert Wyatt, Hugh Hopper and Mike Ratledge. He played on the studio albums *Third* (1970), *Fourth* (1971) and *Fifth* (1972). However, a series of musical disagreements resulted in a continuing string of personnel changes; founding member Robert Wyatt had departed after the album *Fourth*. The results of these changes are commonly judged as driving the band further into jazz-fusion as the release of albums proceeded. The presence of John Marshall (from *Fifth* onwards), and Karl Jenkins (from *Six* onwards) is seen as contributing a different jazz ethos that conflicted with the ideas of Hugh Hopper (who left in 1973) and John Etheridge who, in later years, decided that during his own tenure (from 1975 onwards) the band had not realised its potential. [35]

Soft Machine's jazz was much influenced by the free jazz that itself had acquired a perverse kind of kudos in the mid-1960s, its illogicality being exactly what the fashionable rule-breakers loved. There remain many fans who regard Soft Machine's output as seminal in the field of jazz-fusion, although I suspect that they are not from the community of jazz aficionados.

## 1966: NYC, NY

In my book about the Brecker Brothers [36] I described the early days of jazz-rock fusion in New York. It is clear that Larry Coryell was a strong influence. As a young guitarist, he arrived in New York from Seattle in September 1965, and proceeded to make an indelible mark on the jazz scene with a unique style that was strongly influenced by a mixture of John Coltrane and the Beatles. However, there was a considerable difference between what he was playing on record and what he was playing live. Most of the experimentation in jazz-rock fusion took place in front of live audiences in the New York jazz club scene, but did not make it onto record.

Larry Coryell is often reported as making an early move into jazz-rock fusion, with a band and an album called *Free Spirits* (1966). The great jazz-rock fusion guitarist, Al di Meola, dubbed Coryell the "Godfather of Fusion", and Randy Brecker, a long-time friend and associate is in complete agreement that it was Coryell who was the leading fusioneer in New York. [37] Unfortunately, the evidence of Coryell's recordings does not show it, the main explanation being the influence exerted over album content by the producers of the recordings. Indisputably, it was in live performances that Coryell put down his marker and was heard playing new things by many musicians as soon as he arrived on the

New York club scene in September 1965. Coryell writes about how he was listening to other players like Grant Green, Joe Beck and Charles Lloyd, and how excited he was when he realised there were new directions in which to take jazz, but it was still a long way from actually formulating a style of play for a working band. [38]. His ideas were no doubt better formed when he joined up with Gary Burton, Steve Swallow and Roy Haynes to record *Duster* (1967), an album proposed by Wikipedia as "one of the first jazz fusion albums". [39] Around 1966, in the same undirected haze, saxophonist Charles Lloyd had begun mixing rock rhythms with jazz in his quartet with Jack de Johnette (drums), Ron McLure (bass) and Keith Jarrett (piano), and had clearly influenced Coryell, but contemporary observers and critics seem to have little appetite for lauding Charles Lloyd's band as the forerunner of jazz-rock fusion.

After studying at Boston's Berklee Music College (where he already began to make albums) Gary Burton (b1943) played with George Shearing and Stan Getz before starting his own group at the beginning of 1967 whilst still only 23. He began to play with the likes of drummers Stu Martin and Roy Haynes, and Steve Marcus (saxophone), Steve Swallow (bass) and Larry Coryell. By the mid-60s, all of these young musicians had been influenced by Coltrane, Dylan, Miles and the Beatles. It was inevitable that they would apply features of the music they were hearing around them to their own musical environment. By abandoning the conventions of jazz they drew a significant measure of disapproval from the traditionalists, but by wearing their hair long and despatching suits and ties to the back of the wardrobe they were able to play at venues that other jazzers couldn't reach. They were adored by many young audiences who didn't much care whether they played jazz or not.

Today, when I listen to Burton's *Duster* (1967), it is hard to find anything that sounds like the jazz-rock experiment it is claimed to be. [4] Roy Haynes was a jazz drummer, recently employed by John Coltrane. Steve Swallow was playing acoustic bass and Burton himself acoustic vibraphone – an instrument almost never associated with rock music, its sweet chimes the very antithesis of rock's intestinal burps. Perhaps it was the presence of Larry Coryell's guitar that did at least provide something of the sound of rock music, but he was heavily constrained by the selected material. None of the pieces sound at all like jazz-rock. Mike Gibbs contributed three of the eight pieces that were more in the latest kind of free jazz format. Carla Bley's *Sing Me Softly of the Blues* was even freer and is not even a blues. Swallow contributed two: *Portsmouth Figurations* was essentially an opportunity for a standard jazz drum solo. Only in *General Mojo's Well Laid Plan* can we hear some of the kind of features of the sound of rock guitar. Having said all that, we must remember that what we experience today is not what those 1967 audiences felt. These musicians believed they were making music that was outside the boundaries of their current musical envelope, where it drew upon influences resulting from the turmoil of the music world around them. However, there can be no doubt that this music does not sound like jazz-rock fusion.

Nicholson says that these two records were the first suggestions that "an artistically and aesthetically satisfying synthesis of jazz and rock was possible." [40] Even then, evidence from recordings implies that Burton was unsure about making a wholehearted change to jazz-fusion, seen in some quarters as unpopular and undesirable. Both Burton and Coryell would continue to experiment with jazz-rock fusion ideas with variable results, and the commitment to a working band playing a menu of jazz-rock fusion was absent until later.

Other claims for Coryell must be taken with a pinch of salt. Eyebrows must surely be raised at suggestions that *Spaces* (1970) is "one of the most beautiful perfectly realised albums in a very long while" [41]. It is also claimed that *Spaces* is "one of the great jazz-rock albums" yet of all the tracks, only *Spaces (Infinite)* truly fits the description. For example, track two is *Rene's Theme*, a guitar duet that mimics the style of Django Rheinhardt. Track three is a mainstream version of a number by Scott LaFaro. Similarly, *Wrong is Right* is written in swing time and features Miroslav Vitous playing string bass with his bow. No fusion here then. The counterpoint between John McLaughlin and Coryell is of interest for the rapidity of the solos, although in track two they are often poorly synchronised, making the music sound like a pub jam session. Chick Corea appears on *Chris*, a 3/4 ballad that is played on electric instruments, but there are no rock rhythms here either. Finally, track six is a pointless guitar solo lasting a mere twenty seconds. So to claim this record does anything other than *consider* the fusion of jazz with rock music is disingenuous when five tracks choose normal formats. Today, this album is of curiosity value only. Even four years later, Coryell had still not entirely committed himself to jazz-fusion on *Introducing the Eleventh House* (1974). Burton, on the other hand, had made a far more dedicated attempt with the excellent *Good Vibes* (1971), the opening track *Vibrafinger* being a stunning example of jazz-rock. Coryell's work was frequently disappointing and demonstrated how the drugs/alcohol culture did not succeed in producing excellence for him at least. It is a matter of fact that, although McLaughlin did not choose him for his jazz-fusion band, he did choose Coryell for his guitar trio band, but was forced to let him go because of his unreliability.

There are many other possible examples of early jazz-rock fusion bands. Jeremy and the Satyrs was one, led by Jeremy Steig (flute) and featuring Mike Mainieri (vibes) who would later feature prominently in the 80s with his band Steps Ahead. The album *Jeremy & The Satyrs* (1968) is often promoted as one of the first jazz-rock fusion records, and features Steig on flute with Eddie Gomez (bass) Donald MacDonald (drums), Warren Bernhardt (electric piano) and Adrian Guillery (guitar). Listeners will find there a wide range of musical styles, and an undoubted presence of all of the styles considered to be a part of jazz-rock, but these are, once more, just experiments and no definite formula for jazz-rock fusion is identifiable. And, yet again, in view of what we now know about the London activities, it is rather late in the timescale we are considering.

## 1966: Chicago IL

In retrospect, we could easily say that, in musical terms at least, Chicago was to New York as Liverpool was to London. In other words, in the 1960s, Chicago was an important musical seed that germinated in the clubs of the windy city, but then spread itself in the wind to the music capital of the USA, New York.

Curiously, the British Invasion had a small part to play here too, when the English act, Chad and Jeremy had their first hit in the US with *Yesterday's Gone* (1964). It would seem that during their follow-up tour of America, they hired a nineteen-year-old bass player called Jim Guerico (b1945, Chicago), who also acted as their road manager. It was a period of employment that proved invaluable to the young man, for soon afterwards Guerico was to be found managing a four-piece rock group called the Buckinghams. Fortuitously, Guerico was able to get the band a contract with Columbia. (It seems to be no coincidence that one half of the British duo, Jeremy Clyde, was born in the English county of Buckinghamshire.) Guerico struck gold right from the off with the Buckinghams; the band had a #1 hit single and album with *Kind of A Drag* (1966). His work with the Buckinghams in his native Chicago yielded six more chart hits in the mid-60s.

No sooner had Guerico found success with the Buckinghams, than he was to be found driving other promising fusion bands towards commercial success. For example, in 1968, Guerico signed another Chicagoan band to Columbia called Illinois Speed Press, comprised of Paul Cotton and Kal David. Originally called The Rovin' Kind, the band had become the regular house band at the city's top club, *Whiskey A Go Go*, but the band members changed its name at Guerico's behest. There are many interlinks to be found amongst the top musicians from Chicago in these times. Kal David had previously played with Peter Cetera in an early psychedelic rock band called Aorta. David, Cetera and multi-instrumentalist Marty Grebb had also played together in 1962 in a band led by David. Cetera went on to become a leading light in Chicago, whilst Grebb joined the Buckinghams where he added significantly to the band's influential brass-rock sound.

As if this were not enough, Guerico was a strong background influence in the formation of Chicago Transit Authority (later, simply Chicago), another strongly influential jazz-rock fusion group created in late 1960s Chicago Illinois. As a new venture, Guerico later founded the famous Caribou Ranch recording studio, "a sonically and environmentally unique facility he built on more than 4,000 acres of Colorado's Rocky Mountains." [42]

Throughout the 1970s and 80s, many top musicians chose to record there, including Earth, Wind & Fire, Supertramp, Nitty Gritty Dirt Band, Return To Forever and Elton John, who in 1974 named his eighth studio album after the studio and ranch.

An important facilitator in these successes was Clive Davis at the head of the powerful Columbia Record Company, where he acted as an executive producer responsible for both jazz and rock music and had a lot of input towards their fusion. Clive Davis (b1932) was born into a Jewish family in Brooklyn, New York. After qualifying with excellence from the Harvard Law School, in his thirties he found himself appointed as General Counsel of Columbia Records, for which company he became Vice President and General Manager in 1966. As holder of probably the most powerful position in the music industry, he soon made his mark by recognising the value of rock music to the business. He hired Janis Joplin's Big Brother and the Holding Company in 1967. The Buckinghams, Chicago Transit Authority and Blood Sweat & Tears, all came under the fatherly eye of Davis, who followed up on these decisions with acquisition of many groups and artists who would become top names: Santana, Boz Scaggs, Billy Joel, Bruce Springsteen, Aerosmith and Earth, Wind and Fire, are some examples. In addition, he signed such artists as Neil Diamond, Pink Floyd, Herbie Hancock and The Isley Brothers. [43]

Soon after his appointment, Clive Davis came into personal contact with his unrelated namesake, Miles Davis, who had been Columbia's biggest-selling jazz artist since 1956. However, jazz music, which had been the dominant music form for several decades, fell way behind when the sales of pop and rock music exploded exponentially in the 1960s; jazz was not the lucrative market it had once been. At first, Clive was not alone in finding it hard to bridge the gap between his angle for business and Miles's unique angle on music. At first, the two men had what might be called a 'difficult' business relationship, but, once Miles had sussed Clive out, Miles wrote that, "He and I got along well, because he thinks like an artist instead of a straight businessman. He had a good sense for what was happening; I thought he was a great man." [44] Clive was generously supportive to Miles during the next critical phase in his career, and encouraged Miles to extend jazz into the world of rock and pop music. This was achieved with the albums, *In A Silent Way* (1969) and *Bitches Brew* (1970).

Another band emanating from Chicago as part of the burgeoning jazz-rock fusion scene was called The Flock. Originally formed as a garage band called the Exclusives by Rick Canoff and Fred Glickstein, they became the Flock soon after they discovered the talented violinist, Jerry Goodman. It was Goodman's virtuosity and unusual sound that propelled The Flock to instant success thanks to a contract with Columbia. The members at the time of their 1969 eponymous studio recording were Fred Glickstein (guitar, lead vocals), Jerry Goodman (violin), Jerry Smith (bass), Ron Karpman (drums), Rick Canoff (saxophone), Tom Webb (saxophone) and Frank Posa (trumpet). Unfortunately, the band's second album *Dinosaur Swamps* (1970) failed to live up to the promise of the first record, probably due to a selection of weak compositions. The disappointment encouraged Clive Davis to suggest Jerry Goodman for the position of electric violinist in John McLaughlin's new band, Mahavishnu Orchestra. Goodman's place in music history was secured, but The Flock were unable to survive without him.

## 1967: Blood Sweat & Tears

In the USA, one of the first and most influential bands to indulge in fusion-type music was Blood Sweat & Tears (BS&T), formed in 1967 as a collaboration between keyboardist Al Kooper, drummer Bobby Columby and guitarist Steve Katz, although Kooper was undoubtedly the main driving force. The deliberate aim of the band was to broaden its sound to include elements of jazz and the band was to become a long-term survivor with many albums to their credit, ironically *without* Kooper. It also went through a number of evolutions of personnel, but Bobby Columby stayed with them for most of their existence and retained the commercial rights to the name until this was taken over much later by David Clayton-Thomas. (I describe in another book how, in 1974, Columby was to discover Jaco Pastorius and to produce his astonishing debut album. [45])

Randy Brecker got a job with Al Kooper's new band, Blood Sweat & Tears, formed in 1967. Incredibly, in 1965, Kooper had gate-crashed a Dylan recording session, and then been invited to play a Hammond organ solo! That turned out to be apocryphal for Dylan fans at the start of his electric period. Kooper soon afterwards joined the band, Blues Project, before creating BS&T. Kooper himself said that a source of inspiration for the BS&T project was the #1 hit, *Kind Of A Drag* by The Buckinghams. This was music identified at the time as brass-rock, in which the traditional format of rock bands (electric guitars, bass and drums) was supplemented by a section of trumpets, trombones, and/or saxophones. Saxophone players were usually able to double on flute or other woodwind for added versatility in the band's sound. A brass front line was, for the first time, an integral part of a band, in this case, led by the yet-to-be-famous jazz trumpeter Randy Brecker. The seven-piece (4+3) band structure was very common for a number of years from 1967 onwards. [46]

The first BS&T sessions took place in September 1967. A band consisting of Kooper (keyboards), Steve Katz (guitar), Bobby Colomby (drums) and Jim Fielder (bass) opened the show for Moby Grape at the *Café Au Go-Go* in NYC. However, the band only took on its full-formed fusion style when joined soon afterwards by horn players Fred Lipsius (saxophone), Randy Brecker, Jerry Weiss (trumpet) and Dick Halligan (trombone). The final line-up debuted at the *Café Au Go Go* on 17–19 November, 1967, and then moved to *The Scene* the following week. Recording sessions for tracks that would become *Child Is The Father To The Man* (1968) took place from 11 November to 20 December 1967. The album was released by Columbia on 21 February 1968. It was a minor hit in the Billboard pop album charts where it reach #47. The album did also benefit from a significant transition that took place amongst the record-buying public in 1968, when a change of emphasis from singles to albums took place.

Their output was very quickly noticed as being different and stimulated a rapid move forward in the fusion of jazz and rock amongst the broader American music community. A modern ear finds the music on the album very dated, but the overt blending of both jazz and rock on tracks such as *Refugee From Yuhupitz* and *I Love You More Than You'll Ever Know* was very fresh at the time.

Their success was double-edged, however, as schizophrenia developed between the jazzers and the rockers. An argument about the band's direction led to a split immediately after the first album. Kooper moved on to other work, whilst Colomby and Katz recruited a new, more powerful lead singer, David Clayton-Thomas, with whom the band is strongly associated in the memories of many music fans. Thus, by 1967 the possibilities for fusion had been very obvious for some time on both sides of the Atlantic and BS&T were lucky enough to be able to capitalise on its potential. Pandora's Box had at last been opened and the music industry began a big expansion in scope that affected all forms of music.

Nevertheless, because of its wide distribution, the record's influence was great in the world beyond NYC, and is the reason why many observers attribute the creation of jazz-rock fusion to BS&T. Its impact was almost entirely due to Kooper's creativity, a factor that was largely lost on succeeding albums because Kooper departed from the band after just one album; most opinions concur that the band's best album was the first one.

Coincidentally, Randy Brecker left BS&T at the same time to play with Horace Silver, but there was no correlation with the split that drove Kooper out. Kooper had been unhappy about the band's desire to hire David Clayton-Thomas, who would potentially compete with Al for the lead vocals. Meanwhile, Randy was already negotiating with Horace Silver. The jazzer's musical reasoning prevailed. Brecker: "Well that [BS&T] was a great band but I didn't get to solo much. I played on one tune. That was sad I think. A lot of the guys in the band were really jazz musicians first, too, and they were really great players, Freddy Lipsius, Bobby Colomby... But when Horace called, I really wanted to take that gig. It was a quintet and I could play to my heart's content. So I left Blood Sweat & Tears in early '68 to join Horace." [47] At his final band meeting, Randy's last words to BS&T as he left the room were, "You'll never make it without Al!" [48]

As time went on, BS&T were as much at home in the jazz genre as they were in rock music. Jazz cats listened to their records and attended their gigs. Their recording sessions were attended by jazz luminaries like Herbie Hancock, whose classic composition *Maiden Voyage* appeared on the BS&T album, *New Blood* (1972). However, it was always an uneasy alliance between the rock and jazz factions, each often accusing the other of having too much influence over the band. Arguments were followed by bust-ups and the band went through several metamorphoses. Notable amongst the jazz members were Fred Lipsius (sax), Lew Soloff (trumpet), and Dave Bargeron (trombone). In the mid-1970s, Mike Stern (guitar) and Don Alias (drums/percussion) appeared in the band's line-up on the album *More Than Ever* (1975). When Ron McClure left in late 1975, Bobby Colomby arranged for Jaco Pastorius to join the band, though he stayed for only about three months. Jaco officially joined Weather Report on 1 April 1976 and BS&T recruited Danny Trifan to replace him.

## 1967: Chicago

Another band often cited as having an important early influence on the creation of jazz-rock music is Chicago, a name that only emerged a number of years after the band was formed. Originally called The Big Thing, a group of seven students, mostly belonging to de Paul and Roosevelt Universities, came together in Chicago in 1967. The founding members were Robert Lamm (vocals, keyboards), Terry Kath (guitar), Peter Cetera (bass), and Daniel Seraphine (drums), with a horn section of Lee Loughnane (trumpet), James Pankow (trombone) and Walter Parazaider (woodwinds).

In 1968 after about a year developing their music in the venues around their home city, they moved to Los Angeles under the influence of their manager Jim Guerico. There they secured a contract with Columbia Records and changed the name of the band to the Chicago Transit Authority. The first record, a double album, was recorded in Columbia's New York studios in January 1969, the same venue where just one month later Miles Davis would record *In A Silent Way* (1969). The tracks for *Chicago Transit Authority* (1969) were laid down at night when the facilities were free from the use by stars like Simon & Garfunkel during the day.

The band members never claimed to be anything more than just a rock band with horns - indeed, there were no recognised jazz players on board. The eponymous first album reached #17 in the US Billboard charts and stayed in the charts for a remarkable 171 weeks. It seems inevitable therefore, that such massive popular success had a great influence on contemporary musicians who heard Chicago's music from 1969 onwards. So, despite being an early starter in the rock-jazz fusion genre, their undoubted influence peaked in subsequent years as the paradigm shift to fusion music reached its peak of activity in 1969-71.

The band went on to release a series of numerically titled albums, beginning with *Chicago* (1970) - often called *Chicago II* to maintain the numerical numbering. This was done annually until 1980, and then on a more infrequent basis, almost always sticking to cover designs based upon the band's logo. From 1970 onwards, the continuing use of the logo to mark the band's business endeavours marked the maturation of the brand, and the permanent change of the band's name to Chicago, rather than the clumsier Chicago Transit Authority.

An exception to the logical progress of album names occurred in 1978 with the release of the twelfth album *Hot Streets* (1978). This event marked the death of lead guitarist Terry Kath in an accidental shooting, a split between the band and manager Guerico in favour of Phil Ramone, and a conscious change in the style of music away from fusion and towards soft-rock. In that sense, the perception of soft-rock as a more commercial approach coincided with the general feeling amongst many members the music industry that jazz-rock fusion had had its day. Nevertheless, from 1979, Chicago reverted to its original scheme for numbering its albums and proceeded steadily towards becoming one of the most successful bands of all time.

## 1968: Jon Hiseman's Colosseum

By 1968, the fusion movement was in a mode of rapid growth on *both* sides of the Atlantic with numerous rock-based bands seeking fame and fortune by the inclusion of jazz elements into their material. There were undoubtedly some cross-influences but in many cases, the bands of this period had grown out of locally inspired intercourse, with American musicians often unaware of what was happening in the UK. As a further example, the brilliant polyrhythmic drummer, Jon Hiseman formed a British rock-jazz band called Colosseum deliberately to capitalise on the novel, now recognised concept of fusion.

The young Hiseman (b1944) was entirely self-taught, starting with a limited number of cheap instruments and no overpowering influences to bias his style. As a result, he quickly grew into a uniquely gifted, in-demand, jazz drummer, who always preferred to play by listening to the band, rather than the drums. This characteristic was represented by the title of an excellent book about his musical career. [49] As a jazzer in the early 60s, he found himself an essential part of many creative groupings, especially the New Jazz Orchestra, which he was a part of from its inception in 1963. It was in this band that Hiseman first formed a relationship with his future wife, saxophonist Barbara Thompson. Through the NJO, Hiseman also developed close friendships with other top jazzmen, Tony Reeves, Dave Greenslade, and Dick Heckstall-Smith that proved especially valuable over the years that followed.

By 1968, Graham Bond's drug problems had driven Hiseman and Heckstall-Smith into John Mayall's Bluesbreakers at a time when Mayall was changing to a more jazz-inflected style, but the change was short-lived. Within months, Mayall had fired Heckstall-Smith, who was then in dire need of employment. Dick made his need clear to Hiseman that it was time for them to form their own band, so during a short Italian holiday, and in sight of some of the finer monuments of ancient Rome, Hiseman decided that the time was right for a new band that was promoted as "Jon Hiseman's Colosseum", but which was soon shortened to just "Colosseum".

Hiseman assembled a balanced band of experienced musician: Heckstall-Smith was on saxophones, Dave Greenslade on keyboards, with Hiseman on drums and Tony Reeves on bass. The final recruit was James Litherland on guitar and vocals. This band too was blazing a trail of "white rock drums with jazz solos," although Hiseman's genuine jazz pedigree enabled him to apply true fusion veneer to the band's output. In a retrospective TV interview, Hiseman talked fondly of a brief period "…from 1968-72 when the music was musician-led…" by which he meant that – for once – the record companies were not dictating the content of a band's music. [23] Musicians who had not been seduced by electric instruments were now in a small minority.

Colosseum premiered with the album, *Those Who Are About to Die Salute You* (1969), recorded in late 1968/early 1969. Inspection reveals a collection of mostly instrumental music in which Heckstall-Smith's tenor saxophone is a prominent sound. The compositions themselves are credited to the band, but not especially novel, being almost entirely based upon the common 12-bar blues chord sequence. However, the strong jazz inflections, solos by all of the instruments, and the saxophone/rock guitar presence contribute to make this record a genuine early milestone for British jazz-rock fusion. Two other notable points are the success of the opening track, *Walking In The Park* – a Graham Bond composition that became the band's hit in the pop charts, and the hijacking of the mega-hit, *A Whiter Shade Of Pale* by Procol Harum. This piece was labelled officially on the record as *Beware The Ides of March* and unofficially as *A Whiter Spade Of Mayall*.

Having recorded their first album, the band went on the road, and played almost every night across the UK and Europe. During these gigs, Colosseum not only honed their material to a fine degree, but also developed their style of evolving the music through improvisation. It was not a free style of improvisation, but structured within the boundaries of each composition. Nevertheless, there were constant diversions within each piece that were spontaneous when played, and then debated rigorously in gig post-mortems.

In his book, Hiseman makes a specific remark about the pressure he felt from living with the constant need to be creative each night, in complete contrast to members of pop groups who were content to make the same sounds, note-for-note, every night. Following the example set by Ginger Baker's drum solo in *Toad*, Hiseman was seen as a trail blazing drummer - a competitor to Baker, and therefore expected to deliver drum pyrotechnics every night. As Hiseman came to be regarded as probably the leading drummer on the UK music scene, this element by which Colosseum performances featured showpiece virtuoso drum solos became common in the stage performances of most jazz-rock bands of this period, and there was the added pressure for drummers to create ever more inventive drum solos to satisfy the demands of expectant audiences. Hiseman was quite clear that when either he or his band failed to deliver on any given occasion, he could feel the disappointment of the audience. [50]

In 1967, it became popular to create pop music formats with longer 'suites' of music similar to those that were found in classical music. In England, a very successful pop single *Excerpt from a Teenage Opera* (1966) was created by Mark Wirtz, who had the idea of writing a long suite of music, as in the style of a classical opera, but he never achieved his objective. The Beatles, too, were in the vanguard for originality when they created the *Magical Mystery Tour*, a musical film for TV that led to a concept album. All these ideas began to coalesce by the end of the decade when it became fashionable for progressive music makers (especially those who were subscribing more to the music of the album, rather than the single) to consider creating 'concept music.' Colosseum was no exception, as the band showed with their extended composition called *Valentyne Suite*. This has since been marked out as the formula by which a lot of subsequent progressive music was created. [51]

Once Colosseum's second album, *Valentyne Suite* (1969), had been recorded, the band played at the *Montreux Jazz Festival*, a remarkable accolade, the more so when it is realised that the band's presence there assisted in popularising an event that was considered to be in a struggling genre - jazz! The event is a clear milestone in jazz-fusion history.

Jazz-fusion was by no means a universally accepted genre by 1969. In the UK, there was speculation in the press about the kind of music being played by Colosseum, especially in an article written by a junior reporter called Mark Knopfler. [52] When the band played at the Fillmore West in San Francisco, on the same bill as the Chicago Transit Authority, comments made by a member of that band recognised the originality of the "jazz solos played over rock rhythms" [53], and Peter Cetera later acknowledged that he knew about the jazz-rock credentials of Colosseum by 1969. In Los Angeles, however, during a six-day gig at the *Whiskey-A-Gogo*, there was just general bafflement about what kind of music was being played.

Just after the USA tour, in September, James Litherland was fired and replaced by Clem Clempson. Despite playing guitar, singing and contributing compositions, Litherland had always been a junior partner, and was not seen as a strong enough member of what was clearly a band that was going somewhere. For a time, Clempson had to take on his duties. However, as the band recorded new tracks to help compile a record for release in the USA entitled *The Grass Is Greener* (1970), it became apparent that Clempson's singing voice left something to be desired. Furthermore, music writers began to realise that there was a widening gulf between what bands delivered live and what they could offer on record. This was especially true of progressive bands like Colosseum and King Crimson, who were constantly refining their music live, and therefore leaving behind the rather sterile studio versions, which were best thought of as musical snapshots of the state of development at the time. [54]

By virtue of the origins of the bands' members, there was still a close relationship with the New Jazz Orchestra, run by MD Neil Ardley. Jon, Dick, Tony (and Barbara Thompson) all played with this big band, and there arose opportunities for it to join forces with Colosseum. One memorable occasion was at the Lanchester Arts Festival in Coventry in January 1970, when a kind of 'superconcert' took place, with Colosseum supplemented by the entire NJO, thanks to Ardley's arrangements. Fortunately, this event was recorded and recently released on CD as *Camden '70* (2008).

By mid 1970 Tony Reeves had declared his desire to leave the band for other projects, and the band's lack of new original material to include in their set lists was beginning to be a real problem for Jon. The band was so busy touring and doing live gigs that there was just no time to create new material they so desperately needed. Louis Cennamo was hired to replace Tony just in time for the band to go into the studio to record its fourth album, *Daughter of Time* (1970). However, Cennamo never lived up to expectations and was quickly replaced by Mark Clarke.

By the time the band wound up its sessions for the recording of *Daughter of Time*, Chris Farlowe had been recruited as the lead singer. So the tracks on the album feature both Clempson and Farlowe as lead singers, with Cennamo, Reeves and Clarke all appearing on bass.

By the time the record was released there was a clear gulf between what the band was doing live, and what was recorded in the studio. Indeed, none of the material on the final studio album was ever played live! It led to much controversy amongst professional writers and fans alike as to whether the album was the band's best or worst. The inevitable result was that the band's last album would be a live recording called simply *Colosseum Live* (1971). This too created tension of a different kind, for, despite having a mobile recording set up and following the band over a number of gigs in March 1971, the band members were never satisfied with the music that was recorded. The critics generally liked the album, but there were continual issues, and Hiseman let the pressures of running the band get on top of him. A variety of disagreements ensued between the band members, and the final straw was when Clempson was persuaded to join Uriah Heap. Hiseman folded the band in September 1971 just as the band was preparing a second tour of the USA in support of Deep Purple. All of them had had enough; the band had finally run out of steam.

Hiseman has claimed that Colosseum was "the first ever jazz-rock combo." [55] He said that on a tour of Chicago their American audiences were astonished at the new sounds they were making in fusion. At first sight this is a curious observation in light of the fact that The Wild Things (later Chicago) had been blazing rock-jazz fusion in the Chicago venues during 1967-8. It is here that my distinction between jazz-rock and rock-jazz is helpful. The musicians in Chicago had backgrounds mostly in rock music - hence the labels of rock with horns, or brass rock. Colosseum, on the other hand, was a band composed of musicians with a much deeper background in jazz, and therefore planted firmly in the jazz-rock category. Colosseum remains highly regarded in Europe but largely unrecognised in the USA.

Whilst his friend Dave Greenslade went off to join another seminal jazz-rock fusion band, If, Hiseman spent the year of 1972 in something of a hiatus period. Colosseum was now part of history and a new band was still a figment of his imagination. He spent time participating in other projects, perhaps most notably Dick Heckstall-Smith's solo album *A Story Ended* (1972). Hiseman even held talks with Robert Fripp about a possible collaboration, but there were too many musical differences between them. As the year progressed, Hiseman, under pressure from his manager, Gerry Bron, began to plan his new band, and settled on the name of Tempest. Mark Clarke was a shoe-in for the bass slot, but Jon was inspired to invite the unknown Allan Holdsworth to play lead guitar. The possibility of proceeding as a trio with Clarke doubling as lead vocalist seemed plausible at first, but when Juicy Lucy singer, Paul Williams, suddenly became available, he became the fourth band member. Both Holdsworth and Williams played other instruments too, which gave the band options for change.

In Oct/Nov 1972, the band recorded *Tempest* (1973) and began to tour in January 1973, but this was not a match made in heaven. The strong musical bond between Hiseman and Clarke was not matched with the others, who had doubts about the musical format. Listening to the album provides strong hints of the deep-seated problems. Here were four brilliant musicians with their own strong opinions about how they wanted to present themselves. The music was solidly in the rock genre, and Holdsworth wanted to extend his already remarkable jazz guitar chops, but was limited by the preference for song-type material. No sooner was the material for the album recorded than Holdsworth wanted to leave the band. He even brought his own replacement, Ollie Halsall, who for a short time played alongside Holdsworth in a five-piece outfit as Holdsworth worked through his commitments to the band. Then Holdsworth moved to the USA and took the seat in Tony Williams' Lifetime that had been vacated by John McLaughlin. Paul Williams was also dissatisfied and left, whereupon Tempest was reduced to a threesome. For Hiseman, it was a good result while it lasted. *Living in Fear* (1973), was recorded late in the year, but after a period of touring, the band, which had never really fitted well under a jazz-rock label, but could have impacted upon the growing prog-rock scene, nevertheless folded. Despite the common agreement that it had possessed immense potential because of the top-notch musicianship of its members, the band never really convinced listeners that the compositions possessed the same level of merit.

## 1968: Jazz-Rock Fusion in Hindsight

Since transatlantic influences (in both directions) were overwhelmingly occurring because of exchanges of recordings (Figure 4), we might deduce that many bands were developing their new ideas in isolation.

As I have described, in London, from around 1963 onwards there was a music scene with frantic nocturnal activity by the likes of John McLaughlin, Georgie Fame, Brian Auger, Dick Heckstall-Smith and others that was never recorded, and so the influences derived from the work of these musicians took longer to export. It appears to me, therefore, that the fusion of jazz and rock first took place in the UK, crystallised from the melting pot of art school counterculture. Like the nature of jazz itself, the process was spontaneous, rather than planned. No clear strategy stood out: it wasn't possible in such a cauldron of change. Perhaps the most natural formulation for those, like John Lennon, who came from rock 'n' roll, was to build on their R&B inclinations. Others with backgrounds in jazz often took the path of free-form jazz derivatives with rock connotations. Logically, the spectrum of results ranged from jazz-rock to rock-jazz, though I seem to be the only writer to use these terms in this way.

My analysis shows that there was much more rock-jazz fusion in the UK than in the USA, and I believe the greatest content of British music exported to the USA was rock-jazz, rather than jazz-rock. In the UK, compared to the '50s, the '60s were a lean period for jazz because so much effort was being expended on the explosion of rock and R&B music. Indeed, it was recognised that jazz content in a band's repertoire could actually be a handicap. Although a musician's jazz background was an asset to a band (for it enabled him to add a new dimension to the band's sound in an already crowded marketplace), there was no serious money-earning potential for bands that played pure jazz, especially jazz that contained only acoustic instruments. Thus, from a high level of activity in the '50s, jazz activities diminished to a small volume that was barely self-sustaining yet still able to move forward with a core of dedicated fans in support. But working jazz musicians needed to feed their families like the rest of us, and so many jumped ship to join some of the thousands of newly formed rock and R&B bands where they would inevitably make jazzy contributions.

The ultimate irony is that the large cohort of art school expats, having absorbed all these influences from across the Atlantic, then served it all back, whence it had come, with *Made in Britain* stamped over it. Started by the Beatles with their first visits to the USA, and continued by a stream of high profile and very successful British pop/rock bands, this became known as the 'British Invasion'. Many observers have suggested that for these reasons, jazz-rock fusion was also British-inspired. This is partly true. However, it does not take account of the natural isolationist tendency of Americans to ignore events outside their own boundaries. There was unquestionably a parallel movement in New York, led by the young jazz guitarist, Larry Coryell, and others such as Steve Marcus and Jeremy Steig, to bring about a fusion of jazz and rock. Even Coryell is the first to admit his influence from the Beatles, but his early motivation to draw together strands of rock guitar into jazz - witnessed at first hand by Randy Brecker - took place without reference to the likes of Graham Bond, John McLaughlin *et al.* [56]

In many cases, it was the jazz interests and capabilities of a strong cohort of

British musicians spending time under the influence of art schools that drove the fusion of pop/rock, blues and jazz in the UK. When this jazz-fusion came to be exported back to the United States by bands I shall discuss below, the creature – still a fledgling chick in New York – had already chipped its way out of the London-laid egg.

## 1969: Fusions Everywhere

At the end of 1968, people were starting to write about jazz and rock coming together, even if it hadn't been formally recognised as a new sub-genre. A lot of activity was taking place in California, focussed on the music venue called *Fillmore West* in San Francisco, which was staging a lot of large scale rock gigs with the significant presence on stage of jazz acts, thanks to the sponsorship of promoter Bill Graham. California might as well have been China as far as the New York jazz scene was concerned. If it didn't happen in New York then it didn't matter and, of course, Miles Davis was at the epicentre of the New York activity. But in the second half of the 60s, the rapidly growing 'sex, drugs, rock 'n' roll' culture of California, and in particular San Francisco, now fuelled the change in music. Acid/pot raves at which stoned individuals partied all night were largely facilitated by a certain kind of music that simply went on and on. It was the first "trance" music. Rock music assumed the jazz approach whereby indefinite improvisations – often based on just one chord – were embedded into the rock tunes. Bands such as Jefferson Airplane and Grateful Dead were thus behind a significant evolutionary change in rock music – recorded, certainly, but especially live. And this change was even further catalysed when the barnstorming band Cream played at *Fillmore West* in 1968, performing extended improvisations based on jazz ideas.

By the end of the 1960s, offshoots of the newly christened *rock* music considerably widened that genre. Record stores were faced with the need for sections labelled *baroque-rock*, *shock-rock*, *blues-rock*, *avant-rock*, *prog-rock*, *glam-rock*, *garage-rock*, *art-rock*, *indie-rock*, *hard-rock*, *alternative-rock*, *Krautrock*, *southern rock*, *symphonic-rock*, *punk-rock* and *raga-rock*. No doubt there were more! It took some years for all those derivatives to emerge and be identified as such, but from the very first there was an exciting listening interaction between rock music and jazz, preferred by a certain kind of people as being *trendy*; stereotypical devotees were thought to wear exclusively sandals and beards. The process of overlap mushroomed, and the absorption of each type of music by another became inevitable. In the final years of the 1960s, the music scene was awash with embryonic invention that might or might not develop into more widely accepted sub-genres of rock. One of the most popular and successful of the early fusions was Prog-rock. Primarily a rock formula, it contained *soupçons* of jazz that varied from a smidge to a dollop.

Names of people and the bands they briefly populate swirl around like loose debris in a tornado. Today's senior generations look back with much fondness upon times when music was as exciting as anyone can remember. Descriptions of what is now music folklore are inevitably biased by rose-tinted memories. The music played at live gigs on the hundreds of student campuses across the UK was not necessarily representative of the kinds of music in recordings available today. Nevertheless, these times are not so distant that they are not well remembered by many readers.

Caravan was a band that operated contemporarily with Soft Machine, its core members derived from the Canterbury Scene, and the multi-faceted group, The Wilde Flowers. In that sense, its output continued the philosophy of creating experimental music with whoever was available at the time, resulting in band longevity - the band exists today. Unlike many other bands, they were successful enough to generate an extended sequence of albums with titles that reflected the typically English humour of prog-rock bands. Originally based around Pye Hastings (guitar, vocals), Richard Sinclair (bass, vocals), Dave Sinclair (keyboards), and Richard Coughlan (drums, percussion), the band exhibited significant jazz influences, although there were variations that paralleled the band's variable membership. Early albums are well regarded in the prog-rock catalogue: *Caravan* (1968), *If I Could Do It All Over Again, I'd Do It All Over You* (1970), *In the Land of Grey and Pink* (1971), *Waterloo Lily* (1972), *For Girls Who Grow Plump in the Night* (1973), and *Cunning Stunts* (1975).

Many fans enthuse about wonder-guitarist, Steve Hillage who befriended Dave Stewart (keyboards), Mont Campbell (bass), Clive Brooks (drums) to form a band called Uriel in 1968. An album entitled *Arzachel* (1969) was released a year later under pseudonyms for legal reasons. It has become a much sought-after item because of what these musicians later became involved in. Hillage left home for University in the autumn of 1968, so without him, the other three became a band called Egg in January 1969. After two relatively unsuccessful albums, *Egg* (1970) and *The Polite Force* (1971), the band folded in 1972. In 1975, Stewart and Campbell later went on to contribute to the more successful prog-rock band, National Health.

One especially original band was Henry Cow, formed by two undergraduates, Fred Frith and Tim Hodgkinson, in a Cambridge University blues club in 1968. Throughout most of its existence, the band shunned commercialism as it went about its experimental agenda. With an ever-changing roster of musicians, Frith and Hodgkinson kept Henry Cow on a path that was challenging and highly innovative, mostly in genres we might today define as *avant-garde* and progressive rock. Jazz was not a significant proportion of the band's fusion mix.

For ten years until 1978, Henry Cow made uncompromising music that had significant influence in mainland Europe rather than the UK. Interested readers can find recently remixed editions of the band's *Complete Works* in rather pricey box sets.

A long-lived band that still performs at the time of writing (2015) is Gong, formed by Dævid Allen who was excluded from Soft Machine after he was marooned in France when refused re-entry to the UK. Allen's band attracted its members from a very wide invitation list of musicians of British, French and other nationalities, and included, variously, Steve Hillage, Chris Cutler and Bill Bruford. Of his own brief encounter, Bruford summed up the prevailing intellectually earnest but ultimately vacuous philosophy of Allen's drugs-led hippy lifestyle thus: "Searching Gong for alternative methods of communal music making was like searching a children's playground for paths to higher enlightenment - not immediately fruitful..." [57]

Robert Wyatt recorded *The End Of An Ear* in August 1970 and released it the following December. Described as an album of free jazz, even the most ardent listeners found it tough going. After his departure from Soft Machine in October 1971, he formed a new band called Matching Mole. Later, in the summer of 1973, Wyatt was seriously injured when he fell out of a fourth floor window and was therefore forced to disband his Matching Mole project.

Elton Dean was an influential British jazz saxophone player who famously had his name adopted by Elton John whilst Dean was playing in the Long John Baldry band. Dean had played with Keith Tippett (1968-70) and in Soft Machine (1969-72). His contribution of jazz to Soft Machine's output is significant. In 2002, Dean and three other former Soft Machine members (Hugh Hopper, drummer John Marshall, and guitarist Allan Holdsworth) toured and recorded under the name Soft Works. With another former Soft Machine member, guitarist John Etheridge, replacing Holdsworth, they subsequently toured and recorded as Soft Machine Legacy, playing some pieces from the original Soft Machine repertoire as well as new works. Dean died in February 2006.

After leaving the Rendell-Carr Quintet (1963-69), Ian Carr went on to form the well-known jazz-rock band Nucleus that made twelve albums, some under Carr's name. In their first year they won first prize at the *Montreux Jazz Festival*, released their album *Elastic Rock* (1969), and performed in the United States at both the *Newport Jazz Festival* and the *Village Gate* jazz club.

An important episode occurred in 1971 that proved to have a big effect on British jazz and involved an experiment in jazz-fusion by pianist Keith Tippett.

Tippett came to London in 1967, at age 20, and found it a difficult place for an aspiring jazz musician. Unable to find paying gigs he survived with menial work. Then he won a scholarship to the Barry Summer School Jazz Course in Wales where he met cornet and trumpet player Marc Charig, saxman Elton Dean, and trombonist Nick Evans. In late 1967, Tippett formed his own sextet, the Keith Tippett Group, with Dean, Charig and Evans, and a rhythm section that, at various times, featured bassists Jeff Clyne, Roy Babbington, Harry Miller and Neville Whitehead, and drummers Phil Howard, John Marshall, Bryan Spring and Alan Jackson. The band played regularly at Oxford Street's *100 Club*, which gave them the visibility to secure a contract with the new Vertigo label. Two albums were released: *You Are Here, I Am There* (1970) and *Dedicated To You But You Weren't Listening* (1971). They remain obscure, but Tippett and members of his group also became involved with Robert Fripp's band, King Crimson. Fripp originally asked Tippett to play the piano in the studio band that he assembled to complete *In The Wake of Poseidon* (1970), after the original King Crimson band broke up. By that time, Tippett's group - which included Dean, Charig, Evans, Jeff Clyne (bass), and Alan Jackson (drums), with Giorgio Gomelsky sitting in on bells - had finished *You Are Here I Am There* (1970).

Tippett, Charig, and Evans all played very prominent roles on King Crimson's *Lizard* (1970), and Fripp invited Tippett to join his band, but he declined, preferring to keep his own group. Even as a guest musician, Tippett featured prominently on *Lizard*, his acoustic piano in sharp contrast to the Mellotrons and other electronic instruments. Tippett and Charig played on *Islands* (1971), by which time the Tippett band had released *Dedicated To You* (1971), with Robert Wyatt, Bryan Spring, Phil Howard, and Gary Boyle. Those who were uncomfortable with the idea that they were in any way involved with jazz now began to use the term *prog-rock* to describe their activities, but their origins deep in the birth of jazz-rock fusion were undeniable.

Also in 1971, Tippett formed the Centipede Orchestra project. This huge 50 piece outfit included many familiar names from the now established jazz-rock fusion sub-genre: Roy Babbington (bass), Ian Carr (trumpet) trumpet, Elton Dean (saxophone, cello), Alan Skidmore (saxophone), Karl Jenkins (oboe), John Marshall (drums), vocalists Zoot Money (ex-Animals), Mike Patto, and Julie Tippett (the former Julie Driscoll), and Robert Wyatt (drums). The plan was to perform an extended large-scale work by Tippett called *Septober Energy*. After a few live performances, a recording was arranged with RCA and the resulting album issued in 1971. There is undeniable jazz-rock content on the album, although it is dominated by the free-jazz ideas that were so prevalent at the time. Today, the music sounds quaint, hideously harmonic at times, and extremely dated. At first, Centipede was of interest to fans of both King Crimson and Soft

Machine, but it soon came to be regarded as a disaster, failing to attract either favourable reviews or sales of any significance. Once the novelty of this huge experiment in jazz-fusion had worn off, the British interest in jazz faded to nothing for the next ten years. Market forces took control of the direction of music in the UK and many of the top British jazz musicians were forced into exile in Europe where they were far more appreciated. Jazz musicians need to eat too.

## 1969: Jazz In A Snapshot

It is easy for us to forget the mood of those days in the 1960s when all of the traditional rules and courtesies of life were being dissolved by the new role models – the Beatles, the Rolling Stones and the great protester, Bob Dylan. Freedom of action in all aspects of everyday life was demanded from all quarters. By the end of the decade, it had become a time of protest against the Vietnam War. The contraceptive pill was liberating women and relaxing attitudes towards sex. It was also a time of demand for change in attitudes towards black people. Finally, the drug taking, that had until then generally been limited to the music and art communities, came out of the closet and entered into the daily life of the population at large. The familiar phrase "Sex, drugs and rock 'n' roll" summed it up succinctly.

All these changes were affecting jazz, which was changing to reflect the new moods of Society. Jazz had been breaking the European musical mould throughout the $20^{th}$ century, but now it was time to take the changes to their ultimate limit. Total and complete freedom for the musician was the target of the next jazz revolution – so-called 'Free Jazz' – and a subject that never fails to invoke love-hate situations. There were, of course, many jazz musicians who had constructed a comfortable lifestyle playing conventionally in the jazz 'mainstream'. However, those with progressive outlooks were driven to change: Cecil Taylor, Ornette Coleman and Archie Shepp being the most prominent in the free jazz genre. Their outlook was that 'Modern Jazz' (as opposed to the Dixieland style that was now being called 'Traditional Jazz') was passing through a difficult, but necessary gestation period in which total freedom of expression was the order of the day.

A flavour of the context of this subject is exemplified by the story that, at a 1967 London performance of the Archie Shepp quintet described as a "ferocious collective set", a quarter of the audience walked out and the remainder cheered wildly at the end. Most listeners found Cecil Taylor's wild hammering on a piano keyboard so outrageous that they could not recognise his virtuosity and despised his music. As a result, his career was as unsuccessful during his lifetime as Vincent Van Gogh's was during his. Cook says [58] that free-jazz stylists Albert Ayler, Archie Shepp and Pharoah Sanders were creating high art, whilst the bluesy down-home style of musicians such as Jimmy Smith and Jack McDuff was perfect for the chitlin circuit. Presumably jazz-fusion, funk, soul and the rest represented lowbrow music? Why *should* high art, almost by definition, be removed from (that is, elevated above) popular culture?

Proponents of free jazz (at the time, most players called it 'the free thing') argued that improvisation needed to be completely freed from the traditional rules of harmony, rhythm and form. The straight-jacket of written music, or agreed shape to music, or chord patterns, became anathema to people such as Miles Davis, who wrote in his autobiography about his admiration for the work of German composer Karlheinz Stockhausen. According to another writer: "Stockhausen is unconcerned with musical tradition...He claims that he explores fundamental psychological and acoustic aspects of music. In most of his works, elements are played off against one another, simultaneously and successively: in *Kontrapunkte* (1953) pairs of instruments and extremes of note values 'confront' one another; in *Gruppen* (1959) fanfares and passages of varying speed (based on the harmonic series) are flung between three full orchestras, giving the impression of movement in space." [59] A shorter description for Stockhausen's work is: no rules.

Others, like Dyer have argued the case for free jazz more cogently. By the mid-1960s, to Miles Davis's chagrin, John Coltrane had joined the ranks of the jazz superstars through such momentous works as *A Love Supreme* (1964). Coltrane had tried all there was to try on the saxophone, and now became caught up by the urgency of discovering spirituality and truth through the playing of his tenor tube. He was taking his music extremely seriously indeed and developing it along the lines of free jazz when his life was suddenly ended. Dyer wrote that Coltrane's last music was a "violent landscape filled with chaos and shrieks." He rationalised it as Coltrane "attempting to absorb all the violence of his times into his music in order to leave the world more peaceful." [60] In the world of a musician that was fuelled by substance abuse, that was understandable. Dyer thought the new thing was universally "to be moving toward a scream, as if it had internalised the danger that had once been attendant on the production of jazz." [61] Dyer's implicit equation of music from Coltrane's final period to the famous painting by Edvard Munch is a seductive metaphor. To many observers, jazz was in a parlous state in 1969 - even more so since Coltrane had passed away in 1967 at the age of 40. Others were simply bowled over in excitement when they realised the possibilities demonstrated by his later works.

Nicholson: "Although jazz was thought of as distinctly un-hip, there were several ingredients in the music of Coltrane and Sanders that contributed to their assimilation by the spiritually inclined members of the counter-culture. Sanders' albums such as *Tauhid* (1966) and *Karma* (1969) with their lack of artifice and their simple plea for universal peace and harmony were in matchless synchronicity with the prevailing atmosphere and aspirations of the alternative society in the late 1960s." [62] Perhaps what had really persuaded young people to like free jazz was the fact that the music sounded so awful that their parents hated it!

Coltrane, in particular, was therefore a huge musical influence to musicians, and not just to saxophone players. Guitarists like Carlos Santana and John McLaughlin found Coltrane's free approach to improvisation and harmony stimulating to the ways they wished to use their guitars. James Gurley of Big Brother and the Holding Company played a long solo on *Ball and Chain* from *Cheap Thrills* (1968). The Byrds included a Coltrane motif from *India* on their *Eight Miles High* track and lead guitarist Roger McGuinn tried to emulate Coltrane's soprano sax solo on 12-string guitar. Coltrane's *A Love Supreme* (1964) with its chanting and strong spiritual content pressed many buttons and was a perfect medium for encouraging crossover into the popular Buddhist-based activities that were sweeping through American society as the opposition to the war in Vietnam and Civil Rights issues occupied many consciences.

Many musicians used heroin because they wanted to reach the same pinnacle of creativity as Bird or Trane: they thought it could only be achieved by taking drugs. [63] Dyer saw jazz as a description of the lives of its creators - much more so than the technical ability to play their instruments. Albert Ayler said: "I have lived more than I can express in bebop terms." It was his reason for moving into free jazz. [64]

Some musicians discovered that they could achieve unparalleled levels of spirituality playing free jazz. Herbie Hancock gives one of the best descriptions in his recent autobiography. [65] Hancock led a free jazz band called Mwandishi in the early 70s and the musicians developed a particularly special mental relationship together. This came to a climax at Chicago's *London House* jazz club one night. He wrote, "As we started that [third] set I watched my fingers as I played. To my shock, they seemed to be moving by themselves. I wasn't controlling them; they were just playing of their own accord. Yet everything my fingers played was connecting perfectly to everything Buster [Williams] was playing, and Benny [Maupin] was playing, and Billy [Higgins] was playing. As we got deeper into the music we became one big, pulsating creature – all of those guys somehow became me, and I became all of them. It was as if were inside each other, in a way I had never felt before and have never felt since."

These were the high points, but there were many low points too. Herbie wrote about occasions when Mwandishi played to audiences that expected "mellow versions of *Speak Like A Child* or *Dolphin Dance*" and booed when they were subjected to free jazz. [66] Eventually, Herbie realised that Mwandishi's output was too unpredictable to be commercially successful and the members of his band were not getting the rewards they deserved. "There were times we shared so much empathy and connection onstage that it really did feel spiritual. At our peak those experiences happened regularly. But when Mwandishi was off – when we didn't connect – the experience wasn't pleasant, and what we were playing just sounded like noise, even to us." [67]

Another ex-member of Miles Davis's bands was Joe Zawinul, who set up Weather Report to play in a freestyle approach, especially when live. After a couple of years, he concluded that when the musicians found symbiosis, the music was great, but that too often it didn't work. Too much freedom led to unacceptable levels of inconsistency. [68] Zawinul's subsequent honing of the Weather Report format led to the band becoming one of the most successful in jazz-rock fusion history, and it was achieved with the acceptance of at least some rules.

So, even in the early 1970s, there were doubts about the longevity of the free jazz philosophy. Charles Mingus was one top jazz musician who was certainly progressive, but was not much impressed by free jazz. "You can't improvise on nothin', man." "At best," says Dyer speaking for his character Mingus, "free jazz was a diversion, which might even help in the long run: after a while, people would see it was a dead end... Twenty years from now, once they'd all got the squawking out of their systems, people like Shepp would go back to playing the blues." [68] Life (and music) without rules can only ever be transitional and is, in any case, contrary to the nature of the Universe.

## 1969: Miles Davis Experiments

In 1969 Miles Davis was by far the biggest star in the jazz night sky and was able to attract whichever musician he wanted by offering top wages. Musicians derived from Miles Davis line-ups of the early 1970s all moved on to populate the leading bands in the jazz-fusion movement.

In September 1968, Miles Davis was planning his own trail-blazing foray into jazz-fusion, but we now know that the foundations for it were already solidly in place both in the USA *and* in the UK. Davis came to London and visited *Ronnie Scott's* jazz club to hear British bass player Dave Holland. He liked what he heard and Holland was given 72 hours notice to turn up in New York to play with the Davis band on *Filles de Kilimanjaro* (1968). Typically for Miles, it was a strange appointment given that Holland's CV indicated he would be quite unsuitable - he had only ever played acoustic bass in the jazz mainstream environment. Soon afterwards, in February 1969, John McLaughlin made the move across the Atlantic, ostensibly to join Tony Williams's now highly regarded band, Lifetime, which a few months later recorded the album *Emergency!* (1969). On arrival in the USA, however, McLaughlin was almost immediately drafted into Davis's band as the maestro's pulling power was exercised. As for Davis's own role, Milkowski writes that *Bitches Brew* (1970) "is generally cited as the galvanising statement in fusion" but agrees that it was not actually the *first* fusion recording. [69] Milkowski's inevitable American perspective suggests that fusion began when "jazz-trained hippies in Greenwich village began picking up on the energy of rock music and boldly blending both aesthetics at nightclubs like *Cafe au Go-Go, the Scene* and *the Gaslight.*" [70] Clearly, the usually accurate Milkowski was not on this occasion inclined to include the contributions from the Brits in his analysis. It is more accurate to say that the two centres of activity - namely, London and New York - were not in close contact. Developments went ahead independently, in many ways, with New York fusioneers mostly influenced by the Beatles, and London fusioneers mostly influenced by Rhythm & Blues, and black soul music. It took a little time for the cross-fertilisation of ideas to shuttle the Atlantic.

There can be no doubt that, once Miles Davis moved decisively into a marriage with electric instruments, his immense influence indicated that it was now 'OK' to blend rock into jazz. This was the sense of jazz-rock creation that became the 1969 version of a 2015 tweet. But what kind of jazz ingredients did he use to convey his new jazz-rock fusion credentials?

Practising endlessly, Coltrane developed saxophone playing to such a degree that he became almost a godlike figure, even arguably eclipsing Charlie Parker, but after his death his deification was completed. Deep down, Miles Davis resented the attention being showered on someone he regarded as one of his apprentices, but the fashionable trend towards free jazz was irresistible, and in any case, it happened to suit Davis's own minimalist style of composition and musical direction.

In some ways, the concurrence of the rock revolution, the abandonment of rules, and the fashionableness of free jazz, misdirected Miles away from the most profitable avenues of jazz-fusion instead of towards them. There is no question that the music laid down on Miles's albums from 1969-75 was highly influential and created moods for Western culture that resonate to this day, but the music itself was inclined too much towards free jazz, and was consequently unmelodic, unstructured, and unfocussed. My own opinion is that it did not extract the sublime performance levels of which his superb band members were capable. It did, however, contain the heavy rhythms and white-hot energy typically found in Miles's live gigs. This was generally transmitted to audiences who responded enthusiastically.

Those not fortunate enough to attend the gigs had no such advantage. Nevertheless, on record, the blending of electric instruments – guitar and keyboard first, and then bass later - with this kind of unstructured jazz environment had a strongly polarising effect. Some listeners found it life-changing; others thought it was deeply unsatisfying. Davis didn't care, however, for he never listened to his own records once they were made and (to his credit) was always looking forward to the next project. However, his musicians rapidly moved on. Professing unending love and affection for Davis (they still do), some admitted that they soon ran out of ideas whilst improvising night after night for 30 minutes in the key of C. Miles's musicians left to form bands of their own. At first, they *did* carry on the Davis improvisational legacy, but when they discovered more popular and rewarding styles, they evolved, as all good jazzers should. Bluntly, they soon realised they could make more money by pleasing their audiences than alienating them.

Of course, the A&R men inside the record companies exerted influence wherever they could and artists could lose their recording contracts if they did not produce records having at least some commercial merit. Larry Coryell was a typical victim. Artists don't like to think about these crude, cynical arguments, but they are a fact of the hard commercial world in which they all earn a living. Even with a conscious change of direction towards black audiences for *On The Corner* (1972), Miles was nonplussed to find his efforts largely ignored by the very people he was targeting. By the early 1970s the public were failing to buy Davis's records in the kinds of numbers that were expected for such a superstar. The record-buying public preferred the more appealing brands of jazz-fusion provided by Davis's disciples: Herbie Hancock, Chick Corea, Joe Zawinul, Wayne Shorter, Billy Cobham and John McLaughlin. That proved a pretty good stimulus to drive jazz-rock music in new directions.

Less well-read commentators claim that Miles Davis invented jazz-rock fusion. However, it is simply not true. For all his other achievements, we *can* be sure that this is one development that cannot be claimed for Davis. I have already discussed at length how jazz-rock fusion came about, albeit in those days before it was a clearly definable movement. In a sense, we could agree that Miles *formalised* the sub-genre because of his powerful outreach. He was certainly at the forefront of the jazz movement, and his records produced in the period 1968-1971 are frequently touted as being some of the most influential in the creation of jazz-fusion. That assertion is undeniable. *Miles in the Sky* (1968) and *Filles de Kilimanjaro* (1968) are cited as being early jazz-rock fusion experiments, but really only on the basis of the presence of electric guitar on a very few tracks. With *In A Silent Way* (1969) there was a bigger transformation that set thousands of tongues wagging, but the release was still *after the event*. I have already provided sufficient evidence that Miles did not initiate the jazz-rock fusion process himself, but, with the loudest of voices, he told jazz fans that it was OK to play electric jazz, and in that sense, he was the unequivocal trailblazer. He *was* at the top of his game and kept himself well informed of what other leading musicians were doing, especially in the UK. Davis quickly realised that jazz-fusion was the inevitable next step in the development of his art and, besides wanting to communicate more directly with young blacks, he also had sufficiently canny business acumen to recognise a profitable corner of the market, even if it didn't go strictly to plan.

Davis's influence was great, but not just because of the actual music he made. Everyone spoke of him fusing jazz with rock: the very fact that he was using electric guitars in his bands caused others to do the same. When he decided to blend rock with the particular kind of jazz that had surfaced at the end of the sixties – a strongly rhythmic but otherwise rule-free jazz - he chose a direction that was enormously influential. On *Bitches Brew* (1969) his ingredients suited the fashionistas, but produced a strange concoction like cold soup (perhaps I should call it curry and ice-cream – see my story at the start of the Pat Metheny book) that contained unusual, even unpleasant sounds that were alien to the hearing of most audiences. Some listeners found that was life-changing; others hated what he had done to jazz.

Open as ever to what was going on in the wider world of art, Davis had been strongly influenced by the worlds of Warhol and Stockhausen that mostly appealed to the art intellectuals but not to ordinary people whom Miles wanted to buy his records. Unlike lesser mortals who had just as much to say, but couldn't get their music heard, Miles was given plenty of exposure for his new music, but it was often as a supporting act to rock bands – and he never wanted to play second fiddle to anybody. (At one point, his band played as a support act to Herbie Hancock, his own protégé!) Miles was perhaps too keen to try to outshine his recently-deceased (1967) arch-competitor, John Coltrane. It took others to make the best step forward by using a more acceptable mix and Miles was left behind in their wake. By 1976, at the peak of popularity of jazz-rock, he was exhausted and retired into complete seclusion for four years. It is arguable whether he would have done this if his records had been as successful as he had hoped.

## 1969: If

One of the most highly regarded bands formed in the late 1960s was a seven-piece outfit called If (the band's moniker was always presented as 'if'). The nucleus for the band's formation was, yet again, around some of the best British jazz musicians seeking to take advantage of the opportunity to create new music and commensurate wealth. The band had all the essential ingredients, including tenor saxophone, electric guitar and vocals, but the feature that distinguished the band from Chicago and BS&T was the absence of a trumpet in favour of a second saxophone.

The lead saxophone player was Dick Morrissey (1940-2000), regarded by many as the best British tenor sax player of his time. He had already served his apprenticeship and become well established on the jazz scene playing hard bop music at the *Marquee* from 1960 onwards. He recorded his first solo album aged only 21, and had his own quartet with Harry South (piano), Phil Bates (bass) and Phil Seamen (drums), making records from 1963-66, and appearing regularly at *Ronnie Scott's* London club. Then, in 1969 aged 29, he turned towards jazz-rock fusion.

The guitarist who teamed up with Morrissey was Terry Smith (b1943), a natural jazzer who was equally at home in the rock/pop world. In the early 1960s, he became a regular on the London club circuit, playing box and cox with John McLaughlin for bands such as Georgie Fame's Blue Flames and Brian Auger's Trinity. In 1967, he was named "Best Jazz Guitarist" in the annual *Melody Maker* poll. In 1968, he became MD for Scott Walker of the famous Walker Brothers pop duo.

The third member of the tripartite creators of If was Dave Quincy (b1939), another saxophonist with alto *and* tenor leanings. It was the presence of all three men in the band of American soul singer J J Jackson that led them to form If. Morrissey and Smith became close friends playing with Jackson in the UK from the time of the hit single, *But Its Alright* (1966). They appeared consistently with Jackson for the next three years, including the album *The Greatest Little Soul Band In The Land* (1969).

Jackson's manager was American producer, Lew Futterman, who had already a proven track record producing American jazz acts Benny Golson, Jimmy Witherspoon and Jack McDuff. With Futterman's strong backing, Morrissey, Smith and Quincy came together in an honest attempt to emulate Chicago and BS&T. John (J W) Hodkinson (aka Hodgkinson) (1942-2013) was chosen to be the lead vocalist, having already begun a modestly successful pop recording career for Phillips under the name of Tony Allen. Once the core players had been established, with Quincy included, it seemed like the perfect time to form If, by joining with John Mealing (b1942) on keyboards and backing vocals, Jim Richardson (b1941) on bass guitar, and Dennis Elliott (b1950) on drums.

Working on both sides of the Atlantic, the band recorded a series of albums each of which remains highly regarded today: *If* (1970), *If 2* (1970), *If 3* (1971), *If 4* (1972) released in the USA as *Waterfall* (1972). These albums are often cited as the most influential series of recordings in British jazz-fusion, recorded at the height of the jazz-rock phenomenon. The albums were supported with extensive tours of USA and Europe, and the band attracted strong public support, without breaking into the premier league of bands. Its musicians felt that the recordings did not do the band justice, and that they were at their best only after the tunes had been honed to perfection on the road. Thus, the recently released album *Europe '72* (1997) is regarded by many as more representative of the band's performance qualities at the height of its popularity.

At the end of this series of albums there was a hiatus in which the band members went in different directions. Elliott joined Foreigner, whilst Quincy and Smith joined Zebra. However, in 1973, Morrissey reformed the band for the second part of the band's existence, and released albums *Double Diamond* (1973), *Not Just Another Bunch Of Pretty Faces* (1974), *Tea Break Is Over, Back On Your 'eads* (1975). After this, Morrissey teamed up with another British jazz guitarist, Jim Mullen, to form Morrissey-Mullen with the initial help of their friends, Average White Band and an album called *Up* (1976) recorded in the USA under AWB's production.

## 1969: Dreams

An American band that competed directly with If was Dreams. This band quickly made a mark, but then melted into the mists of New York's rapidly changing scene. Inspired by a brief stint with BS&T, and an appearance on their first album *Child is Father to the Man* (1967), Randy Brecker felt that their formula for success could work for him too. In 1969, Randy was soon at the centre of a new grouping made up of brother Michael, Barry Rogers (trombone), Doug Lubahn (bass), Jeff Kent (keyboards), John Abercrombie (electric guitar), Eddie Vernon (lead vocals) and Billy Cobham (drums).

At first, the music was almost all written by Kent or Lubahn. The first eponymous album was released in 1970. The first four songs, *Devil Lady*, *15 Miles to Provo*, *The Maryanne* and *Holli Be Home* are clearly targeted at airplay with their short, simple song formats. From then on, the album develops far more into jazz-fusion as a long, uninterrupted section fills the whole of the second side of the vinyl disc: *Dream Suite: Asset Stop / Jane / Crunchy Grenola* Finally, the album goes out in a blaze with *New York*.

The demonstrably successful BS&T format required the music to be almost entirely vocal, with room for only short instrumental solos, but it was not the context to make jazzers feel comfortable. However, this recipe resulted in the placement of the band's albums in the record shop racks labelled 'pop music'. The jazzers, disgruntled by having to play 'below themselves' in such bands, could thus be pacified by thoughts of pecuniary advantage. Another approach, however, was to counterbalance a subset of pop-targeted content with another of chunky instrumentals. This was the Dreams formula. Most of us already know the outcome: from a commercial point of view, the BS&T (and the Chicago) formula was enormously successful; sadly, the Dreams formula wasn't.

After the first album, there was a feeling that the band had not reached its full potential with the first line-up. The jazzers in the band could not contain their disappointment with rockers for their perceived lack of ability to improvise. A certain amount of disagreement ensued in the leaderless ranks of Dreams. Two of the band's founding members, Jeff Kent and Doug Lubahn (both rockers), left after just one record, "fired by the band" according to Billy Cobham.

Kent and Lubahn were replaced by Don Grolnick (keyboards) and Will Lee (bass). John Abercrombie also left, to be replaced by jazz guitarist Bob Mann. Most members of the band contributed to the vocals, again led by Eddie Vernon. With a regular gig at the *Village Gate*, Dreams became well known as a horn band and it was very much this unit that eventually evolved into the Brecker Brothers Band.

The new band recorded its second and final album, *Imagine My Surprise* (1971). It contained a further collection of vocal tracks with a strong brassy-jazz backing, but because of the significant personnel changes, the music is very different from the band's first album. Sadly, from a commercial point of view it was no more successful than the first.

After two modestly successful albums aimed at the pop market, the band parted. The jazzers were frustrated with the lack of commercial impact and the constant need to suborn themselves to singers with small talents and large egos. The Brecker Brothers were destined to make their own mark in 1975 with another configuration by successfully developing the funky style of jazz-fusion, but before that they would take on other exciting challenges.

## So, Which Was The First Jazz-Rock Fusion Band?

The title of this section is such an apparently simple question to pose, but a difficult and controversial question to answer. The essence of the difficulty in answering the original question is in deciding upon the year in which it really happened: should we be considering 1962 or 1966? There is no firm agreement about the precise date when jazz-rock fusion began, but much of the reason for that is due to there being a poor consensus about *what jazz-rock actually is!* Let's review the situation...

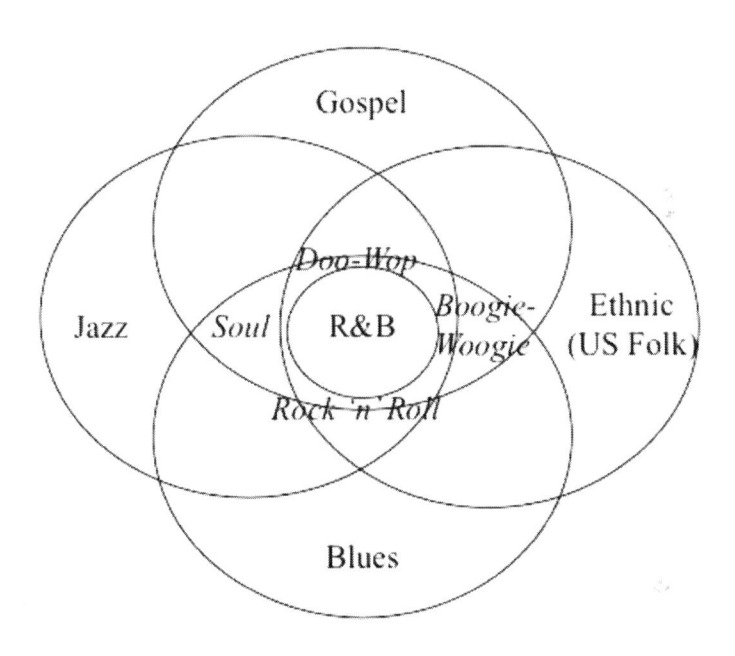

*Figure 5: A Venn diagram that is more representative of the fusion occurring in 1962.*

Part of the difficulty arises from the fact that 'rock' as a defined musical genre did not really exist until the mid-1960s. At the beginning of the 1960s, the relevant genres were R&B, rock 'n' roll and jazz; soul music also has some relevance (Figure 5). Rhythm and blues contained elements of blues, jazz, gospel and boogie-woogie. Clearly, the strong rhythmic elements of boogie-woogie and rock 'n' roll were relevant, and its exposition mostly on electric instruments is an essential feature. Similarly, soul music contained elements of rhythm and blues, gospel and doo-wop. Most of this musical essence had African-American origins, although the rock 'n' roll was mostly formulated by

Elvis and his friends.

Thus, although rock music did not formally exist in the first half of the 60s, all of its elements did. From 1960, several key changes were in play, initiated largely by the Beatles in Liverpool, where a new style of music quickly evolved called 'Beat music'. According to Wikipedia, it was "a pop and rock music genre that developed in the United Kingdom in the early 1960s. Beat music is a fusion of rock and roll, doo-wop, skiffle and R&B." [71] Is it illogical to say that the kind of music played by the Beatles, but not yet identified as 'rock' music played no part in the fusion of jazz with rock?

At first, music was developed in parallel, whether in Liverpool's Cavern Club, or with the intense activities involving R&B at the Marquee and the Flamingo in London, led by Cyril Davies and Alexis Korner in their band Blues Incorporated. Once the momentum for development had been initiated, and the top Merseyside acts had moved from Liverpool and Manchester to London, an incendiary sequence of changes began that drew Beat music into its formula, and resulted in the emergence of rock music around 1964. Now, it is clear to this author at least, that jazz was already part of this mix, emphasised by the fact that many of the musicians were self-identified jazz musicians, excited by the possibilities of leaving an increasingly unpopular genre – jazz - in favour of one with enormous potential for popularity. And here hangs a point of some consequence: those musicians who took their jazz sensibilities into the world of R&B and Beat music, were consciously leaving jazz behind, so the earliest music being played was higher in proportion of rock 'n' roll / R&B / soul than it was in jazz.

Discussions of 'Jazz fusion' create problems of both definition and interpretation. I have already identified problems with the current definition of 'Jazz fusion', not least of which is the misuse of term itself and its constant confusion with 'Jazz-rock'. Wikipedia uses the statement that "...until around 1967, the worlds of jazz and rock were nearly completely separate." [72]. If we agree that the definition of rock music, as defined by the same publication, is accurate, then we conclude that rock music was not definable as such until the mid 1960s, by which time the 'Beat music' that had defined the 'British Invasion' had morphed into 'rock'. If you, dear reader, are prepared to accept this argument, then there could have been no jazz-rock fusion until around 1966 when the likes of Larry Coryell, Gary Burton, Steve Marcus and Jeremy Steig began to consider using elements of this newly identified 'rock' music in jazz.

My own conclusion is that to argue that jazz-rock fusion could only take place once rock was an identifiable genre is pedantic and pointless, because the fusion of all the *elements* of jazz and rock was occurring from around 1961-2. Clearly, there was a very big difference between what was occurring in 1962 and the musical environment of 1966. Therefore, I propose that Figure 5 is a more accurate representation of the jazz-fusion occurring in London in 1962, whilst Figure 3 (p55) is more relevant to the more widespread movements of 1966.

It would seem sensible to assert that no original jazz-rock fusion group could have been formed without the presence of self-identified jazz musicians. This should be a minimum requirement, but a clear desire to employ electric instruments – i.e. keyboards, guitar and bass – in a jazz combo should be involved. Blues Incorporated was formed in 1961 jointly led by Cyril Davies and Alexis Korner. It had a fluid line-up of players, but a reasonably consistent combination of instruments: harmonica, organ, electric guitar, saxophone and drums. Focussing at first on blues and the purer forms of R&B, Davies – a supporter of pure blues - left the band early in 1963 when Korner wanted to take the music towards jazz, from which point the musicians were mostly recruited from the world of jazz. This clear change of direction is an unambiguous decision for jazz-rock fusion, even though rock had not then been identified as such. It clears the way for me to nominate Blues Incorporated (1963), with its associated musicians such as Korner, Graham Bond, Jack Bruce, Ginger Baker, Dick Heckstall-Smith and Herbie Goins, as the earliest jazz-rock fusion band.

For the sake of completeness, I should at least discuss the other candidates that have been put forward. Undoubtedly, there are sound reasons for their nominations by other writers, based upon various interpretations of the definition of jazz-rock fusion.

Nicholson champions an almost unknown band called The Fourth Way as one of the first genuine jazz-rock bands from 1969. [73] Led by Mike Nock (keyboards), it included Michael White (electric violin), Ron McLure (electric bass) and Eddie Marshall (drums). This is clearly too late to be considered in this argument. As for Nock, well, he had played with Steve Marcus's Count's Rock Band in early 1967 and had apparently clearly seen the future of jazz. Now with an eponymous 1969 release he laid down a marker for others to follow. The trouble was that, like much of what was happening in the UK, his work went mostly unobserved: the band failed to attract any comment at all in *Down Beat*, the major opinion-former in jazz. This was almost entirely due to Nock's location in San Francisco - not New York. Nock reportedly had one of the most advanced keyboard setups in use at the time and his band succeeded in encapsulating all of the major elements of jazz-rock. He was unquestionably the trailblazer of jazz-rock on the West Coast of the USA.

There is no doubt that, beginning in December 1967, Blood Sweat &Tears was a band that achieved great success with a jazz-rock fusion formula, even identifying the music more accurately as rock-jazz because of the music being centred on vocals and song-based material. (Indeed, Randy Brecker is quite clear that he wanted to leave the band in 1968 because it did not offer him, as a jazz musician, enough satisfying solos. However, it is not difficult to conclude that BS&T was the first band put together specifically to play the new kind of material. Those wishing to cast their vote against BS&T would argue that this was a band not performing enough jazz music to count as jazz-rock, and that the later Brecker combo, Dreams is a more authentic candidate.

In 1962, there is no question that the USA was playing no part in any kind of jazz-rock fusion. Let's be clear. The British Invasion had not yet happened: the Beatles were only just starting their journey when John McLaughlin was doing in London, in 1962, what Larry Coryell was doing in New York more than *three years later*. As a true jazzer, McLaughlin was sitting in with all of the hot acts of the time, rather than playing for just one outfit, so it is not possible to identify a single band as the progenitor of jazz-R&B-soul fusion, even though the process was just beginning. I hope we can now agree that this was too early a period to talk about 'rock' as such, but then, what is rock if not a fusion of its own progenitors – rock 'n' roll, blues (R&B) and folk/ethnic (country) music?

With regard to the argument about the earliest jazz-rock fusion *band*, I believe that the final words must be spoken in favour of Graham Bond. (Blues was, after all, the mission for Alexis Korner's Blues Incorporated.) Inspection of my timescales at the back of this book leads to the inevitable conclusion that it was Jazzer Bond, with his affinity for both alto saxophone and electronic Mellotron synthesiser, playing alongside (variously) Jack Bruce, Ginger Baker, John McLaughlin and Dick Heckstall-Smith, who formed a recognisable jazz-rock fusion band in 1963, even if the music is perhaps better described as jazz-R&B-soul fusion. If this band was slightly later than the version of Blues Incorporated in which Bond was influenced by Alexis Korner, then I may be splitting hairs. Each of these musicians was an experienced professional or semi-professional performing artist by the early 1960s, and each made his own mark on Graham Bond's bands. At the very least, the coming-together of Clapton, Baker and Bruce in Cream in the summer of 1966 (before BS&T) must qualify as a kind of rock-jazz fusion, but it was surely the experiences of these musicians in Bond's band that were expressed in Cream.

If there was a single factor that gave these British musicians the edge, it was the unique environment offered by the pulsating London club scene during the period 1961-64, the inspiration offered by American rock 'n' roll, blues and soul music, and the market forces created by the need to entertain US servicemen living 3,000 miles away from home.

In the influential allmusic.com website, Unterberger presents a short, mostly accurate account of Graham Bond's activities, and admits that "their [the Graham Bond band's] records were admirably tough British R&B/rock/jazzsoul..." but then contradicts himself by saying that "though Bond has sometimes been labelled as a pioneer of jazz-rock, in reality it was much closer to rock than jazz." This assertion is used nonsensically as if to disqualify Bond from his rightful position as creator of jazz-rock fusion. Whether we call it jazz-rock or rock-jazz is irrelevant here. Bond's achievements should not be so easily dismissed, for his activities with John McLaughlin, Jack Bruce and Ginger Baker took place in 1963, and Gary Burton's work with Coryell did not take place until 1967. [74] Bond is the focus, but it is the activities of the group of British jazz musicians led by Bond, McLaughlin, Bruce, Baker, Fame, Auger, Korner and Heckstall-Smith amongst others that set the jazz-R&B-soul fusion scene alight from 1962 onwards. Even if we cannot call it jazz-rock (or rock-jazz) fusion because rock was as yet undefined, *it is jazz-rock in all but name.* Much of this activity was never recorded on disc, but anyone who is in any doubt about the validity of the case for the London scene as the most fertile ground for fusing jazz with R&B and soul in the early 1960s should consult the definitive work by Harper. [75]

In no way does this diminish the efforts made on the Western side of the Atlantic Ocean from 1965/6 onwards, because the kinds of instantaneous contact and opportunities for sharing that we enjoy today were absent then. The fusion of these two music genres was always an obvious development, and so it is not surprising that it went on in parallel in at least two centres.

As of 2015, Wikipedia, referencing the influential Allmusic Guide, asserts that "until around 1967, the worlds of jazz and rock were nearly completely separate." It goes on to describe the London scene from 1962 in terms similar to those I have used above, yet declines to accept what is clearly evident. The assignment of the invention of 'jazz-rock' or 'jazz fusion' to Coryell, Burton and Miles Davis in the late 1960s depends upon your own viewpoint. If you are a jazzer, interested in the time when jazz evolved to include elements of rock, but remained identifiable as jazz, then you will probably look towards the records by these musicians made from around 1966-1970.

## New Instruments: The Electric Piano

The post-war period was, then, like no other in human history, and the confluence of great cultural change and remarkable scientific advances may never be repeated. Much has been said until now of the musicians, but little of the new kinds of instruments they chose to play. This deficiency will now be addressed, for it is crucial to the fusion of jazz and rock.

One of the biggest driving forces in the creation of jazz-rock fusion music was the availability for the first time of a new range of instruments, made possible by the electronics revolution that had begun with the invention of the transistor in 1949. The electric piano was developed by Harold Rhodes (1910-2000), who spent most of his long life involved with either the teaching of piano or the design and manufacture of new kinds of piano. In the whole of the 20th century he was one of the great contributors to the piano as an instrument. Rhodes began to develop his electromechanical instruments in the late 1950s. The notes were made by mechanical means, as they are in all other non-electronic instruments. In a conventional piano, hammers strike tensioned wire strings in response to the press of a lever called a piano key. Rhodes invented and patented his own system whereby similar hammers struck specially designed metal tuning forks that had one prong longer than the other (called asymmetrical). Now a solid-bodied electric guitar does not have the hollow sound box of the acoustic guitar to naturally amplify its sound. It requires pick-ups and electronic circuitry to amplify the inaudible sounds produced by the plucked string. Likewise, Rhodes' piano had no built-in natural amplification, so he used the same electronic technology to amplify the sound from his piano. Unlike the guitar, in which the amplifier and speaker are separate, he incorporated the amplifier into the body of the piano.

Once the great promise of his work was evident, Rhodes' company was taken over by Leo Fender (the guitar designer and manufacturer) in 1959 and from then until 1965 development of the Fender-Rhodes electric piano was disappointing. Following another buy-out by CBS in 1965, Rhodes was given the freedom of action to further develop his instrument. The Fender-Rhodes piano (it continued to use that name until 1974) went from strength to strength and became the favourite keyboard for many musicians. The very electromechanical nature of the piano gave it a distinctive sound that many musicians liked, especially for jazz. Unlike other instances in which a particular instrument became the favourite, there was no competition in this case. Consequently, the Fender-Rhodes or Rhodes piano, as it later became known, defined the sound of a large part of the musical output of the 70s and 80s, characterised by such tracks as *Angela*, the very well-known theme from the TV series *Taxi* (1978-83), played by keyboardist Bob James. Much of the output of Joe Sample, keyboardist for the Crusaders, was also created with this instrument. There are, of course, many other examples.

There wasn't much more to do in development of the Fender-Rhodes, but there was a whole new world of development waiting around the corner in keyboard technology.

## Keyboard Synthesisers

The mid-60s and 70s were an important time in the development of new electronic instruments - one of which was the electronic synthesiser. The Mellotron, which we now know was used extensively by Graham Bond, was an early sample player that used tape loops. Some versions played string sounds or flute sounds, and the instrument was used in movie soundtracks and on recordings.

Early synthesisers were large, odd-sounding machines based on old analogue electronics – modern digital electronics using low d.c. voltages were still some years away. These analogue devices used a.c. electric voltages to create and control sounds produced by variable magnitude alternating magnetic fields in the inbuilt speaker systems. The principle was simple. The pitch of the note varied with voltage. Thus, higher voltages would make higher notes and lower voltages made lower notes. Several companies began to make instruments, all based on the concept of Control Voltage. Short electrical cables called patch cords would feed the control voltages around these instruments to manipulate the sound character and shape (pitch and timbre). These early synthesisers could play only a single note (monophonic) at a time, so to add more notes it was necessary to use more synthesisers. Some people realised that you could record multiple parts on tape and so around 1968 bands such as the Beatles and the Beach Boys started to experiment with single electronically-generated sounds mixed onto tapes, as in *Good Vibrations* (1966), *Strawberry Fields Forever* (1967) and tracks from *Pet Sounds* (1966), *Revolver* (1966) and *Sergeant Pepper's Lonely Hearts Club Band* (1967).

These monophonic synthesisers were difficult to set up, use and maintain, but they gave musicians something they could get no other way - fresh new sounds. King Crimson released *In the Court of the Crimson King* (1969), an album that featured a fusion of sound experimentation with rock. It influenced the next generation of prog-rock and *avant-garde* artists, much of which went on in Europe, rather than the USA. Thus Kraftwerk released *Kraftwerk 2* (1971) featuring early drum machines, whilst Neu! released their debut album *Neu!* (1972), an innovative work of experimental rock featuring some of the most pioneering punk and minimalist music from the 20th Century.

## Drum Machines

Early drum machines were often referred to as *rhythm machines* and played only pre-programmed rhythms. The first were included in organs in the late 60s, and intended to accompany the organist. The first stand-alone drum machine was the Rhythm Ace, released around 1970 by a company then called Ace Tone, later called Roland. It only had pre-sets; the user could not alter or modify the pre-programmed rhythms. The first programmable rhythm machine was the Roland CR-78, which allowed users to create their own beats. Later that same year, Roland produced the Boss DR-55, the first fully programmable drum machine for under $200. The Linn LM-1 was the first drum machine to use digital samples. Released in 1980 and at a price of $5,000, it has a distinctive sound that can be heard on many records from the early 1980s, such as The Human League's *Dare* (1981) and albums by the band Men Without Hats. The Roland TR-808 followed soon after; but was cheaper for not having any sampling functions. The TR808 was ahead of its time, becoming more popular later in the late 1980s after it had been discontinued. Until the musical instrument digital interface (MIDI) became mass-produced in 1983, the design of drum machines to interface with other electronic instruments, such as keyboards, was problematic and designs frequently required various devices to enable sound engineers to synchronise the rhythm with the music. MIDI revolutionised the technology at a stroke. Now all instruments and recordings could be easily manipulated through a desk or master computer, commonly the Apple/Macintosh. Herbie Hancock was one of the first to use the Apple for creating and controlling his music on *Mr Hands* (1978).

## Electrifying Music

Stevie Wonder released *Talking Book* in 1972, and it became one of the most influential albums in the decade that made much use of electronically produced music. The same year, Vangelis started experimenting and composing with electronic synthesisers and sequencers. Pink Floyd's album *The Dark Side of the Moon* (1972) was also released with the help of ensembles of synthesisers. It combined techniques of loops, sequential synthesis, sampling, and drew a creative bridge between rock and ambient experimental and *avant-garde* music.

By 1973 the monophonic Moog and ARP brands of synthesisers were in extensive use by bands such as Emmerson, Lake and Palmer, Genesis and others. Then the Oberheim company introduced the first commercial polyphonic (able to play several notes at a time) keyboard synthesiser. With built-in keyboard, it was much simpler to use and could make four notes at a time. An array of knobs and switches made it possible to quickly create rich, new sounds. Compared to the heavy, cumbersome Mellotron, it was far more portable and easy to program than most of its predecessors. Other improved polyphonic synthesisers quickly followed from such manufacturers as Sequential Circuits, Yamaha, Moog, Roland and ARP.

After the arrival of polyphonic instruments, the next important advance came with the use of electronic memory devices. In that year Rick Wakeman released

*The Six Wives of Henry VIII* (1973) featuring numerous electronic instruments and Wakeman became the first solo artist specialising in electronic instruments in the history of pop music to reach the status of superstar. In that year also, programmable memory became available for instruments. Polyphonic synthesisers were given a small built-in computer that could use memory chips to store and recall sounds created by the user. Rock musicians such as Keith Emerson became famous for playing on stage in front of stacks of electronic keyboards. Prior to programmable memory, both he and Wakeman required these extravagant keyboard set-ups because each of the instruments could only be set-up to produce a single sound per show. Hours of preparation were needed to patch together the sounds and the different instruments. Then, when keyboards had memory, a single synthesiser could be used for many different sounds during a live show or recording session simply by pressing one button. In 1973, Emerson was the first artist to perform live playing a modular system, a system of numerous and independent synthesis devices - such as filters, and controllers - that could be interconnected through a patching system with the capability of controlling and producing synthesised sounds in an unlimited number of combinations. This patching system makes the devices look like an old telephone switchboard. The first modular synthesiser had been made in 1964 by Robert Moog in collaboration with Walter Carlos, who was the first musician to record the Moog synthesiser on his legendary album *Switched On Bach* (1964).

Herbie Hancock released the wonderful jazz-fusion album *Head Hunters* (1973) and introduced the use of synthesisers and modular systems in jazz. Hancock had many of his electronic instruments custom-modified to connect with each other, allowing him to mix and match sounds any way he wished. For the first time, instruments of different makes were connected with each other by means of a common, though custom, digital connection. It would not be until 1983 that the Musical Instrument Digital Interface (MIDI) would become a standard device for making such interconnections between electric musical instruments. Other major events from that year include the release of *No Poosyfooting* by Fripp and Eno, a pioneering work of ambient and electronic music. Mike Oldfield released *Tubular Bells* (1973), another progressive work of ambient music that used a Farfisa organ amongst other new instruments. Tangerine Dream released *Phaedra* (1974) starting a series of records that drew the guidelines of the electronic spatial music. Other companies who produced modular systems during the 70s were Roland, ARP, Buchla, and Emu.

Synclavier keyboards were developed from about 1972 onwards at Dartmouth College, a private liberal arts institution in Hanover, New Hampshire by Sydney Alonso, Cameron Jones and Jon Appleton. Developing their own hardware – notably the ABLE mini-processor - and software in these early days of digital electronics, Alonso and Jones created the first version of the Synclavier in 1975 with their company, New England Digital (NED). By 1979, the potential of the system was realised and the company produced the Synclavier II, Systems were enormously expensive at first, with typical models costing anything from $100,000 to $500,000. Synclavier II had an upgraded sampling capacity and memory, as well as a velocity- and pressure-sensitive keyboard. The Synclavier was adopted by a host of top musicians, including bands such as the Cars, Genesis and Duran Duran. Michael Jackson's *Thriller* (1982) used its sounds on *Beat It* (1983) and Frank Zappa used it to compose his Grammy-winning album *Jazz from Hell* (1986). The original system used FM sampling in mono, but was later converted to stereo simply by having two mono cards and software that allowed *panning* the sound from one card to the other. By 1984 the Synclavier II had become the world's leading keyboard synthesiser with only the Fairlight CMI III to compete.

## Guitar Synthesisers

Guitar synthesisers took rather longer to arrive on the scene. One development that took place from the late 1970s was of the Roland guitar synthesiser, an electronic device that allowed a guitarist to play his guitar, whilst translating the sounds of plucked strings into entirely new sounds. Suddenly guitarists could make the same kinds of sounds that keyboardists had been making since the 70s.

The 1978 GR500 system was Roland's first attempt at guitar synthesis. It consisted of the guitar controller (GS500), a 24-way cable and the synthesiser unit (GR500). The Ibanez-made guitar was based on the Gibson Les Paul shape but with more controls and different pickups. Roland released a second generation of synth systems in 1980 - the GR-100 system. This included three types of guitar controllers in many different finishes: the G505 - a Telecaster style with three single coils, the G303 - a Gibson SG derivative - and the deluxe version, the G202 with dual humbucker pick-ups was a Stratocaster-shaped cross between the G505 / G303 and the G808. All of these controllers could operate the GR100 or the later GR300 synthesiser units via a 24-way cable. This system generally did not track well, forcing the guitarist to play slowly, deliberately and precisely.

The blue GR300 had six VCOs – one for each guitar string – with each controlled by the string pitches. There were also hexa-fuzz, an LFO, tuning pre-sets and control over the attack of each note. The decay of each note was controlled by the way the guitar was played and this made the system far more versatile. New techniques were available. For example, it was now possible to apply vibrato to open strings, and each string could now produce two notes (one from the divided pickup and one from a VCO). The pitch of the VCOs could be offset by two pre-set controls selected by footswitches. Envelope attack could be slowed down and the strings that could have a synthesised tone applied to them could be individually selected. Many of the functions such as compression could be selected by footswitches and the state of each was indicated by LEDs.

The guitar controllers for the GR300 were the same as those offered for use with the GR100. The controls on the guitars allowed control of the sound parameters such as VCF frequency and resonance, guitar / synth balance, oscillator / hexa-fuzz selection and LFO on / off through the use of two concealed touch plates. All this was achieved on guitars that looked very conventional. Examination of the back of the guitar, however, showed a large amount of electronics inside. [76]

There is some doubt about the precise history of the Synclavier guitar synthesiser. Pat Metheny and Lyle Mays were amongst the first jazz musicians to use the Synclavier I during December 1981 for their sessions that led to *Off Ramp* (1982). Metheny was reportedly using a "Synclavier guitar". In reality this was a box of electronics that acted as an interface between a modified guitar and the Synclavier electronics. An early instrument was the Roland GR300, which linked a guitar to the Synclavier II system. It was released in late 1983 and John McLaughlin was one of the first to try it out. According to Milkowski [77], McLaughlin worked over a period of months for up to fifteen hours a day, learning how to programme the device and exploring the countless new sounds he could make with it.

Devices from different manufacturers were generally not compatible with each other and could not easily be interconnected. Audio engineer and synthesiser designer Dave Smith of Sequential Circuits Inc. proposed the MIDI standard in 1981 and the MIDI Specification 1.0 was formally published in August 1983. Thus any connection of a guitar to a device such as the Synclavier was done only by means of bespoke electronics.

Various musicians adopted guitar synthesisers. Pat Metheny used the Synclavier again on *First Circle* (1984). John McLaughlin had encouraged Katia Labeque to play the Synclavier keyboard synthesiser on *Belo Horizonte* (1981), but he did not use the guitar synth himself on record until his album *Mahavishnu* (1984). The early 8-bit versions of the Synclavier were noted for their warm sounds, but were limited technically and replaced in 1982-3 by new designs that, for the first time, sampled sounds directly to hard disk.

Electronic instruments have played a major role in the very existence of jazz-fusion as a genre. Consequently, they have attracted their fair share of criticism. A notably eloquent critic is Dyer who said, using Charlie Haden's *Silence*

(1987) as an example: "Electronic instruments define themselves in relation to - and partake of the quality of - din. Acoustic instruments define themselves in relation to - and partake of the quality of - silence. For this reason, acoustic instruments will always have a greater purity. [78]

## The Electronic Wind Instrument (EWI)

At this point, it is necessary to discuss important developments that took place in the mid '70s to early '80s regarding the development of new electronic 'saxophones'. In the early 1970s, a musically inclined inventor called Bill Bernardi designed an analogue electronic wind instrument that he named the Lyricon. With engineering assistance from Roger Noble and an enthusiastic player called Chuck Greenberg, Bernardi set up a company called Computone in Massachusetts. By 1974 two models were available, the first a silver coloured straight model that resembled a soprano saxophone, and a second black model based on the look of a clarinet. In terms of use and performance, the Lyricon was most successful. Musicians were excited by the potential it offered and by its usability. As a result, many well-known instrumentalists took it up, such as Ian Anderson, Sonny Rollins and Roland Kirk. Tom Scott had the nickname "Mr Lyricon" pinned upon him by the manufacturers, perhaps because of his famous performance on Steely Dan's *Peg* (1977) using it. Commercially, however, Computone was put into financial difficulty by the fast-changing digital electronics and the adoption of MIDI into electronic musical systems. The company closed in 1981, but where the commerce had failed, the idea was a great success.

The digital Electronic Wind Instrument was, like its analogue sibling, an electromechanical device operated by the breath and fingers of the player. Its main difference was that it could create an electronic signal that could be fed via MIDI to a synthesiser. In fact, this instrument had started out as a new kind of trumpet, called an electronic valve instrument (EVI) by its inventor, Nyle Steiner.

Steiner was an experienced trumpet player who had worked with the Utah Symphony Orchestra in the 1960s. He first had the idea of an electronic trumpet in the 1960s, and used his manufacturing skills to build a prototype in his own workshop in the early '70s. His first playable EVI was completed in 1975, which he called the Steiner Horn. At an early stage, Michael's brother, Randy, had examined the EVI to see how it might fit with his own playing, but he found it to be too different from the traditional trumpet. He felt that playing it would have been like learning an entirely new instrument.

Shortly afterwards, Steiner developed a woodwind version of his device that he called, the Electronic Wind Instrument (EWI), known to most people as the 'ee-wee'. Michael found the EWI entirely to his liking. Steiner: "I developed my own transducer using whatever - I tried a lot of things out. A lot of the main parts I had to build myself. The first one was just a switch. You blew, and it turned on and off - just like pressing a key. Later, I built a proportional transducer." [79]

The early models consisted of two parts: a wind controller to convert the player's actions into an electronic signal, and a synthesizer to create whatever sound was desired through suitable programming. Steiner built everything himself. Recent models, such as the Akai EWI4000S or Yamaha WX7, are self-contained with the synthesiser in the lower part of the controller. The instrument has the same fingering system as a soprano saxophone, and is similar in size and shape.

The wind controller part of the EWI has a mouthpiece with sensors for both air pressure (to control volume) and lip pressure (to control vibrato). It can be played fast, because there is no movement of the keys; the positions of the musician's fingers are sensed by changes in the electrical conductivity beneath his fingertips; a set of rollers under the left thumb is used to change octaves. A particular advantage is the span of eight (!) octaves offered by most instruments, compared to the maximum of three on regular saxophones.

A recording exists of Michael playing an early version of the EWI during a gig with a Don Grolnick band called Idiot Savant at the Breckers' club, *Seventh Ave South*, on 18-20 August, 1984. [80] It is likely that he got the instrument directly from Nyle Steiner in 1983, studied a lot, and tried it a lot during gigs in the club. The early model Michael used can be seen in videos posted on the Internet. [81]

In 1986, Steiner met representatives of the instrument manufacturers, Akai, to discuss the commercial production of EWIs. It was agreed that Akai would adopt the project. "Soon they had a model ready for production, it was very buggy at first, but soon it was all worked out. This first model was the EWI 2000, and EVI 2000". [82]

## Bob Dylan and Folk-Rock Fusion

Many looked upon folk music as precious, but Bob Dylan soon showed that it too was not immune to the rock revolution. Martin Scorsese's documentary about Bob Dylan's early years is the most revealing film so far made about him. [83] Up to 1966 folk music had always been acoustic solo material, but the film contains footage of the 1966 gig in Newcastle UK when Dylan appeared on stage with a Fender Stratocaster electric guitar and a band. It was in utter contrast to the accepted image of him held by many of his fans - what Schiller called the "hipster troubadour" image. [84] Dressed in a dark suit and tie, he looked like John Lennon. Many in the crowd saw a traitor to their cause and booed. Leaving aside his unexpected attire, the change to his music had been more attributable to the guitar he carried. Dylan's perhaps unwitting plan to create folk-rock fusion had begun by using electric guitar at the Newport Folk Festival in 1965. Intense emotions were evoked there too. Top folk singer Pete Seeger was so incensed he threatened to cut the cable to Dylan's amplification. The parallels with the unpopularity of fusion of jazz and rock that were already beginning are remarkable.

Dylan is presented in Scorsese's documentary as the greatest songwriter of all time, and there are few who would argue with that. Analysis of his greatness is all about the songs as songs. These songs are hailed as capturing the public mood of the time like no others did. Whilst Lennon and McCartney were still singing about love, Dylan was already a social commentator, telling us that - *The Answer is Blowing in the Wind*, *The Times They Are a Changing* and *Don't Think Twice, It's All Right*. These songs are as famous as any that have ever been written. It was a time of social revolution in the western civilisation. People did care, and took Dylan's songs into their hearts. They remain inside many peoples' heads forty years after they were written, but not necessarily because of the lyrics. Today, most people couldn't get beyond the first few lines of the song in terms of words, yet the music is well remembered as great melody. Dylan was quite a good guitarist, but most people agree that he was a very poor singer, his vocal style involving serious slurring of the notes so that the melody in his songs was often as unrecognisable as his diction. It is therefore ironic that, long after Dylan's lyrics lost their political relevance, it is the melodies that are best remembered.

In the film, Dylan himself seems bemused about his own abilities. He genuinely seems to have no comprehension of the source of his creative powers, even today. When asked questions in the mid-1960s by the music press about his work, he was mostly unable to provide any sensible answers at all and this led to him developing contempt for the press because of their continued "stupid" questions. His rude response was mistakenly seen as being "hip" and many began to copy him. The truth is that he genuinely was unable to answer. On the whole, there seems to be no deep inspiration behind the songs. Maybe Dylan just does not see it. He never claimed to have any sincere motivation to "Save the World" or to be the original protest singer. [85] (He wasn't anyway, for Mingus' *Fables of Faubus* (1959) and Rollins *Freedom Suite* (1958) had already established the link between music and protest. Sure, Dylan cared about what he saw around him. We were all quite fearful about the threat of nuclear destruction: the Cuban missile crisis was still fresh in our minds in the early

1960s, as were the TV images of Russian thermonuclear weapons exploding in the Siberian wastelands. So it was natural to protest about that. Dylan seems to believe that the songs just flowed out of him at the appropriate time as if he was some kind of conductor of socio-political electricity.

Above all, Dylan was passionate about his music. He hated having to fit music into the three-minute slot allocated for airtime. "The sociologists were saying that TV ...was destroying the minds and imaginations of the young - that their attention spas were being dragged down. Maybe that's true but the three-minute song also did the same thing. Symphonies and operas are incredibly long, but the audience never seems to lose its place or follow along. With the three-minute song the listener doesn't have to remember anything as far back as twenty or even ten minutes ago. There's nothing you have to be able to connect. [86]

Dylan: "My style was too erratic and hard to pigeonhole for the radio, and songs, to me, were more important than just light entertainment. They were my preceptor and guide into some altered consciousness of reality, some different republic, some liberated republic...It wasn't that I was anti-popular culture or anything, and I had no ambitions to stir things up. I just thought of mainstream culture as lame as hell and a big trick." [87]

Dylan needed the time to be able to develop his ideas and had little time for the 45-rpm vinyl disc. "Folk singers, jazz artists and classical musicians made LPs, long playing records with heaps of songs in the grooves - they forged identities and tipped the scales, gave more of the big picture. LPs were like the force of gravity. They had covers back and front that you could stare at for hours. Next to them, 45s in their cheap wrappers were flimsy and primitive. They just stacked up in piles and didn't seem important." [88]

The style of music he chose to present his songs did not seem of any concern to him at all, yet music was important enough for him to make the transition from acoustic to electric instruments. In 1965 he had already achieved great success as a folk singer and did not need to turn to rock. It may be that he had deep-seated ambition to repeat the success of the Beatles, who were by now sending shock waves all around the world. He liked the Beatles' music and made efforts to befriend them at the time. America had nothing to compare with them in 1965, so maybe he harboured the notion of filling the gap. Throughout the Scorsese film, it is Dylan's pragmatism that is most enlightening. He is candid and revealing, but afterwards there remains a sense of frustration that the magical, mystical part of his character that we all suspect lurks inside him somewhere is missing on the outside.

## Funk

In earlier pages I wrote about the fusion of jazz with R&B and soul that took place in London in the early 1960s. Records made by African-American artists in the late 1950s and early 1960s were strongly influential amongst the best young musicians in the UK at the time. Of course, it was James Brown who led the field as a singer with roots in gospel, R&B and soul music, so that by the mid-sixties he had attracted the nickname "Godfather of Soul." To some extent this was left behind when he released a single from his album of the same name, *Cold Sweat* (1967), described as "a watershed event in the evolution of funk music" [89]

Brown's inspirational idea turned the whole band into a drum, with more emphasis on bass and drum locking. The result was that the music "became more intense with less." Previously, with R&B, rock 'n' roll and soul music, the emphasis was on beats 2 and 4 in each bar. Now, Brown stressed beat 1, and this became the bedrock of funk music, called 'The rhythm of the One'.

Music that came to be described as funk was in a strongly African musical style. Always considered to have strong sexual connotations, funk music consists of a groove with rhythm instruments such as electric guitar, electric bass, organ, and drums playing interlocking rhythms. But besides the celebration of physical pleasures, funk was also associated with the black people's identity in a time of stark inequality; it was described variously as "a state of mind", "the sound of rebellion", "a celebration of being black", and "unapologetic blackness." With its pulsating rhythms "…in its essence, funk makes you dance, makes you move." [90] The "groove" had arrived in music.

Somehow, funk music resonated with the cultural challenges that America found for itself. In the 1960s life as an African-American was hard because of prejudice, discrimination and segregation. It was observed that the "Vanilla pop of Motown was the only black music that got through to the charts." [90] However, by the mid 1970s, as the nation finally faced up to its racist past, African-Americans had become totally absorbed by funk music, thanks mostly to James Brown. As Brown's popularity grew from 1967 onwards, he took on a significant role in the Civil Rights movement. Brown used his fame to talk to black people and inspire them to succeed in a world dominated by whites. He recognised that money was the way for black people to gain power. A share in his optimistic vision was offered through his funky music, and especially with a lyric to a song that became an anthem for African-Americans, "Say it loud, I'm black and I'm proud."

But James Brown's influence and leadership soon garnered support from a new direction thanks to a young musician called Sylvester Stewart, aka Sly Stone. Stewart's style was to promote an agenda of sharing, a sense of togetherness for musicians of mixed race and gender. Clothes and hair were a part of the image, but the music was original and strong as hit songs were generated from jams.

Sly and the Family Stone became an extremely influential band from 1967 to 1975, and through its highly visible public image the band promoted the idea of an integrated society to the whole of America. Both Miles Davis and Herbie Hancock were so smitten with this music that they both created a large volume of their own work based on it.

Stewart formed the group in 1967, along with three of his siblings. The Stewarts were an exceptionally musical family that would inevitably make its mark on the music world. From their earliest days, the youngest four Stewart children had formed a group called the Stewart Four and released a record on 78 rpm vinyl. As a teenager Sylvester released several pop singles under the name of Danny Stewart. In 1963, Sly was working as a DJ in San Francisco and as a record producer, totally immersed in the business.

In 1966, Sly formed a band called Sly and the Stoners, with Cynthia Robinson on trumpet. Concurrently, his brother Freddie founded a band called Freddie and the Stone Souls, which included Gregg Errico on drums. It was Sly's friend, saxophonist Jerry Martini, who suggested that Sly and Freddie combine bands and they created Sly and the Family Stone in 1967. Sly and Freddie were both guitarists so Sly made Freddie the official Family Stone guitarist, and taught himself to play the electronic organ. Bassist Larry Graham completed the original line-up, and within a year, sister Rose, joined as well. Rose (Rosemary) played electric piano and sang, while Vet (Vaetta) provided background vocals. She and her friends Mary McCreary and Elva Mouton had formed a gospel group called The Heavenly Tones. Sly recruited the three teenagers directly out of high school to become Little Sister, background vocalists for Sly and the Family Stone.

Of the non-family members, perhaps the most famous was Larry Graham. A special feature of the music was the way Graham emphasised the funky sound with a new method of playing called 'slap' bass. He had originally developed it because of the need to make up for not having drums, so it was a percussive style that mimicked drums. Graham stayed with Family Stone from its creation until 1972 when he began to have serious problems with Sly's drug abuse.

The band's debut single was *I Ain't Got Nobody*, which was a big hit in the San Francisco area. This came to the attention of Clive Davis, an executive with CBS Records and (in effect) Miles Davis's boss. Davis (who was, of course, no relation to Davis) signed Sly and the Family Stone to the Epic Records label, a brand of CBS. Family Stone's first album was *A Whole New Thing* (1967), which received critical acclaim but sold poorly. It was now that record company 'experience' came into play. Advice from Davis and others at CBS resulted in Sly writing the single *Dance to the Music* (1968), which became a big hit. Just before its release, Rose Stewart Stone, who had previously been somewhat reluctant to leave her steady job, joined the group as a vocalist and a keyboardist.

The band began to tour and were characterised by energetic performances and outrageous costumes. *Dance to the Music* and the follow-up album *Life* (1968) became highly influential across the music industry because of a recipe of particularly unusual ingredients. It had one of the most eclectic fusions of cultures and influences of any band yet seen. The music was a heady mix of James Brown proto-funk, Motown pop, Stax soul, Broadway show tunes, and psychedelic rock music. Wah-wah guitars, distorted fuzz bass lines, church-styled organ lines, and horn riffs provided the musical backdrop for the vocals of the band's four lead singers, who by sharing out the vocals almost on a bar-by-bar basis created a style of vocal arrangement both unusual and revolutionary at that time in popular music. Cynthia Robinson would shout ad-libbed vocal directions to the audience and/or the band. The lyrics, meanwhile, were universal pleas for peace, love and understanding, sung by a fully integrated inter-racial band with men and women treated equally as both vocalists and musicians. The band's gospel-styled singing endeared them to black audiences, while their rock music elements and wild costuming—including Sly's large Afro hairstyle and tight leather outfits, Rose's blonde wig, and the other members' loud psychedelic clothing—caught the attention of mainstream audiences.

So, the smooth, piano-based *Motown sound* was out; *psychedelic soul* was in. Rock-styled guitar lines similar to the ones Freddie Stone played began appearing in the music of artists like The Isley Brothers (*It's Your Thing*) and Diana Ross & the Supremes (*Love Child*). Larry Graham's *slapping* technique of bass guitar playing became synonymous with funk music. Some musicians changed their sound completely to co-opt that of Sly & the Family Stone, most notably Motown in-house producer Norman Whitfield, who took his main act The Temptations into *psychedelic soul* territory starting with the Grammy-winning *Cloud Nine* (1968).

By 1975 everybody wanted to make funky music including the Brecker Brothers who created a strong brand of jazz-funk fusion where the funk elements had, by definition, already included blues, R&B, soul etc. The Jackson Five had started out in the Motown genre, but soon moved into funk. Stevie Wonder became one of the superstars of popular genres with his unique style, typified by songs such as the superfunky *Superstition* (1972) and the astonishing album *Songs In The Key Of Life* (1976). Even the Brits started playing funk, and Average White Band (with a little help from the Brecker Brothers) made a great impact with *Pick Up The Pieces* (1974).

Another very important musician in the fusion of genres was George Clinton, who took funk music up another gear, so that by the end of the 1970s he had turned funk into a way of life. George Clinton took funk and fused it with psychedelic rock. At first, his band Funkadelic was acid rock with a huge dose of funk. Clinton even stole James Brown's band after an internal dispute created discontent amongst the ranks. At first Clinton's experimental sound was too challenging for both black and white audiences. Then he evolved it into a theatrical dance-oriented act and exaggerated the beat even more. Although he kept the beat on the One, he freed it up and allowed musicians to *ad lib* in the way jazz musicians had always done. Clinton put pure creative freedom in studio and stage.

The history of Clinton and his bands is one of the most complicated stories in music. From the mid 1970s, P-Funk was a combined outfit derived from Parliament and Funkadelic. Gigs had everything from performance art to spaceships and aliens in elaborate costumes. Music evolved into continuous songs performed by up to thirty musicians onstage simultaneously. The music created strong feelings of unity amongst audiences and offered the 'stadium rock' experience that had not previously been presented to black audiences.

Clinton expanded his operation into a business empire as a kind of franchise. As musicians under his auspices each wanted to record their own projects, Clinton offered them the opportunity to perform and record in different ways. George Clinton can be credited as an important catalyst and liberator of the black imagination, for the music of his small army of bands offered African-American people real freedom. Clinton's funk music was at the centre of a cultural shift that gave them a strong sense of their own identity

In the early 1970s, a new genre of so-called 'Blaxploitation' movies gained prominence, most notably *Shaft* (1971), for which the funky score, written by Isaac Hayes and Johnny Allen won an Oscar for "Best Score Soundtrack album". Once again, the growing voice of African-American people was acting as a driving force towards empowerment. Soon, the funk-soul-jazz fusion was conquering the airwaves, adopted almost universally for TV themes.

Kool and the Gang was an American band who had started out in jazz in the 1960s, but took their jazz boots into the more lucrative world of funk with hit songs such as *Jungle Boogie* (1973).

In the second half of the 1970s, Earth Wind and Fire became a supergroup that made funk music more popular than ever, and incorporated gospel, funk, soul and jazz in a more polished format. The band used catchy melodies that were mostly absent from George Clinton's line-ups; Funkadelic was simply too weird for many tastes. With EW&F a lighter style embracing catchy pop songs with universal appeal were more appealing to whites and members of the black middle classes. The. music somehow smoothed the paths for black people to move up in the social world. EW&F made so much money they could expand on their P-Funk-style stage antics. Audiences could feast their eyes and ears on astonishing new theatrical effects, many using Egyptology for their inspiration.

In the late 1970s and early 1980s, a new kind of groove took a hold of live music. It was christened 'Disco' music because of its origins, and like many crazes spread like wildfire, but killed off funk acts. Disco music retained elements of funk, but the rhythm of the 'One' was gone. This was known as 'Four on the floor'; there was no syncopation because all beats were emphasised. It was assisted by electronic rhythm machines and computer controlled rhythms. The precision of the beats gave drummers the distinct impression they would soon be out of work. Even Earth, Wind And Fire took the difficult decision to modify their style of groove and took on disco beat with *Boogie Wonderland* (1979). As keyboardist Larry Dunn remembered, it was "… a slippery slope to walk between staying current and staying true to what made you current." [91]

To remain vibrant and high in the popularity charts of the record-buying public, change was necessary. Some of the original pioneers of funk found it hard and became marginalised, but those that did change, like Kool and the Gang, EW&F, and George Clinton, reaped great benefits. Even so, Sly and the Family Stone had disbanded by the end of the 1970s, and the George Clinton empire began to break up in the late 80s.

Hip hop then took over from funk as a direct reflection of black life, yet the introduction of sampling took funk to its heart. Prince developed his style out of funk and then went into many styles, always underpinning his music with funk roots. Today, as with jazz, many original acts continue with strong elements of funk in their performances; Daft Punk and Ferrell Williams, for example, use funk extensively.

## The Impact of Jazz on Popular Music: Pop-Jazz

The fusion of jazz and rock music was, of course, approached from both sides of the fence. From the jazz camp, various musicians showed how elements from rock music could be incorporated into jazz. This is where the term *jazz-fusion* best applies. Other rock-based bands showed how jazz sounds could be used to advantage in rock music – remember, I'm calling this *rock-jazz fusion*. So, fusion music fell into one of two camps. On the one hand were rock-oriented musicians (Jeff Beck, for example) playing music with an electric guitar-focussed rock beat and using jazz musicians to provide a wider tonal spectrum. On the other were jazz musicians, such as John McLaughlin, playing music with a keyboard or saxophone focus and flavours of rock-based tonalities that are based on instrumental, rather than sung, compositions.

The Beatles showed how good brass instruments sounded in pop records such as *Yellow Submarine* (1965), *Penny Lane* (1966) and *Sergeant Pepper's Lonely Hearts Club Band* (1967). The guitar-dominated rock band was suddenly fair game for the inclusion of wind instruments, if only as a guest appearance on a single recording. The Beatles were not influenced by jazz, but they were open to any idea that extended their original sound into new areas, the most obvious being Indian music. Other rock bands, however, certainly were hearing jazz in their rock music and included jazz musicians in their formal line-up. Artists such as Van Morrison and Jesse Colin Young recorded albums that were not rock, yet which were song-based and contained significant amounts of jazz. One very successful album was Stevie Wonder's *Talking Book* (1972) that featured a host of musicians with fusion already part of their psyche. By the end of the 70s the rock superstar Sting was routinely using jazz musicians in his line-ups (Vinnie Colaiuta was his drummer of choice for several years) and famously played a duet with the jazz saxophone virtuoso Branford Marsalis at the 1985 London *Live Aid* concert. No-one could claim that this was in any way a deliberate progression. The young musicians of the 70s had been kids during the 60s and were simply playing in the directions their ears were leading them.

Today, much popular music is a fusion of two or more styles that were popular in previous decades, simply because the musicians playing it have grown up listening to different styles of music and have inevitably been influenced by them. Few musicians could claim that their creations have been entirely uninfluenced by other musicians. Jazz has often been called musicians' music. It tends to be more difficult to play and young, inexperienced musicians who are attracted by the sounds of jazz recognise and respect the skills of the musicians playing it. Al Kooper, co-founder of the early rock-jazz group Blood Sweat & Tears, was the man who gave Bob Dylan his electronic organ sound on *Like A Rolling Stone* (1967). As Kooper was recruiting for BS&T, he came into close contact with numerous jazz musicians - sax player, Fred Lipsius was one, and trumpeter Randy Brecker was another. Their skill and versatility knocked him out.

Prince is an artist who has always had jazz influences and this was recognised by Miles Davis who befriended the singer and was reportedly influenced by him. Similarly, Donald Fagen and Walter Becker of Steely Dan have used jazzers extensively for all of their albums, and their music is easily categorised as jazz-fusion whilst still residing in the category of pop. Jazz also influenced the styles in which vocalists went about their business. Listen to Sting, Witney Houston, Mariah Carey, or Christina Aguillera and you will realise just how much they owe to jazz. Indeed, Sting has built his post-Police career on a considered blending of jazz into his rock music. The term *crossover* was applied to jazz that was intended for sale in the popular marketplace and, on the whole, the transition from jazz to pop/rock was smoothed by using jazz-rock fusion styles. Even so-called *easy-listening* music can have significant jazz influences.

Many pop musicians recognised that their works were best realised by the use of session musicians from the jazz world, and many of the top jazz musicians made a very comfortable living as hired-hands on pop records. Rhythm players make up the core of any band and were an obvious first choice. Thus drummers like Steve Gadd, Jeff Porcaro and Vinnie Colaiuta, bass players like Nathan East, James Jamerson and Anthony Jackson Jr, and keyboard players like Michael Omartian and Clifford Carter appeared as session men on many popular albums. Guitarists were also, of course, much in demand. The best were extremely versatile and, as they could usually read music, were competent enough to come into a studio, lay down a solo or track and, with almost clinical efficiency, be out of the door by teatime. The likes of Larry Carlton, Paul M Jackson Jr, David T Walker and Robben Ford are to be found across the whole spectrum of recorded popular music.

Horn players could add a great deal too, from a solo to liven up a middle-eight-bar section, to an entire horn sub-band that added great new colours and depth. By the early 70s, it was common to use a saxophone for a middle-eight bar solo in a pop record. Indeed, some popular songs are memorable for the extraordinary saxophone solos they contain. Two of the very best are by Phil Woods on Billy Joel's *Just the Way You Are* (1977) and Bob Messenger's stunningly beautiful sax on the Carpenters' *A Song For You* (1972). Two of the most prolific soloists were Michael Brecker and Tom Scott; for example, Brecker played on Paul Simon's *Still Crazy After All These Years* (1975) and Scott on Paul McCartney's *Listen To What the Man Said* (1974).

Horn sections, too, became a must-have accessory. Many bands featured them strongly as, for example, Sly and the Family Stone on their first album *A Whole New Thing* (1967), George Clinton's Parliament/Funkadelic bands in the mid-1970s, or Earth Wind and Fire. The Brecker Brothers, Michael and Randy, became famous for their tight sound and for years were the number one choice to lead horn sections on rock and pop albums. Michael Jackson achieved the greatest success in popular music on his albums *Off The Wall* (1979), *Thriller* (1982), *Bad* (1987) and *Dangerous* (1991) with jazz musicians at his back. Of course, Jackson himself was no jazz musician, but his producer Quincy Jones was one of the most respected in the business. Jazzer Q was very much responsible for the selection of musicians and thus for the stunning sounds achieved on all of these albums. Jackson's horn section would make most jazz fans mouths water: Kim Hutchcroft and Larry Williams (saxophones), Jerry Hey and Gary Grant (trumpets), Bill Reichenbach (trombone) were a hornman's dream team. This formidable group of musicians appeared on many other albums, including the work of Al Jarreau, George Benson and Maroon 5. The Tower of Power horn section made up of Greg Adams and Lee Thornburg (trumpets), Emilio Castillo, Richard Elliot, and Stephen 'Doc' Kupka (saxes) was extremely popular with musicians such as Huey Lewis, Elton John and Rod Stewart. All of this represented the homogeneous absorption of jazz sounds and styles into popular music. The irony was that many listeners heard jazz sounds in popular music without necessarily realising it. Jazz-rock or rock-jazz had almost ceased to exist as a separate genre, except in a historical sense.

A final, very important influence was from film and TV theme music, which is something I mostly only allude to in this series of books. Throughout the 1980s and early 90s, much film and TV music was written and played by jazz musicians. The result was a subliminal influence on the minds of the mass audiences who were exposed to the sounds of jazz whilst they were concentrating on the next twist in the plot of *Starsky and Hutch* or *Miami Vice*. The impact of this on the absorption of jazz into popular music should not be underestimated.

Steely Dan is a band that emerged from the pop/rock genre with a strong leaning towards jazz flavours and this has continued to this day. The two main musicians, Walter Becker and Donald Fagen have pursued solo careers, besides coming together for the Steely Dan albums. These guys have always focussed on the song format for their compositions, but have never been afraid to use extended instrumental sections, usually with jazz musicians front and back. Good examples are the well-known *Deacon Blues* (1977) and *Everything Must Go* (2003). This was a particularly jazz-influenced band, but many others employed jazz elements on a lesser scale. Thus rock-fusion permeated popular music extremely quickly.

By the late 1960s, the development of the rock/pop industry had reached a stage where it was so highly developed compared to its embryonic structure in the early 60s that it needed to create an upper tier of superstars. Paul Simon had the good fortune to emerge as one of the first to find himself on the same earning potential with the likes of Paul McCartney, John Lennon, Bob Dylan and Jimi

Hendrix. Simon had benefited from the spectacular success of the film *The Graduate*, which brought him many awards, but reached the pinnacle of his musical relationship with Art Garfunkel and the multi-award-winning album *Bridge Over Troubled Water* (1969). Suddenly he surprised everybody by announcing their divorce. Garfunkel was emasculated because Simon was clearly the musical genius in the pair. Simon then went on to develop his career with several solo albums that were marked by a combination of brilliant composition in the popular music genre and some very distinctive musical arrangements. Gone was the contemporary guitar music duo and in its place was a pop superstar. Along with his newfound status came a budget that allowed him, like Steely Dan, to hire the best musicians for whatever band he thought was necessary to create milestone albums. Like Steely Dan, he hired the same musicians that were appearing on the jazz-fusion albums I describe here. Unlike Steely Dan, his music remained firmly planted in the pop music genre, ostensibly uninterested in jazz flavours and tints. Subconsciously, though, he could not avoid jazz-fusion.

His first solo album was *Paul Simon* (1972) followed by *There Goes Rhymin' Simon* (1973) and *Still Crazy After All These Years* (1975). For these records Simon was hiring such jazz-fusion musicians as Michael Brecker, David Sanborn, Steve Gadd, Ralph MacDonald, Bob James, Richard Tee, Phil Woods, Toots Thielemans, Hugh McCracken and Tony Levin. Saxophone solos on pop records were in vogue and *Still Crazy* was no exception. Michael Brecker played a short 16-bar solo on the title track, whilst Phil Woods got the plum job of playing a frantic cadenza at the end of *Have a Good Time*. (Phil Woods was an unlikely jazz sax star in the pop world. As a hard-nosed bebop, specialist he has at least two claims to fame: he created one of the great saxophone solos of all time for Billy Joel's *Just the Way You Are* from *Stranger* (1977), a piece that won the Grammy for "Song of the Year". He also married Charlie Parker's widow.) But with so many funk-loving musicians in Simon's bands, and spending much time with them on the road, it was inevitable that jazz would break through in places. Thus *You're Kind* has a beautiful brass track in the background. David Sanborn clearly enjoyed *I Do It For Your Love* because he used it, along with another Simon track, *Smile* on his debut album, *Taking Off* (1975) recorded in the same year as the *Still Crazy* tour in which he participated. Simon's *Graceland* (1986) was, of course, a true fusion album in the sense that he embraced South African rhythms with pop/rock and influenced a new round of what later became known as World Music.

## Acid Jazz and Smooth Jazz: Kinds of Jazz-Pop

The question you might now ask is, "Did jazz-fusion spawn any other more recent styles?" The answer, of course, is "Yes". Many people use the term *acid-*

*jazz* to refer to a genre that grew out of jazz-fusion. Once more, *Wikipedia* defines it as follows: "Acid jazz (also known as groove jazz or more recently club jazz) is a musical genre that combines jazz influences with elements of soul music, funk, disco and also 90s English dance music, particularly repetitive beats and modal harmony. It developed over the 1980s and 1990s and could be seen as taking the boundary crossing of jazz fusion or jazz-funk onto new ground." [92]

We see at once that this still fits inside the definition of jazz-fusion. I feel that acid-jazz is an especially poor term because, for people who do not know what it represents, the term *acid* gives entirely the wrong impression of the style of music. The use of the term *R&B* has also taken on new musical connotations recently.

Another very significant development was Smooth Jazz, a term invented to describe the commercial, more melodic forms of music that had their origins in jazz-fusion, and which tried to retain an identifiable jazz content, whilst also residing in the popular music genre. Many observers who disliked the hi-jacking of their art by business interests saw it as undesirable – an artefact of the music business to promote the development of FM radio stations. As the number of stations grew and developed their own identities, the demand for 24/7 coverage on a Jazz FM station, for example, could not be satisfied by playing only the kinds of music described in this series of books. It was judged that the FM radio fan of the 1980s demanded something softer that would appeal to a wider range of audiences. This, in turn, would attract the kind of financial sponsorship needed for the stations to survive. Smooth jazz was the result, and many jazz musicians were content to work in this sub-genre. Just as jazz-fusion had become a by-word for 'crap' from the late 1970s, the jazz puritans almost universally condemned smooth jazz, and critics writing for the music press unfairly vilified many of its exponents. My own opinion is that jazz, being a specialist interest that needs all the support it can get, needed the visibility offered by FM radio stations. How are young people ever to get exposure to the wonderful sounds of jazz if it is not through stations like these and the albums they promote?

George Benson played a big part in the creation of the smooth jazz genre with his incredibly successful album, *Breezin'* (1976). Soon afterwards, Larry Rosen and Dave Grusin created the GRP label, and their company was responsible for smoothing the rougher edges of jazz, and making it a more user-friendly art-form. The 1980s saw a trend away from the scatty, free-jazz-riddled experiments of the 1960s and the decibel-fuelled chaos of 70s jazz-rock into a considered, organised, clean-cut form of jazz-fusion. It percolated into most corners of everyday life in western culture, especially TV and film, as well as in shops, restaurants and – yes, elevators. In many other arenas, this might have been considered another of the great successes of jazz, comparable with its immense popularity in the dance halls of the 1930s and 40s. In a sense, jazz-fusion was becoming the bedrock of popular music that the leading artists used for their own purposes. Instead, preferring to see jazz occupying elitist space on the frontiers of art, the jazz puritans found new reasons to hate the music. Now they hated what they saw as simplifications introduced into smooth-jazz. As a result, many talented 1980s jazz-fusion musicians and bands were openly despised: Spyro Gyra, the Rippingtons, Lee Ritenour, Bob James, Dave Grusin, David Benoit - even the brilliant Yellowjackets suffered from the backlash. Then there was Kenny G. "Kenneth Gorelick (Kenny G) is possibly, poor fellow, the most despised musician with any jazz associations," wrote Cook, who went on to describe him as an "instrumental pop artist" with "almost no improvisation in his records." [93] Well, there are other established jazz artists who fit that description once they have become successful: doing what they prefer instead of what they must. Anyone doubting Kenny G's jazz abilities should listen to *Silhouette* (1988). So, in these senses, much to the chagrin of serious jazz lovers, jazz-fusion is alive and well and resides – often incognito - all around us, encapsulated into jazz-pop - and many other places too!

## Jazz: The End of the Road?

If you look again at the definition of jazz-fusion with which I began this part of the book, you will see that it remains today as valid as ever. However, as you read about music in books, on the Internet and elsewhere, you realise that there is a multitude of other names used to describe similar musical sub-genres. Whether we talk about jazz-rock or rock-jazz fusion, the focus is, by definition, on the electric guitar, which is a great clarification. Clearly, when jazz absorbed the elements of guitar-based rock music a new genre was created that is clearly identifiable. This came at a time when technological advances were giving new tools to the musicians and they took full advantage of the new electronic instruments. But we have seen that there have been other fusions too, which need not include electronics, but which often do. When a guitar is not the centrepiece of an otherwise electric jazz group, it is not really appropriate to call it jazz-rock, hence the need for a jazz-fusion label.

Up to the 1970s, there was a kind of unwritten duty to respect musicians who could actually apply serious technical skill to their art, Eric Clapton, Jimmy Page, Jeff Beck and Jimi Hendrix being just some examples. Even the "you can do it too" motto of 1950s skiffle was a prelude to interested parties acquiring better instruments and learning to improve their skills. However, the 1960s fashion for the abandonment of all rules finally turned the tide of increasing demand for instrumental virtuosity, with the invention of punk music from 1974 onwards by bands such as the Ramones, the Sex Pistols and the Clash. No instrumental talent was required – only the knack of finding the pulse of the latest youth fashion. In many groups of aspiring rock musicians, the bass guitar was handed to the person who played the guitar least well, or not at all. Guitars were raped rather than skilfully played in the way they had been with Clapton and Co. and playing guitar became more about self-expression than musical performance. Keyboards were even easier to play than guitars and allowed the creation of music by people with virtually no musical knowledge. And finally, computers generated monotonous, uninteresting drum rhythms at the click of a mouse instead of being the result of years of practising paradiddles. Bands like the Human League demonstrated that anyone could be successful in pop music without ever learning to play an instrument. I could argue that disrespect for the playing of instruments was fuelled by those who delighted in smashing them onstage.

Fortunately, this indictment of musical progress has never applied to jazz, a genre that has continued to be defined far more by creativity and skill than commercial appeal. As a genre of minority interest, however, jazz has been in serious decline since the late 1990s, assisted by the age of the download that has mostly killed interest in the CD format. The present age of "whatever you want, whenever you want it" has meant that young listeners can be held more tightly inside the popular mainstream and avoid the more creative musical arts. As a result, most people today have no idea what jazz is, and are therefore unable to name a single jazz musician.

At first, jazz-fusion appeared to be the way forward for the future development of the genre, even whilst most of the major characters thought that the jazz-fusion *thing* was finished by around 1978. The patriarch, Miles Davis, was in retirement, along with the Mahavishnu Orchestra and Tony Williams' Lifetime. Chick Corea's career in Return to Forever was over, as also was Herbie Hancock's with Head Hunters. Some, notably Weather Report, soldiered on, very much against the perceived tide that was ebbing from its door and leaving behind a foul smell of rotting weed.

Joe Zawinul was one major innovator who not only refused to be categorised, but continued to make music in the fusion vein. In his case, the fusion that resulted was categorised as World Music. Pat Metheny, speaking in 2000, said about him: "I think it's hard in the climate right now for Joe to be appreciated because we're in an era when all things electronic having to do with backbeats and that sort of thing – it all comes under this banner of this word 'fusion', and it has absolutely no positive connotations. It's the same as putting it under the category of 'shit.'" [94] Dyer too thought the 1970s fusion was a Dark Age of jazz. [95]

Metheny, of course, spoke with extra despair because he too had been tarred and feathered with the label of fusion and knew what an uphill struggle it had been and how illogical it all was. This pervading impression of the death of jazz-fusion in 1978 remains today, largely because from that year on, new terms were coined to describe the various sub-genres that had been created. Importantly, however, these new musics that flowed from the original jazz-fusion *did* continue to flourish, either labelled differently or embodied within other forms.

The Pat Metheny Group (PMG) was formed in 1976 and continued to release albums at regular intervals until 2005 when it reached a remarkable zenith with *The Way Up*. In some ways, after a period of searching, Metheny has reinvented it with his new band, the Pat Metheny Unity Band, and their very successful album *Kin (<-->)* (2014). Metheny might not like being labelled as a jazz-fusioneer, but everyone else considers PMG music to be jazz-fusion. People like Joe Zawinul and Billy Cobham continued regardless playing jazz-fusion with their bands. In 1980 Miles Davis came out of retirement and, typically, continued to do his own thing that was as deep into jazz-fusion as ever. In doing so, he trained a large cohort of new generation jazz-fusion musicians such as Bill Evans, Mike Stern, Marcus Miller and Kenny Garrett. Chick Corea, Herbie Hancock and the Brecker Brothers were independent enough to be able to follow whatever path they wanted. Thus, being musicians with the broadest of musical interests, their acute musical noses led them into widely disparate areas of music, many of them innovative in their own right.

Corea's complex career brought him back to jazz-fusion in a big way in the mid-1980s with the very successful Elektric Band. In this band, just like Miles, he tutored his own students of jazz-fusion, John Patitucci, Eric Marienthal, Dave Weckl and Frank Gambale; they all carry the jazz-fusion torch today (although Patitucci has mostly reverted to 'mainstream' acoustic bass).

Herbie Hancock was in love with technology - the very foundation of jazz-fusion - so as the electronics industry invented more and more amazing instruments, it was natural for him to continue to create new kinds of jazz-fusion with the many new toys he acquired. However, his supreme contribution to mainstream *freebop* jazz within and without the Miles Davis Bands gave him plenty of opportunities for a parallel career in more standard styles of jazz.

In 2008, Return to Forever was reformed in its original line-up for a big tour. The same year Chick Corea and John McLaughlin joined forces with Kenny Garrett, Christian McBride and Vinnie Colaiuta to form a completely new jazz-fusion band called Five Peace Band. Sadly, it was a one-off.

One of those most dedicated to the jazz-fusion cause is John McLaughlin. John spent many years exploring the Indian musical tradition and becoming the leading proponent of Indo-jazz fusion, as well as creating some amazing acoustic guitar megatrios. Today we find some of the very best jazz-fusion on his albums. *Industrial Zen* (2006) and *Floating Point* (2008) were a demonstration that his ideas were still as unique and relevant to fusion as they had ever been. Since then, McLaughlin has continued in a band called 4$^{th}$ Dimension, and released two exceptionally beautiful and creative albums, *To The One* (2010) and *Now Hear This* (2012). Supported by a brilliant live recording at Berklee Music College, *The Boston Record* (2014), the latest format of the band, with the exceptional Gary Husband (keyboards and drums), Ranjit Barot (drums), and Etienne M'Bappe (bass) has proved to be a stable and popular unit, completing extensive tours of Europe and the USA throughout 2014 and 2015.

As the members of the old guard grow yet older, most have tended to return to their purer jazz roots where acoustic jazz is without doubt physically less demanding in the absence of the bulky, heavy, complicated high tech kit used in the past. The idea of gigging with simple setups appeals to sixty- and seventy-something jazzers. However, the torch of jazz-fusion has been repainted in different colours and passed to other bands that parallel much of the characteristics of the 1960s but with none of the fanfare. Today's most extraordinarily gifted musicians are largely unknown except to small groups of enlightened listeners to niche genres. It may come as a surprise to some readers that there is a lot of wonderful jazz-fusion to be found in less obvious corners of Europe, and that as the UK continues to reject jazz as a desirable art form, Europeans are embracing it with even more enthusiasm than in the past. The evidence is clear from the profitable gigging circuit that finds plenty of venues across the European Union, yet can often find only one venue in the UK – London.

The Norwegian band, Jaga Jazzist, was formed in the mid-1990s, but did not make much impact until the release of its first album *Living Room Hush* (2002). Propelled to popularity by such great tracks as *Going Down*, *Airbourne*, *Made For Radio* and the excellent *Lithuania*, the record sold very well, and the band was signed by a London-based independent label called Ninja Tune. Led by its founder Lars Horntveth, and supported by his brothers Line and Martin, the nine-piece band has released a series of outstanding albums, *The Stix* (2003), *What We Must* (2005), and *One Armed Bandit* (2010). In 2013, the band's London connection led to a collaboration with the Britten Sinfonia, and an album of superbly orchestrated live performances of some of the band's most successful compositions was released: *Jaga Jazzist Live With The Britten Sinfonia* (2013). In this recording, band favourites from the studio albums take on a new, exciting character. In particular, *Oslo Skyline* makes a superb climax to what is an outstanding album.

One of the band's trademarks is a complicated multi-layered structure. Typical tracks begin with a strong motif, helically looped so that the DNA is burned into our memories. Then new layers are added that may or may not have tendrils of amino-acid links to the harmonic strands already established. They may be improvised or orchestrated, but they always build over minutes into multi-coloured models of new musical life forms. It is these extensive creations that represent a large proportion of the band's innovations and they are responsible for the ever-present feelings of surprise that come with listening to this band.

There is so much that is new, but with identifiable influences. The rhythmic properties can be conventional, but may also be highly syncopated; they may be so ethereal that the listener finds herself in a state of weightlessness. There is a strong sense of repetition, of phrases, of rhythmic patterns, of harmonic foundations, of melody. Sometimes, it is a drone in the style of Joe Zawinul's Syndicate, but then it might be a surprising chord sequence of the Metheny/Mays ilk. Sometimes the melody lines flow in comfortable harmony. Other times, there could be a dissonant match of two lines in the style of the Brecker Brothers *Some Skunk Funk*. And as with the Breckers, it works, and leaves a satisfying aftertaste like a ginger biscuit enjoyed with a cup of Darjeeling tea.

Lars Horntveth is one of the creative geniuses behind the music. His blend of unusual instruments is a real strength. The courageous juxtaposition of bass clarinet and flute is one such. And when he falls back on a more conventional sound of the tenor saxophone, he still finds the presence of mind to embellish it with heavy breathing, thus creating another new texture. He might use a very repetitive phrase and let it run like a spaniel unleashed in a field of scents. His enthusiasm is predictable, but then the dog might root around in the undergrowth and find a jewel like the one found by Pat Metheny in his remarkable piece, *Something To Remind You* from *We Live Here* (1995). Like Metheny, he puts his gem in direct sunlight and rotates it so that it creates a miasma of sparkling harmonies, unpredictable and vibrant.

This music is joyful, at times introspective and extrovert at others. It is exciting, and frequently tuneful. It is music to be enjoyed - not endured. And because it is unusual, you should play it once, and then play it again. Then play it again. Hopefully, you will find rich and unexpected rewards lying deep inside these colourful Scandinavian tapestries of 21st century jazz. The English titles convey just enough information to stimulate our interest. This is not impressionistic music, yet somehow the titles are very appropriate - tempting us to indulge. The band's output is modest compared to its longevity, but is a sad reflection of the fact that its members make their living from other activities. We should be grateful that it is still extant.

Another band that has recently attracted a great deal of attention is the American outfit, Snarky Puppy. The band operates along similar lines to Jaga Jazzist in that, at any moment, it consists of somewhere between ten and twenty musicians, depending upon who is available. The flexibility of collectives such as these allows them to move forward in the way that traditional big bands cannot because of the very great overheads. Top quality musicians can earn living wages doing gigs for smaller bands, whilst perhaps accepting smaller remuneration from their casual employment in the collective.

Formed in Denton Texas in 2004, largely from students at the University of North Texas, the band now operates out of Brooklyn, NY under the leadership of bassist, composer and producer, Michael League. The band's output is not easily classifiable, as it crosses seamlessly the normal boundaries, between classical, jazz, blues, rock, electronic, metal etc. Perhaps the biggest factor leading to their current popularity was the award in 2014 of a Grammy in the category "Best R&B Performance" for the song *Something*, performed with Lalah Hathaway on the band's 7$^{th}$ album *Family Dinner - Volume 1* (2013). That was rather ironic in view of the fact the band has made its name with largely instrumental performances, even though it has readily included a wide range of guest musicians.

Although there are plenty of exceptions, a typical piece of Snarky Puppy music is instrumental, unpredictable in form (and hence length), fluidly orchestrated whilst allowing plenty of scope for improvised solos, and – perhaps most importantly - melodic. As a result, pieces like *Thing of Gold* from the album *groundUP* (2012) exhibit striking similarities with the feel of early Pat Metheny Group albums and the open-road atmosphere of Jack Kerouac. [96] Like PMG, Snarky Puppy appeals to all age ranges, but has made an indelible mark with the young generation thanks to relentless touring and a strong presence on the YouTube website. Its strong alliance with video has meant that most of the later CD albums have been released with very successful DVDs of the actual recording sessions. Many of these occur at smaller venues in which the musicians encircle the audience and everyone present is fed a live mix through headsets. The spontaneity, enthusiasm and abandonment of formulaic music in these videos is a joy to behold, and provides plenty of evidence for the rejuvenation of 21$^{st}$ century progressive music.

Other remarkable music is being created under the banner of 'progressive metal' by bands such as Blotted Science, with their two albums, *The Machinations of Dementia* (2007), *The Animation of Entomology* (2011); Exivious with their two albums *Exivious* (2009) and *Liminal* (2013); and Animals As Leaders with their three albums, *Animals as Leaders* (2009), *Weightless* (2011), and the *Joy of Motion* (2014). The music is hard to classify, and any labels we care to apply to it can be seen as misleading by some listeners. The music is strongly directed towards the highest technical standards of instrumentalism, especially through guitarists with a great deal of experience and solid reputations such as American, Ron Jarzombek, and the rising stars, Tosin Abasi, a Nigerian-American, and Tymon Kruidener from the Netherlands. Other players such as Alex Webster (bass with Blotted Science) and Hannes Grossman (drums with Blotted Science) set the standards of musicianship at very high levels. The innovative French guitarist Christophe Godin is another who, with his band Mörglbl, is contributing enormously to progressive music.

Recordings of these types demonstrate a new formula of high-energy instrumental music that is improvisation-dominated and may also have strong electronic content. Interested listeners should not be put off by the classification of these albums as 'metal', although there is little doubt that lovers of 'metal' music will probably enjoy these albums.

An Italian band called Slivovitz is also making remarkable jazz-fusion music of a more jazz-rock flavour. Formed in Naples as far back as 2001, the band took five years to release their first eponymous album, by which time the musicians had proved to be as formidable and creative as most of their contemporaries. At the time of writing, Slivovitz continues to secure its presence in the top rank of fusion bands through its live performances, notably at the many European Jazz and Arts Festivals taking place each year. Meanwhile its recording prowess has been expanded to four excellent albums with *Hubris* (2009), *Bani Ahead* (2011) and *All You Can Eat* (2015).

Even those listeners more inclined to serious rock music will find it hard to deny the jazz content of music by the Hedvig Mollestad Trio as it blazes its way through a repertoire that is highly charged with positive ions. A more recent arrival on the scene, guitarist Mollestad (Hedvig Mollestad Thomassen is her full name) is another Norwegian with much to say that is fresh and interesting.

Categorisation is of no consequence for music that is of such presence and quality. The network of followers of what most now regard as niche music is easy to penetrate once awareness of the existence of these bands has been raised by the internet or social media, through which channels – ironically - the music is now more visible to the world's population than ever before. Today, maybe 'fusion' is still an unfashionable word for it; maybe the best word to describe the spirit of experiment in which the music is made is 'progressive', or is that tarnished too? Whatever, jazz-fusion is surely alive and well in its niche bunker.

## Concluding remarks

During the twentieth century, the music industry has both benefited from enormous growth and suffered depressing slump. Jazz too has seen the same peaks and troughs, though not necessarily at the same time. An important watershed came in the early 1980s as the age of the twelve-inch vinyl disc came to an end and the benefits of digital technology, in particular the compact disc, came to be recognised. Today, a similar revolution is occurring with the growth of on-line activities. It looks as if the end of the CD is nigh and with so many people opting to download their music as short items for playback in a mixed musical context, the concept of the album may even be dead too. It's a sobering thought that the killing of the album format is like telling a painter he can no longer use oil paints or a sculptor that marble is banned. Even jazz itself seems to be in major decline, for reasons I gave at the start of this book: jazz is not being passed on from parent to child and our kids get no exposure to it in their daily environment. Essentially a live music medium, jazz suffers from the disinterest more and more people have in leaving their homes. They prefer to get their entertainment on-line and that entertainment does not involve playing or listening to jazz. As if all that were not bad enough, jazz no longer has a wider social role. In the early days of jazz it was the music of the poorest black communities. In the 1930s and 40s it was the popular form of entertainment for people of all ethnic backgrounds. Today, jazz is too sophisticated to express the music of the ghetto: that role has, for some time, been better expressed by hip-hop. [97]. If jazz is too incompatible with most popular appetites, what role remains?

# References to Part 2

Stuart Nicholson's book *Jazz-Rock, A History* is the deserved cornerstone in the narrow archway of available literature on this subject. Disgracefully, it has been unavailable for a number of years and is obtainable only on the haphazard used-books market. Sadly it took me two years from commencement of this project to obtain my copy. Nicholson's excellent book deserves a far wider recognition and readership, despite too many irritating spelling mistakes. Its deep, detailed coverage is supported by a discography by Jon Newey that promises more than it delivers. There is, however, a most valuable index. If you buy only one book, buy this one.

There are a number of first-hand accounts now available of the turbulent period of the 1960s. An essential purchase is Bill Bruford's book, *Bill Bruford: The Autobiography: Yes, King Crimson, Earthworks and More* (2009), Jawbone Press, ISBN 9781906002231. This book is funny, beautifully written and informative, as it presents not only a detailed account of Bruford's career, but also a charming description of life as a top-rank musician.

A recently published original study of the London scene in the early 1960s is by Colin Harper, *Bathed In Lightning* (2014) Jawbone Press, ISBN 9781908279514. The paper edition is essential and sufficient for most readers, but the digital download version contains a great deal more detail.

Sax player, Dick Heckstall-Smith has also written (with Pete Grant) a funny, vital book entitled, *Blowing the Blues: A Personal History of the British Blues* (2004), Clear Press Ltd. ISBN 9781904555040. It also includes a music CD.

Paul Stump's book called, *The Music's All That Matters: A History of Progressive Rock*, (1997) Quartet Books, ISBN 9780704380363 is clearly focussed on prog-rock, but its early pages provide excellent material that is relevant to this discussion, even if his vocabulary ranges from difficult to extravagant.

Martyn Henson's book, *Playing the Band: The Musical Life of Jon Hiseman* published by Temple Music (2010) is another jewel that adds much to the story.

No-one who is interested in the Beatles should be without Ian MacDonald's book, *Revolution in the Head: The Beatles' Records and the Sixties*, 3rd revised edition (2008), Vintage Books, ISBN 9780099526797.

There are numerous other books written by famous musicians about their exploits in the 1960s. Those I found useful are:

Barry Miles: *Paul McCartney: Many Years From Now*, (1997) Secker and Warburg, ISBN 9780436280221.

Keith Richards: *Life*, (2010), Weidenfield and Nicolson / Orion, ISBN 9780297854395.

Pete Townsend: *Who I Am*, (2012), Harper Collins, ISBN 9780007466030.

Al Kooper, *Backstage Passes and Backstabbing Bastards: Memoirs of a Rock 'n' Roll Survivor*, (2008) Backbeat Books, ISBN 9780879309220.

Larry Coryell: *Improvising: My Life In Music* (2007), Backbeat Books, ISBN 9780879308261.

George Cole: *The Last Miles: The Music of Miles Davis 1980-1991*, (2005), Equinox, London, ISBN 9781845531225.

Quincy Jones: *Q: The Autobiography of Quincy Jones*, Sceptre Books (2001).

For the disentanglement of the rock genealogy, I found the following BBC programme very useful: *Rock Family Trees: The British R&B Boom*, Screen Resource for BBC (2001).

Specific References
1. Wikipedia, *Jazz fusion*, retrieved 9 Feb 2015.
2. Wikipedia, *Rock music*, retrieved 9 Feb 2015.
3. Bill Milkowski: *Fusion* in Bill Kirchner (ed): *Oxford University Press* (2000).
4. Nick Coleman, *ABC Magazine*, In *Independent on Sunday* (10 April, 2005), London.
5. Bob Dylan: *Chronicles*, Vol 1, Pocket Books (2004), p5.
6. Ian Macdonald: *Preface to the First Revised Edition*, in *Revolution in the Head: The Beatles Records and the Sixties*, Vintage (2005).
7. MacDonald, p xvii.
8. MacDonald, p368.
9. Paul Stump: *The Music's All That Matters: A History of Progressive Rock* (1997), Quartet Books.
10. S. Frith and H. Horne, *Art Into Pop*, Methuen, London (1987), p81.
11. Stump, p16.
12. Stuart Nicholson, *Jazz Rock: A History*, Schirmer Books 1998, p5.
13. Nicholson, p6.
14. JP Jones, quoted in Colin Harper: *Bathed in Lightning* (2015) Jawbone,

p141.
15. Harper, p122.
16. *John Mayall: The Godfather of British Blues*, Focus Productions for BBC (2003).
17. Harper, p55.
18. Graham Bond, *Melody Maker*, London, 10 October 1964.
19. Interview by Paul Gallan, First published in *GRAMBO*, issue 28 (July, 1993).
20. Dick Heckstall-Smith, *Blowing the Blues: A Personal History of the British Blues* (2004), Clear Press Ltd. ISBN 9781904555040.
21. David Schiller: *Guitars - A Celebration of Pure Mojo* (2008) Workman Publishing, New York, p2.
22. Alexis Petridis, *The Guardian*, London (Tuesday May 3, 2005).
23. *Jazz Britannia*, (Part 2), BBC (2005).
24. Eric Clapton with Christopher Simon Sykes: *Eric Clapton: The Autobiography*, Century, London (2007), p82.
25. Clapton, p96.
25a. Clapton, p66.
26. Clapton, p78.
27. DVD: *Jimi Hendrix, Band of Gypsys*, MCA Records.
28. Wikipedia, *Canterbury Scene*, retrieved 20 November 2014.
29. Stump, p30.
30. Arnold Shaw, notes to album *The Soft Machine*, in 2009 CD edition p17.
31. Mark Powell, in notes to *The Soft Machine, Volume Two* (2009) Polydor.
32. *Free Will and Testament: The Robert Wyatt Story*, Something Else Productions for BBC (2003).
33. BBC Review, Amazon website, retrieved 2014.
34. Chris Jones, Amazon review, retrieved 2014.
35. Graham Bennett: *Out-Bloody-Rageous*, (2008) ISBN 0-946719-8-5) p324.
36. Ken Trethewey, *The Brecker Brothers: Funky Sea, Funky Blue*, Jazz-Fusion books (2014).
37. Randy Brecker, personal communication.
38. Larry Coryell, *Improvising: My Life in Music*, Backbeat Books (2007) p33-5.
39. Wikipedia, *Duster*, downloaded 9 February 2015.
40. Nicholson, p32-3.
41. Larry Coryell, sleeve notes to *Spaces* (1970), Vanguard VMD 79345.
42. http://www.denverpost.com/business/ci_26071845/caribou-ranch-will-close-its-gates-guericos-focus
43. CliveDavis.com retrieved 2013.
44. Miles Davis with Quincy Troupe; Miles: *The Autobiography* (1990), Picador p287.

45. Ken Trethewey, *Weather Report: Electric Red*, Jazz-Fusion Books (2012).
46. Al Kooper: *Backstage Passes and Backstabbing Bastards*, Backbeat Books, NY (2008) Hal Leonard Corporation.
47. Personal interview with Randy Brecker, (17 May 2013).
48. Bone2Pick Randy Brecker Interview Pt 1 with Michael Davis hip-bonemusic.com 28 Sep 2012
49. Martyn Hanson: *Playing the Band: The Musical Life of Jon Hiseman*, Temple Music (2010).
50. Hanson, p115.
51. Hanson, p128.
52. Hanson, p131.
53. Hanson, p136.
54. Hanson, p155.
55. Hiseman talking to Gavid Gallant in *Jazzwise* (Dec 07/ Jan 08), Issue 115, p73.
56. Ken Trethewey, *The Brecker Brothers: Funky Sea, Funky Blue*, (2014) Jazz-Fusion Books, pp19-21
57. Bill Bruford, *The Autobiography – Yes, King Crimson, Earthworks and More*, Jawbone (2009) p90.
58. Richard Cook, *Jazz Encyclopedia*, Penguin Books (2005) p183.
59. David Ake, *Jazz Cultures*, University of California Press (2002).
60. Dyer, p204.
61. Dyer, p201.
62. Nicholson, p109.
63. Dyer, p199.
64. Dyer, p119.
65. Herbie Hancock, *Possibilities*, Viking (2014) p129.
66. Hancock, p140.
67. Hancock, p169.
68. Brian Glasser, *In A Silent Way: A Portrait of Joe Zawinul*, Sanctuary (2001).
69. Milkowski, p502.
70. Milkowski, p503.
71. Wikipedia, *Beat music*, downloaded 9 February 2015.
72. Wikipedia, *Jazz fusion*, downloaded 9 Feb 2015.
73. Nicholson, p108.
74. Richie Unterberger, *Graham Bond Biography*, allmusic.com, downloaded 8 Feb 2015.
75. Colin Harper: *Bathed in Lightning* (2015) Jawbone
76. Bill Hillman: *History of Roland guitar synthesisers*; http://www.hillmanweb.com/guitsyn.html.
77. Bill Milkowski, *Woodshedding With The Heavenly Timbres*. "John

McLaughlin: Mahavishnu's hot new band allows the master to rock out on his Synclavier", *Guitar World* (March 1985).
78. Dyer, p215.
79. http://www.patchmanmusic.com/NyleSteinerHomepage.html
80. The Louis Gerrits Michael Brecker Collection, personal communication, August 2013.
81. http://www.synthtopia.com/content/2013/02/03/steinerphone-ewi-synth-jam/ retrieved 2013.
82. Joel C Peskin: *The EWI Story* http://members.aol.com/lreedman1/ewi.htm retrieved 2013.
83. Arena: *No Direction Home – Bob Dylan. A Film by Martin Scorsese*, UK BBC2 TV (26/7 Sep 2005).
84. Schiller, p6.
85. Bob Dylan: *Chronicles*, Vol 1, Pocket Books (2004).
86. Dylan, p56.
87. Dylan, p34-5.
88. Al Kooper, p89.
89. Wikipedia, *Cold Sweat*, downloaded 9 Feburary 2015.
90. *One Nation Under A Groove: The Story of Funk*, BBC4 (2014), Narrated by Soweto Kinch
91. Larry Dunn, keyboard player with Earth, Wind and Fire, quoted in *One Nation Under A Groove: The Story of Funk*, BBC4 (2014), Narrated by Soweto Kinch.
92. Wikipedia: *Acid Jazz*, downloaded 9 Feburary 2015.
93. Cook, p215
94. Brian Glasser, *In a Silent Way – A Portrait of Joe Zawinul*, Sanctuary Publishing Ltd, 2001, p288-9.
95. Dyer, p204.
96. John Bungey, *Who Let the Dogs Out?* Saturday Review, *The Times*, London, 20 Jun 2015
97. Dyer, p205.

# A Timeline of the Main Events in Jazz-Fusion

| *Timeline Approximate years* | *Event* |
| --- | --- |
| 1900 | Pianist Jelly Roll Morton becomes active as one of the first exponents of a new genre of music known as jazz. |
| 1908 | Joseph "King" Oliver starts to play cornet in New Orleans jazz bands. |
| 1912 | Louis Armstrong starts to be recognised as a jazz cornet player. |
| 1915 | Morton publishes one of the very first jazz compositions. |
| 1917 | The Original Dixieland Jass Band makes the first jazz record. |
| 1918 | King Oliver takes his band to Chicago. |
| 1922 | Louis Armstrong moves to Chicago. |
| 1920s | Armstrong makes a big impact with his Hot Five and Hot Seven bands. |
| 1927 | Duke Ellington begins his career in the Cotton Club of New York City. |
| 1933 | Duke Ellington takes his band to the UK. |
| 1935 | The Swing Era begins. |
| Late 1930s | Birth of bebop as Dizzy Gillespie and Kenny Clarke begin their experiments. |
| 1940s | Continuation of the Swing Era of the Big Bands; Domination of jazz as the most popular music genre. |
| Early 1940s | Bebop development continues: Charlie Parker, Dizzy Gillespie, Thelonius Monk, Kenny Clarke. |
| 1945 | Celebration of the end of WWII. Embrace of hard-won freedoms. |
| Late 40s | Birth of the Cool: Miles Davis, Gil Evans, Gerry Mulligan. |
| 1950s | Commencement of the abandonment of rules in Western Society. Enhanced social awareness. |
| mid-1950s | Bebop evolves into hard bop. |
| 1956 | Rock 'n' roll comes to town (Elvis Presley); electric guitar comes to prominence in popular culture. Jazz becomes less popular and takes on more classical styles – evolves to higher art forms. |
| Late 50s | Rock 'n' roll developed (Buddy Holly and others, Cliff Richard and the Shadows in UK). Skiffle invented in UK (Lonnie Donnegan). |
| 1959 | Free jazz created (Ornette Coleman). |

| | |
|---|---|
| 1960s | The age of the Permissive Society: sex, drugs and rock 'n' roll.<br>Fight begins for civil rights in the USA.<br>Free jazz develops: Ornette Coleman, John Coltrane, Archie Shepp, Cecil Taylor. |
| 1961 | Rhythm and Blues popularised (John Mayall, Alexis Korner, Paul Butterfield). |
| 1962 | The Beatles' first record for Parlophone: *Love Me Do*.<br>Creation of the 'Beat music' genre.<br>Jazz becomes minority interest, abandoned by popular audiences in favour of other music forms (Miles Davis, John Coltrane).<br>The injection of American styles into British R&B played by jazz-trained musicians takes place in the London club scene. (John McLaughlin, Brian Auger, Dick Heckstall-Smith, Ginger Baker, Jack Bruce, Graham Bond.) |
| 1965 | Cult of the electric guitar begins with Hendrix, Clapton, Page, Green and Beck.<br>Rock music emerges as a developed form.<br>First keyboard synthesisers appear.<br>Recognised fusions begin: rock with jazz (Blood Sweat & Tears, Hendrix, Cream, Colosseum, Soft Machine), jazz with rock (Graham Bond); folk with rock (Bob Dylan); funk with jazz (Sly Stone); soul with jazz (James Brown) |
| 1968-9 | Miles Davis embraces jazz-rock-ethnic fusion. |
| 1970s | Fusions continue: jazz with world music, jazz with classical (third stream), jazz with electronic music.<br>Commercialisation of fusion music grows: pop with jazz (Paul Simon, Steely Dan, Quincy Jones, Van Morrison); funk/ soul with jazz (The Brecker Brothers, Stevie Wonder, the Crusaders); folk with jazz (Joni Mitchell, Jesse Colin Young)<br>Keyboard synthesiser technologies mature |
| 1975-6 | Punk rock kills the need for skill in music (Sex Pistols, The Clash). |
| 1976-80 | Miles Davis 'retires'. |
| Late 70s | Jazz-rock is considered 'dead'.<br>Return to Forever and Mahavishnu Orchestra disband.<br>Weather Report soldier on into the 80s.<br>New forms of jazz-fusion emerge: Pat Metheny Group, Brecker Brothers. |

| | |
|---|---|
| 1980s | Guitar synthesisers developed and taken up by Pat Metheny, John McLaughlin. |
| | Wind synthesisers (EWI) developed and taken up by Michael Brecker and Tom Scott. |
| | Jazz-fusion thrives despite much criticism. |
| | Miles Davis returns to it, Chick Corea Elektric Band formed. |
| | Joe Zawinul reinvents himself. |
| | Herbie Hancock invents hip-hop. |
| | Mahavishnu Orchestra reforms. |
| | Jaco Pastorius stuns. |
| | Pat Metheny Group soars. |
| | Steps Ahead impress. |
| | David Sanborn permeates everywhere |
| | Jazz-pop evolves into smooth jazz (Yellowjackets, Spyro Gyra, Kenny G, Rippingtons, Nelson Rangell). |
| Mid-80s | Computers revolutionise music making and recording (Herbie Hancock). |
| | CD format displaces vinyl discs. |
| Late 80s | Smooth jazz peaks with the likes of the GRP record label and Jazz FM radio. |
| | Jazz-fusion becomes a natural part of TV and film themes. |
| 1990s | Many serious jazzers revert to traditional forms of acoustic jazz. |
| | Homogenisation of jazz-fusion into popular forms complete. |
| 2000s | The age of the music download; demise of the CD commences. |
| | Jazz becomes a 'niche' art form, mysterious to the general public. |
| 2008-9 | Chick Corea rediscovers jazz-fusion briefly with Five Peace Band and reformed Return To Forever. |
| 2010s | John McLaughlin's 4$^{th}$ Dimension continues to develop jazz-fusion. |
| | Jazz-fusion is best thought of as 'progressive' music, played by a range of bands formed across broad geographical areas. |

# PART 3: Significant Contributions to Jazz-Fusion

## Early jazz-fusion

Many people speak of a favourite album that had a big effect on their lives, usually at an early age when they are musically immature and impressionable. For me, it was *Collaboration* (1964), a disc by the Modern Jazz Quartet with Laurindo Almeida. It was one of the first jazz albums that I had ever heard. At the time, in early 1969, I was 18 years old and had been playing guitar seriously for five years. I had specialised in classical music and flamenco that I played on nylon-stringed Spanish acoustic instruments. In those days, my record collection was almost non-existent. I had not been exposed to jazz at all, except for what in the UK was called 'Trad Jazz' played by the likes of Kenny Ball or Acker Bilk, music that is perhaps better described as a version of Dixieland Jazz. I had just become aware of the sound of the bossa nova. A couple of songs – *Girl From Ipanema* and *One Note Samba* had been hits in the pop charts – so when I heard the magnificent version of the second of these tunes played by Laurindo Almeida, I was bowled over for a number of reasons. First, Almeida was a magnificent guitarist playing my own instrument in the classical style. Second, he seemed to have taken the classical music that I had been studying so hard and mixed a large dollop of the Brazilian sound that I, and many others, found exciting. Third, there were some chords that were so colourful that they literally made my spine tingle. That was jazz!

The tune *One Note Samba* was the real start of it. After a classical solo introduction (with no obvious rhythm) that lasted for a couple of minutes, the wonderful bossa nova rhythm suddenly broke out, only to be engulfed by a mouth-watering swash of sound from Milt Jackson's vibraphone. The music swung in a way that I had not experienced before and it gave me an irresistible desire to spend all my time learning to play the piece, especially the difficult solo introduction. I have been playing it ever since.

From the first time I heard this music, I was, of course, listening to my first jazz-fusion album. Of course, I did not recognise it as fusion: the idea had not been coherently formulated at this point. What we now see is that the album was very significant indeed. At the time of its recording in 1964, some jazz musicians had a strong interest in playing classical music. One was Jacques Loussier who, in 1959, formed the Play Bach Trio to do just that. Four albums were released on Decca Records in sequential years in which the musicians simply took Bach compositions and added a jazz rhythm. It was an example of what became known as the Third Stream, a term that was intended to describe the true hybridisation of jazz with classical music – a jazz-fusion, in other words. Stan

Getz had already played some Third Stream music on *Focus* (1961), a collaborative project with composer Eddie Sauter. The idea of jazzing-up Bach gained much currency. Thus, for example, the Modern Jazz Quartet (with Almeida) used it on *Collaboration* (1964), for the fourth track, *Fugue in A Minor* by J S Bach. In most instances, the fusion was minimal, as Bach's notes remained largely unaltered, but with bass and drums added to make the music swing. In the MJQ recording, even with Brazilian musician Almeida in the quintet, this is also the case, except for a lovely flourish from Jackson's vibes at the end, as if to say, "OK, that's classical music. Now listen to THIS!"

From where we are today, Almeida's presence in this context was unusual enough, but the jazz-fusion represented an entirely new level. The MJQ included three tracks, *Silver*, *Trieste* and *Valeria* that were straight jazz pieces, with Almeida included in the arrangements. It is true that, in these, there is a minimal amount of guitar improvisation in the true jazz style, and he could hardly have been expected to play like American jazz electric guitarists Jim Hall, Herb Ellis or Wes Montgomery, especially since he was using an unamplified nylon-stringed acoustic instrument (like me). Nevertheless, Almeida played some very pleasing solo passages, mostly in his usual chordal style, with the melody emphasised from within. There was a short track called *Foi A Saudade* that allowed Almeida to play more in his Brazilian style. The final track, however, was another popular inclusion with Almeida playing the slow movement of Rodrigo's *Concierto de Aranjuez*; the MJQ played a John Lewis arrangement of the orchestral score. This *Concierto* had been written in the early twentieth century and with its strong Spanish flavours had become the most popular piece for classical guitar and orchestra; British guitar virtuoso John Williams was kept busy playing it in front of a symphony orchestra throughout the 1960s. It was Miles Davis who had made the *Concierto* visible to jazz musicians by including an arrangement of it on his album *Sketches of Spain* (1959). Hence, it is not surprising to find it included on *Collaboration*. What we find on this recording is a most interesting combination of Third Stream music, mainstream jazz and bossa nova, in which four American jazz musicians join forces with a Brazilian acoustic guitarist. The album is a triumph, but it was not the first in this particular kind of jazz-fusion.

The 1960s craze for bossa nova was initiated by the release of the Brazilian film *Black Orpheus* (1959) with a soundtrack of rich Brazilian rhythms and melodies created by Luis Bonfa (1922-01) and Antonio Carlos Jobim (1927-94), both of whom – like Laurindo Almeida (1917-95) – played Spanish acoustic guitars. "The gentle laid-back qualities of the samba seemed ideally suited for blending with the American Cool Jazz idiom and for a period of five years or so the music was a huge popular success, led by the great American saxophonist Stan Getz (1927-91), and thanks to his friendships with Bonfa, Jobim and others." [1]

Naturally, it was music focussed very much on the acoustic nylon-stringed Spanish-style guitar, and there was an emerging bridge into Brazilian-American jazz from the popular British interest in classical guitar-based music as popularised by such musicians as Julian Bream and John Williams. I, for one, was seduced into jazz through this route, a young guitarist learning the classical style, but with inevitable teenage love of pop music thanks to the Beatles. This was my own natural bridge into jazz, the bossa nova was my port of entry and I never afterwards sought repatriation. My late teens and early twenties were spent perfecting as many of the wonderful guitar sounds on the Getz/Byrd/Gilberto/Jobim albums as my technique would allow. Later, the seduction was completed when, totally in love with the sound of Stan Getz, I set aside my guitar in favour of the saxophone.

Bossa nova was a true fusion. Beginning as a "soft, pared-down version of the samba" [1] the minimalist rhythm was then infused with sophisticated chords and harmonies derived from American jazz. This process was driven primarily by Brazilian guitarists Jobim, Bonfa and Joao Gilberto (b1931), aided and abetted from the American side by Getz and guitarist Charlie Byrd (1925-99). Jobim was a musician and composer who collaborated with lyricist Vinicius de Moraes to provide inspiration for *Black Orpheus*. It resulted in two smash hits, *The Girl from Ipanema* and *Insensatez*. The former will be forever associated with its vocalist, Astrud Gilberto (b1940), Joao's wife. Joao Gilberto first collaborated with Jobim in the early 1950s and in 1958 wrote *Bim Bom Chega de Saudade*. This single gave rise to Gilberto's first album in Brazil in 1959 and these were the first bossa nova recordings. Almeida was already earning a living in the USA when the bossa waves broke on the shore and he was one of the first to capitalise on what would become a new jazz form. Although he was spotlighted through his tour with MJQ in 1964, he had already made recordings and many performances with Stan Getz.

It was Charlie Byrd who introduced Getz to the bossa nova in 1961 and the two men recorded *Jazz Samba* (1962), which drew heavily on Gilberto's music and made famous the tune *One Note Samba*. Master-craftsman Getz's smooth style and tone were perfectly suited to the current taste of the American public and the album was a huge hit. Unusually for a jazz-fusion, it was well received by the critics. At last, jazz had entered the popular music marketplace. A follow-up album, *Getz/Gilberto* (1963), became one of the biggest jazz-pop hits of all time as it promoted the songs that were now familiar to many listeners – *Girl from Ipanema*, *Desafinado* and *Corcovado*. Realising a good thing when they saw it, Getz's record company, Verve, capitalised on the unexpected but very welcome popularity by issuing yet more recordings. *Jazz Samba Encore* (1963) was a recording of Getz with Luiz Bonfa, and in the same year Verve released *Stan*

*Getz with Guest Artist Laurindo Almeida* (1963). The following year came a repeat of the successful formula with *Getz/Gilberto #2* (1964).

Although the bossa nova soon faded from the jazz scene, the music became entirely absorbed into western culture and remains popular today. Brazilian music had graduated and made a permanent mark on the history of jazz. It was the first penetration of a new foreign ethnic music culture into jazz from outside the USA. Later, that phenomenon would be extended to include music from a number of cultures, and musicians such as Miles Davis, Wayne Shorter, Joe Zawinul, Herbie Hancock and Pat Metheny would drive forward the new jazz genre known as World Music. These were new jazz-fusions in their own right for in each case jazz had been mixed with folk music from a variety of different ethnic origins – mostly Africa and Latin America. The principle of jazz-fusion was now well established and it was clear that any kind of music from anywhere in the world could be blended with jazz.

## Jazz-rock fusion

Although the jazz-fusion with Brazilian music was important to me, it is the fusion with rock that I would now like to concentrate on once more. I have described the events quite thoroughly in Part 2 so now it is time to explore the work of the most significant musicians. A diagram is included on p161 which shows where I think their styles belong.

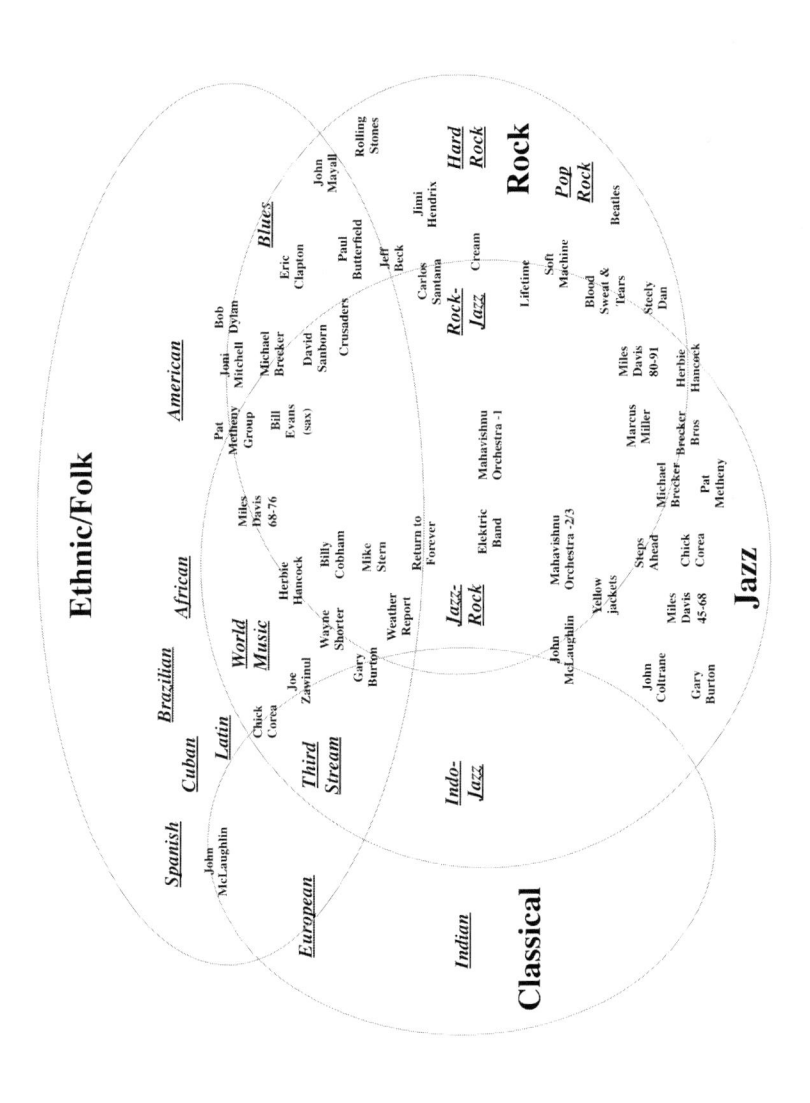

*Figure 6: A Venn diagram showing the approximate positions of musicians discussed in these pages.*

# Miles Davis (1926-91)

*Miles Davis, 28 June 1985, at the Théâtre St-Denis in Montreal.
(Photo courtesy of Festival International de Jazz de Montréal 1985)*

Miles Davis's footprints are to be found over a large proportion of the jazz space in the diagram shown in Figure 5 - more than any other musician. Yet here lies another Davis paradox. Miles never had a popular hit, but he did succeed in making himself the most influential and successful jazz musician of all time, an influence that spread far beyond mere jazz music. His album *Kind of Blue* (1959) was Number 12 in the list of 500 greatest albums of all time. [2] Today, more than two decades after his death, Davis probably sells more CDs than any other jazz musician.

His career began in the mid-1940s when bebop was becoming established in the clubs of New York and Chicago. Davis worked with all of the important jazz musicians of the time, most notably Charlie Parker and John Coltrane. However, Davis was not a great technical trumpet player and, although he is widely regarded as a major contributor to bebop jazz, his natural style did not sit comfortably with the bebop style of rapid, complex melodies and brash, energetic performances. Furthermore, his playing was prone to frequent mis-hit notes, but Miles turned the resulting fragility of sound to his own advantage. Curiously, fans of Miles Davis profess that this irregularity is actually one of the great strengths of his style, especially when muted. Davis soon realised that he was more comfortable in situations that required a slower, more thoughtful melodic approach. As a result, with the help of composer/arranger Gil Evans, he set himself at the forefront of a new school of jazz known as 'The Cool'. This was characterised by moods that were more introspective, melodies and tempos that were less frantic. As important was the movement's extrapolation beyond music and into an entirely new social style or fashion. These 'hip' people dressed in smart clothes (threads). A relaxed, laid-back approach and overt sexuality was underpinned by a necessarily covert (it was illegal) but still strong association with hard drugs. In a word, it was 'Cool'. Even his first name was synonymous with cool, and when the name 'Miles' was uttered, everyone knew who was being discussed.

The addictive drugs, however, became a serious impediment to musical progress and the early 50s were a time when Davis should have been in his prime. Several years were wasted in the fight against heroin addiction that could well have cost him his life. Davis kicked his habit and from 1955 became engaged in several projects. First he got a contract for a substantial series of recordings released on the Prestige label. Of particular note was a series of albums released in 1956 called *Relaxin'*, *Workin'*, *Steamin'* and *Cookin' with the Miles Davis Quintet*. Following the death of Charlie Parker, the cult's leader, Davis made such an impact at the 1955 Newport Jazz Festival that he landed a far more lucrative contract with market leader Columbia Records and soon released the major album entitled *'Round About Midnight* (1956).

Miles worked with Gil Evans again from 1957. It was to be a masterstroke, for Miles could concentrate on developing and applying his cool approach to trumpet playing, which included his trademarked sound with a Harmon mute. Even if Davis was to have no clear presence in the pop music arena, the sound of his muted trumpet is probably the one that most people came to associate with jazz. Miles's latest project with Evans was with a large group of musicians, and resulted in a rare recording with what was essentially a Big Band. *Miles Ahead* (1957) was released under the grouping Miles Davis +19 and it was another of many triumphs for Davis. He continued to record with his small groups, and another important album was *Milestones* (1958), but the successes of his partnership with Gil Evans continued in parallel. Another joint album contained arrangements of Gershwin's music, *Porgy and Bess* (1958). Almost by definition this was jazz-fusion of a kind, since it was strongly focussed on the blues. However, Miles's first real step into jazz-fusion was another project with Gil Evans that mixed jazz with ethnic Spanish flavours, represented by *Sketches of Spain* (1959). Its commercial success greatly assisted in the popularisation of Rodrigo's composition for guitar and symphony orchestra, *Concierto de Aranjuez*.

These were casual jazz-fusions: there was no intention by anybody to create a new sub-genre of music. Each project was individually inspired and, even if it extended to a second or third album, there was no great change in philosophy, no revolution or paradigm shift of the kind that would occur ten years later with the hybridisation of jazz and rock. So, in the late 1950s, it was business as usual, except that for Miles, nothing was 'usual' – for him, everything at this point in history was exceptional.

In 1958 Miles formed a new quintet with Cannonball Adderley (alto saxophone), John Coltrane (tenor saxophone), Bill Evans (piano), Paul Chambers (bass) and Jimmy Cobb (drums). This band would become known as Miles's 'First Great Quintet'. It was also a move that, in many ways, enabled Coltrane to develop from an unknown, comparative novice into the major musician he would soon become. Coltrane was inexperienced and, though he was clearly gifted, it was by no means obvious that he was a musical genius. Under Davis's leadership, there is no doubt that Coltrane acquired the experience he needed to move on to greater things. In January 1959, this band recorded what is now regarded as the best jazz album of all - *Kind of Blue*. There was no fusion here - just the redefinition of what people call the 'mainstream' of jazz. Mainstream was always the centre, the middle-ground of the genre, but the music was continuously evolving. Jazz mainstream could not remain forever rooted in its Dixieland, swing-time roots, or even in its bebop or cool phases, no matter how popular or how successful. Jazz needed to move on and Miles Davis was its unelected leader with his own personal philosophy of 'living in the moment'. *Kind of Blue* had a massive impact on everyone – it still does when people hear it for the first time. It introduced into jazz a new way of playing, but it was not jazz-fusion.

No band, no matter how good, lasts for ever, especially when it is populated with great artists. Coltrane was destined for even greater things and he soon moved on towards the highest planes of artistry. Davis needed to consider his own next moves. Soon it all came together when he recruited two very young, new and brilliant musicians: pianist Herbie Hancock and the 17-year-old drumming phenomenon, Tony Williams. Alongside the rather older (but equally brilliant) Wayne Shorter and bassist Ron Carter, Davis formed a new quintet that would eclipse even his earlier band. The series of albums that was released from 1963-68 by the 'Second Great Quintet' is regarded as one of the most remarkable in the history of jazz. Again, there were no signs of fusion, but, with the amazingly gifted composer Shorter at his side, Davis led jazz music to some of its greatest intellectual heights. This was truly music for the connoisseur - difficult to approach without a great deal of concentration, yet offering the most intellectually rewarding experiences to those who made the effort. This band was so far ahead of all others in jazz that the step up in achievement seemed almost supernatural.

Davis's Second Great Quintet was, of course, making its mark at a time when the rest of the music world was in total revolution. The move towards an ever-increasing level of sophistication in music was contrary to the intellectual direction of popular culture. Davis's band, no matter how good it was, could not achieve the levels of record sales necessary to sustain him in the style to which he (and his record company) had become accustomed. Davis knew that things had to change and he needed a new style. Towards the end of the 1960s, he began to associate with rock musicians and others from beyond the world of jazz. His wife, Betty Mabry was a strong influence. She had many friends in the rock music business and encouraged Miles to listen to their records. Gradually, Miles began to see the way forward. He knew that his own music must include recognition of what was happening in the world of rock music.

He began to experiment with various ideas that drew upon some aspects of rock within a jazz environment. Electric guitar seemed an essential ingredient, but at first he couldn't quite get what he wanted. He tried several recordings with electric guitar players that seemed to come to nothing, and then began to focus more upon the use of electric keyboards at the expense of guitar. Many writers report that the first real jazz-fusion album was *In a Silent Way* (1969), a project that involved three electric keyboards played by Herbie Hancock, Joe Zawinul and Chick Corea. There *was* an electric guitar too. John McLaughlin had been invited to the USA from England to join Tony Williams' new band, Lifetime, but almost at once was drafted in to play electric guitar in Miles's experimental recording sessions. Earlier, Dave Holland had himself been invited to join Miles from England; he played acoustic (oddly, not electric) bass. Davis chose this very unusual combination of instruments in a way that seemed to miss the whole point of what he'd been looking for; it really did not draw in the rock content that we might have expected. Having decided to include electric guitar sounds, he didn't want to hear rock sounds. Instead, he focused on free jazz ideas, building on just musical fragments with no strong element of composition to back it all up. He rationalised that, having planted the seed of an idea in the minds of his musicians he expected them to do the rest. His philosophy of living in the moment created spontaneous, but often incoherent collections of improvisations with little to hold them all together. The recorded music that resulted was generated by his producer, Teo Macero, who introduced another novel idea into jazz – that of splicing together segments of music after the recording had been completed. Many listeners, for whom Miles could do nothing wrong, loved this new music. They proclaimed it as the new jazz-fusion, one that genuinely hybridised rock and jazz.

Forty years on, it is almost impossible to appreciate the effect that *In A Silent Way* (1969) and the follow-up album, *Bitches Brew* (1970), had on listeners. When people heard these albums for the first time, they felt it was truly life-changing music. The music was just a small part of the overall impact, which seemed to convey an entirely new philosophy of life with resonances of Ginsberg, Kerouac and Timothy Leary. The albums became icons for societal changes that young people wanted so badly. Sting, for one, wrote how he was played *Bitches Brew* by a friend who "places the needle on the edge of the turning disc and then lies back indulgently on a pile of cushions to observe its effect on me, as if he's just administered a powerful drug." [3] There were many others who felt that way.

The period of Davis's career from 1970 until 1976 is probably the most controversial, with commentators in stark disagreement about the merits or otherwise of the music. Miles continued to develop these ideas, expanding his use of complex African rhythms through percussion instrumentation, and giving electric guitarists increasing amounts of freedom to blow their fuses. The exciting sound and mature presence of Wayne Shorter's tenor sax was replaced by rabid soprano saxophone sounds from a series of clever players like Steve Grossman and David Liebman. In accordance with Miles's mantra of living 'in the moment', it was a style that thrived on live performance. Thus the albums from this period are almost exclusively concert recordings, both official and unofficial. The presentational format of Davis's gigs took on almost surreal proportions as his own performances became increasingly bizarre and, to many ears, unmusical. This jazz-fusion formula did not stand up well alongside other things that were being done by the very musicians who had played alongside him in 1969-70. They had left his band to capitalise on their own new kinds of jazz-fusion.

In my opinion, the period from 1970-76 was the least successful in the history of Miles Davis, so that by 1976 he was exhausted and, though idolised, still commercially unsuccessful compared to his earlier sidemen. To his credit, Davis recognised that too. The disappointment contributed to his tiredness and he withdrew from the world for four years, a time of personal darkness with little hope for the future. Eventually, some close friends coaxed him out of retirement, notably his nephew Vincent Wilburn, who persuaded him to reform his band and go out on the road with a newer version of jazz-fusion. Since, by definition, the music was intended to be more commercial, it displeased many of the jazz *cognoscenti* who regard this period of Davis's career as his worst. Others, like me, who loved the sounds of this new jazz-rock formula, found the new music far more to their liking. There was colour and composition. There was energy and rhythm, funk and genuine rock in the music. To us, the final decade from 1980 until his death in 1991 was a period of great excitement and entertainment, when Miles did what he had always done best - to encourage and develop some of the best new talent around.

The release of the *Man With the Horn* (1981) was another of the many milestones that marked this exceptional musician's life. At last, playing alongside Mike Stern (guitar) and Bill Evans (sax) we could hear that he had finally assimilated the obvious, logical formula for jazz-rock fusion. Once again, Miles Davis's popularity was great, but this time lodged amongst the ordinary people that he had originally set out (and failed) to reach in the early 70s. By now, his trumpet style didn't matter much. His playing was thin and quite minimal, although his tone and accuracy, especially in his weaker high registers were better than ever, but it was his very presence that brought out the best from his sidemen. As a result, Miles was responsible for the appearance of a new generation of wonderful musicians like Bill Evans (saxophone), Mike Stern, John Scofield, Marcus Miller and Kenny Garrett, as well as a clutch of very good albums. His work with Marcus Miller is probably the most innovative from this period, and resulted in the remarkable albums *Tutu* (1986) and *Amandla* (1989). Another project with Danish jazz composer Palle Mikkelborg resulted in *Aura* (1989), an album that was inspirational in the writing of this series of books. Apart from these works, and a few somewhat haphazard studio recordings such as *Star People* (1983), *Decoy* (1983) and *You're Under Arrest* (1985), most of his final output was focussed on recordings of his live performances. This new, unexpected phase in his career revitalised Davis and allowed him to continue to create jazz and entertain live audiences right up to the time of his death in September 1991. He was 64 - a very good age for someone who had abused his body so seriously for so long.

Many have argued that Miles Davis led the way in the formulation of jazz-rock fusion. I find it hard to accept that a trumpeter could be credited with the creation of this new genre of music, but of course it is not as a trumpeter that he is being examined. Miles Davis was the undisputed leader of the jazz movement, and from 1968 at least, the word from him was that jazz-rock was cool. Miles was a musical fashion designer with the same kind of influence in his world that Bill Gates has exerted over software. Bill Gates didn't write much of the code for Windows software, but he sure as hell contributed a lot towards its existence.

In 1968, at the formal start of the period of jazz-rock fusion, Miles Davis was the undisputed King, and led the way with his own brand of fusion that, whilst it included electric instruments, had free jazz as a significant part of its formula. His albums *In a Silent Way* (1969) and *Bitches Brew* (1970) are regarded by many as two of the most important in jazz. He progressed into the early 1970s with greater emphasis on electric guitars and percussion-led polyrhythms, but was not able to develop the popularly successful albums that he so earnestly desired. His insistence on keeping total spontaneity, minimum forms and a tedious monochordal drone or vamp was, in my opinion, the wrong choice. The evidence of the 1980s and 90s is that the best jazz-fusion needed to contain a lot more than just the primal elements. Of the many top musicians he attracted into his bands at this time, some, like Keith Jarrett and David Liebman, preferred to remain in the jazz mainstream and decided not to pursue the jazz-fusion front. Others, like John McLaughlin, Chick Corea, Joe Zawinul, Wayne Shorter and Herbie Hancock, moved on to create their own bands and to release albums that became the jazz-fusion milestones of music history.

Partial Discography of Miles Davis
1948: The Complete Birth Of The Cool, Miles Davis
1954: Walkin', Miles Davis All Stars
1955: Blue Moods, Miles Davis
1955: Miles Davis And Milt Jackson Quintet/Sextet, Miles Davis
1955: Miles Davis Volume 1, Miles Davis
1955: Miles Davis Volume 2, Miles Davis
1955: The Musings Of Miles, Miles Davis
1956: 'Round About Midnight, Miles Davis
1956: Collectors' Items, Miles Davis
1956: Dig, Miles Davis and Sonny Rollins
1957: Bags Groove, Miles Davis
1957: Blue Haze - Prestige, Miles Davis
1957: Cookin' With The Miles Davis Quintet, Miles Davis Quintet
1957: Miles Ahead, Miles Davis + 19
1958: Ascenseur Pour L'Echafaud, Miles Davis
1958: Miles Davis And The Modern Jazz Giants, Miles Davis
1958: Milestones - Columbia, Miles Davis
1958: Porgy And Bess, Miles Davis
1958: Relaxin' With The Miles Davis Quintet, Miles Davis Quintet
1959: Kind Of Blue, Miles Davis
1959: Workin' With The Miles Davis Quintet, Miles Davis Quintet
1960: Sketches Of Spain, Miles Davis
1960: With John Coltrane In Copenhagen 1960, Miles Davis Quintet with John Coltrane
1961: In Person: Friday And Saturday Nights At The Blackhawk Complete, Miles Davis Quintet
1961: In Person: Friday Night At The Blackhawk San Francisco Volume 1, Miles Davis Quintet
1961: In Person: Saturday Night At The Blackhawk San Francisco Volume 2, Miles Davis Quintet
1961: Miles Davis At Carnegie Hall: The Legendary Performances Of May 19, 1961, Miles Davis
1961: Someday My Prince Will Come, Miles Davis Sextet

1961: Steamin' With The Miles Davis Quintet, Miles Davis Quintet
1962: Miles Davis At Carnegie Hall: The Complete Concert, Miles Davis Quintet
1963: Miles In Antibes, Miles Davis Quintet with John Coltrane
1963: Quiet Nights, Miles Davis
1963: Seven Steps To Heaven, Miles Davis
1964: At Newport 1958, Miles Davis
1964: Miles Davis In Europe, Miles Davis Quintet with John Coltrane
1964: The Complete Concert 1964, Miles Davis
1965: E.S.P., Miles Davis
1965: Miles In Berlin, Miles Davis Quintet
1965: My Funny Valentine, Miles Davis
1966: Four And More, Miles Davis
1967: Miles Smiles, Miles Davis
1967: Sorcerer, Miles Davis
1968: Miles In The Sky, Miles Davis
1968: Nefertiti, Miles Davis
1969: Filles de Kilimanjaro, Miles Davis
1969: In A Silent Way, Miles Davis
1969: Miles Davis - Village, Miles Davis
1969: Miles In Tokyo, Miles Davis
1970: At Fillmore: Live At The Fillmore East, Miles Davis
1970: Bitches Brew, Miles Davis
1970: Isle Of Wight, Miles Davis
1971: A Tribute To Jack Johnson, Miles Davis
1971: Live-Evil, Miles Davis
1972: On The Corner, Miles Davis
1973: Black Beauty: Miles Davis At Fillmore West, Miles Davis
1973: In Concert: Live At Philharmonic Hall, Miles Davis
1973: Jazz At The Plaza, Miles Davis Sextet
1974: Big Fun, Miles Davis
1974: Get Up With It, Miles Davis
1975: Pangaea, Miles Davis
1976: Agharta, Miles Davis
1976: Water Babies, Miles Davis
1977: Dark Magus: Live At Carnegie Hall, Miles Davis
1977: In Paris: Live At The Festival International de Jazz, Miles Davis, Tadd Dameron
1979: Circle In The Round, Miles Davis
1979: First Miles, Miles Davis
1981: Directions, Miles Davis
1981: The Man With The Horn, Miles Davis
1982: We Want Miles, Miles Davis
1983: Star People, Miles Davis
1984: Decoy, Miles Davis
1985: At Last!, Miles Davis and the Lighthouse All-Stars
1985: You're Under Arrest, Miles Davis
1986: Tutu, Miles Davis
1987: Live Miles: More Music From The Legendary Carnegie Hall Concert, Miles Davis
1987: Music From Siesta, Miles Davis / Marcus Miller
1989: Amandla, Miles Davis
1989: Aura, Miles Davis
1989: Double Image - Crown, Miles Davis
1989: Greek Theater '88 Oslo '87, Miles Davis
1990: Live In 1958-59. Featuring John Coltrane, The Miles Davis All-Stars
1990: Miles Davis - Jazz Door, Miles Davis
1990: Miles In Paris 1989 [DVD], Miles Davis
1991: Dingo, Miles Davis, Michel Legrand
1991: Doo-Bop, Miles Davis
1991: Live At The Hi-Hat / Boston, Miles Davis and the Hi-Hat All Stars
1991: Sing In Singen, Miles Davis
1991: XV. Miles Davis And John Coltrane: Their Greatest Concert, Miles Davis, John Coltrane
1992: Black Devil, Miles Davis
1992: In Stockholm 1960 Complete, Miles Davis, John Coltrane, Sonny Stitt
1992: Miles! Miles! Miles! Live In Japan '81, Miles Davis
1992: No (More) Blues, Miles Davis Quintet
1993: 1969 Miles: Festiva de Juan Pins, Miles Davis Quintet
1993: Live In Zurich 1960, Miles Davis Quintet with John Coltrane
1993: Miles And Quincy: Live At Montreux, Miles Davis

1993: Miles Davis And The Jazz Giants, Miles Davis
1993: Time After Time USA 1989 - Jazz Door, Miles Davis
1994: En Concert Avec Europe 1: Olympia 11 Juillet 1973, Miles Davis
1994: Live At Newport 1958 And 1963, Miles Davis, Thelonius Monk
1995: Another Bitches Brew: Two Concerts In Belgrade, Miles Davis
1995: Live: From his Last Concert In Miramas, Miles Davis
1996: Gemini - Crown, Miles Davis
1996: Live Around The World, Miles Davis
1996: Live At The Barrel, Jimmy Forrest / Miles Davis
1997: Fat Time, Miles Davis
1998: Live, Miles Davis
1998: Panthalassa: The Music Of Miles Davis 1969-1974, Miles Davis
1999: Perfect Way - Delta, Miles Davis
1999: Time After Time - Delta, Miles Davis
2000: Live Directions Switzerland 22.10.71, Miles Davis
2000: Live In Avignon 1988, Miles Davis
2000: Paris Jazz Concert Olympia Jul. 11th, 1973, Miles Davis
2000: The Essential Live In Stockholm, Miles Davis / John Coltrane
2001: At La Villette [DVD], Miles Davis
2001: Live At The Fillmore East (March 7, 1970): It's About That Time, Miles Davis
2001: Live: Olympia 20 Mars 1960 Part 1, Miles Davis
2001: Live: Olympia 20 Mars 1960 Part 2, Miles Davis
2001: Sorcery In Antwerp, The Miles Davis Quintet
2002: 1960/61, Miles Davis Quintet with John Coltrane
2002: Live In Munich [DVD], Miles Davis
2002: Olympia Oct. 11th, 1960 First Concert, Miles Davis and Sonny Stitt
2002: Olympia Oct. 11th, 1960 Second Concert, Miles Davis and Sonny Stitt
2002: Olympia: Mar. 20th 1960 Part 1, Miles Davis

2002: Olympia: Mar. 20th 1960 Part 2, Miles Davis
2002: The Complete Live Recordings 1948-1955, Miles Davis
2003: Complete Performances With The Lighthouse All-Stars, Chet Baker & Miles Davis
2005: Amsterdam Concert, Miles Davis Quintet featuring Barney Wilen
2005: Ezz-Thetic, Lee Konitz, Miles Davis, Teddy Charles, Jimmy Raney
2005: Human Nature Live, Miles Davis
2005: It's About That Time: Live In Montreux 1969, Miles Davis Quintet
2005: Live In Montreal [DVD], Miles Davis
2005: Miles Davis: The Cool Jazz Sound [DVD], Miles Davis
2005: Munich Concert, Miles Davis
2006: Complete Live In Paris 1949, Miles Davis - Tadd Dameron Quintet
2006: European Tour '56, Miles Davis with the Modern Jazz Quartet and Lester Young
2006: Live In Den Haag, Miles Davis Quintet featuring John Coltrane
2006: Live In Germany 1988 [DVD], Miles Davis
2006: Live In Saint Louis 1956, Miles Davis Quintet with John Coltrane
2006: Manchester Concert: Complete 1960 Live At The Free Trade Hall, Miles Davis
2006: Winter In Europe 1967, Miles Davis Quintet
2007: At Hammersmith Odeon, London 1982 [DVD], Miles Davis
2007: Live At The 1963 Monterey Jazz Festival, Miles Davis Quintet
2007: Live In Milan 1964, Miles Davis Quintet
2007: Michel Legrand Meets Miles Davis, Michel Legrand/ Miles Davis
2007: Milan 1964 - DVD, Miles Davis Quintet
2007: Miles And Coltrane Quintet 'Live', Miles Davis / John Coltrane
2007: So What [DVD], Miles Davis
2007: The Complete Live Recordings 1956-1957, Miles Davis

2008: Live In Poland 1983, Miles Davis Septet
2008: Live In Poland 1983 [DVD], Miles Davis
2008: The 1971 Berlin Concert [DVD], Miles Davis / Keith Jarrett
2008: Time After Time Live At The Philharmonic Concert Hall Complete Edition [DVD, Miles Davis
2009: Birdland Jam Session June 30 1950, Miles Davis
2009: Live In Vienna 1973, Miles Davis Septet
2009: Milestones - Hallmark, Miles Davis
2010: Complete Live At The Blue Coronet 1969, Miles Davis
2010: Live At Newport 1966 And 1967, Miles Davis
2010: Live At The Hollywood Bowl 1981, Miles Davis Sextet
2010: Live In Berlin 1969, Miles Davis Quintet
2010: Live In Rome And Copenhagen 1969, Miles Davis Quintet
2010: Live In Stockholm 1973 [DVD], Miles Davis
2010: The 1960 German Concerts, Miles Davis Quintet with John Coltrane
2010: The 1969 Berlin Concert [DVD], Miles Davis Quintet
2010: The Montreal Concert, Miles Davis
2010: Warsaw Concert 1983, Miles Davis
2011: Bitches Brew Live, Miles Davis
2011: The Unissued Japanese Concerts, Miles Davis Quintet
2011: Live In Europe 1967: The Bootleg Series, Miles Davis Quintet

## Joe Zawinul (1932-2007), Wayne Shorter (b1933): Weather Report

Wayne Shorter, jazz composer *par excellence* and member of Miles's Second Great Quintet had stood alongside Miles during his experiments for *In A Silent Way* (1969) and *Bitches Brew* (1970). So too had Joe Zawinul, whom Miles recruited in November 1968 to provide additional electronic piano. Indeed, it was Zawinul who had composed the title track for *In a Silent Way*. Their presence in the new moment for Miles was short-lived, however, for Wayne and Joe saw their own version of the new direction for jazz and the opportunities it presented. In early 1970 they left Miles to form, along with Miroslav Vitous, a new jazz-fusion band called Weather Report.

The band was intended to be about spontaneous group improvisation and based its output upon the strengths of Zawinul and Shorter's compositions. The music was electric and had a unique blend of tonal colours. Some of it was a hybrid with classical European ethnic content, and in the albums *Weather Report* (1971), *I Sing the Body Electric* (1972) and *Live in Tokyo* (1972) there was little evidence of fusion with rock music. With no electric guitar and with Vitous rooted in a rather different jazz genre that was more associated with free jazz than jazz-rock, his presence prevented the band from progressing far into the jazz-rock arena. It didn't take Zawinul long to realise the band's limitations with Vitous in it. In particular, by 1972 John McLaughlin's Mahavishnu Orchestra had achieved a level of commercial success so far achieved only by rock bands. It was clear that something had to change. Vitous, with his classical acoustic upright bass was squeezed out of the band during the recording of *Sweetnighter* (1973). This album stepped away from the original aim of collective improvisation as the business reality won the battle with artistic merit. Though Wayne continued to provide music for the band, there was a greater emphasis on Zawinul's songs, which were more forceful and groove-based. Two major tracks *Boogie Woogie Waltz* and *125th Street Congress*, were augmented with four other tracks and the transition to a proper jazz-rock group had now genuinely begun.

Electric bass guitar exponent Alphonso Johnson was hired for *Mysterious Traveller* (1974). Unusually for a jazz-fusion band, Weather Report almost never used an electric guitar, which was probably just as well, for its absence allowed Joe and Wayne to exploit their unique brand of jazz. *Mysterious Traveller* was a big success and Johnson's funky electric bass was a big part of that. Once it became clear that far greater commercial success was to be achieved by adopting a formula that contained larger amounts of American ethnic music, i.e. blues, funk and rock, the band never looked back. The content of the music became much more orchestrated and Americanised. It was a formula for great success. With the Mahavishnu Orchestra now disbanded, *Tale Spinnin'* (1975) secured the band's place as the leading jazz-fusion band of the time, despite growing competition from Chick Corea (Return to Forever) and Herbie Hancock (Head Hunters) – more of that below. Then, Zawinul was unexpectedly confronted with the electric bass phenomenon called Jaco Pastorius. Joe tried to remain loyal to Johnson, but Pastorius was so extraordinary that, when Johnson decided to move on (perhaps the pressure got to him, who knows?) Pastorius was instantly hired. *Black Market* (1976) contained contributions from both Pastorius and Johnson and was a superb album, but the real storm was created with *Heavy Weather* (1977), an album so exceptionally different that many people would list it as the *best* jazz-rock fusion album. Hurricane Jaco had arrived and the weather conditions became more turbulent by several orders of magnitude.

Jaco Pastorius was at his very best during the years from 1975-80, a period of time when he played for Weather Report. However, he also had a great impact upon other musicians, most notably Joni Mitchell, whose music reached a peak at the same time as she too was investigating the power of jazz-fusion.

Although all of Weather Report's promotional material gave Zawinul and Shorter equal billing, inevitably it was Zawinul's intensely strong personality that came to dominate everything they did. Although he would say different, detached observers saw the self-effacing Wayne occupy less and less of the limelight, culminating in the release of an album *Mr Gone* (1978) which seemed to tacitly admit the disappearance of the saxophone player. Shorter's profile was not helped by the presence of Jaco, whose ego was in continual competition with Zawinul for maximum attention. Shorter didn't give in; he simply didn't compete. He was content to retreat into the shadows during this period, even though the success of Weather Report grew increasingly strong.

In spite of the band's immense success, it did suffer in some way because of an inability to retain a regular drummer. Only when Peter Erskine arrived for *Mr. Gone* (1978) did the situation begin to resolve itself. At last there were five band members who could get on with each other and contribute consistently. The albums *8.30* (1979), *Night Passage* (1980 and *Weather Report 2* (1982), followed, at which point Jaco left the band, fired at last by Zawinul for his extreme misbehaviour. (He was by now, often uncontrollable through severe reactions to drugs and alcohol.) Indeed, the band was slowly disintegrating in any case, and it was only the strong bond between Joe and Wayne that kept things together. The excellent Victor Bailey replaced Jaco, but the writing for the band's demise was on the wall. After four further albums, *Procession* (1983), *Domino Theory* (1984), *Sporting Life* (1985) and *This is This* (1986) the band finally dissolved. Too loyal to make the break he needed, Wayne continued to support Joe, even though his own role was almost reduced to nothing. By the time of the last two albums, his contributions were very small indeed. It is remarkable that Weather Report lasted as long as it did, a fact that bears testament to the strong friendship that Wayne and Joe formed, despite their different personalities.

By the mid-1980s, separation had become inevitable and, as if to prepare for it, the two men began to re-direct their attentions. Wayne began to record music that seemed to refocus on a new kind of jazz-fusion with Brazilian ethnic music. Likewise, Joe began to direct his own attentions to a new jazz-fusion with elements of both North African and European ethnic folk music because of his own roots in Austria. With a continuously varying multinational cohort of talented musicians at his side, Zawinul created a new jazz-fusion that became known simply as World music. His band, the Zawinul Syndicate, lasted until his death in 2007.

Despite making major contributions to both jazz and jazz-fusion since then, both men will always be remembered for Weather Report, a band that existed for 16 years and released as many albums, until 1986. Many people would rate the band amongst the very best jazz-fusion bands of all time, although the range of output varied considerably over the entire period. There is little doubt that the zenith of the band's career occurred during the tenure of Jaco Pastorius on bass, a musician of such creativity and skill that he carried Weather Report to even higher levels than they would otherwise have achieved. The albums *Black Market* (1976) and *Heavy Weather* (1977) were at the pinnacle of jazz-fusion, and today are considered to be uniquely placed in the jazz pantheon. The compositions in those collections were so strong that they moved almost everyone that heard them, in contrast to most of the later output that, whilst still very good by most standards, were not in the same stratospheric level of achievement. By the time that Jaco Pastorius moved on to direct his own career, Weather Report was past its best, although still able to attract some of the largest revenues in jazz at that time. To most observers, Wayne Shorter had become dominated by Joe Zawinul and it had become essential for these two great musicians to split in order for them to realise their own true potentials, rather than be constrained by a partnership that had begun to run dry of inspiration. As one of the world's great saxophone players, Wayne was never limited to playing in jazz-fusion, but his compositional skills were put to great use in the more conventional jazz mainstream. Zawinul, on the other hand, showed just how big a part he had begun to play in the overall direction of Weather Report and, as one of the great jazz electric keyboard/ synthesiser players (along with Herbie Hancock), moved on to become a leader of the World music genre. Perhaps it was his non-American birthright that, in the end, sealed Zawinul's role as arguably the most consistent member of the jazz-fusion group of musicians.

Once his eyes were focussed on jazz-fusion, he never made another record beyond the boundaries he had helped to define.

## Discography of Joe Zawinul

1959: To You with Love, Joe Zawinul Trio
1959: What A Difference A Day Makes, Dinah Washington
1960: The Two Of Us, Dinah Washington and Brook Benton
1961: Nancy Wilson / Cannonball Adderley, Nancy Wilson / Cannonball Adderley
1961: Jazz Casual, Cannonball Adderley, Charles Lloyd
1962: Cannonball In Europe: Live At Comblain-La-Tour, The Cannonball Adderley Sextet
1962: Jazz Workshop Revisited, The Cannonball Adderley Sextet
1962: An Orderly Evolution, The Cannonball Adderley Sextet
1962: Sextet In New York, The Cannonball Adderley Sextet
1962: This Here, The Cannonball Adderley Sextet
1963: Hooray For Cannonball, Cannonball Adderley
1963: The Sextet, Cannonball Adderley
1963: Soulmates, Ben Webster and Joe Zawinul
1963: Lugano 1963, The Cannonball Adderley Sextet
1966: Mercy, Mercy, Mercy! Live At The Club, The Cannonball Adderley Quintet
1966: Money In The Pocket, Joe Zawinul
1966: Money In The Pocket, Cannonball Adderley
1966: Cannonball In Japan, Cannonball Adderley Quintet
1967: 74 Miles Away, The Cannonball Adderley Quintet
1967: Why Am I Treated So Bad?, The Cannonball Adderley Quintet
1967: Radio Nights, Cannonball Adderley
1968: The Rise And Fall Of The Third Stream, Joe Zawinul
1969: Mercy, Mercy, Mercy, Cannonball Adderley
1969: Soul 69, Aretha Franklin

1969: In A Silent Way, Miles Davis
1970: Purple, Miroslav Vitous
1970: Concerto Retitled [live], Joe Zawinul
1970: Country Preacher: Live At Operation Breadbasket, The Cannonball Adderley Quintet
1970: Bitches Brew, Miles Davis
1971: Weather Report 1, Weather Report
1971: Zawinul, Joe Zawinul
1972: I Sing The Body Electric, Weather Report
1973: Sweetnighter, Weather Report
1974: Big Fun, Miles Davis
1974: Mysterious Traveller, Weather Report
1975: Tale Spinnin', Weather Report
1976: Live At Montreux 1976 [DVD], Weather Report
1976: Black Market, Weather Report
1977: Heavy Weather, Weather Report
1977: Live In Tokyo, Weather Report
1978: Mr. Gone, Weather Report
1979: Havana Jam II, Various Artists (Weather Report)
1979: Circle In The Round, Miles Davis
1979: 8-30, Weather Report
1979: Havana Jam, Various Artists (Weather Report)
1980: Night Passage, Weather Report
1982: Weather Report 2, Weather Report
1983: Procession, Weather Report
1984: Domino Theory, Weather Report
1984: Japan Domino Theory: Weather Report Live In Tokyo, Weather Report
1985: Sportin' Life, Weather Report
1986: Dialects, Joe Zawinul
1986: This Is This, Weather Report
1988: The Immigrants, The Zawinul Syndicate
1989: Black Water, The Zawinul Syndicate
1989: Back On The Block, Quincy Jones
1990: Best Of Weather Report Vol. I, Weather Report
1990: Weather Report: The Collection, Weather Report

1992: Black Devil, Miles Davis
1992: Lost Tribes, The Zawinul Syndicate
1992: Joe Zawinul And The Austrian All Stars, Joe Zawinul
1992: En Concert Avec Europe 1: Salle Pleyel 27 Mars 1969, Cannonball Adderley and his Quintet
1996: Stories Of The Danube, Joe Zawinul
1996: My People, The Zawinul Syndicate
1996: Weather Report - This Is Jazz, Weather Report
1997: Original Jazz Classics Collection, Cannonball Adderley
1998: World Tour [live], Joe Zawinul & The Zawinul Syndicate
1998: The Complete Bitches Brew Sessions (August 1969 - February 1970), Miles Davis
2000: Mauthausen: Chronicles From The Ashes, Joe Zawinul
2000: Cannonball Adderley, Cannonball Adderley
2001: At La Villette [DVD], Miles Davis
2001: The Complete In A Silent Way Sessions, Miles Davis
2002: The Best Of Weather Report, Weather Report
2002: The Definitive Cannonball Adderley, Cannonball Adderley
2002: Paris Jazz Concert 1969, Julian Cannonball Adderley
2002: Live And Unreleased, Weather Report
2002: Faces & Places, The Zawinul Syndicate
2005: Vienna Nights: Live At Joe Zawinul's Birdland, Joe Zawinul & The Zawinul Syndicate
2005: Joe Zawinul - A Musical Portrait, Joe Zawinul
2006: Brown Street, Joe Zawinul
2006: Forecast: Tomorrow, Weather Report
2007: Weather Report - Columbia Vol. 1, Weather Report
2008: Collections, Weather Report
2008: Weather Report - Cambden, Weather Report
2009: 75th, Joe Zawinul & The Zawinul Syndicate

2009: Weather Report: L'Eclat Du Jazz Fusion, Weather Report
2009: 75, Joe Zawinul & The Zawinul Syndicate
2010: Live In Germany 1971 [DVD], Weather Report
2010: The Very Best Of Weather Report, Weather Report
2010: Absolute Zawinul, Absolute Ensemble and Joe Zawinul
2010: Live In Berlin 1975, Weather Report
2011: Live In Offenbach 1978, Weather Report
2011: Live In Cologne 1983, Weather Report
2011: The German Concerts: Berlin 1975, Offenbach 1978, Cologne 1983, Weather Report
2011: Live In Offenbach 1978 [DVD], Weather Report
2011: Live In Cologne 1983 [DVD], Weather Report
2012: Weather Report - Columbia Vol. 2, Weather Report
2015: The Legendary Live Tapes 1978-1981, Weather Report

## Discography of Wayne Shorter
1959: Kelly Great, Wynton Kelly
1959: Live In Copenhagen, Art Blakey and the Jazz Messengers
1959: Live In Stockholm, Art Blakey and the Jazz Messengers
1960: Like Someone In Love, Art Blakey and the Jazz Messengers
1960: Lausanne 1960, Art Blakey and the Jazz Messengers
1960: More Birdland Sessions, Lee Morgan
1960: The Big Beat, Art Blakey and the Jazz Messengers
1960: A Night In Tunisia, Art Blakey and the Jazz Messengers
1960: Paris Jam Session, Art Blakey and the Jazz Messengers
1960: Live In Stockholm 1960, Art Blakey and the Jazz Messengers
1960: Introducing Wayne Shorter, Wayne Shorter
1960: The Young Lions, The Young Lions

1960: Meet You At The Jazz Corner Of The World, Art Blakey and the Jazz Messengers
1961: Roots And Herbs, Art Blakey and the Jazz Messengers
1961: A Day With Art Blakey 1961, Art Blakey and the Jazz Messengers
1961: Art Blakey!!!!! Jazz Messengers!!!!!, Art Blakey and the Jazz Messengers
1961: Ready For Freddie, Freddie Hubbard
1961: Olympia, May 13th 1961 (Second Concert), Art Blakey and the Jazz Messengers
1961: Mosaic, Art Blakey and the Jazz Messengers
1961: Olympia, May 13th 1961 (First Concert), Art Blakey and the Jazz Messengers
1961: The Witch Doctor, Art Blakey and the Jazz Messengers
1961: Buhaina's Delight, Art Blakey and the Jazz Messengers
1961: Pisces, Art Blakey and the Jazz Messengers
1961: Free Form, Donald Byrd
1961: Second Genesis, Wayne Shorter
1961: The Freedom Rider, Art Blakey and the Jazz Messengers
1962: Three Blind Mice Vol 2, Art Blakey and the Jazz Messengers
1962: Three Blind Mice Vol 1, Art Blakey and the Jazz Messengers
1962: Wayning Moments, Wayne Shorter
1962: Just Jazz!, Benny Golson
1962: The African Beat, Art Blakey and the Jazz Messengers
1963: Caravan, Art Blakey and the Jazz Messengers
1963: Here To Stay, Freddie Hubbard
1963: Ugetsu - Art Blakey's Jazz Messengers At Birdland, Art Blakey and the Jazz Messengers
1963: The Body & The Soul, Freddie Hubbard
1964: Kyoto, Art Blakey and the Jazz Messengers
1964: Night Dreamer, Wayne Shorter
1964: The Individualism Of Gil Evans, Gil Evans
1964: Indestructible, Art Blakey and the Jazz Messengers
1964: Juju, Wayne Shorter
1964: Search For The New Land, Lee Morgan
1964: Free For All, Art Blakey and the Jazz Messengers
1964: Some Other Stuff, Grachan Moncur III
1965: E.S.P., Miles Davis
1965: Et Cetera, Wayne Shorter
1965: The Gigolo, Lee Morgan
1965: The Soothsayer, Wayne Shorter
1965: Speak No Evil, Wayne Shorter
1965: Miles In Berlin, Miles Davis Quintet
1965: Spring, Tony Williams
1966: Delightfulee, Lee Morgan Orchestra
1966: The Soul Man!, Bobby Timmons Quartet
1966: The All Seeing Eye, Wayne Shorter
1966: Adam's Apple, Wayne Shorter
1967: Standards, Lee Morgan
1967: The Procrastinator, Lee Morgan
1967: Schizophrenia, Wayne Shorter
1967: Sorcerer, Miles Davis
1967: Lush Life, Lou Donaldson
1967: Miles Smiles, Miles Davis
1967: Sweet Slumber, Lou Donaldson Nonet
1968: Miles In The Sky, Miles Davis
1968: Nefertiti, Miles Davis
1969: In A Silent Way, Miles Davis
1969: Super Nova, Wayne Shorter
1969: Filles de Kilimanjaro, Miles Davis
1969: Miles Davis - Village, Miles Davis
1970: Expansions, McCoy Tyner
1970: Odyssey Of Iska, Wayne Shorter
1970: Bitches Brew, Miles Davis
1970: Moto Grosso Feio, Wayne Shorter
1971: Weather Report 1, Weather Report
1971: Zawinul, Joe Zawinul
1972: I Sing The Body Electric, Weather Report
1973: Sweetnighter, Weather Report
1974: Mysterious Traveller, Weather Report
1974: Big Fun, Miles Davis
1975: Tale Spinnin', Weather Report
1975: Native Dancer, Wayne Shorter
1975: Man-Child, Herbie Hancock

1976: Water Babies, Miles Davis
1976: Black Market, Weather Report
1976: Jaco Pastorius, Jaco Pastorius
1976: Live At Montreux 1976 [DVD], Weather Report
1976: Identity, Airto Moreira
1976: Milton, Milton Nascimento
1977: V.S.O.P., Herbie Hancock
1977: Heavy Weather, Weather Report
1977: The Quintet, V.S.O.P.
1977: Don Juan's Reckless Daughter, Joni Mitchell
1977: Aja, Steely Dan
1977: Live In Tokyo, Weather Report
1977: Tempest In The Colosseum, V.S.O.P. The Quintet
1978: Mr. Gone, Weather Report
1979: 8-30, Weather Report
1979: Havana Jam II, Various Artists (Weather Report)
1979: V.S.O.P. - Live Under The Sky, Herbie Hancock
1979: The Swing Of Delight, Carlos Santana
1979: Circle In The Round, Miles Davis
1979: Havana Jam, Various Artists (Weather Report)
1980: Night Passage, Weather Report
1981: Word Of Mouth, Jaco Pastorius
1982: Confidence, Narada Michael Walden
1982: Conrad Silvert Presents Jazz At The Opera House, Various Artists
1982: Weather Report 2, Weather Report
1982: Wild Things Run Fast, Joni Mitchell
1983: Procession, Weather Report
1984: Domino Theory, Weather Report
1984: Sound System, Herbie Hancock
1984: Japan Domino Theory: Weather Report Live In Tokyo, Weather Report
1985: Dog Eat Dog, Joni Mitchell
1985: Atlantis, Wayne Shorter
1985: Sportin' Life, Weather Report
1986: Round Midnight, Dexter Gordon / Herbie Hancock
1986: Mo' Wasabi, Randy Bernsen
1986: The Other Side Of Round Midnight, Dexter Gordon
1986: This Is This, Weather Report
1986: Power Of Three, Michel Petruciani / Jim Hall / Wayne Shorter
1986: Spontaneous Inventions, Bobby McFerrin
1987: Diamond Land, Toninho Horta Quintet
1987: Phantom Navigator, Wayne Shorter
1987: Yauraete, Milton Nascimento
1988: If This Bass Could Only Talk, Stanley Clarke
1988: Chalk Mark In A Rain Storm, Joni Mitchell
1988: Joy Ryder, Wayne Shorter
1989: The Manhattan Project, The Manhattan Project
1989: American Odyssey, Larry Coryell
1989: Something More, Buster Williams
1989: The Art Of Jazz, Art Blakey and the Jazz Messengers
1989: Double Image - Crown, Miles Davis
1989: Real Life Story, Terri Lyne Carrington
1989: Silent Will, Andrea Marcelli
1989: The Best Of Art Blakey And The Jazz Messengers, Art Blakey and the Jazz Messengers
1990: First Instrument, Rachelle Ferrell
1990: Miles Davis - Jazz Door, Miles Davis
1990: Double Image - Moon, Miles Davis
1990: Clarke / Duke Project III, Stanley Clarke and George Duke
1990: Cookin' At The Plugged Nickel, Miles Davis Quintet
1990: Pandoga: Select Live Under The Sky '90, Masahiko Satoh
1990: Best Of Weather Report Vol. I, Weather Report
1990: A Galactic Odyssey, Haru
1990: Song Of The Sun, Jim Beard
1990: Weather Report: The Collection, Weather Report
1991: Davisiana, Miles Davis Quintet
1991: Night Ride Home, Joni Mitchell
1991: Capri, Paolo Rustichelli
1992: Paraphernalia, Miles Davis Quintet
1992: A Tribute To Miles, Herbie Hancock / Wayne Shorter / Ron Carter / Wallace Roney / Tony Williams
1992: No (More) Blues, Miles Davis

Quintet
1992: Black Devil, Miles Davis
1993: The Sun Don't Lie, Marcus Miller
1993: 1969 Miles: Festiva de Juan Pins, Miles Davis Quintet
1993: The Miles Davis Gold Collection, Miles Davis
1993: Holiday For Pans, Jaco Pastorius
1994: Turbulent Indigo, Joni Mitchell
1995: Highlights from The Plugged Nickel, Miles Davis Quintet
1995: High Life, Wayne Shorter
1995: The Complete Live At The Plugged Nickel 1965, Miles Davis Quintet
1996: Weather Report - This Is Jazz, Weather Report
1996: Gemini - Crown, Miles Davis
1996: Quiet, John Scofield
1997: 1 + 1, Herbie Hancock and Wayne Shorter
1998: Taming The Tiger, Joni Mitchell
1998: The Complete Bitches Brew Sessions (August 1969 - February 1970), Miles Davis
1998: The Complete Columbia Studio Recordings (1965-68), Miles Davis
1998: Africaine, Art Blakey and the Jazz Messengers
1998: Gershwin's World, Herbie Hancock
2000: Les Incontournables, Jaco Pastorius
2000: Both Sides Now, Joni Mitchell
2001: Live At The Fillmore East (March 7, 1970): It's About That Time, Miles Davis
2001: Future 2 Future, Herbie Hancock
2001: Sorcery In Antwerp, The Miles Davis Quintet
2001: At La Villette [DVD], Miles Davis
2001: The Complete In A Silent Way Sessions, Miles Davis
2001: M2, Marcus Miller
2002: The Best Of Weather Report, Weather Report
2002: Footprints Live, Wayne Shorter
2002: Live And Unreleased, Weather Report
2002: Travelogue, Joni Mitchell
2003: Alegria, Wayne Shorter
2004: Footprints: The Life And Music Of Wayne Shorter, Wayne Shorter
2005: Beyond The Sound Barrier, Wayne Shorter Quartet
2005: Live At The 1988 Montreux Jazz Festival [DVD], Carlos Santana, Wayne Shorter
2005: In Tokyo - Live At The Big Sight [DVD], Herbie Hancock / Wayne Shorter / Dave Holland / Brian Blade
2005: It's About That Time: Live In Montreux 1969, Miles Davis Quintet
2006: Winter In Europe 1967, Miles Davis Quintet
2006: Forecast: Tomorrow, Weather Report
2006: The Definitive Collection, Steely Dan
2007: River: The Joni Letters, Herbie Hancock
2007: Weather Report - Columbia Vol. 1, Weather Report
2007: Milan 1964 - DVD, Miles Davis Quintet
2007: Shine, Joni Mitchell
2007: Live In Milan 1964, Miles Davis Quintet
2008: 32 Festival de Jazz de Vitoria-Gasteiz, Various Artists
2008: Weather Report - Cambden, Weather Report
2008: Collections, Weather Report
2009: 75, Joe Zawinul & The Zawinul Syndicate
2009: 75th, Joe Zawinul & The Zawinul Syndicate
2009: Weather Report: L'Eclat Du Jazz Fusion, Weather Report
2009: Live At Montreux 1996 [DVD], Wayne Shorter
2010: The Very Best Of Weather Report, Weather Report
2010: Live In Berlin 1975, Weather Report
2010: Live In Germany 1971 [DVD], Weather Report
2010: The Complete Columbia Studio Recordings, Miles Davis, Gil Evans
2010: Live In Rome And Copenhagen 1969, Miles Davis Quintet
2010: Live In Berlin 1969, Miles Davis Quintet
2010: The 1969 Berlin Concert [DVD],

- Miles Davis Quintet
- 2010: The Imagine Project, Herbie Hancock
- 2010: Complete Live At The Blue Coronet 1969, Miles Davis
- 2011: Live In Cologne 1983 [DVD], Weather Report
- 2011: Live In Offenbach 1978, Weather Report
- 2011: Live In Europe 1967: The Bootleg Series Vol. 1, Miles Davis Quintet
- 2011: Live In Cologne 1983, Weather Report
- 2011: The German Concerts: Berlin 1975, Offenbach 1978, Cologne 1983, Weather Report
- 2011: Live In Offenbach 1978 [DVD], Weather Report
- 2012: Weather Report - Columbia Vol. 2, Weather Report
- 2013: Without A Net, Wayne Shorter Quartet.
- 2015: The Legendary Live Tapes 1978-1981, Weather Report

*The Wayne Shorter Quartet performing at the Barbican in London, 2007. Left to right: Danilo Perez, Wayne Shorter, John Patitucci, Brian Blade. (Photo: Ken Trethewey)*

# Herbie Hancock (b1940)

*Herbie Hancock performing at the Lighthouse Centre, Poole, UK in 2006. (Photo: Ken Trethewey)*

Of all the musicians described in these works, Herbie Hancock is probably the most eclectic - the musician whose work extends the farthest from his jazz roots. Herbie is one of the few jazz musicians who genuinely became famous in popular music culture. It was very early on in his career that he wrote *Watermelon Man* (1962), a song that became a hit for Mongo Santamaria and made Hancock a great deal of money. When it was released the popular jazz-fusion was the Brazilian-derived bossa nova sub genre; it was cool and carried a measure of sophistication that appealed more to the thirty-somethings. With *Watermelon Man*, Hancock had success with a Latin-flavoured popular hit tune, much less sophisticated and, appealing to a younger audience, was eminently suited for the rapidly expanding market for music in discotheques.

Then, Herbie was hired at a very young age to occupy the piano seat in the leading jazz group of the time - the second great quintet of Miles Davis, a role that is cemented in jazz history as one of the great bands of all time. After appearing briefly on Miles's *In a Silent Way* (1969), he lost his job after a late return from honeymoon.

After leaving Miles, Herbie took a little time to discover the best route into successful jazz-fusion. His early attempts were in a band called Mwandishi and, like Weather Report's early albums, strongly based in free jazz improvisation, difficult harmonies and minimal form. Herbie and his fellow band members found their experiences to be extremely satisfying – even inspirational, from an artistic standpoint, but record-buying audiences mostly found the music unpalatable. However, once he recognised that the must commercially successful formula was based on jazz mixed with the soul and funk sounds of musicians like Sly Stone, Herbie formed the Head Hunters band and never looked back. The album *Head Hunters* (1974) was one of the most successful jazz-fusion albums of all time, and served as a base to move forward.

Herbie's interest in the technology of music led him to become one of the leading exponents of electronic keyboards, synthesisers and computer music. For a period, he moved into jazz-disco dance music, with powerful collaborations with musicians like Quincy Jones and Rod Temperton who had worked at the centre of the Michael Jackson *Thriller* phenomenon. Herbie became expert in the rapidly developing technology of electronic keyboard and synthesiser music, applying his performances to the more popular styles at the softer end of rock music. He sold many records as a result and became by far the most successful musician to 'cross-over' from jazz into popular music. Success inevitably attracted the kind of insults that derive from jealousy. It wasn't helped by his singing, which, even though he had a good voice, employed an electronic synthesiser called the vocoder, a much-hated device that characterised a lot of his work in the late 1970s.

Then, with the support of the New York musician Bill Laswell, he recorded *Rockit*, a piece that appeared on *Future Shock* (1983). The original style and sound of the music was stunning and would become extremely influential for a group of young musicians who would be inspired to invent Hip Hop. By now, he was involved with the integration of computers into music and became well known for trying out every new development that became available. Of course, his success meant that he had the financial resource to allow himself to indulge himself in such luxuries, but because he was so skilled at finding good ways to use all these new devices, it paid off. He became famous for being the most technical jazz musician and was a leading user of the now established Apple Macintosh computer in music. More recently, Herbie has used his position of influence to work on a series of projects with leading artists.

Herbie Hancock could occupy a large part of the space on the diagram in Figure 5, for he has also worked in the classical and jazz-classical spaces, often alongside Chick Corea. He has played a role at the heart of the jazz mainstream with his VSOP band in the 1970s and 80s and has remained a leading exponent of acoustic jazz piano as well as his remarkable contributions to electronic keyboard instruments. All of his efforts came to fruition in 2008 when he was awarded the Grammy for Album of the Year, a project with Joni Mitchell and

Larry Klein entitled *The River* (2007) that showcased (although not exclusively) Joni Mitchell's music. He made history by becoming only the second jazz musician to be given this major honour. It was a stunning achievement and a fitting tribute to one of the greatest jazz musicians in history.

## Discography of Herbie Hancock

1960: With John Coltrane In Copenhagen 1960, Miles Davis Quintet with John Coltrane
1961: Rock Your Soul, Herbie Hancock
1961: Day Dreams, Herbie Hancock
1961: Free Form, Donald Byrd
1961: Royal Flush, Donald Byrd
1961: Out Of This World, Donald Byrd, Pepper Adams
1961: The Essential Herbie Hancock, Herbie Hancock
1961: Chant, Donald Byrd
1962: Gaslight 1962, Eric Dolphy
1962: Takin' Off, Herbie Hancock
1963: A New Perspective, Donald Byrd
1963: Vertigo, Jackie McLean
1963: Straight, No Filter, Hank Mobley
1963: Illinois Concert, Eric Dolphy
1963: My Point Of View, Herbie Hancock
1963: No Room For Squares, Hank Mobley
1963: Seven Steps To Heaven, Miles Davis
1963: Miles In Antibes, Miles Davis Quintet with John Coltrane
1963: Step Lightly, Blue Mitchell
1963: Inventions And Dimensions, Herbie Hancock
1963: Hub-Tones, Freddie Hubbard
1964: It's Time!, Jackie McLean
1964: The Complete Concert 1964, Miles Davis
1964: Some Other Stuff, Grachan Moncur III
1964: Search For The New Land, Lee Morgan
1964: Empyrean Isles, Herbie Hancock
1964: Miles Davis In Europe, Miles Davis Quintet with John Coltrane
1964: In Memory Of, Stanley Turrentine
1964: Lifetime, Tony Williams
1965: The Turnaround, Hank Mobley
1965: E.S.P., Miles Davis
1965: Maiden Voyage, Herbie Hancock
1965: Miles In Berlin, Miles Davis Quintet
1965: Spring, Tony Williams
1965: Components, Bobby Hutcherson
1965: Cornbread, Lee Morgan
1965: My Funny Valentine, Miles Davis
1965: Et Cetera, Wayne Shorter
1965: I'm Tryin' To Get Home, Donald Byrd
1965: Speak No Evil, Wayne Shorter
1965: Freedom, Kenny Burrell
1966: Blow-Up - The Original Soundtrack, Herbie Hancock
1966: Four And More, Miles Davis
1966: Cantaloupe Island, Herbie Hancock
1966: The All Seeing Eye, Wayne Shorter
1966: Adam's Apple, Wayne Shorter
1966: Happenings, Bobby Hutcherson
1967: Miles Smiles, Miles Davis
1967: Oblique, Bobby Hutcherson
1967: Schizophrenia, Wayne Shorter
1967: Sorcerer, Miles Davis
1967: Black Jack, Donald Byrd
1967: The Procrastinator, Lee Morgan
1967: Standards, Lee Morgan
1968: Nefertiti, Miles Davis
1968: Speak Like A Child, Herbie Hancock
1968: Miles In The Sky, Miles Davis
1969: Uptown Conversation, Ron Carter
1969: Miles In Tokyo, Miles Davis
1969: In A Silent Way, Miles Davis
1969: Fat Albert Rotunda, Herbie Hancock
1969: Infinite Search, Miroslav Vitous
1969: The Prisoner, Herbie Hancock
1969: Filles de Kilimanjaro, Miles Davis
1970: Straight Life, Freddie Hubbard
1970: Red Clay, Freddie Hubbard
1971: Zawinul, Joe Zawinul
1971: Mwandishi, Herbie Hancock
1971: First Light, Freddie Hubbard
1971: He Who Lives In Many Places, Terry Plumeri

1971: A Tribute To Jack Johnson, Miles Davis
1972: On The Corner, Miles Davis
1972: Moon Germs, Joe Farrell
1972: Crossings, Herbie Hancock
1973: Sextant, Herbie Hancock
1973: The Spook Who Sat By The Door, Herbie Hancock
1973: Head Hunters, Herbie Hancock
1974: Get Up With It, Miles Davis
1974: Big Fun, Miles Davis
1974: Dedication, Herbie Hancock
1974: Death Wish, Herbie Hancock
1974: Thrust, Herbie Hancock
1975: Native Dancer, Wayne Shorter
1975: Man-Child, Herbie Hancock
1975: Flood, Herbie Hancock
1976: Water Babies, Miles Davis
1976: Milton, Milton Nascimento
1976: Jaco Pastorius, Jaco Pastorius
1976: Identity, Airto Moreira
1976: Songs In The Key Of Life, Stevie Wonder
1976: Corea/Hancock/Jarrett/Tyner, Corea / Hancock / Jarrett / Tyner
1976: Secrets, Herbie Hancock
1977: V.S.O.P., Herbie Hancock
1977: The Quintet, V.S.O.P.
1977: The Herbie Hancock Trio (1977), Herbie Hancock
1977: Tempest In The Colosseum, V.S.O.P. The Quintet
1978: Sounds ... And Stuff Like That!!, Quincy Jones
1978: An Evening With Herbie Hancock And Chick Corea In Concert, Herbie Hancock and Chick Corea
1978: Sunlight, Herbie Hancock
1978: Everyday Everynight, Flora Purim
1978: Third Plane, Ron Carter, Herbie Hancock, Tony Williams
1979: The Swing Of Delight, Carlos Santana
1979: The Joy Of Flying, The Tony Williams Lifetime
1979: CoreaHancock: An Evening With Chick Corea And Herbie Hancock, Chick Corea / Herbie Hancock
1979: Circle In The Round, Miles Davis
1979: Mingus, Joni Mitchell

1979: V.S.O.P. - Live Under The Sky, Herbie Hancock
1979: Michel Colombier, Michel Colombier
1979: Feets Don't Fail Me Now, Herbie Hancock
1979: The Piano, Herbie Hancock
1979: Direct Step, Herbie Hancock
1980: Monster, Herbie Hancock
1980: Mr. Hands, Herbie Hancock
1981: What Cha' Gonna Do For Me, Chaka Khan
1981: Magic Windows, Herbie Hancock
1981: Morning Sun, Alphonse Mouzon
1981: Word Of Mouth, Jaco Pastorius
1981: The Dude, Quincy Jones
1981: Herbie Hancock Trio With Ron Carter And Tony Williams (1981), Herbie Hancock Trio
1981: GB, George Benson
1982: Conrad Silvert Presents Jazz At The Opera House, Various Artists
1982: Herbie Hancock Quartet, Herbie Hancock Quartet
1982: Lite Me Up, Herbie Hancock
1983: Future Shock, Herbie Hancock
1984: Sound System, Herbie Hancock
1984: The Herbie Hancock Trio In Concert, Herbie Hancock Trio
1984: Live In Lugano - Supertrio In Concert [DVD], Herbie Hancock / Ron Carter / Billy Cobham
1985: Village Life, Herbie Hancock, Foday Musa Suso
1986: The Other Side Of Round Midnight, Dexter Gordon
1986: Round Midnight [DVD], Dexter Gordon / Herbie Hancock
1986: Round Midnight, Dexter Gordon / Herbie Hancock
1986: Hideaway, Stanley Clarke
1986: Mo' Wasabi, Randy Bernsen
1986: Ornella E..., Ornella Vanoni
1987: Total Happiness (Music from The Bill Cosby Show, Vol. 2), Various Artists
1987: Yauraete, Milton Nascimento
1987: Jazz Africa, Herbie Hancock, Foday Musa Suso
1988: Don't Try This At Home, Michael

Brecker
1988: The Best Of Herbie Hancock - The Blue Note Years, Herbie Hancock
1988: Perfect Machine, Herbie Hancock
1988: Joy Ryder, Wayne Shorter
1988: Summer Cooler, Various Artists
1988: Nightwind, Mike Lawrence
1989: Something More, Buster Williams
1989: Back On The Block, Quincy Jones
1990: Parallel Realities Live, De Johnette, Metheny, Hancock, Holland
1990: Live In Concert [DVD], De Johnette / Hancock / Holland / Metheny
1990: Cookin' At The Plugged Nickel, Miles Davis Quintet
1990: A Jazz Collection, Herbie Hancock
1991: Capri, Paolo Rustichelli
1991: The Very Best Of Herbie Hancock, Herbie Hancock
1991: Davisiana, Miles Davis Quintet
1992: The Best Of Herbie Hancock Vol. 2, Herbie Hancock
1992: A Tribute To Miles, Herbie Hancock / Wayne Shorter / Ron Carter / Wallace Roney / Tony Williams
1992: No (More) Blues, Miles Davis Quintet
1992: Black Devil, Miles Davis
1993: The Miles Davis Gold Collection, Miles Davis
1994: The Herbie Hancock Quartet Live, Herbie Hancock Quartet
1994: Urbanator, Urbanator
1994: Dis Is Da Drum, Herbie Hancock
1994: Live In New York, Herbie Hancock Trio
1994: Head To Head, Jonathan Butler
1994: Mwandishi: The Complete Warner Bros. Recordings, Herbie Hancock
1994: Vinnie Colaiuta, Vinnie Colaiuta
1995: Jammin' With Herbie, Herbie Hancock
1995: Antonio Carlos Jobim: An All Star Tribute [DVD], Various Artists
1995: Q's Jook Joint, Quincy Jones
1995: Highlights from The Plugged Nickel, Miles Davis Quintet
1995: The Complete Live At The Plugged Nickel 1965, Miles Davis Quintet
1996: Urbanator II, Michal Urbaniak

1996: The New Standard, Herbie Hancock
1996: Gently, Liza Minnelli
1996: The New Standard Special Edition, Herbie Hancock
1997: 1 + 1, Herbie Hancock and Wayne Shorter
1997: Wilderness, Tony Williams
1998: Gershwin's World, Herbie Hancock
1998: Return Of The Headhunters, Headhunters
1998: Blue Breakbeats, Lee Morgan
1998: The Complete Blue Note Sixties Sessions, Herbie Hancock
1998: The Complete Columbia Studio Recordings (1965-68), Miles Davis
1998: This Is Jazz, Herbie Hancock
1999: Blue Break Beats, Volumes 1-4, Various Artists
1999: The Best Of Herbie Hancock - The Hits, Herbie Hancock
1999: Backtracks, Quincy Jones / Herbie Hancock
1999: The Best Of Herbie Hancock, Herbie Hancock
1999: Dr. Jazz, Herbie Hancock
1999: Voyager, Herbie Hancock
1999: Mr Funk, Herbie Hancock
1999: Riot: The Newly Discovered Takes from Blue Note Sixties Sessions, Herbie Hancock
2000: Touchstone, Donald Byrd, Pepper Adams
2000: The Definitive Herbie Hancock, Herbie Hancock
2000: Les Incontournables, Jaco Pastorius
2000: Night Walker, Herbie Hancock
2000: Jammin' With Herbie Hancock, Herbie Hancock
2000: Both Sides Now, Joni Mitchell
2000: Portrait: Herbie Hancock, Herbie Hancock
2001: The Complete In A Silent Way Sessions, Miles Davis
2001: Nearness Of You: The Ballad Book, Michael Brecker
2001: M2, Marcus Miller
2001: Sorcery In Antwerp, The Miles Davis Quintet
2001: Future 2 Future, Herbie Hancock
2001: At La Villette [DVD], Miles Davis

2002: Future 2 Future Live [DVD], Herbie Hancock
2002: Directions In Music, Herbie Hancock
2002: The Columbia Years: '72 - '86, Herbie Hancock
2002: Travelogue, Joni Mitchell
2002: Jazz Profile, Herbie Hancock
2003: Herbie Hancock Trio [DVD], Herbie Hancock
2003: Left Alone, Eric Dolphy
2004: Rockit, Herbie Hancock
2004: Jazz Moods: Round Midnight, Herbie Hancock
2004: Herbie Hancock Box, Herbie Hancock
2004: Herbie Hancock Special with Bobby McFerrin And Michael Brecker [DVD], Herbie Hancock
2005: Hit The Rhodes, Jack, Various Artists
2005: De Luxe, Herbie Hancock
2005: The X Tracks: Best Of Andy Summers, Andy Summers
2005: Live Detroit / Chicago, Herbie Hancock
2005: Baraka, Herbie Hancock
2005: Possibilities, Herbie Hancock
2005: In Tokyo - Live At The Big Sight [DVD], Herbie Hancock / Wayne Shorter / Dave Holland / Brian Blade
2006: World Of Rhythm [DVD], Herbie Hancock
2006: The Very Best Of Herbie Hancock, Herbie Hancock
2006: Winter In Europe 1967, Miles Davis Quintet
2006: The Essential Herbie Hancock, Herbie Hancock
2006: Great Sessions - Herbie Hancock, Herbie Hancock
2006: Piano Fiesta, Herbie Hancock / Chick Corea
2006: The Collection: A Selection Of Tracks From The Blue Note Years, Herbie Hancock
2006: Virgin Forest, Lionel Louecke
2006: Hot And Heavy, Herbie Hancock
2006: Anthology, Herbie Hancock
2006: Manchester Concert: Complete 1960 Live At The Free Trade Hall, Miles Davis
2006: Givin' It Up, George Benson, Al Jarreau
2007: The Finest In Jazz, Herbie Hancock
2007: Jazz To Funk, Herbie Hancock
2007: The Jewel In The Lotus, Benny Maupin
2007: Pilgrimage, Michael Brecker
2007: River: The Joni Letters, Herbie Hancock
2007: Milan 1964 - DVD, Miles Davis Quintet
2007: Live At The 1963 Monterey Jazz Festival, Miles Davis Quintet
2007: Herbie Hancock Trio In Concert [DVD], Herbie Hancock
2007: Live In Milan 1964, Miles Davis Quintet
2007: Jazz Biography, Herbie Hancock
2008: Watermelon Man [DVD], Herbie Hancock's Headhunters
2008: Then And Now - The Definitive Herbie Hancock, Herbie Hancock
2008: Awake Live, Josh Groban
2008: Late Night Jazz Favourites, Herbie Hancock
2008: Herbie Hancock: The Collection, Herbie Hancock
2008: Dancin' Grooves, Herbie Hancock
2008: The Very Best Of Herbie Hancock, Herbie Hancock
2008: The Collection, Herbie Hancock
2008: Hear, O Israel: A Prayer Ceremony In Jazz, Various Artists
2008: 32 Festival de Jazz de Vitoria-Gasteiz, Various Artists
2009: Shape Of My Heart, Katia Labeque
2009: The Best Of Herbie Hancock (3 CD Box Set), Herbie Hancock
2009: One Night In Japan [DVD], Herbie Hancock & The New Standard All Stars
2010: The Imagine Project, Herbie Hancock
2010: Live in Lugano – Supertrio in Concert, Herbie Hancock, Ron Carter, Billy Cobham
2011: Live In Europe 1967: The Bootleg Series Vol. 1, Miles Davis Quintet

# John McLaughlin (b1942)

*John McLaughlin backstage in 2013. (Photo: Gary Husband)*

John McLaughlin was the first jazz musician to dedicate an entire phase of his career to jazz-fusion. John's albums did not contain only a couple of jazz-fusion tracks, or make a few obscure references to rock rhythms buried inside solid jazz compositions. McLaughlin created a band that recorded nothing but jazz-fusion and blew its listeners away. If that sounds like hyperbole, then you should read the book by Kolosky. [4]

McLaughlin had been a guitar prodigy since teenage in England. It didn't take him long to move to London after turning professional, and he became an in-demand session player for a lot of early 60s pop music, but failed to make any impact on the bigger scale. However, moving around the London music scene quickly got him many friends and gigs. One important gig was with the Graham Bond Quintet along with Ginger Baker and Jack Bruce. He was fortunate enough to make an exceptional jazz album called *Extrapolation* (1969) just before he received an invitation to go to the USA to play with drummer Tony Williams in his proposed new jazz-rock band that would be called Lifetime. Remarkably, almost immediately after arriving in New York, he found himself recording with Miles Davis and appeared on some of the most written-about albums of all time, *In a Silent Way* (1969) and *Bitches Brew* (1970). It was truly the stuff of dreams, but John was quite unfazed by it, preferring to play alongside Williams and his chosen organ player Larry Young. His experiences right at the centre of profound change gave him the edge he needed to set up his own band at the earliest opportunity. He left Davis and Williams to become the leader of a truly spectacular outfit called Mahavishnu Orchestra that, amidst all the brouhaha and froth that was early 1970s jazz-rock fusion, actually put down the most significant markers of any other band in the fledgling genre.

The first three Mahavishnu Orchestra albums, *Inner Mounting Flame* (1971) *Birds of Fire* (1971) and *Between Nothingness and Eternity* (1972) represent an unparalleled advance in jazz music and I have awarded them all five stars. Far from being dated, they are essential listening even today, some forty years later. The band members are still revered in the annals of jazz musicianship. Drummer Billy Cobham was an exceptional talent and almost everybody who heard him recognised an incomparable musician. Jan Hammer was a keyboard player who, early on in the development of synthesisers, was able to take their playing to a higher level. Both men established huge footprints in the jazz-fusion world long after the band broke up in 1972. The band's unique sound was much assisted by the presence of electric violin player Jerry Goodman, who introduced a sound into jazz-rock that until then had been confined to the classical platform and the folk club. Bassist Rick Laird was the dark horse of the outfit, not John's first choice, but by no means a poor cousin, even amidst some of the loudestenergetic and most complicated music that had yet been created.

So great was the success of the first Mahavishnu Orchestra that, when it disbanded, the next formation was inevitably very different from what had gone before. The critics were unimpressed with the second line-up and the albums were perceived to be failures. McLaughlin became very disillusioned with the reception his work was getting in the USA, and retreated from the front line of jazz-rock into a slightly Europeanised form of Indian music with a band called Shakti. Here he extended the role of the guitar in a musical genre that was, to Western ears, what might be called today 'specialist' or 'niche'. McLaughlin turned his attention away from the energy-intensive sounds of electric guitar towards the more earthy and ethnic acoustic sounds compatible with those that had been part of the Indian sub-continent for centuries. He developed a kind of

Indo-Jazz fusion in the footsteps of John Mayer in the late 1950s/ early 1960s, and made some beautiful albums that have stood the test of time.

Next, he embarked upon a period of playing in guitar super-trios with premier guitarists Al di Meola and Paco de Lucia. Di Meola had made a mark as McLaughlin's equivalent role in Return to Forever, and had been voted Best Guitarist by *Down Beat* readers on several occasions. De Lucia was one of flamenco's top exponents and provided legitimacy to those pieces that were drawn from Spanish music. The resulting performances were popular and enervating to live audiences, but on record it was often difficult to interpret who was playing what. The albums were varied and entertaining but lacked coherent identities and were not especially innovative.

By the mid-80s, McLaughlin tried again with a third Mahavishnu Orchestra, with limited success. This time he developed a friendship with saxophonist Bill Evans who had helped Miles Davis out of retirement and had played in Miles's bands of the early 1980s. Bill had many high quality jazz-fusion-oriented friends so John did not find it hard to build some exciting new line-ups. However, once again, many critics considered the music unsuccessful simply because of what the first band had achieved. However, the recorded works demonstrate many fine qualities at a time when guitar synthesisers and other new electronic tools were becoming available. Along with Pat Metheny, McLaughlin became a leading exponent of guitar synthesiser. The sounds of jazz-fusion produced in this middle period of his career were innovative and exciting, even if some critics were viewing jazz-fusion as a passé technique. Others lamented his surrender of the rock guitar to the silicon chip.

McLaughlin has never given up on the music he loves and has remained true to his original jazz-fusion credentials, despite his occasional forays into the wider territory of acoustic guitar music and more Indo-jazz. For example, around the turn of the century, he reran his Indian band with the name Remember Shakti and made another three good albums that were along the same lines as before. He has produced more top-rated (by me) jazz-fusion albums than any other artist apart from Pat Metheny, whose style is entirely different. With his band Heart of Things, John also released two stunning jazz-fusion albums called *The Heart of Things* (1997) and *Live in Paris* (1998). By the mid-noughties he was back to his best with *Industrial Zen* (2006) and in 2008 John released a startling jazz-fusion album that may be the best Indo-jazz fusion album of all time. It was as if all his years of work with jazz-rock and Indian music had finally given him the inspiration to make the ultimate fusion. Although his previous albums under the names of Shakti and Remember Shakti have been creditable Indo-jazz albums, *Floating Point* (2008) is a genuine Indo-jazz-fusion album and is uniquely placed in the catalogue of fusion music. McLaughlin received a Grammy nomination, but did not win. Then, just when he was expected to take this music on tour, he turned in 2008 back into his jazz-rock orientation. Many artists would have simply drawn upon the success of an earlier band name, but John ignored the Mahavishnu moniker and called his new group the 4th Dimension.

Amazingly, the same year, he joined up with Chick Corea to form a one-off project called the Five Peace Band. Another successful tour followed and the excellent album with the same name was released in 2009.

But the 4$^{th}$ Dimension had now gelled into a unit capable of creating some of the finest jazz-rock fusion ever recorded. John had chosen the multi-talented genius, Gary Husband to play keyboards, even though Gary had developed primarily as a percussionist. John saw it as a real bonus and was happy to use every one of Gary's talents to the full. Now able to recruit widely from a new generation of unbelievably skilled electric bass guitar players, John chose Etienne M'Bappe, another brilliant product of Cameroon who had been recognised by Joe Zawinul and employed in his band, Syndicate. These three musicians appeared on the first album to be released by the 4$^{th}$ Dimension, called *To The One* (2010), alongside John's favoured drummer Mark Mondesir. However, soon afterwards Indian-born Ranjit Barot, recognised by John himself as a virtuoso drummer, occupied the drum seat. This line-up of the 4$^{th}$ Dimension has proved to be more successful than maybe even John could have hoped and has toured extensively since 2011. Two more albums have attracted my five star rating: the studio-recorded *Now Hear This* (2012) and *The Boston Record* (2014) recorded live in the Performance Center at Boston's Berklee Music School. His last release, *Black Light* (2015) is yet another fine example of this band's output. Besides being progressive, and powered by John's compositions that draw upon his cosmic inspiration and six decades of experience, the music on offer today from this awesome group of musicians is as wonderful – if not better than – any of the output by the Mahavishnu Orchestra.

## Discography of John McLaughlin

1969: Extrapolation, John McLaughlin
1969: Emergency, The Tony Williams Lifetime
1969: In A Silent Way, Miles Davis
1969: Infinite Search, Miroslav Vitous
1969: Super Nova, Wayne Shorter
1970: Things We Like, Jack Bruce
1970: Moto Grosso Feio, Wayne Shorter
1970: Purple, Miroslav Vitous
1970: Spaces, Larry Coryell
1970: Bitches Brew, Miles Davis
1970: Turn It Over, The Tony Williams Lifetime
1970: Solid Bond, Graham Bond Organisation
1970: Marbles, John McLaughlin
1970: Devotion, John McLaughlin
1971: Live-Evil, Miles Davis
1971: A Tribute To Jack Johnson, Miles Davis
1971: Where Fortune Smiles, John McLaughlin, John Surman, Karl Berger, Stu Martin, Dave Holland
1971: My Goal's Beyond, John McLaughlin
1971: Escalator Over The Hill, Carla Bley,

1971: The Inner Mounting Flame, Mahavishnu Orchestra, Paul Haines
1971: Innovations, Duffy Power
1972: On The Corner, Miles Davis
1973: Welcome, Santana
1973: Between Nothingness And Eternity, Mahavishnu Orchestra
1973: Love Devotion Surrender, John McLaughlin and Carlos Santana
1973: Birds Of Fire, Mahavishnu Orchestra
1974: Get Up With It, Miles Davis
1974: Apocalypse, Mahavishnu Orchestra
1974: Big Fun, Miles Davis
1975: Shakti with John McLaughlin, Shakti
1975: The Essential Larry Coryell, Larry Coryell
1975: Metamorphosis, Rolling Stones
1975: Journey To Love, Stanley Clarke
1975: Visions Of The Emerald Beyond, Mahavishnu Orchestra
1976: Inner Worlds, Mahavishnu Orchestra
1976: A Handful Of Beauty, Shakti
1976: School Days, Stanley Clarke
1977: Natural Elements, Shakti
1978: Johnny McLaughlin - Electric Guitarist, John McLaughlin
1979: Circle In The Round, Miles Davis
1979: Electric Dreams, John McLaughlin with the One Truth Band
1981: Friday Night In San Francisco, Al DiMeola, John McLaughlin, Paco De Lucia
1981: Belo Horizonte, John McLaughlin
1982: Music Spoken Here, John McLaughlin
1983: Passion Grace And Fire, John McLaughlin, Al di Meola, Paco de Lucia
1984: Mahavishnu, Mahavishnu Orchestra
1985: You're Under Arrest, Miles Davis
1985: The Alternative Man, Bill Evans
1986: Round Midnight, Dexter Gordon / Herbie Hancock
1986: The Other Side Of Round Midnight, Dexter Gordon
1986: Adventures In Radioland, John McLaughlin and Mahavishnu
1987: Making Music, Zakir Hussain
1989: Aura, Miles Davis
1990: Live At The Royal Festival Hall, John McLaughlin Trio
1990: The Mediterranean Concerto For Guitar And Orchestra, John McLaughlin
1992: Black Devil, Miles Davis
1992: Que Allegria, John McLaughlin Trio
1993: Time Remembered - John McLaughlin Plays Bill Evans, John McLaughlin
1994: Tokyo Live, The Free Spirits featuring John McLaughlin
1995: After The Rain, John McLaughlin
1995: Molom - A Legend Of Mongolia, John McLaughlin
1996: The Guitar Trio, Paco De Lucia, Al Di Meola, John McLaughlin
1996: The Promise, John McLaughlin
1997: The Heart Of Things, John McLaughlin
1998: The Heart Of Things Live In Paris, John McLaughlin
1998: The Complete Bitches Brew Sessions (August 1969 - February 1970), Miles Davis
1999: Remember Shakti, Remember Shakti
1999: The Lost Trident Sessions, Mahavishnu Orchestra
2000: The Believer, Remember Shakti
2001: At La Villette [DVD], Miles Davis
2001: Saturday Night In Bombay, Remember Shakti
2001: The Complete In A Silent Way Sessions, Miles Davis
2003: Thieves And Poets, John McLaughlin
2003: Universal Syncopations, Miroslav Vitous
2003: Finally The Rain Has Come, Leni Stern
2003: The Complete Jack Johnson Sessions, Miles Davis
2005: The Cellar Door Sessions 1970, Miles Davis
2006: Industrial Zen, John McLaughlin
2007: Original Album Classics (5 CD Box

Set), John McLaughlin
2007: Trio Of Doom, John McLaughlin, Jaco Pastorius, Tony Williams
2008: The Complete On The Corner Sessions, Miles Davis
2008: Floating Point, John McLaughlin
2008: Meeting Of The Minds - The Making Of Floating Point [DVD], John McLaughlin
2009: Montreux Jazz Festival 2009 [DVD], The CTI Jazz All-Star Band
2009: Five Peace Band, Chick Corea and John McLaughlin
2010: To The One, John McLaughlin and the 4th Dimension
2012: Now Hear This, John McLaughlin and the 4th Dimension
2014: The Boston Record, John McLaughlin and the 4th Dimension
2015: Black Light, John McLaughlin and the 4th Dimension

# Chick Corea (b1941)

*Chick Corea playing at the Royal Festival Hall, London, 1992.
(Photo by Ken Trethewey)*

Chick Corea is one of the very best and most highly respected jazz musicians. An exceptionally talented pianist, he soon established himself at the cutting edge of jazz at a time when fashion demanded the abandonment of rules. Chick Corea's career began modestly. As an ambitious young musician in the 1960s he was fortunate to be able to make albums of contemporary jazz that were much influenced by the trends around him. With saxophonist Anthony Braxton, his early work involved many experiments with free jazz and he established a reputation as a creative *avant-garde* musician.

Then he received the call to join the Miles Davis band. It was to be a life-changing event, not just because of his involvement with the phenomenon that was Miles Davis, but also because Miles persuaded him to take up the electric piano, an instrument that was new to him and that he hated at first. However, he was a rapid convert to electric piano. Corea played a big part in the seminal Miles Davis albums at this critical point in history: *In A Silent Way* (1969), *Bitches Brew* (1970) and *Live Evil* (1970).

In 1972 Corea started his own jazz-rock band, Return to Forever. In these early days, and with no clear recipe for successful jazz-fusion, it took time for him to become established in jazz-fusion. His first attempt was a grouping that included Airto Moreira (percussion) and Flora Purim (vocals), as well as Stanley Clarke (bass) and Joe Farrell (sax and flute). Though successful in many ways, it quickly became clear that the band's focus was somewhat short of the marks being set by the likes of Mahavishnu Orchestra. It simply wasn't electric enough, so in 1974 Chick rebuilt the band by retaining Clarke and adding Al di Meola (guitar) and Lenny White (drums). It was the key to success and a string of great albums followed: *Hymn of the Seventh Galaxy* (1973), *Where Have I Known You Before* (1974), *No Mystery* (1975) and *Romantic Warrior* (1976). With this line-up Chick established Return to Forever as one of the most important jazz-rock bands of all time.

Over the course of his career, Chick's major influence has been his Latin heritage and, time and again, we find him basing his music strongly on harmonies and rhythms derived from the Spanish-Moorish cultures. Nevertheless, as a pianist of the highest standard, a large quantity of Chick's output has been in the jazz-classical European fusion category. Some of his recordings of his own compositions stand proud in the category of classical European music, but again, it is his roots in the ethnic Spanish folk culture that join up with his brilliant jazz brain and shine through much of what he does.

As the momentum for jazz-fusion began to dissipate around 1978, Chick's path was diverted back towards the jazz middle ground. There he made a large number of albums with an equally large number of jazz musicians. However, his attentions were drawn back to jazz-fusion in the mid-1980s and resulted in the formation of a new band, The Chick Corea Elektric Band. Six more albums were produced: *The Chick Corea Elektric Band* (1986), *Light Years* (1988), *Eye of the Beholder* (1990), *Inside Out* (1991), *Beneath the Mask* (1992) and *Paint the World* (1993). Each album was innovative and different from the one that preceded it, and fans of jazz-fusion believe that this was a rare purple period for the genre at a time when everyone thought that jazz-fusion was *passé*.

Chick later reformed the Elektric Band to record a final album, *To the Stars* (2004). It turned out to be a sad junior cousin and seemed to be more about a promotion of Scientology than a serious attempt to build upon a brilliant set of albums. Then in 2008, Chick looked even farther back to Return to Forever and made the most of the opportunity to reform the band for a money-spinning world tour. An album called *The Anthology* (2008) was released that was a compilation of the band's original tracks. Then came *Returns* (2008), a double CD that contained fresh recordings of old material. In 2009 he recorded a brilliant partnership with John McLaughlin and the album *Five Peace Band* (2009).

## Discography of Chick Corea

Discography of Chick Corea
1966 Tones For Joan's Bones, Chick Corea
1968 Filles de Kilimanjaro, Miles Davis
1968 Now He Sings, Now He Sobs, Chick Corea
1969 In A Silent Way, Miles Davis
1969 Is, Chick Corea
1969 Supernova, Wayne Shorter
1969 Sundance, Chick Corea
1970 Bitches Brew, Miles Davis
1970 Black Beauty - Miles Davis at Fillmore West, Miles Davis
1970 Live at the Fillmore East: It's About That Time, Miles Davis
1970 Arc, Chick Corea
1970 Spaces, Larry Coryell
1970 Live Evil, Miles Davis
1970 At Fillmore, Miles Davis
1970 The Song Of Singing, Chick Corea
1970 Moto Grosso Feio, Wayne Shorter
1971 Piano Improvisations Vol. 2, Chick Corea
1971 Piano Improvisations Vol. 1, Chick Corea
1972 Light As A Feather, Return to Forever
1972 On The Corner, Miles Davis
1972 Inner Space, Chick Corea
1972 Return To Forever, Return To Forever
1973 Crystal Silence, Chick Corea and Gary Burton
1973 Hymn of the Seventh Galaxy, Return to Forever
1974 Big Fun, Miles Davis
1974 Where Have I Known You Before, Return to Forever
1975 Journey To Love, Stanley Clarke
1975 No Mystery, Return to Forever
1975 Chick Corea, Chick Corea
1976 Water Babies, Miles Davis
1976 The Leprechaun, Chick Corea
1976 Romantic Warrior, Return To Forever
1976 Land of the Midnight Sun, Al di Meola
1976 My Spanish Heart, Chick Corea

1976 Corea/Hancock/Jarrett/Tyner, Corea/Hancock/Jarrett/Tyner
1978 The Mad Hatter, Chick Corea
1978 Friends, Chick Corea
1978 Corea Hancock, Corea/Hancock
1978 Johnny McLaughlin - Electric Guitarist, John McLaughlin
1978 An Evening With Herbie Hancock and Chick Corea In , Herbie Hancock and Chick
1978 Secret Agent, Chick Corea
1979 Delphi 1, Chick Corea
1979 Circle in the Round, Miles Davis
1979 Duet, Chick Corea and Gary Burton
1980 Tap Step, Chick Corea
1980 Delphi 2 and 3, Chick Corea
1980 In Concert Zurich October 28 1979, Chick Corea and Gary Burton
1981 Live In Montreux, Chick Corea
1981 Three Quartets , Chick Corea
1981 Trio Music, Chick Corea
1982 Touchstone , Chick Corea
1982 Echoes Of An Era 2, Corea/White/Clarke/Henderson/Hubbard
1982 Griffith Park Collection, Corea/White/Clarke/Henderson/Hubbard
1982 Echoes Of An Era, Corea/White/Clarke/Henderson/Hubbard
1983 On Two Pianos, Chick Corea and Nicolas Economu
1983 The Meeting, Chick Corea and Friedrich Gulda
1983 Lyric Suite For Sextet, Chick Corea and Gary Burton
1983 Again and Again - Jo'berg Sessions, Chick Corea
1984 Mozart Double Piano Concerto Fantasy For Two Piano, Chick Corea and Friedrich Gulda
1984 Children's Songs, Chick Corea
1985 Voyage, Chick Corea and Steve Kujula
1985 Septet, Chick Corea
1985 Works, Chick Corea

1986 Chick Corea Elektric Band, Chick Corea Elektric Band
1987 Trio Music Live In Europe, Chick Corea
1987 Phantom Navigator, Wayne Shorter
1987 Chick Corea Compact Jazz, Chick Corea
1988 GRP Super Live In Concert, Chick Corea and Friends
1988 John Patitucci, John Patitucci
1988 Light Years, Chick Corea Elektric Band
1989 Happy Anniversary Charlie Brown, Chick Corea and Friends
1989 On the Corner, John Patitucci
1989 Chick Corea Akoustic Band, Chick Corea Akoustic Band
1990 Master Plan, Dave Weckl Band
1990 Eye of the Beholder, Chick Corea Elektric Band
1991 Inside Out, Chick Corea Elektric Band
1991 Alive, Chick Corea Akoustic Band
1992 Beneath the Mask, Chick Corea Elektric Band
1992 Play, Chick Corea and Bobby McFerrin
1993 Paint The World, Chick Corea Elektric Band II
1994 Expressions (Solo Piano), Chick Corea
1994 Vinnie Colaiuta, Vinnie Colaiuta
1995 Time Warp, Chick Corea Quartet
1996 The Beginning, Chick Corea
1996 From Nothing - Chick Corea Solo Piano (Japan Only), Chick Corea
1996 Live From Elario's (First Gig) Chick Corea Elektric Band, Chick Corea Elektric Band
1996 Circle 2 Gathering (Japan Only), Chick Corea
1996 Live From The Blue Note Tokyo (Japan Only), Chick Corea Akoustic Band
1996 Live From The Country Club (Japan Only), Chick Corea Trio
1996 Forever & Beyond (5-Cd Boxed Set), Chick Corea
1997 Priceless Jazz Collection, Chick Corea
1997 Native Sense - The New Duets, Chick Corea and Gary Burton
1997 Remembering Bud Powell, Chick Corea and Friends
1998 Origin Live at the Blue Note, Chick Corea and Origin
1998 Like Minds, Burton Corea Metheny Haynes Holland
1999 Change, Chick Corea and Origin
1999 Concerto, Chick Corea and the London Philharmonic Orchestra
2000 Solo Piano - Standards, Chick Corea
2000 Solo Piano - Originals, Chick Corea
2001 Past Present & Futures, Chick Corea Trio
2003 Rendezvous In New York, Chick Corea
2004 To the Stars, Chick Corea Elektric Band
2005 Rhumba Flamenco, Chick Corea
2005 The Song is You, Chick Corea
2005 Rendezvous In New York (10-DVD Boxed Set), Chick Corea
2006 The Ultimate Adventure, Chick Corea
2007 The Enchantment, Chick Corea and Béla Fleck
2008 The New Crystal Silence, Chick Corea and Gary Burton
2008 Duet: Chick and Hiromi, Chick Corea and Hiromi Uehara
2008 The Anthology, Return to Forever
2009 Five Peace Band, Chick Corea and John McLaughlin
2009 Returns, Return to Forever
2011 Orvieto, Chick Corea and Stefano Bollani
2011 Forever, Corea, Clarke and White
2011 Live & Let Live – Love For Japan, Makoto Ozone
2012 Hot House, Chick Corea and Gary Burton
2012 The Continents: Concerto for Jazz Quintet and Chamber Orchestra, Chick Corea
2013 Trilogy, Chick Corea Trio
2013 The Vigil, Chick Corea
2014 Solo Piano – Portraits, Chick Corea
2015 Two, Chick Corea and Béla Fleck

## Tony Williams (1945-1997)

Tony Williams is one of the most highly rated and widely respected drummers in the history of jazz, an enviable reputation largely created by his pivotal role in the Miles Davis Second Great Quintet during the 1960s. Davis's selection of the precocious and highly talented 16-year-old was a sufficient statement of Williams' potential. By 1969 he was already one of the most famous drummers in the world to the extent that he was able to attract the similarly talented John McLaughlin from across the Atlantic to join his fledgling jazz-rock fusion band, Lifetime. When Williams encountered a short delay in securing commercial support for his band, Davis poached McLaughlin for his own jazz-fusion recordings. Fortunately for Williams, McLaughlin turned down Davis's invitation to join his band, remaining committed to the Lifetime project with Williams.

Along with organist Larry Young, this formidable trio created a great impact with its own jazz-rock music. The highly respected writer Stuart Nicholson says that Lifetime's first album, *Emergency!* (1969), is one of the most important of all jazz-fusion albums. [5] First hand accounts say that the band was truly astonishing in a live environment, but listening to these recordings in the 21st century can be a very disquieting experience. The music is badly recorded, with poor, unimaginative compositions. Its only positive quality is its energy, which is heterogeneously distributed. Tony Williams was an entirely self-taught drummer who had not demonstrated any particular compositional skills up to this point and even McLaughlin seemed to have been dragged down by it. It may be the case that McLaughlin's experience in the band inspired him directly to produce the stunning results in his own Mahavishnu Orchestra, in which case, the existence of Lifetime had been very worthwhile, but listening to the records is not especially pleasurable. Williams was able to solidify his reputation as a jazz-fusion bandleader with a series of albums throughout the 1980s and 90s, perhaps the best being *Wilderness* (1997). Williams did not play with Davis again after leaving in 1969, although he did maintain a professional relationship with Herbie Hancock until Williams' premature death in 1997.

Discography of Tony Williams
1963 My Point of View, Herbie Hancock
1963 Seven Steps to Heaven, Miles Davis
1964 Four and More, Miles Davis
1964 My Funny Valentine, Miles Davis
1964 The Complete Concert 1964, Miles Davis
1964 Miles in Tokyo, Miles Davis
1964 Lifetime, Tony Williams
1964 Miles Davis in Europe, Miles Davis

1964 Empyrean Isles, Herbie Hancock
1965 Maiden Voyage, Herbie Hancock
1965 The Soothsayer, Wayne Shorter
1965 E.S.P., Miles Davis
1965 Spring, Tony Williams
1966 Miles Smiles, Miles Davis
1966 Cantaloupe Island, Herbie Hancock
1967 Nefertiti, Miles Davis
1967 Sorcerer, Miles Davis
1968 Filles de Kilimanjaro, Miles Davis

1968 Miles in the Sky, Miles Davis
1969 Emergency, The Tony Williams Lifetime
1969 In A Silent Way, Miles Davis
1970 Turn It Over, The Tony Williams Lifetime
1971 Ego, The Tony Williams Lifetime
1972 The Old Bums Rush, The Tony Williams Lifetime
1974 Captain Marvel, Stan Getz
1974 Stanley Clarke, Stanley Clarke
1975 Believe It, The New Tony Williams Lifetime
1976 Water Babies, Miles Davis
1976 Million Dollar Legs, The Tony Williams Lifetime
1977 V.S.O.P., Herbie Hancock
1977 The Quintet, V.S.O.P.
1977 The Herbie Hancock Trio (1977), Herbie Hancock
1978 Sunlight, Herbie Hancock
1978 Mr Gone, Weather Report
1978 The Joy of Flying, Tony Williams
1978 Third Plane, Ron Carter, Herbie Hancock, Tony Williams
1978 Johnny McLaughlin - Electric Guitarist, John McLaughlin
1979 Circle in the Round, Miles Davis
1979 Live Under the Sky, V.S.O.P.
1980 Mr. Hands, Herbie Hancock
1981 Herbie Hancock Trio (1981), Herbie Hancock Trio
1982 Herbie Hancock Quartet, Herbie Hancock Quartet
1985 Foreign Intrigue, Tony Williams
1986 Civilisation, Tony Williams
1988 Angel Street, Tony Williams
1989 Native Heart, Tony Williams
1991 The Story of Neptune, Tony Williams
1992 Tokyo Live, Tony Williams
1992 A Tribute to Miles, Herbie Hancock
1993 The Sun Don't Lie, Marcus Miller
1997 Wilderness, Tony Williams
1998 Young at Heart, Tony Williams
2001 Future 2 Future, Herbie Hancock
2007 Trio of Doom, John McLaughlin, Jaco Pastorius, Tony Williams

# Billy Cobham (b1944)

*Billy Cobham playing with his band, Asere, October 2006*
*(Photo: Ken Trethewey)*

Thanks largely to his musical father and his Panamanian heritage, Billy Cobham had been infused with rhythm since the day he was born. Even after his family had immigrated into the United States, he continued to be immersed in fierce, energetic Latin rhythms. By the time that a spell in the US Army (where he was a musician) came to an end, he was a remarkable drummer and was quickly picked up by the top jazz musicians. He recorded with George Benson (guitar) on *Giblet Gravy* (1968), but his first high point was reached the same year when he joined Horace Silver's band alongside Randy Brecker, Bennie Maupin and others. In March 1968, he recorded some tracks for Silver at Rudy van Gelder's studio and in January 1969 recorded the Blue Note album *You Gotta Take a Little Love* (1969).

Billy recognised the music of jazz-fusion early in his career and, with the Brecker Brothers, was one of the members of the original jazz-fusion band Dreams. By now, his reputation was exploding with energy and, with a base in New York, it was inevitable that Miles Davis would check him out as he investigated the talent available for his experimental bands. When Miles returned from a tour of Europe in November 1969, Billy was invited to some studio recording sessions. The recordings he made then were not released for some years afterwards, but it was here in Columbia's Studio E that he met Bennie Maupin, Steve Grossman, Chick Corea, Herbie Hancock and John McLaughlin. Miles liked what Cobham played and Billy appeared on several Davis albums, but it was his new friendship with John McLaughlin that would perhaps be most important to him at this time because Cobham was John McLaughlin's first choice for his new band Mahavishnu Orchestra.

The short lifetime of the Orchestra caused Cobham to focus on leading his own bands on albums starting with *Spectrum* (1973), *Crosswinds* (1974) and *Total Eclipse* (1974). These very good jazz-fusion albums were a showcase for the kind of skills that had already made him, according to many, the best drummer in the world. They also brought into sharper focus his pals from Dreams, Michael and Randy Brecker, bassist Lee Sklar and guitarist Tommy Bolin, later famous for playing with Deep Purple. John Abercrombie, another friend from the days of Dreams, became a regular sideman. On keyboards we find George Duke, with whom Billy would also make many albums. By 1976, the two men were frequently playing alongside bass megastar Stanley Clarke, and Billy played on Clarke's important landmark album *School Days* (1976).

Despite some moments of disagreement, Cobham remained friends with McLaughlin after the break-up of the first Mahavishnu Orchestra, and was present for at least some of the time during subsequent reincarnations of the band. He has also remained loyal to all his musical friends throughout his career, returning time and again to each one for further recorded projects. For example, Billy played on Larry Coryell's *Spaces* (1970) and on *Spaces Revisited* (1997). Whilst never attaining those amazing heights of performance and prolific appearances that he did in the 1970s, Cobham has had an impressive career. In 1980, influenced by the moves to Europe that some other jazz musicians had made, Cobham did the same and never looked back. Since then he has been prolific number of projects across the whole spectrum of jazz.

Discography of Billy Cobham
1969 Dreams, Dreams
1970 Live Evil, Miles Davis
1970 Spaces, Larry Coryell
1970 Imagine My Surprise, Dreams
1971 The Inner Mounting Flame, Mahavishnu Orchestra
1971 A Tribute To Jack Johnson, Miles Davis
1971 My Goal's Beyond, John McLaughlin
1973 Spectrum, Billy Cobham
1973 Birds of Fire, Mahavishnu Orchestra
1973 Love Devotion Surrender, John McLaughlin and Carlos Santana
1973 Between Nothingness and Eternity, Mahavishnu Orchestra
1974 Total Eclipse, Billy Cobham
1974 Crosswinds, Billy Cobham
1974 Big Fun, Miles Davis
1974 Get Up With It, Miles Davis
1975 A Funky Thide of Sings, Billy Cobham
1975 Shabazz, Billy Cobham
1976 Life and Times, Billy Cobham
1976 School Days, Stanley Clarke
1976 Live on Tour in Europe, The Billy Cobham - George Duke Band
1977 Magic, Billy Cobham

1977 Alivemutherfoya, Billy Cobham
1978 Inner Conflicts, Billy Cobham
1978 Johnny McLaughlin - Electric Guitarist, John McLaughlin
1978 Simplicity of Expression: Depth of Thought, Billy Cobham
1979 Circle in the Round, Miles Davis
1979 B.C., Billy Cobham
1980 Live: Flight Time, Billy Cobham
1981 Atlantis, Clarke/Duke Project
1981 Stratus, Billy Cobham
1982 Smokin', Billy Cobham
1982 Observations and Reflections, Billy Cobham
1982 Observatory, Billy Cobham
1984 A Jazz Hour with the Herbie Hancock Trio in Concert, Herbie Hancock Trio
1984 Mahavishnu, Mahavishnu Orchestra
1985 Consortium, Billy Cobham
1985 Warning, Billy Cobham
1986 Power Play, Billy Cobham
1987 Picture This, Billy Cobham
1988 Billy's Best Hits, Billy Cobham
1989 Incoming, Billy Cobham
1990 No Filters, Billy Cobham
1991 By Design, Billy Cobham
1993 The Traveler, Billy Cobham
1994 Live At The Greek, Stanley Clarke
1996 Paradox: The First Second, Billy Cobham
1996 Paradox, Billy Cobham
1996 Nordic, Billy Cobham
1997 Spaces Revisited, Larry Coryell
1998 Focused, Billy Cobham
1998 Mississippi Nights Live, Billy Cobham
1999 The Lost Trident Sessions, Mahavishnu Orchestra
1999 Nordic: Off Color, Billy Cobham
1999 Ensemble New Hope Street, Billy Cobham
2001 North By Northwest, Billy Cobham
2001 The Art of Three, Billy Cobham
2001 Many Years BC, Billy Cobham
2002 Drum and Voice, Billy Cobham
2003 The Art of Five, Billy Cobham
2005 Caravaggio, Billy Cobham
2006 Drum 'n' Voice 2, Billy Cobham
2006 Meeting of the Spirits, Billy Cobham/ Colin Towns HR-Big Band
2007 The Art of Four, Billy Cobham
2007 Fruit From The Loom, Billy Cobham
2008 De Cuba y de Panama, Billy Cobham and Asere
2009 Slippin' and Trippin', Victor Bailey
2010 Palindrome, Billy Cobham
2010 Drum 'n' Voice Vol. 3, Billy Cobham
2010 Live in Lugano: Supertrio in Concert, Herbie Hancock, Ron Carter, Billy Cobham
2011 Live at Leverkusen Jazzfestival, Billy Cobham Band
2012 The Fusion Syndicate, The Fusion Syndicate
2013 Compass Point, Billy Cobham
2014 Tales From The Skeleton Coast, Billy Cobham

2015 Spectrum 40 Live, Billy Cobham

# Pat Metheny (b1954)

*The Pat Metheny Group performing at the Lighthouse Centre, Poole, UK in 2002. Left to right: Pat Metheny, Antonio Sanchez, Richard Bono. (Photo: Ken Trethewey)*

Pat began his career with jazz-fusion pioneer Gary Burton, although it was not for the purposes of taking part in that kind of music. Pat's apprenticeship was served playing a form of jazz that was at the higher intellectual levels of art, during which time he raised his own academic level by a number of notches. Soon he was out on his own, creating new kinds of guitar and group sounds based upon a kind of American folk music that included improvisation. Immediately it was novel, wide-ranging and popular. He soon formed a band, the Pat Metheny Group that, because of its style and personnel, was at once inserted into the jazz-fusion genre by marketing people keen to promote his music to the record-buying public. Whilst Pat was always uncomfortable with that categorisation, it was beyond his control and critics were constrained to describe his music in that context from the start. Pat was immediately successful with his own proprietary formula. The band's first eponymous album, known colloquially as the *'White'* album), was released in 1977 and began a hugely important series of releases that continued with *American Garage* (1979). Soon the popular success was impossible to ignore and the organisation of his peers responsible for awarding Grammys gave "Best" awards to no fewer than eight albums by the Pat Metheny Group: *Offramp* (1982), *First Circle* (1984), *Still Life (Talking)* (1987), *Letter From Home* (1989), *We Live Here* (1995), *Imaginary Day* (1997), *Speaking of Now* (2002) and *The Way Up* (2005).

As a solo artist, Pat gravitates more strongly back into the mainstream of jazz with an acoustic focus, whilst often trying to integrate other sub-genres of jazz into his music. Pat made it his business to get to know as many of the top jazz musicians as possible and to play and record with them. He was also humble enough to seek out the best emerging talent and to do the same with musicians who were much younger than he was. From time to time, his music may draw upon influences of eastern and Latin flavours, as well as entering the fields of free jazz and only occasionally the blues. There is a strong desire to expand the heritage of solo jazz electric guitar, exemplified by the likes of Jim Hall, Wes Montgomery and Barney Kessel, but ultimately, his work draws upon his roots in Missouri and his love of American culture.

I regard Pat Metheny as one of the foremost jazz musicians alive today. It's true to say that such stars as Wayne Shorter, Chick Corea, John McLaughlin and Herbie Hancock command the highest levels of respect as jazz artists, but as a contributor to jazz, whether playing, composing, arranging or producing, Pat has now made a bigger contribution to his art than anyone. Not only has he moved the art of guitar playing forward into the next generation, but, more relevant to this discussion, he has also invented an entirely new form of jazz-fusion. Based upon two musical traditions in the USA, Pat's creation is a blend of jazz itself and the country/folk traditions of the European settlers to the mid-Western United States. Pat's career is so extensive that I cannot represent it properly in a few paragraphs: interested readers should see my book about him.

It is his work with the Pat Metheny Group that is of most significance to a study of jazz-fusion. Anyone who buys the albums listed above - which are amongst the very best albums in jazz - will soon discover why he is such an important player in this part of jazz. The sounds are unique and instantly recognisable, as colourful as any that have been laid down on tape and the music cuts through to the very soul of its listeners. It is focussed on all of the positive aspects of the human condition, love for family, honour amongst our fellow humans, respect for the beauty of the natural world. Many observers are uncomfortable with such an overt display of human characteristics, especially in a world that fashionably seems to revel in the darker side of humanity. Nevertheless, Pat's approach to melody and harmony has gone down well with the public and his impact on music and the world at large has been immense. However, since PMG's last (and maybe final) album, the ten-year-old *The Way Up* (2005), Pat has, by some accounts, lost direction amongst a series of curious and unrelated projects. With much more of his career still remaining, only in the fullness of time will his true achievements be properly analysed.

Discography of Pat Metheny
1974 Ring, The Gary Burton Quintet with Eberhard Weber
1974 Jaco, Pastorius Metheny Ditmas Bley
1976 Bright Size Life, Pat Metheny
1976 Dreams So Real: Music of Carla Bley, Gary Burton Quartet
1977 Passengers, Gary Burton Quartet with Eberhard Weber
1977 Watercolors, Pat Metheny
1978 Pat Metheny Group, Pat Metheny Group
1979 New Chautauqua, Pat Metheny
1979 American Garage, Pat Metheny Group
1980 Shadows and Light, Joni Mitchell
1980 80/81, Pat Metheny
1981 As Falls Wichita, So Falls Wichita Falls, Pat Metheny and Lyle Mays
1982 Offramp, Pat Metheny Group
1983 Travels, Pat Metheny Group
1984 Rejoicing, Pat Metheny Trio
1984 Works, Pat Metheny
1984 First Circle, Pat Metheny Group
1985 The Falcon and the Snowman, Pat Metheny Group
1987 Still Life (Talking), Pat Metheny Group
1987 Michael Brecker, Michael Brecker
1988 Works II, Pat Metheny
1989 Letter From Home, Pat Metheny Group
1989 Different Trains/Electric Counterpoint, Steve Reich, Pat Metheny
1990 Parallel Realities Live, de Johnette, Metheny, Hancock, Holland
1990 Question and Answer, Pat Metheny Trio
1990 Reunion, Gary Burton
1991 Blue Asphalt, Pat Metheny Group
1991 The Road To You, Pat Metheny Group
1992 Till We Have Faces, Gary Thomas
1992 Secret Story, Pat Metheny
1993 In Concert, Pat Metheny Group
1993 Wish, Joshua Redman
1993 Harbor Lights, Bruce Hornsby Band
1994 Te Vous / Praise, Roy Haynes
1994 I Can See Your House From Here, John Scofield and Pat Metheny
1994 Zero Tolerance for Silence, Pat Metheny
1995 We Live Here, Pat Metheny Group
1995 Blues for Pat - Live in San Francisco, Joshua Redman Quartet
1996 Hot House, Bruce Hornsby Band
1996 We Live Here - Live in Japan, Pat Metheny Group
1996 Tales From the Hudson, Michael Brecker
1996 Passagio per il Paradiso, Pat Metheny
1996 Pursuance: The Music of John Coltrane, Kenny Garrett Quartet
1996 Quartet, Pat Metheny Group
1997 Imaginary Day, Pat Metheny Group
1997 Beyond the Missouri Sky (Short Stories), Charlie Haden and Pat
1997 The Elements - Water, Dave Liebman Quartet
1997 Across the Sky, Pat Metheny Group
1997 Wilderness, Tony Williams
1997 The Sign of 4, Derek Bailey, Pat Metheny, Gregg Bendian, Paul Wertico
1998 Like Minds, Burton Corea Metheny Haynes Holland
1999 The Sound of Summer Running, Marc Johnson
1999 Jim Hall and Pat Metheny, Jim Hall and Pat Metheny
1999 A Map of the World, Pat Metheny
1999 Time is of the Essence, Michael Brecker
2000 Trio 99-00, Pat Metheny Trio
2000 Trio Live, Pat Metheny Trio
2001 Reverence, Richard Bona
2001 Nearness of You: The Ballad Book, Michael Brecker
2001 Nocturne, Charlie Haden
2001 Imaginary Day Live, Pat Metheny Group
2002 Speaking of Now, Pat Metheny Group
2003 Speaking of Now Live, Pat Metheny Group

2003 One Quiet Night, Pat Metheny
2004 Selected Recordings, Pat Metheny
2005 The Way Up, Pat Metheny Group
2005 Song X: Twentieth Anniversary, Pat Metheny
2005 The Song is You, Chick Corea
2006 The Way Up Live, Pat Metheny Group
2006 Metheny Mehldau, Pat Metheny and Brad Mehldau
2007 Metheny Mehldau Quartet, Metheny Mehldau Quartet
2007 Pilgrimage, Michael Brecker
2007 Migration, Antonio Sanchez
2008 Day Trip, Pat Metheny
2008 Upojenie, Pat Metheny and Anna Maria Jopek
2008 Tokyo Day Trip, Pat Metheny, Christian McBride, Antonio Sanchez
2009 Quartet Live, Gary Burton, Pat Metheny, Steve Swallow, Antonio Sanchez
2010 Orchestrion, Pat Metheny
2011 What's It All About, Pat Metheny
2012 Unity Band, Pat Metheny
2014 Kin (<-->), Pat Metheny

*Pat Metheny performing with his band at the Hammersmith Appollo in London, 2005. (Photo: Ken Trethewey)*

# The Brecker Brothers: Randy (b1945) and Michael (1949-2007)

*The Brecker Brothers, Michael and Randy. (Photo courtesy of Randy Brecker)*

The story of the Brecker Brothers is long and convoluted. Both men came from a strong musical family and were extremely gifted. Both were in at the very start of the jazz-fusion boom when, as members of the band Dreams, they participated in the early albums *Dreams* (1969) and *Imagine My Surprise* (1970). Based together in New York, older brother Randy had got a head start by his early arrival there and by his membership of the seminal band Blood Sweat and Tears. Randy played on the band's first album *Child is Father to the Man* (1968) before there was a major change of personnel. He was soon joined in the Big Apple by his brother Michael, and it was as a horn twosome that they began to play all across the city in bands such as Dreams, White Elephant, Larry Coryell's Eleventh House, Billy Cobham and Average White Band. Both men were soon in great demand as session musicians, and flitted daily around the New York studios, involved in a large proportion of the cutting-edge jazz-fusion projects of the early 1970s. Their core of friends – David Sanborn, Don Grolnick, Steve Gadd, Will Lee and Ralph MacDonald – all became leading jazz-fusion musicians, largely through the huge popular success of one of the funkiest bands of the 1970s, the Brecker Brothers. The sequence of albums they released is well worth listening to today: *The Brecker Brothers* (1975), *Back to Back* (1976), *Don't Stop the Music* (1977), *Heavy Metal Bebop* (1978), *Détente* (1980) and *Straphangin'* (1981). They were so successful that by 1980 they had their own jazz club, 7th Ave South, and their even closer involvement with jazz resulted in Michael's joining a new band called Steps (later, Steps Ahead) led by vibraphone player Mike Mainieri.

The careers of the two men now began to diverge somewhat. For example, Michael continued to play extensively on albums by other jazz stars such as Tony Williams' *The Joy of Flying* (1979) and Joni Mitchell's *Shadows and Light* (1980), as a result of which he developed a close friendship with Pat Metheny. He also played with such widely ranging people as Charles Mingus and Herbie Hancock, as well as being a popular choice for the notoriously demanding sessions for Steely Dan. It was probably Michael's work for Steps Ahead that is of most interest to us in this period because he became a leading exponent of the electronic wind instrument (EWI), adding an extra dimension to the whole ethos of what jazz-fusion music could achieve. A particular peak of achievement was reached with his performances on *Magnetic* (1986).

Remarkably, Michael had not recorded any albums as leader until well into the middle part of his career. In 1987, aged 38, Michael finally began a series of albums that would move away somewhat from the more clearly defined forms of jazz-fusion towards an attempt to use his supreme gifts to make a mark on the purer forms of jazz. A self-effacing man, he would have been embarrassed to admit to just how good he was, but it is unarguable that, with his hero John Coltrane for inspiration, Brecker set out to push back the frontiers of just what could be achieved on his instrument. Many would argue that he was entirely successful and became the leading exponent of tenor saxophone of his generation. However, that remarkable achievement was done in a universe almost parallel with his fabulous contributions to jazz-fusion, which were still incomplete.

Randy, meanwhile, was to be found on albums with other tenor saxophone players such as Bob Mintzer and Tom Scott, but would always be reunited with his brother on albums by their many musician friends. Perhaps it was always possible that the Brecker Brothers would reunite one day in the band that scored a deep mark into the 1970s, and eventually it took place for two superb albums *Return of the Brecker Brothers* (1992) and *Out of the Loop* (1994). For a complete history of the work of these two jazz legends, you should read my book in this series, *The Brecker Brothers, Funky Sea, Funky Blue*.

Discography of Michael Brecker
1969 Dreams, Dreams
1970 Imagine My Surprise, Dreams
1972 In The Public Interest, Gary Burton
1972 In Pursuit of the 27th Man, Horace Silver
1972 White Elephant, White Elephant
1973 The Real Great Escape, Larry Coryell
1974 Crosswinds, Billy Cobham
1974 Total Eclipse, Billy Cobham
1974 AWB, Average White Band
1975 The Brecker Brothers, The Brecker Brothers
1975 Shabazz, Billy Cobham
1975 Still Crazy After All These Years, Paul Simon
1975 Taking Off, David Sanborn
1975 A Funky Thide of Sings, Billy Cobham
1976 (Eleventh House) Aspects, Larry Coryell
1976 Jaco Pastorius, Jaco Pastorius
1976 Back to Back, The Brecker Brothers Band
1977 Don t Stop the Music, The Brecker Brothers
1977 Love Play, Mike Mainieri
1977 Heads, Bob James
1978 Heart To Heart, David Sanborn
1978 Heavy Metal Bebop, The Brecker Brothers
1978 Strokin, Richard Tee
1978 Me, Myself, An Eye, Charles Mingus
1978 The Joy of Flying, Tony Williams
1978 Difference, Larry Coryell
1978 Inner Conflicts, Billy Cobham
1979 Morning Dance, Spyro Gyra
1979 Lucky Seven, Bob James
1980 Détente, The Brecker Brothers
1980 80/81, Pat Metheny
1980 Carnaval, Spyro Gyra

1980 Shadows and Light, Joni Mitchell
1980 Step By Step, Steps
1980 Smokin' in the Pit, Steps
1980 Something Like a Bird, Charles Mingus
1981 Freetime, Spyro Gyra
1981 Straphangin', The Brecker Brothers
1981 Wanderlust, Mike Mainieri
1981 Magic Windows, Herbie Hancock
1981 Word of Mouth, Jaco Pastorius
1981 Three Quartets , Chick Corea
1982 Paradox, Steps
1982 Cityscape, Claus Ogerman with Michael Brecker
1982 Peter Erskine, Peter Erskine
1982 The Nightfly, Donald Fagen
1983 Papa Lips, Bob Mintzer and the Horn Man Band
1983 Friends, Larry Carlton
1983 The Genie, Bob James
1983 An Innocent Man, Billy Joel
1983 Steps Ahead, Steps Ahead
1984 Gaucho, Steely Dan
1984 Works, Pat Metheny
1984 Straight To The Heart, David Sanborn
1984 Modern Times, Steps Ahead
1985 Brothers In Arms, Dire Straits
1986 Live in Tokyo 1986, Steps Ahead
1986 From All Sides, Hiram Bullock
1986 Magnetic, Steps Ahead
1986 Obsession, Bob James
1987 A Change Of Heart, David Sanborn
1987 Michael Brecker, Michael Brecker
1987 Members Only, Nelson Rangell
1987 Give It What U Got, Hiram Bullock
1988 Time In Place, Mike Stern
1988 John Patitucci, John Patitucci
1988 Don't Try This at Home, Michael Brecker
1988 Works II, Pat Metheny
1988 Times Like These, Gary Burton

1988 Motion Poet, Peter Erskine
1989 Bottom's Up, Victor Bailey
1989 Jigsaw, Mike Stern
1989 On the Corner, John Patitucci
1990 Sketchbook, John Patitucci
1990 Master Plan, Dave Weckl Band
1990 Grand Piano Canyon, Bob James
1990 Toe to Toe, Randy Brecker
1990 Life Colors, Chuck Loeb
1991 In the Door, Joey Calderazzo
1991 Song of the Sun, Jim Beard
1992 Now You See It (Now You Don't), Michael Brecker
1992 Return of the Brecker Brothers, The Brecker Brothers
1993 Two T's, Bob Mintzer
1993 Another World, John Patitucci
1994 Restless, Bob James
1994 Out of the Loop, The Brecker Brothers
1994 The Birthday Concert, Jaco Pastorius
1994 Tenderness, Al Jarreau
1994 Is What It Is, Mike Stern
1995 Medianoche, Don Grolnick
1996 The New Standard, Herbie Hancock
1996 The Music Inside, Chuck Loeb
1996 The Promise, John McLaughlin
1996 Tales From the Hudson, Michael Brecker
1997 Wilderness, Tony Williams
1997 Give and Take, Mike Stern
1997 One More Angel, John Patitucci
1997 East River, The Brecker Brothers
1998 Now, John Patitucci
1998 Two Blocks from the Edge, Michael Brecker
1999 Scenes From My Life, Richard Bona
1999 Time is of the Essence, Michael Brecker
1999 Inside, David Sanborn
2000 The London Concert, Don Grolnick
2000 Celebrating the Music of Weather Report, Various Artists
2001 Hangin in the City, Randy Brecker
2001 Voices, Mike Stern
2001 Nearness of You: The Ballad Book, Michael Brecker
2001 Reverence, Richard Bona
2002 Score, Randy Brecker
2002 Directions in Music, Herbie Hancock
2002 34th N Lex, Randy Brecker
2003 Wide Angles, Michael Brecker Quindectet
2004 Selected Recordings, Pat Metheny
2005 Some Skunk Funk, Randy Brecker, Michael Brecker
2006 Sneakin' Up Behind You: The Very Best of, The Brecker Brothers
2007 Copenhagen Live, Steps Ahead
2007 Pilgrimage, Michael Brecker
2010 Live in Tokyo U-Port Hall 1995 [DVD], The Brecker Brothers
2010 Angle of Repose [DVD], Michael Brecker Quindectet
2012 The Complete Arista Collection, The Brecker Brothers

Discography of Randy Brecker
1969 Dreams, Dreams
1970 Imagine My Surprise, Dreams
1972 In Pursuit of the 27th Man, Horace Silver
1972 In The Public Interest, Gary Burton
1974 AWB, Average White Band
1974 The Eleventh House, Larry Coryell
1974 Total Eclipse, Billy Cobham
1974 Crosswinds, Billy Cobham
1975 A Funky Thide of Sings, Billy Cobham
1975 Taking Off, David Sanborn
1975 The Brecker Brothers, The Brecker Brothers
1976 Jaco Pastorius, Jaco Pastorius
1976 Back to Back, The Brecker Brothers Band
1977 Don t Stop the Music, The Brecker Brothers
1978 Heart To Heart, David Sanborn
1978 Heavy Metal Bebop, The Brecker Brothers
1979 Morning Dance, Spyro Gyra
1980 Détente, The Brecker Brothers
1981 Straphangin', The Brecker Brothers
1982 The Nightfly, Donald Fagen
1983 Papa Lips, Bob Mintzer and the Horn Man Band
1983 Invitation, Jaco Pastorius
1985 Amanda, Randy Brecker, Eliane Elias

1985 Hearts and Numbers, Don Grolnick
1986 In the Idiom, Randy Brecker
1988 Street Dreams, Lyle Mays
1988 Live at Sweet Basil, Randy Brecker
1990 Toe to Toe, Randy Brecker
1991 Art of the Big Band, Bob Mintzer Big Band
1992 Return of the Brecker Brothers, The Brecker Brothers
1992 Heads Up, Dave Weckl Band
1992 Born Again, Tom Scott
1992 Upfront, David Sanborn
1993 Standards and Other Songs, Mike Stern
1993 Kamakyriad, Donald Fagen
1994 Out of the Loop, The Brecker Brothers
1995 Into the Sun, Randy Brecker
1996 Songs From The Night Before, David Sanborn
1997 East River, The Brecker Brothers
1997 A Prescription for the Blues, Horace Silver Quintet
1998 Focused, Billy Cobham
2000 Celebrating the Music of Weather Report, Various Artists
2000 The London Concert, Don Grolnick
2000 The JazzTimes Superband, Bob Berg, Randy Brecker, Dennis Chambers, Joey DeFrancesco
2001 Hangin in the City, Randy Brecker
2002 34th N Lex, Randy Brecker
2002 Score, Randy Brecker
2003 Timeagain, David Sanborn
2004 Soul Bop Band Live, Bill Evans, Randy Brecker
2005 Some Skunk Funk, Randy Brecker, Michael Brecker
2006 Sneakin' Up Behind You: The Very Best of, The Brecker Brothers
2006 Both / And, Marc Copland, Randy Brecker
2007 The Other Side of Something, Bill Evans
2008 Randy in Brasil, Randy Brecker
2008 Seraphic Light, Saxophone Summit
2009 Nostalgic Journey: Tykocin Jazz Suite, Randy Brecker
2010 Live In Tokyo U-Port Hall 1995 [DVD], The Brecker Brothers
2012 The Complete Arista Collection, The Brecker Brothers
2013 Randy Brecker Plays Wlodek Pawlik's Night In Calisia, Randy Brecker, Wlodek Pawlik
2013 The Brecker Brothers Band Reunion, Randy Brecker
2013 One Way Road To My Heart, AMC Trio with Randy Brecker
2014 Trumpet Story, The Bill Warfield Big Band featuring Randy Brecker
2015 Dearborn Station, Randy Brecker with the DePaul University Jazz Ensemble
2015 RandyPOP Live, Randy Brecker

*Left: The Brecker Brothers performing at the North Sea Jazz Festival in 1992. (Photo: Louis Gerrits)*

# David Sanborn (b1945)

*David Sanborn (centre) performing with Hiram Bullock (left) at the Royal Festival Hall, London in 1992. (Photo: Ken Trethewey)*

David Sanborn was an early member of the jazz-fusion movement, like his friends Michael and Randy Brecker with whom he recorded numerous albums. Sanborn views himself not as a jazz musician but as a soul-blues music player. Nevertheless, his music fits well into the jazz-fusion sub-genre, and with many of the top fusion musicians at his side he was able to develop the art of saxophone playing so much that he played a significant role in its absorption into the popular mainstream. We could therefore argue that he was a leading exponent of jazz-pop or 'smooth jazz' as many would call it. Fortunately, his reputation remained high despite his great exposure in shopping malls, restaurants and elevators.

David's reputation as a bluesman began with his membership of the Paul Butterfield Blues Band, an outfit remembered by many people for the famous blues guitar sound of Mike Bloomfield. Paul Butterfield became well known all across the USA as one of the few serious competitors against the foreign invasion by British blues bands in the mid-1960s. After Bloomfield's departure for other projects, Butterfield changed his line-up to include saxophone, and

Sanborn was hired. This gave him much deep experience of life on the road with a popular live band, but did not provide him with the profile he needed for the next big step up. It was perhaps Sanborn's performances with Stevie Wonder that gave him that extra recognition, especially on *Talking Book* (1972), yet his solo recording career began only with his debut album, *Takin' Off* (1975). In parallel, he was by now a member of the Brecker Brothers cutting edge funky outfit, appearing on *The Brecker Brothers* (1975) and *Back to Back* (1976). He also made guest appearances for John McLaughlin on *Johnny McLaughlin – Electric Guitarist* (1978) and *Electric Dreams* (1979). But it was his work as leader that quickly found success and the financial necessity for session work was diminished. Sanborn began to record and tour, and released albums that illustrated a progressive and rapid improvement both in musical style and in saxophone technique. His hard, penetrating tone became the model for others to copy, whilst his fluency with "off-the-top" (extremely high) notes was especially awesome to less experienced players.

He gained his first Grammy for Best R&B Instrumental Performance for *All I Need is You*, a track from the hit album *Voyeur* (1981), by which time he had established relationships with most of the top jazz-fusion musicians who were used on his albums. For example, the Breckers played on Sanborn's *Heart to Heart* (1978), whilst session supremo, drummer Steve Gadd, became a Sanborn regular during this period. Guitarist Hiram Bullock was a long-time member of Sanborn's bands, and pianist Don Grolnick was likewise in many of Sanborn's line-ups.

Perhaps the most significant relationship Sanborn formed was with the uniquely talented bass player and multi-instrumentalist Marcus Miller. Sanborn's music developed significantly through the 1980s, with Miller taking on more and more of the production role, as well as contributing some of the most rhythmic bass lines in the business. Miller's strongly funk/soul/blues- based style was a perfect match for Sanborn's background. A string of very good albums ensued: *As We Speak* (1982), *Backstreet* (1983), *Straight to the Heart* (1984) and *Double Vision* (1986), a record with pianist Bob James. For contemporary Sanborn watchers like me, each release seemed to be an advance on the previous one, and much of that progress was attributable to Miller. The rise and rise of Sanborn's career culminated with his two finest albums, *A Change of Heart* (1987) and *Close Up* (1988).

There is no doubt that throughout the 1980s, David Sanborn was one of a small elite of the best jazz-fusion saxophone players. His saxophone sound was the most instantly recognisable (and his style was the most widely imitated) simply because of the astonishing amount of exposure he received. After *Close Up*, he took a break from his established style and surrendered to the regression made by many jazzers to purer forms of jazz. *Another Hand* (1991) was a poor album and a rare blip in what had until then been a remarkable career. David Sanborn has continued to release very acceptable harmonic and lyrical albums steadily over the years since then, but it was from that high pinnacle in 1988 that he had completed his best work.

Discography of David Sanborn
1967 The Resurrection of Pigboy Crabshaw, The Paul Butterfield Blues Band
1972 Talking Book, Stevie Wonder
1975 The Brecker Brothers, The Brecker Brothers
1975 Taking Off, David Sanborn
1976 Back to Back, The Brecker Brothers Band
1976 Sanborn, David Sanborn
1976 Jaco Pastorius, Jaco Pastorius
1977 Promise Me the Moon, David Sanborn
1978 Heart To Heart, David Sanborn
1978 Johnny McLaughlin - Electric Guitarist, John McLaughlin
1979 Electric Dreams, One Truth Band
1980 Hideaway, David Sanborn
1981 Voyeur, David Sanborn
1982 As We Speak, David Sanborn
1982 Casino Lights, Various Artists
1983 Neesh, Mike Stern
1983 Backstreet, David Sanborn
1983 Suddenly, Marcus Miller
1984 Gaucho, Steely Dan
1984 Straight To The Heart, David Sanborn
1986 Double Vision, David Sanborn and Bob James
1986 Upside Downside, Mike Stern
1987 A Change Of Heart, David Sanborn
1988 Close Up, David Sanborn

1991 Another Hand, David Sanborn
1992 Upfront, David Sanborn
1992 Return of the Brecker Brothers, The Brecker Brothers
1993 The Sun Don't Lie, Marcus Miller
1994 The Best of David Sanborn, David Sanborn
1994 Hearsay, David Sanborn
1995 Pearls, David Sanborn
1995 Into the Sun, Randy Brecker
1995 Love Songs, David Sanborn
1995 Big Girl, Candy Dulfer
1996 Songs From The Night Before, David Sanborn
1996 The Promise, John McLaughlin
1997 Give and Take, Mike Stern
1999 Inside, David Sanborn
2000 Celebrating the Music of Weather Report, Various Artists
2002 34th N Lex, Randy Brecker
2002 The Essentials, David Sanborn
2003 Timeagain, David Sanborn
2005 Closer, David Sanborn
2006 Sneakin' Up Behind You: The Very Best of The Brecker Brothers
2007 Rendezvous, Jorge Dalto and Superfriends
2010 Only Everything, David Sanborn
2013 Quartette Humaine, Bob James and David Sanborn
2014 Enjoy the View, Bobby Hutcherson
2015 Time and the River, David Sanborn

## Jaco Pastorius (1951-1987)

Electric bass was an instrument that played a significant role in the formulation of successful jazz-fusion. The character of its sound was gutsier, it lent itself more to the stronger male feel that was the essence of rock music and, when amplified it could compete with the high volume demanded by rock music. Instead of the genteel, elegant – even professorial - rhythm of the acoustic bass, the electric bass kicked ass with a feral intensity that had been unknown in jazz up to that time. And amplification lent itself to signal transformations that produced entirely new kinds of sounds. Technique too played a part, perhaps the most obvious innovation being the slap-style of playing that characterised much of the funky jazz-fusion when soul was added to the mix.

Jaco Pastorius was a self-taught electric bass player from Miami Florida who entirely revolutionised his instrument. In a world in which the term 'genius' is often too liberally used, many observers believe the term truly applies to Jaco. After a short apprenticeship on the road with Wayne Cochrane and the CC Riders, Pastorius began to astonish audiences with his incomparable skills and his unique sound using a bruised and battered Fender Jazz bass instrument from which he had crudely removed the frets and filled the holes with wood-filler. Hence, the sound of a fretless electric bass is associated more with Pastorius than any other player.

Jaco began to appear on albums from 1974 onwards. Pastorius played on all tracks for *Jaco* (1974) that featured a quartet put together by pianist Paul Bley and contained Pat Metheny. Pastorius had already formed a relationship with Metheny because of their association with the University of Florida, and it was Jaco that Pat invited to play bass on his own debut album *Bright Size Life* (1976). He made an appearance on the suite *Golden Dawn* from Al di Meola's *Land of the Midnight Sun* (1976). But Jaco's biggest early break came when he was recommended to pop star Joni Mitchell by blues guitarist Robben Ford. Mitchell was captivated by Jaco's unique sound and his treatment of the bass as a solo instrument, rather than just another rhythm device. Consequently, Jaco contributed as much – possibly more - to Mitchell's "jazz period" as any other musician.

His stunning debut album *Jaco Pastorius* (1976) took the jazz world by storm, as also did his own self-styled title as "The World's Greatest Bass Player". His brash, egotistical approach was, however, backed up by immense ability and he was able to talk Joe Zawinul into giving him a job with the leading jazz-fusion band of the time, Weather Report. Once he appeared alongside these top musicians, his future was in large measure assured by the remarkable albums *Black Market* (1976), *Heavy Weather* (1977) and *Mr Gone* (1978).

Unfortunately, influenced by Joe Zawinul, a notorious heavy-drinker and a man he respected enormously, Jaco became badly affected by the abuse of alcohol. His behaviour became increasingly destructive both on and off the stage and Zawinul eventually fired him because of it. Pastorius did his best to continue his amazing career by forming his own band, Word of Mouth, in the company of such great musicians as Randy and Michael Brecker and Peter Erskine, but despite making some good records, his decline because of substance abuse continued. He suffered several mental breakdowns and his behaviour became so outrageous that he was shunned by almost all who knew him. Guitarist Mike Stern was one of the few musicians who could hang out with Jaco and it was Stern who gave Jaco one of his last opportunities to appear on record with *Upside, Downside* (1986). Pastorius died in 1987 after being beaten up outside a nightclub. However, his musical legacy remains as a testament to his supreme abilities on electric bass, and many people - including me - continue to regard him as the "World's Greatest Bass Player".

Discography of Jaco Pastorius
1974 Jaco, Pastorius Metheny Ditmas Bley
1976 Land of the Midnight Sun, Al di Meola
1976 Hejira, Joni Mitchell
1976 Bright Size Life, Pat Metheny
1976 Jaco Pastorius, Jaco Pastorius
1976 Black Market, Weather Report
1977 Don Juan's Reckless Daughter, Joni Mitchell
1977 Heavy Weather, Weather Report
1978 Sunlight, Herbie Hancock
1978 Mr Gone, Weather Report
1979 8-30, Weather Report
1979 Mingus, Joni Mitchell
1980 Night Passage, Weather Report
1980 Shadows and Light, Joni Mitchell
1980 Mr. Hands, Herbie Hancock
1981 Word of Mouth, Jaco Pastorius
1982 Weather Report 2, Weather Report
1983 Invitation, Jaco Pastorius
1985 Source, Bob Mintzer
1986 Jaco Pastorius in New York, Jaco Pastorius
1986 Upside Downside, Mike Stern
1988 Works II, Pat Metheny
1994 The Birthday Concert, Jaco Pastorius
2002 Live and Unreleased, Weather Report
2004 Selected Recordings, Pat Metheny
2005 Word of Mouth Revisited, Jaco Pastorius Big Band
2006 The Word is Out, Jaco Pastorius Big Band
2006 Forecast: Tomorrow, Weather Report
2007 Trio of Doom, John McLaughlin, Jaco Pastorius, Tony Williams
2007 Live at the Aurex Jazz Festival [DVD], Jaco Pastorius and Word of Mouth Big Band
2008 Live in Japan and Canada 1982 [DVD], Jaco Pastorius
2010 Trilogue – Live in Berlin 1976 [DVD], Jaco Pastorius
2011 Live in Offenbach 1978 [CD and DVD], Weather Report
2015 The Legendary Live Tapes 1978-1981, Weather Report

## Stanley Clarke (b1951)

Stanley Clarke is widely regarded as one of the world's top bass players. Although he has frequently been compared to Jaco Pastorius, conservatory-trained Clarke has a range with his instrument that is much wider than Jaco's and there are many who consider Clarke to be easily the greatest all-round bass player. At home on acoustic or electric instruments, he is also a fine jazz composer and orchestrator who has spent much of his working career on scores for film and TV. However, it was on electric bass in the jazz-rock band Return to Forever that he first made his mark and he is therefore inevitably described as primarily a jazz-fusion musician.

Born in Philadelphia, Clarke made a great start to his career by joining Chick Corea in 1972, with whom he has recorded many times over the years since then. Corea was forming his first version of the very important jazz-fusion band Return to Forever and alongside Clarke was saxophonist Joe Farrell and percussionist Airto Moreira with his wife Flora Purim. Within a month of recording the band's first eponymous album, Clarke was recording Corea compositions in the studio with Chick, Stan Getz and Tony Williams for Getz's album *Captain Marvel* (1974). But in these early times of jazz-fusion, the real formula had not yet been evaluated and the music that Chick presented to his musicians was Latin-based rather than jazz-rock. Farrell, for example, was already established as a leading mainstream saxman, whilst Moreira and Purim were Brazilians who embroidered the early RTF music into the style of Getz's mid-60s successes. A second RTF album in the same Latin flavour entitled *Light as a Feather* (1972) was released the same year, and at the end of that year Farrell chose Clarke to play on his own mainstream/free jazz album *Moon Germs* (1972) along with Herbie Hancock and Jack de Johnette.

Although RTF made a big impact in the jazz world, it was not in the same league of importance as Chick's second line-up. Largely inspired by the massive success of the Mahavishnu Orchestra, Chick wanted to do something similar. Thus, Clarke found himself in the spotlight of one of the great jazz-fusion bands of all time, alongside guitar heavyweight Bill Connors and drummer Lenny White. (Al Di Meola replaced Connors for later RTF albums). Clarke continued to appear on all subsequent albums by Return to Forever, during which time he forged a very strong bond with Corea. Thus after the break-up of RTF he was often Chick's first choice bass player on albums such as *My Spanish Heart* (1976), *Tap Step* (1980) and *Touchstone* (1982).

As a solo artist too, Clarke's career was solid, if not prolific. His first eponymous album of 1974 was followed by the highly influential *School Days* (1976). From then on, the steady stream of albums that followed did not somehow hit the same mark as many of his albums with other musicians. Thus *Modern Man* (1978), *Rock, Pebbles and Sand* (1980) and *Let Me Know You* (1982) did not live up to expectations as he seemed to find it difficult to extract himself from the bull's eye scored by *School Days*.

Clarke's slightly unexciting solo career was more than compensated for by his work alongside other jazz giants. Thus, when Lenny White brought a project of his own to fruition involving Clarke with Chick Corea, Freddie Hubbard and Joe Henderson, *Griffith Park Collection* (1982) and *Echoes of an Era* (1982) were the result. The album *East River Drive* (1994) was a great artistic success with Stanley supported by an army of jazz stars, and that studio album was followed up with another collaborative project involving Larry Carlton, Billy Cobham, Najee and Deron Johnson entitled *Live at the Greek* (1994). *Rite of Strings* (1995) with Al di Meola and Jean-Luc Ponty was another exciting collaboration, whilst Tony Williams' *Wilderness* (1997) with Clarke, Herbie Hancock, Pat Metheny and Michael Brecker was a particularly special album.

Clarke was also one of a relatively small number of jazz-fusion musicians who successfully made the cross-over to the music world beyond jazz where his jazz-fusion credentials and his slap technique made him a prince of the disco and his fiery energy turned him into a jazz-rock-bass superstar. In particular, he was part of a rock band called Animal Logic, formed by ex-Police drummer Stewart Copeland, and two albums bearing the band's name were released in 1989 and 1991. Clarke's work in a long-term partnership with the flamboyant keyboardist George Duke helped to gain him much crossover popularity thanks to Duke's reputation with extrovert jazz-rocker Frank Zappa. Clarke and Duke released three albums (1981, 1983, 1990) under the heading of the *Clarke/Duke Project*.

During the period from 1995 to 2007, as sales of jazz albums declined, Clarke directed his attention towards the lucrative work offered by the composition of TV and film scores. However, a scattering of recording projects slowly emerged, notably with pianist McCoy Tyner in 1999-2000, and a bass supergroup project with Marcus Miller and Victor Wooten that was released as *Thunder* (2008). A wide-ranging solo album called *The Toys of Men* (2007) reminded jazz fans of what they had been missing for all these years. Then in 2008 the world was stunned when Corea (who had in 2004 unsuccessfully reformed the Elektric Band) finally reformed Return to Forever in its premier jazz-rock format. Two albums resulted, the first *Anthology* (2008) was a retrospective of earlier recordings, the second was an entirely new album and DVD of the band playing the older material live and called *Returns* (2009).

Today, as a solo artist Clarke is still best remembered for his composition *School Days*, which he has performed on numerous albums. However, his presence in one of the greatest jazz-fusion bands will always be his crowning achievement.

Discography of Stanley Clarke
1971 Black Unity, Pharoah Sanders
1972 Moon Germs, Joe Farrell
1972 Return To Forever, Return To Forever
1972 Light As A Feather, Return to Forever
1973 Hymn of the Seventh Galaxy, Return to Forever
1974 Captain Marvel, Stan Getz
1974 Stanley Clarke, Stanley Clarke
1975 No Mystery, Return to Forever
1975 Journey To Love, Stanley Clarke
1976 School Days, Stanley Clarke
1976 Romantic Warrior, Return To Forever
1976 Land of the Midnight Sun, Al di Meola
1976 My Spanish Heart, Chick Corea
1977 Musicmagic, Return To Forever
1978 Return To Forever Live - The Complete Concert, Return To Forever
1978 Johnny McLaughlin - Electric Guitarist, John McLaughlin
1978 RTF Live (4-Record Set), Return To Forever
1978 Modern Man, Stanley Clarke
1980 Tap Step, Chick Corea
1980 Rocks, Pebbles And Sand, Stanley Clarke
1980 The Best Of Return To Forever, Return To Forever
1981 Clarke / Duke Project, Stanley Clarke and George Duke
1981 Atlantis, Clarke/Duke Project
1982 Griffith Park Collection, Corea/ White/ Clarke/ Henderson/ Hubbard
1982 Echoes Of An Era, Corea/ White/ Clarke/ Henderson/ Hubbard
1982 Touchstone, Chick Corea
1982 Let Me Know You, Stanley Clarke
1983 Clarke / Duke Project II, Stanley Clarke and George Duke
1984 Time Exposure, Stanley Clarke
1986 Hideaway, Stanley Clarke
1988 If This Bass Could Only Talk, Stanley Clarke
1990 Clarke / Duke Project III, Stanley Clarke and George Duke
1993 East River Drive, Stanley Clarke
1994 Live At The Greek, Stanley Clarke
1994 I Wanna Play For You, Stanley Clarke
1995 The Rite of Strings, Al di Meola, Stanley Clarke, Jean-Luc Ponty
1996 Return To The 7th Galaxy Anthology Of Return To Forever, Return To Forever
1997 Wilderness, Tony Williams
2007 The Toys of Men, Stanley Clarke
2008 Thunder, Stanley Clarke, Marcus Miller and Victor Wooten
2008 The Anthology, Return to Forever
2009 Returns, Return to Forever
2009 Jazz In The Garden, Stanley Clarke Trio
2010 The Stanley Clarke Band, The Stanley Clarke Band
2011 Forever, Corea, Clarke & White
2014 Up, The Stanley Clarke Band
2015 D-Stringz, Stanley Clarke, Birelli Lagrene, Jean-Luc Ponty

# Marcus Miller (b1959)

Miller commenced a musical education at the High School of Music and Art (now the LaGuardia School of Performing Arts), where he studied recorder, clarinet and saxophone. He followed that up with further music courses at Queens College, NY where he continued to study clarinet. However, he had by now earned himself a considerable reputation as a funky bass player in the New York area, and it was this that persuaded him to take up a career as a full-time musician. He was soon a member of the house band for the popular American TV show, *Saturday Night Live* (1978-9) and playing on many recordings by top pop musicians such as Luther Vandross's *Never Too Much* (1981), Roberta Flack's *Bustin' Loose* (1981), Carly Simon's *Hello Big Man* (1983), Bryan Ferry's *Boys and Girls* (1985) and Billy Idol's *Whiplash Smile* (1986). He was a popular sideman with top jazz musicians too, notably Grover Washington Jr., for whom he played on *Winelight* (1980) and *Come Morning* (1981), and McCoy Tyner's *It's About Time* (1986).

Miller's great break came when Miles Davis invited him to make the album *Tutu* (1986). This superb album became one of the significant milestones of Davis's final career phase and Miller's contribution to the album was enormous, whether as composer, musician, arranger or producer. It set him on the road to much later success, despite the much poorer album with Davis, *Music From Siesta* (1987), although he made up for this with *Amandla* (1989). More recently, Miller has focussed his efforts on production, but his reputation as one of the great electric bass players is secure.

Discography of Marcus Miller
1980 Hideaway, David Sanborn
1980 Détente, The Brecker Brothers
1980 Winelight, Grover Washington Jr
1981 We Want Miles, Miles Davis
1981 Voyeur, David Sanborn
1981 Straphangin', The Brecker Brothers
1981 Come Morning, Grover Washington
1981 Standing Tall, The Crusaders
1982 Cityscape, Claus Ogerman with Michael Brecker
1982 The Nightfly, Donald Fagen
1982 Casino Lights, Various Artists
1982 As We Speak, David Sanborn
1983 Suddenly, Marcus Miller
1983 Backstreet, David Sanborn
1983 Star People, Miles Davis
1984 Marcus Miller, Marcus Miller
1984 Straight To The Heart, David Sanborn
1985 Hearts and Numbers, Don Grolnick
1985 The Alternative Man, Bill Evans
1986 Tutu, Miles Davis
1986 Double Vision, David Sanborn and Bob James
1986 It's About Time, McCoy Tyner
1987 A Change Of Heart, David Sanborn
1987 Music From Siesta, Miles Davis / Marcus Miller
1988 Close Up, David Sanborn
1989 Amandla, Miles Davis
1991 Another Hand, David Sanborn
1991 Healing the Wounds, The Crusaders
1992 Upfront, David Sanborn
1993 The Sun Don't Lie, Marcus Miller
1994 Push, Bill Evans
1994 Hearsay, David Sanborn
1995 Love Songs, David Sanborn
1995 Tales, Marcus Miller
1995 Pearls, David Sanborn

1995 High Life, Wayne Shorter
1996 Escape, Bill Evans
1998 Live and More, Marcus Miller
1999 Inside, David Sanborn
2000 Celebrating the Music of Weather Report, Various Artists
2000 Best of 82-96, Marcus Miller
2001 M2, Marcus Miller
2002 The Ozell Tapes, Marcus Miller
2003 Dreyfus Night in Paris, Miller Petrucciani Lagrene White Garrett
2005 Silver Rain, Marcus Miller
2005 Word of Mouth Revisited, Jaco Pastorius Big Band
2006 Sneakin' Up Behind You: The Very Best of, The Brecker Brothers
2007 Free, Marcus Miller
2008 Thunder, Stanley Clarke, Marcus Miller, Victor Wooten
2008 Marcus, Marcus Miller
2008 Cannon Re-Loaded, All-Star Celebration of Cannonball Adderley
2011 A Night In Monte Carlo, Marcus Miller
2012 Renaissance, Marcus Miller
2015 Afrodeezia, Marcus Miller
2015 Tutu Revisited, Marcus Miller

*One of the great all-round drummers, Vinnie Colaiuta on tour with Herbie Hancock at the Roundhouse, London, in 2007. (Photo: Ken Trethewey)*

# Bill Evans (b1958)

Bill Evans (not to be confused with the well-known bebop pianist of the same name) is one of the second generation of fusion stars who began his career in the 1980s. David Liebman recommended Evans to Miles Davis in 1980 just at the time when Miles was considering coming out of retirement. As a consequence, Evans played in the Davis bands from 1981-84 and on the four albums that Miles recorded during this period. After this, Evans left to embark on his own solo career and his first album as leader was *Living in the Crest of a Wave* (1984), a record that clearly established him as an original jazz-fusion musician. By this time he had already befriended Mark Egan and Danny Gottlieb after they parted company with the Pat Metheny Group, and Evans (with keyboardist Clifford Carter) played on the album *Elements* (1983) for Egan and Gottlieb's band Elements. Over many years, Evans has continued to record with Egan and Gottlieb, whether on their solo or group albums, whilst apparently not becoming a formal member of Elements.

Through his association with Miles Davis, Evans also befriended John McLaughlin and played in a later incarnation of the Mahavishnu Orchestra. With this band he helped to cement McLaughlin's presence in the new post-70s era of jazz-fusion. Evans' work as a sideman is quite limited compared to many of his peers, but his work as leader of some excellent jazz-fusion bands has resulted in a very innovative career and a series of albums of very high quality. His second release as a leader was the stunning jazz-fusion album *Alternative Man* (1985) which I have awarded five stars. Later, Evans was a leading exponent of the fusion of jazz with the rap/urban style of music on *Push* (1994) and *Escape* (1996). Another attempt at innovation was his Soul Bop Band with Randy Brecker of 2003/4. More recently he has been involved with the fusion of jazz and blue grass music, playing with Béla Fleck on *Soul Grass* (2005) and *The Other Side of Something* (2007).

Discography of Bill Evans (sax)
1981 The Man With The Horn, Miles Davis
1981 We Want Miles, Miles Davis
1983 Elements, Elements
1983 Decoy, Miles Davis
1983 Star People, Miles Davis
1984 Living in the Crest of a Wave, Bill Evans
1984 Forward Motion, Elements
1984 Mahavishnu, Mahavishnu Orchestra
1985 Blown Away, Elements
1985 The Alternative Man, Bill Evans
1986 Adventures in Radioland, John

McLaughlin and Mahavishnu
1988 A Touch of Light, Mark Egan
1989 Liberal Arts, Elements
1989 Summertime, Bill Evans
1990 Spirit River, Elements
1990 Let the Juice Loose - Live at the Blue Note Tokyo, Bill Evans
1991 The Gambler - Live at the Blue Note Tokyo 2, Bill Evans
1991 Beyond Words, Mark Egan
1992 Petite Blonde, Petite Blonde
1994 Push, Bill Evans
1995 Live in Europe, Bill Evans and Push
1996 Escape, Bill Evans

1997 Starfish and the Moon, Bill Evans
1999 Touch, Bill Evans
2000 Soul Insider, Bill Evans
2001 Freedom Town, Mark Egan
2002 Big Fun, Bill Evans
2004 Soul Bop Band Live, Bill Evans, Randy Brecker
2005 Soul Grass, Bill Evans
2006 Industrial Zen, John McLaughlin
2007 The Other Side of Something, Bill Evans
2009 Vans Joint, Bill Evans
2012 Dragonfly, Bill Evans

*Dave Weckl drumming for the Chick Corea Elektric Band at the Royal Festival Hall, London in 1991. (Photo: Ken Trethewey)*

# Dave Weckl (b1960)

After working with George Benson, Dave Weckl really came to prominence as the astonishing drummer in Chick Corea's Elektric Band, 1986-92. His vision and rhythmic capabilities caused many to see him, for a time, as the world's best drummer, especially in view of his own very remarkable five-star solo album *Master Plan* (1990). Corea is one of the most demanding jazz musicians to work alongside, because of his complex compositions, but Weckl's profile soared to great heights as he showed just how creative he could be with some of the most difficult charts any musician could be asked to play. By the time the original Elektric Band split, Weckl was already appearing on a great number of jazz-fusion albums, yet still formed his own band and released a series of very good jazz-fusion albums. Since the turn of the century, Weckl has continued a career in the premier league of jazz, alongside all of the finest musicians of earlier decades.

Discography of Dave Weckl
1984 20/20, George Benson
1986 Chick Corea Elektric Band, Chick Corea Elektric Band
1986 Upside Downside, Mike Stern
1988 John Patitucci, John Patitucci
1988 Light Years, Chick Corea Elektric Band
1989 Chick Corea Akoustic Band, Chick Corea Akoustic Band
1989 Round Trip, Eric Marienthal
1989 On the Corner, John Patitucci
1990 Eye of the Beholder, Chick Corea Elektric Band
1990 Master Plan, Dave Weckl Band
1991 Inside Out, Chick Corea Elektric Band
1991 Alive, Chick Corea Akoustic Band
1992 Heads Up, Dave Weckl Band
1992 Beneath the Mask, Chick Corea Elektric Band
1993 Another World, John Patitucci
1994 Hard Wired, Dave Weckl Band
1995 Mistura Fina, John Patitucci
1996 Live From Elario's (First Gig) Chick Corea Elektric Band, Chick Corea Elektric Band
1996 Between the Lines, Mike Stern
1996 Live From The Blue Note Tokyo (Japan Only), Chick Corea Akoustic Band
1998 Rhythm of the Soul, Dave Weckl Band
1999 Synergy, Dave Weckl Band
2000 Transition, Dave Weckl Band
2001 The Zone, Dave Weckl Band
2002 Perpetual Motion, Dave Weckl Band
2003 Live (and very plugged in), Dave Weckl Band
2004 To the Stars, Chick Corea Elektric Band
2005 Multiplicity, Dave Weckl Band
2006 Who Let the Cats Out? Mike Stern
2014 Convergence, Dave Weckl and Jay Oliver
2015 Of the Same Mind, Dave Weckl Acoustic Band

# The Crusaders: Joe Sample (b1939), Wilton Felder (b1940), Nesbert 'Stix' Hooper (b1938), Wayne Henderson (b1939)

*The Crusaders performing at Knebworth Park, Hertfordshire, UK in 1982. Wilton Felder is second right and Joe Sample far right. (Photo: Ken Trethewey)*

In his entertaining memoirs, Al Kooper was quite clear about the difference between the musical atmospheres of the two main centres of American music, New York and Los Angeles. That disparity is probably best summed up by the obvious differences in climate and lifestyle, with the gentle, warm, relaxed Californian climes clearly very different from the harsher, edgier, frenetic pace of life in the Big Apple. [6] There is no doubt that the LA music industry has had the greatest impact of the assimilation of jazz into popular everyday music forms. As a result, there is a clear group of musicians whose output belongs to what has been called, the 'West Coast Sound'. Of these, the Crusaders can be promoted as leaders in their field.

The Crusaders began as a group of four school friends in Houston Texas. While continuing their education by day, Joe Sample, Wilton Felder, Wayne Henderson and Nesbert 'Stix' Hooper formed a band called the Swingsters that by night played a mixture of R&B, blues and jazz in clubs and bars around the city. It was a very early kind of jazz-fusion in its own right. But for them, the life of the music student was limiting. Henderson: "We were playing everything - opera, and with the Houston Symphony, and dance music, but jazz-wise we were suffering and just had to get out; we wanted to blow and had to have a place to do it." [7] They decided to move to Los Angeles where the number of opportunities for jazz was far greater. They played amongst the community of jazz musicians as the Modern Jazz Sextet. At first, it was tough to get started as a serious modern jazz group. They were forced to change their identity to the Nite Hawks playing a more popular style of R&B music, in a sense reproducing the way they had gone about their music back home in Texas. After spending over four months playing in Las Vegas, the group finally got an audition with jazz producer Richard Bock, owner of the Pacific Jazz label. He hired them and they changed the name of the band to the Jazz Crusaders. Beginning with *Freedom Sound* (1961) the Jazz Crusaders went on to release a long sequence of popular jazz recordings, around half of them studio albums and the remainder recorded in locations such as the Lighthouse Jazz Club at Hermosa Beach in Los Angeles.

By the late 1960s, jazz was becoming less popular as the commercial market became dominated by rock music. The Jazz Crusaders recognised that they needed to refocus their work in a more popular genre. With the benefit of their strong background playing all styles to many kinds of audiences in Houston, they were well placed to go forward as a new band called the Crusaders playing their own brand of jazz-fusion that blended jazz with funk, soul and blues. They added the guitar and electric bass to their line-up and, starting with the album *Crusaders I* (1972), commenced a long sequence of jazz-fusion albums with a strong funky soul content: *Second Crusade* (1973), *Southern Comfort* (1974), *Scratch* (1975), *Chain Reaction* (1975). By 1976, however, Wayne Henderson had left to become a producer and Larry Carlton, who had been a regular with the band until then, had decided to pursue a solo career. He would continue to appear with the Crusaders, although on an infrequent basis.

Next, the Crusaders developed another very successful formula whereby they recorded music with a number of extremely good vocal artists. The first was Randy Crawford, largely unknown until she recorded *Street Life* (1978) with the Crusaders. It made her an international star. Then came recordings with Bill Withers who was already a heavyweight star from the world of soul music. His brilliant song *Soul Shadows* appeared on *Rhapsody and Blues* (1979). This was followed by Joe Cocker's recordings of *This Old World's Too Funky for Me* and *I'm So Glad I'm Standing Here Today*, both of which appeared on *Standing Tall* (1980).

By now all the band members were involved in parallel solo careers and the band's output became rather more disjointed. Nevertheless, albums were released throughout the 1980s such as *The Good and the Bad Times* (1986) and *Life in the Modern World* (1988). Although little appears in print on the subject, there seemed to have been more than a little disagreement in the air, as the titles of some of the albums attest. The band's final album for many years was *Healing the Wounds* (1991), although they did make a last reappearance together (without Hooper) in 2003 and recorded the album *Rural Renewal* (2003). From 1991, Wayne Henderson (with Wilton Felder in support) generated acrimony from the use of the band's original name, the Jazz Crusaders, against the wishes of Joe Sample. For a time, Wayne's new Jazz Crusaders continued with a different sound and emphasis on a newer brand of jazz-fusion. Wayne died in April 2014, Joe in September 2014 and Wilton in September 2015.

As with many bands of long standing, it is possible to identify several stages in the band's existence. For the Crusaders these are: (1) The period of the Jazz Crusaders from 1961-1970 when they performed mostly jazz mainstream music, but with some blues and funk influences (2) The period of the Crusaders from 1972-76. This was the time when Henderson and Felder concentrated the sounds of trombone and tenor sax in unison to produce the band's trademarked soul-funk sound. It was their most fertile period during which they were extremely influential for their special kind of jazz-fusion. (3) The period during which Felder was the lone horn but the albums were supplemented with a series of fine vocal tracks. (4) A post-Crusaders period from 1991 when Henderson and Felder continued as the Jazz Crusaders and identified with a different style of popular jazz-fusion.

Discography of the Crusaders
1961 Freedom Sound, The Jazz Crusaders
1962 Lookin' Ahead, The Jazz Crusaders
1963 At the Lighthouse, The Jazz Crusaders
1963 Tough Talk (1963), The Jazz Crusaders
1963 Heat Wave, The Jazz Crusaders
1964 Stretchin' Out, The Jazz Crusaders
1965 The Thing, The Jazz Crusaders
1965 Chile Con Soul, The Jazz Crusaders
1966 Live at the Lighthouse 66, The Jazz Crusaders
1967 Talk That Talk, The Jazz Crusaders
1967 The Festival Album, The Jazz Crusaders
1967 Uh Huh, The Jazz Crusaders
1968 Lighthouse 68, The Jazz Crusaders
1968 Powerhouse, The Jazz Crusaders
1969 Lighthouse 69, The Jazz Crusaders
1969 Live Sides, The Jazz Crusaders
1969 Tough Talk (1969), The Jazz Crusaders
1976 Young Rabbits, The Jazz Crusaders
1970 Give Peace A Chance, The Jazz Crusaders
1970 Best of the Jazz Crusaders, The Jazz Crusaders
1971 Old Socks New Shoes, New Socks Old Shoes, The Jazz Crusaders
1971 Pass the Plate, The Crusaders
1972 Crusaders I, The Crusaders
1973 The 2nd Crusade, The Crusaders
1973 Unsung Heroes, The Crusaders
1973 Hollywood, The Jazz Crusaders
1974 Southern Comfort, The Crusaders
1974 Scratch, The Crusaders
1975 Chain Reaction, The Crusaders
1976 Those Southern Nights, The Crusaders
1976 Best Of The Crusaders, The Crusaders

1977 Free As the Wind, The Crusaders
1978 Images, The Crusaders
1979 Street Life, The Crusaders
1980 Rhapsody and Blues, The Crusaders
1981 Standing Tall, The Crusaders
1982 Royal Jam, The Crusaders
1984 Ghetto Blaster, The Crusaders
1986 The Good And Bad Times, The Crusaders
1987 The Vocal Album, The Crusaders
1987 Soul Shadows, The Crusaders
1988 Life In The Modern World, The Crusaders
1990 The Golden Years, The Crusaders
1991 Healing the Wounds, The Crusaders
1993 Live in Japan 1993, The Crusaders
1994 The Crusaders Best, The Crusaders
1994 And Beyond, The Crusaders
1995 Happy Again, The Jazz Crusaders
1995 The Ultimate Compilation, The Crusaders
1995 The Greatest Crusade, The Crusaders
1996 Louisiana Hot Sauce, The Jazz Crusaders
1996 Way Back Home, The Crusaders
1996 Best of the Crusaders (2), The Crusaders
1998 Break N Da Rulz, The Jazz Crusaders
2000 Power of our Music - The Endangered Species, The Jazz Crusaders
2000 Finest Hour, The Crusaders
2002 The Crusaders At Their Best, The Crusaders
2002 Priceless Jazz, The Crusaders
2003 Rural Renewal, The Crusaders
2003 Live at Montreux 2003, The Crusaders
2003 The Pacific Jazz Quintet Studio Sessions, The Jazz Crusaders
2003 Groove Crusade, The Crusaders
2003 Very Best of the Crusaders, The Crusaders
2004 Soul Axess, The Jazz Crusaders
2005 Live in Japan 2003, The Crusaders
2006 Alive in South Africa, The Jazz Crusaders
2007 Global Warning - Jazz in the Hip Hop Generation, The Jazz Crusaders
2007 Gold, The Crusaders
2008 Kick the Jazz, The Jazz Crusaders

*Popular British jazz-fusion band of the 1980s, Shakatak plays on the same bill as the Crusaders at Knebworth Park. Left to right: Jackie Rawe, Nigel Wright, Gill Saward, Roger Odell, Keith Winter, George Anderson, Bill Sharpe. (Photo: Ken Trethewey)*

## Tom Scott (b1948)

Throughout the early part of the 1970s the Crusaders, as one of the leading jazz groups of the West Coast for the previous decade, played a highly influential role in the style and output of music from the West Coast region. Tom Scott was one musician who quickly adopted a similar style of jazz-fusion, thanks to his friendship with Joe Sample. Scott had been playing in a North Hollywood club called the *Baked Potato* alongside Sample, bassist Max Bennett and drummer John Guerrin. He soon found himself playing Crusaders-style grooves and decided to form a band based on that style of music. Hence, the LA Express was born. The band recorded its first album for the Ode label, *Tom Scott and the LA Express* (1974). Apart from the excellent jazz-fusion content, the remarkable thing about the album is that he was employing two current Crusaders, Joe Sample and Larry Carlton. Whether this was intended to be a one-off for this recording or whether he had ambitions of luring them from their own band we do not know. If it was the latter, his plan didn't work.

Clearly, Scott intended to have his own existence in the jazz world for he quickly followed up his first recording with *Tom Cat* (1974). He replaced Carlton with Robben Ford and Sample with Larry Nash. The successes achieved with these two albums led to a third album, *New York Connection* (1975) with the same musicians. At the end of 1974, the band (and numerous other musicians) was hired by George Harrison for his one and only US tour, *Dark Horse*. Scott also won a commission to write the theme music to the very popular TV show *The Streets of San Francisco* (1972-80) and followed that up with the theme for the TV cop series *Starsky and Hutch* (1975-79). This famous piece of music is imprinted on the memories of many of us who watched the series and the piece entitled *Gotcha* became the opening track on Scott's fourth album *Blow It Out* (1977). Tom Scott maintained his own stream of solo recordings, now without a regular band, but with his own nucleus of session guest musicians. He was a founder member of the Blues Brothers, and played in bands for some of the world's most famous pop musicians. He became an important figure in the GRP family of artists and took a central role as arranger and member of the GRP Big Band that made a great impact on the jazz scene at the end of the decade.

Discography of Tom Scott
1968 Honeysuckle Breeze, Tom Scott
1969 Rural Still Life, Tom Scott
1970 Hair to Jazz, Tom Scott
1971 Paint Your Wagon, Tom Scott
1972 Great Scott, Tom Scott
1972 For the Roses, Joni Mitchell
1974 Tom Scott and the LA Express, Tom Scott and the LA Express
1974 Court and Spark, Joni Mitchell
1974 Miles of Aisles, Joni Mitchell
1974 Tom Cat, Tom Scott and the LA Express
1976 New York Connection, Tom Scott
1976 Silk Degrees, Boz Scaggs
1976 Hejira, Joni Mitchell
1977 Aja, Steely Dan

1977 Blow It Out, Tom Scott
1978 Intimate Strangers, Tom Scott
1979 Street Beat, Tom Scott
1981 Apple Juice, Tom Scott
1981 Voyeur, David Sanborn
1981 Word of Mouth, Jaco Pastorius
1984 Desire, Tom Scott
1984 Gaucho, Steely Dan
1985 Target, Tom Scott
1986 One Night, One Day, Tom Scott
1987 Picture This, Billy Cobham
1987 Streamlines, Tom Scott
1988 Flashpoint, Tom Scott
1990 Them Changes, Tom Scott
1991 Keep This Love Alive, Tom Scott
1992 Born Again, Tom Scott
1994 Reed My Lips, Tom Scott
1994 I Wanna Play For You, Stanley Clarke
1995 Night Creatures, Tom Scott
1996 Bluestreak, Tom Scott and the LA Express
1997 Priceless Jazz, Tom Scott
1999 Smokin' Section, Tom Scott
2002 Newfound Freedom, Tom Scott
2006 The Very Best of Tom Scott, Tom Scott
2006 Bebop United, Tom Scott
2008 Cannon Re-Loaded: All-Star Celebration of Cannonball Adderley, Tom Scott

## Joni Mitchell (b1943)

Joni Mitchell was born Roberta Joan Anderson on November 7 1943 in Fort McLeod, Alberta, Canada. In 1963, aged 19, she moved to Toronto and entered the world of folk music. As the music evolved, so did the descriptions: she stopped being a folk singer and became a singer / songwriter, a genre populated with the likes of Bob Dylan, Gordon Lightfoot, Leonard Cohen and Neil Young. Besides the obvious bonus of being in her early twenties, attractive, blonde and with a good voice, Mitchell was already using unusual guitar tunings to help define her sound. All these positive features marked her out as different from the start.

In 1967 she met ex-Byrdman David Crosby who helped her get her first recording contract. Even at such an early stage in her career, Crosby recognised jazz influences in her songs. While her manager Elliot Roberts prepared her first contract, she and Crosby planned the first album *Song to a Seagull* (1968). This, and the following two records, *Clouds* (1969) and *Ladies of the Canyon* (1971) followed the simple voice/guitar format. Crusader Wilton Felder played on Joni Mitchell's album *Blue* (1971), which shows that Joni was already mixing with top jazz musicians. On the credits for her next album, *For the Roses* (1972) we find Felder again, this time with Joe Sample playing electric keyboards and Tom Scott contributing woodwind sounds. Though she was working with jazz musicians, her music was still in a transitional phase between folk music and jazz-fusion.

Joni now extended her work by employing Tom Scott's band LA Express on the milestone album *Court and Spark* (1974) released early in the year. Joni used a rhythm section for the first time on the album, a serious venture into a fusion of jazz with pop/folk. It was a big hit and at the Grammy awards ceremony following the album's release it received a nomination for Album of the Year (1974). Joni's jazz credentials were at last revealed fully. To promote the album, Joni went on tour with her band in February 1974 and a series of shows at the Universal Amphitheater in Los Angeles was recorded on 14-17 August and released as the live album *Miles of Aisles* (1975). For Mitchell's next album *The Hissing of Summer Lawns* (1975) the LA Express were now formally dropped as an accompanying band as she used musicians just for the sessions (yet they *did* tour with her – without Scott.) Wayne Shorter replaced 'Tommy' Scott as her preferred saxophonist, although the other band members, including Robben Ford were present. In addition, Crusaders Wilton, Joe and Larry returned to her studio for appearances on several of the tracks.

In 1975, Robben Ford introduced Joni to the sound of Jaco Pastorius and her world was transformed again, as evidenced by the music on *Hejira* (1976) and *Don Juan's Reckless Daughter* (1977). In 1978, Joni began working on a collaboration with the great jazz bassist Charlie Mingus who was by now very ill. Joni released the album *Mingus* (1979), by which time Mingus had died. It was a great thing that Pastorius - seen by many as the greatest bass player the world had seen since Mingus himself - performed on the album. A year later, Joni took her music on the road once more for a grand tour known as *Shadows and Light* (1980). Her band was to be one of the greatest of its type ever assembled, with Pastorius on bass, Pat Metheny (guitar), Lyle Mays (keyboards), Michael Brecker (saxophone) and Don Alias (drums/percussion). Although the course of Joni's career changed again after that, and she became more focussed on the studio and less on overt jazz, she still relied heavily upon the creativity of Wayne Shorter. You could say that the jazz was now totally integrated into her music - implicit instead of explicit - as it was becoming across the music world.

Discography of Joni Mitchell
1968 Song to a Seagull, Joni Mitchell
1969 Clouds, Joni Mitchell
1970 Ladies of the Canyon, Joni Mitchell
1971 Blue, Joni Mitchell
1972 For the Roses, Joni Mitchell
1974 Court and Spark, Joni Mitchell
1974 Miles of Aisles, Joni Mitchell
1975 The Hissing of Summer Lawns, Joni Mitchell
1976 Hejira, Joni Mitchell
1977 Don Juan's Reckless Daughter, Joni Mitchell
1979 Mingus, Joni Mitchell
1980 Shadows and Light, Joni Mitchell
1982 Wild Things Run Fast, Joni Mitchell
1985 Dog Eat Dog, Joni Mitchell
1988 Chalk Mark in a Rain Storm, Joni Mitchell
1991 Night Ride Home, Joni Mitchell
1994 Turbulent Indigo, Joni Mitchell
1998 Taming the Tiger, Joni Mitchell
2000 Both Sides Now, Joni Mitchell
2002 Travelogue, Joni Mitchell
2007 Shine, Joni Mitchell

# Larry Carlton (b1948)

Larry Carlton is very famous for his work as a member of the Crusaders, yet he has recorded prolifically both as a session man and as a leader on his own albums. In 1975, Carlton played a guitar solo on *Kid Charlemagne*, the opening track of Steely Dan's album *The Royal Scam* (1975). Fagen and Becker's obsession for perfection paid off handsomely, for they ensured that the solo was nothing but the best Carlton could do. To listeners, it was sensational and made him the hottest jazz-fusion guitarist on the West Coast. He was inundated with employment as a session guitarist and it was hardly surprising that his appearances for the Crusaders began to dwindle from this point on. Warner Bros. offered him a solo recording contract that resulted in a series of albums: *Larry Carlton* (1977), *Mr 335 - Live in Japan* (1978), *Strikes Twice* (1979), *Sleepwalk* (1981) and *Eight Times Up* (1983). As Tom Scott had found, Carlton's new profile brought in other work too. He got the job (with Mike Post) of writing the theme for another TV cop series, *Hill Street Blues* and it won a Grammy award in 1981 for Best Pop Instrumental Performance.

The early 80s in LA were dominated by the Michael Jackson era during which disco music strongly dominated the music scene. Many of the top LA-based musicians were involved with the recordings of Jackson. Larry Carlton continued to release solo albums, although in 1985 he changed course somewhat with a pair of albums displaying his beautiful skills with acoustic guitar, *Alone But Never Alone* (1985) and *Discovery* (1986). There was a terrible moment in 1989 when he was shot and almost killed in an event of random violence. Fortunately he recovered and the event is now marked by the release of his album *On Solid Ground* (1989). Larry continued with his career, which embraced a wide range of gigs and recordings across the jazz diaspora, many of which remain high in the memories of cool, melodic jazz.

Discography of Larry Carlton
1968 With A Little Help From My Friends, Larry Carlton
1972 Crusaders I, The Crusaders
1973 The 2nd Crusade, The Crusaders
1973 Singing / Playing, Larry Carlton
1974 Southern Comfort, The Crusaders
1974 Scratch, The Crusaders
1975 Katy Lied, Steely Dan
1976 Those Southern Nights, The Crusaders
1976 Best Of The Crusaders, The Crusaders
1976 The Royal Scam, Steely Dan
1976 Hejira, Joni Mitchell
1977 Aja, Steely Dan
1977 Larry Carlton, Larry Carlton
1977 Free As the Wind, The Crusaders
1977 Don Juan's Reckless Daughter, Joni Mitchell
1978 Mr 335 - Live in Japan, Larry Carlton
1979 Off the Wall, Michael Jackson
1979 Strikes Twice, Larry Carlton
1981 Sleepwalk, Larry Carlton
1981 Standing Tall, The Crusaders
1982 The Nightfly, Donald Fagen
1982 Wild Things Run Fast, Joni Mitchell
1982 Casino Lights, Various Artists
1983 Eight Times Up, Larry Carlton

1983 Friends, Larry Carlton
1984 Gaucho, Steely Dan
1984 Against All Odds, Larry Carlton and Michael Colombier
1986 Last Nite, Larry Carlton
1986 The Good And Bad Times, The Crusaders
1986 Discovery, Larry Carlton
1986 Alone But Never Alone, Larry Carlton
1989 On Solid Ground, Larry Carlton
1990 Collection, Larry Carlton
1991 Renegade Gentleman, Larry Carlton
1992 The Best of Mr 335, Larry Carlton
1992 Kid Gloves, Larry Carlton
1994 Live At The Greek, Stanley Clarke
1995 Happy Again, The Jazz Crusaders
1995 Christmas At My House, Larry Carlton
1995 Larry & Lee, Larry Carlton and Lee Ritenour
1996 The Gift, Larry Carlton
1997 The Larry Carlton Collection Vol 2, Larry Carlton
2000 Twentieth Century Masters - The Millenium Collection, Larry Carlton
2000 Fingerprints, Larry Carlton
2000 Today and Tomorrow, Larry Carlton
2001 Deep Into It, Larry Carlton
2001 No Substitutions - Live in Osaka, Larry Carlton and Steve Lukather
2003 Sapphire Blue, Larry Carlton
2005 The Very Best of Larry Carlton, Larry Carlton
2006 Fire Wire, Larry Carlton
2007 Live in Tokyo With Special Guest Robben Ford, Larry Carlton and Robben Ford
2008 Greatest Hits Rerecorded Volume 1, Larry Carlton
2010 Take Your Pick, Larry Carlton, Tak Matsumoto
2015 @Billboard Live Tokyo, Larry Carlton, David T. Walker

## Yellowjackets

The 1980s were also notable for the emergence of new jazz-fusion bands whose existence was a direct result of the activities of the 1970s. One such was the Yellowjackets, a band first formed in 1977 by Robben Ford a blues guitarist well known for his 1974-6 membership of Tom Scott's LA Express. Ford was a friend of keyboardist Russell Ferrante, and in 1977 when Ford was a free agent once again they joined forces with Jimmy Haslip (bass) and Ricky Lawson (drums) to become The Robben Ford Band. Together they made an album for Elektra called *The Inside Story* (1979) that contained a mixture of jazz and blues styles and a couple of vocal tunes, but was very much in the jazz-fusion category. However, Ford's contract was for himself, not the band. His sidekicks wanted to create their own momentum in instrumental jazz, whilst Ford wanted to concentrate on a more popular vocal-based blues style. The result was a friendly split. Ford set about initiating his own solo career, whilst, with the aid of a great demo tape (on which Ford played), Ferrante, Haslip and Lawson got their own contract with Warner Bros. thanks to Warners' A&R man, Tommy LiPuma, who became their first producer. Using the name Yellowjackets (a name that in non-American English equates to 'wasps') the three musicians then recorded that first eponymous album, released in 1981, with Ford as a guest. (The CD edition of the album released in 2003 contains those tracks from the original demo tape.)

Right from the start, the LA-based band was successful for playing a warm, melodic style of electric jazz that was typical of the free-and-easy Californian sunshine lifestyle. But popularity was not gained at the expense of quality, largely thanks to the efforts of Russell Ferrante, the brilliant composer of much of the band's music. Almost at once, the band started to receive Grammy nominations. *Mirage à Trois* (1983) was a candidate for the honour, as also was *Samurai Samba* (1985). In 1986, the Yellowjackets transferred their affiliation from Warners to the booming GRP jazz label. They immediately struck Californian oil with the fourth album *Shades* (1986) that scooped the award (ironically) for Best R&B album, even though the band could hardly be described as R&B. It appeared that Ford's influence was still clearly at work!

Some changes in personnel took place. After appearing as guest on several albums, Ford was replaced in 1985 by Marc Russo, a technically gifted, energetic alto saxophone player with a strong tonal similarity to David Sanborn and who played in the highest registers of the instrument as if he had been born doing it. At this point, the band took on the focus of the saxophone, rather than the guitar, which was a big change in its ethos. Although initially the band got its music from many different sources, gradually, Ferrante took on a bigger share of the compositional duties. In 1986, drummer Ricky Lawson also moved on to greater things and was replaced by William Kennedy who stayed with the band until 2000. Yet again, their next album *Four Corners* (1987) was nominated for a Grammy. The band finally struck it lucky for the next album with Kennedy on drums, *Politics* (1988), which won the band's second - and sadly last - Grammy, now in the more meaningful section of Best Contemporary Jazz album. (If it were not for the extraordinary efforts of Pat Metheny, the band would undoubtedly have scooped many more of the top awards. YJ was surely unfortunate to have been up against such tough opposition!)

In 1989, after the release of *The Spin* (1989), Russo decided it was time for him to leave the band and a relationship was formed with a new (tenor) saxophone player who, at first seemed a rather unlikely candidate for Russo's job. Bob Mintzer had spent much time playing in big bands, notably with the Thad Jones and Mel Lewis Big Band, and also with Buddy Rich, for whom he was an arranger. Besides being a fine all-round instrumentalist, Mintzer was especially gifted in composition and arrangement, and by the time he came under the recruiting scrutiny of the Yellowjackets, he already had a contract of his own with DMP and was leading his own occasional large group, the Bob Mintzer Big Band. Bob was not quite hired when he appeared as a guest saxophonist on *Greenhouse* (1991). However, Mintzer was able to combine both roles as he began to play more and more with Yellowjackets. As a kind of *quid pro quo*, the Yellowjackets appeared on Mintzer's album for DMP, *One Music* (1992). By this time, Mintzer had formally become the fourth Yellowjacket and he has remained so ever since.

With Mintzer on board, they released at roughly annual intervals a series of extremely successful, high quality albums. *Live Wires* (1992) was a brilliant 2-CD collection of live recordings. Then came three seminal recordings that seemed to bring into focus everything the band stood for at that time. Many fans regard *Like A River* (1993), *Run For Your Life* (1994) and *Dreamland* (1995) with great fondness as representative of a time when jazz-fusion had come of age and blended homogeneously into the jazz mainstream. However, by the mid-1990s, the commercial world had undergone radical change thanks to the popularity of the smooth jazz formula. In 1996, with LiPuma now head of GRP, that label was at the forefront of the smooth jazz wave that caused many mainstream jazzers to turn away. For reasons about which we could speculate, the band joined many other top jazz artists and left GRP, in this case to return to the Warner Bros. fold. Recognising the end of something special, GRP held a wake and released *Collection* (1996). Meanwhile, YJ moved on with *Blue Hats* (1997), *Club Nocturne* (1998).

There seemed to follow a period during which the musicians executed other projects. Bob, in particular returned to his Big Band to arrange some Count Basie tunes, and also to take part in a kind of supergroup event with John Abercrombie (guitar), John Patitucci (bass) and Peter Erskine (drums) that was called the Hudson Project.

A further change of label occurred in 2001 when the boys joined their current Heads-Up label, which was then a rapidly expanding outfit dedicated to high quality jazz. Under this banner YJ released *Mint Jam* (2001) and *Time Squared* (2003). The same year, the band indulged themselves with an unusual project in which they recorded a series of popular Christmas songs, *Peace Round - A Christmas Celebration* (2003). The year 2005 saw the release of *Altered State* and the following year a wonderful 2-disc release to celebrate the band's silver anniversary – *Twenty Five* (2006) in which one of the discs was a DVD. Then, after a brief hiatus, they invited guitarist Mike Stern to join them for *Lifecycle* (2008) in a project that was a direct return to the early days of jazz-rock music and resulted in a brilliant jazz-fusion album in all but name. Again, like many of its predecessors, it was nominated for a Grammy, but did not win.

As the 1990s progressed, the Yellowjackets' music evolved gradually, moving away from the louder electrified jazz-fusion style towards the softer, more intricately constructed forms of acoustic-based jazz. Nevertheless, the Yellowjackets have never abandoned their jazz-fusion roots. Even today, Mintzer can be heard playing his EWI, as on *Measure of a Man* from *Lifecycle*

(2008) and the music is - from time to time - as funky and as much derived from jazz-rock as it ever was, for example on *I Wonder* on the same album. The Yellowjackets have never made a conscious decision to avoid this or that style of music. As a band with no leader, the ethos has always been to enjoy what they do, to take whatever music is available at the time (usually from the pen of one of the band) and then to make it available to the rest to work on collectively. The band does not generally use modal harmony, nor does it deliberately set out to shock. Instead, harmonies are unusual and challenging. Tracks on Yellowjackets albums are almost always rooted in conventionally constructed jazz forms, although the melodies can be extremely complicated and difficult to play. Rhythms, as in much of the best jazz, are also extremely complicated, whilst at the same time feeling natural. There are beautiful slow ballads and frantically fast bebop-style romps, yet across the wide range of styles, Yellowjackets music has a clearly identifiable brand, which, when you become used to it, is charming, foot-tapping, sometimes (though not often) singable and usually stimulating.

The musicianship of the individuals and the band is quite simply extraordinary. Mintzer's saxophone sound is rich and mellow. He does not shrink from playing notes off the top, but is not regarded as expert in that area. His playing in the normal range of the instrument is always fluid, superbly inventive and on a par with Michael Brecker. He plays a wide range of instruments, including tenor and soprano saxophones, flute, clarinet and bass clarinet. Like Brecker, he too enjoys playing the EWI. Mintzer is a very special composer and arranger, sharing much of that duty with Russ Ferrante. Far from being entrapped by the demands of membership of a top-class act, Bob has been able to fulfil a demanding parallel career on two other fronts. The first of these is with his Big Band, although this is more restricted to occasional recording sessions and gigs than the rigorous demands of international tours such as he has made with YJ. The catalogue of recordings released by the Big Band now runs to about 18 fine albums. Secondly, Bob has worked in many smaller groupings, making numerous records and playing many gigs. Bob Mintzer is clearly a prolific jazz musician who has contributed greatly to the wider field of jazz.

Russell Ferrante is an exceptional keyboard player, these days concentrating on acoustic piano, but continuing to add layers of colour by means of concurrent synthesiser playing. From the start of the band's existence, Ferrante has been the lead composer for the band, although he has always allowed the others to assist in the development of his compositions. Ferrante's compositions are perhaps the most complex of all of the YJ's music and push the limits of harmony melody and rhythm to the very edges of the band's remit. Ferrante's playing (and his style of composition too) at times sounds influenced by Chick Corea in his own jazz-fusion Elektric Band period, although without the latter's strong Spanish legacy. Nevertheless, Ferrante has his own trademark that becomes apparent to those who listen regularly to his playing.

Jimmy Haslip is a very highly regarded player of electric bass and is probably one of the main anchors that keep the YJ ship moored close to the jazz-fusion jetty. As a primarily electric player, we could be forgiven for thinking he might be somehow limited in the demands of an acoustic jazz setting that Ferrante frequently sets up. However, that is not the case. Haslip's penetrating and perceptive accompaniments are perfectly atoned to the piece being played. As a one-time student of Pastorius, he frequently reminds me of that great master, although Haslip is definitely a player of the generation that succeeded Pastorius. His dextrous licks on his six-string bass are as good as you will hear anywhere (except perhaps for the demonstrative Victor Wooten), although he always plays according to the needs of the number. There are many times when his playing is quite unobtrusive, and many others when his funky slap style brings a piece properly to life. Haslip has been a long-time friend of Bruce Hornsby, and has taken part in many recordings by that artist. In 2012, the long periods of touring with YJ finally took its toll on Haslip, and he took time off from the band, a hiatus that later proved to be permanent. His place was taken by Felix Pastorius, son of Jaco, and the new band recorded *A Rise in The Road* (2013). Felix was himself replaced by Dane Alderson in 2015.

Marcus Baylor became the third Yellowjackets drummer after Ricky Lawson and William Kennedy, both of whom contributed greatly to the reputation of the band today. Marcus is a top-class drummer who, like his predecessors, was given full license to contribute to the development of the pieces. However, in 2015 the band's earlier drummer, William Kennedy returned once more.

As Steven Ivory states joyfully on the sleeve notes of *The Best of the Yellowjackets – The Millennium Collection* (2006), another collection of music from the GRP days: "Yellowjackets were born out of the most honourable intentions that a musical collective can possess: the unflinching resolve of its members to follow their musical instincts." [8] About that, there is no doubt, but there is another strong characteristic about them too, and that is the way that all past and present members have remained strong friends to this day and that they have all enjoyed themselves enormously.

Discography of Yellowjackets
1981 Yellowjackets, Yellowjackets
1983 Mirage a Trois, Yellowjackets
1985 Samurai Samba, Yellowjackets
1986 Shades, Yellowjackets
1987 Four Corners, Yellowjackets
One of 1988 Politics, Yellowjackets

1989 The Spin, Yellowjackets
1991 Greenhouse, Yellowjackets
1992 Live Wires, Yellowjackets
1993 Like a River, Yellowjackets
1994 Run For Your Life, Yellowjackets
1995 Collection, Yellowjackets
1995 Dreamland, Yellowjackets

1997 Blue Hats, Yellowjackets
1998 Club Nocturne, Yellowjackets
1998 Priceless Jazz, Yellowjackets
1999 The Best of Yellowjackets, Yellowjackets
2001 Mint Jam, Yellowjackets
2003 Time Squared, Yellowjackets
2003 Peace Round - A Christmas Celebration, Yellowjackets
2005 Altered State, Yellowjackets
2006 The Millennium Collection: The Best of the Yellowjackets, Yellowjackets
2006 Twenty Five, Yellowjackets
2008 Yellowjackets in Concert, Yellowjackets
2008 Lifecycle, Yellowjackets featuring Mike Stern
2011 Timeline, Yellowjackets
2013 A Rise In The Road, Yellowjackets

*One of the most in-demand session musicians of his time, bassist Nathan East on tour with Herbie Hancock in 2006. (Photo: Ken Trethewey)*

# References to Part 3

1. Stephanie L Stein Crease, *Jazz and Brazilian Music*, in *The Oxford Companion to Jazz*, ed. Bill Kirchner, Oxford University Press, 2000, p548.
2. www.rollingstone.com/news/story/5938174/the_rs_500_greatest_ albums_ of_all_time/
3. Sting, *Broken Music*, Simon and Schuster, 2003 p104.
4. Walter Kolosky, *Power, Passion and Beauty – The Story of the Legendary Mahavishnu Orchestra*, published by Abstract Logix Books, Cary North Carolina, 2006.
5. Stuart Nicholson, *Jazz Rock: A History*, Schirmer Books 1998, p133ff
6. Al Kooper, *Backstage Passes and Backstabbing Bastards: Memoirs of a Rock 'n' Roll Survivor*, Backbeat Books, 2008, p89.
7. Wayne Henderson, sleeve notes to *Freedom Sound* (1961) by the Jazz Crusaders, Pacific Jazz Records.
8. Steven Ivory, sleeve notes to *The Best of the Yellowjackets – The Millenium Collection* (2006) by Yellowjackets, Universal Music Group.

# Selected Albums and DVDs to Illustrate This Book

1948; Miles Davis; The Complete Birth Of The Cool;
1957; Miles Davis + 19; Miles Ahead;
1958; Miles Davis; 1958 Miles;
1958; Miles Davis; Milestones - Columbia;
1959; Miles Davis; Kind Of Blue;
1960; John Coltrane; Coltrane Plays The Blues;
1962; Alexis Korner's Blues Incorporated; R&B From The Marquee;
1962; Stan Getz, Charlie Byrd; Jazz Samba;
1964; Stan Getz, Joao Gilberto; Getz/Gilberto #2;
1964; The Modern Jazz Quartet with Laurindo Almeida; Collaboration;
1964; Wayne Shorter; Juju;
1964; Miles Davis; The Complete Concert 1964;
1965; The Graham Bond Organisation; There's A Bond Between Us;
1965; The Graham Bond Organization; The Sound Of 65;
1965; Miles Davis; E.S.P.;
1965; Herbie Hancock; Maiden Voyage;
1967; Miles Davis; Miles Smiles;
1968; Blood, Sweat & Tears; Child Is Father To The Man;
1968; Miles Davis; Nefertiti;
1969; Colosseum; Valentyne Suite;
1969; Colosseum; Those Who Are About To Die Salute You;
1969; John McLaughlin; Extrapolation;
1969; Miles Davis; Filles de Kilimanjaro;
1969; Miles Davis; In A Silent Way;
1970; Nucleus; We'll Talk About It Later;
1970; The Graham Bond Organisation; Solid Bond;
1970; Dreams; Dreams;
1970; Miles Davis; Bitches Brew;
1971; Hal Galper; Wild Bird;
1971; Michael Gibbs; Tanglewood 63;
1971; Dreams; Imagine My Surprise;
1971; Mahavishnu Orchestra; The Inner Mounting Flame;
1972; Mike Mainieri and Friends; White Elephant Vols 1 and 2;
1972; Hal Galper; The Guerilla Band;
1972; Stevie Wonder; Talking Book;
1972; Return to Forever; Light As A Feather;
1972; Weather Report; I Sing The Body Electric;
1973; Miles Davis; Miles And Coltrane;
1973; Miles Davis; Black Beauty: Miles Davis At Fillmore West;
1973; Mahavishnu Orchestra; Between Nothingness And Eternity;
1973; Mahavishnu Orchestra; Birds Of Fire;
1973; Herbie Hancock; Head Hunters;
1974; Eleventh House; Introducing The Eleventh House With Larry Coryell;
1974; Billy Cobham; Total Eclipse;
1974; Herbie Hancock; Thrust;
1974; Billy Cobham; Crosswinds;
1974; Weather Report; Mysterious Traveller;
1975; Parliament; Mothership Connection;

1975; The Brecker Brothers; The Brecker Brothers;
1975; Herbie Hancock; Flood;
1975; Weather Report; Tale Spinnin';
1976; The Eleventh House featuring Larry Coryell; Aspects;
1976; Parliament; The Clones Of Dr. Frunkenstein;
1976; Jaco Pastorius; Jaco Pastorius;
1976; Return To Forever; Romantic Warrior;
1976; Stanley Clarke; School Days;
1976; Weather Report; Black Market;
1977; Shakti; Natural Elements;
1977; Steely Dan; Aja;
1977; Weather Report; Heavy Weather;
1978; Frank Zappa; Zappa In New York;
1978; The Brecker Brothers; Heavy Metal Bebop;
1978; Weather Report; Mr. Gone;
1978; Pat Metheny Group; Pat Metheny Group;
1979; Warren Bernhardt, Michael Brecker, Randy Brecker, Mike Mainieri; Blue Montreux Vols 1 and 2
1979; Pat Metheny Group; American Garage;
1979; The Crusaders; Street Life;
1980; Joni Mitchell; Shadows And Light;
1980; Steps; Smokin' In The Pit;
1980; The Brecker Brothers; Détente;
1980; Weather Report; Night Passage;
1980; The Crusaders; Rhapsody And Blues;
1981; Yellowjackets; Yellowjackets;
1981; The Brecker Brothers; Straphangin';
1981; Jaco Pastorius; Word Of Mouth;
1981; David Sanborn; Voyeur;
1981; Pat Metheny and Lyle Mays; As Falls Wichita, So Falls Wichita Falls;
1981; The Crusaders; Standing Tall;
1982; Michael Jackson; Thriller;
1982; Pat Metheny Group; Offramp;
1982; Weather Report; Weather Report 2;
1982; David Sanborn; As We Speak;
1983; Weather Report; Procession;
1983; Jaco Pastorius; Invitation;
1983; David Sanborn; Backstreet;
1984; Steely Dan; Gaucho;
1984; Mahavishnu Orchestra; Mahavishnu;
1984; David Sanborn; Straight To The Heart;
1984; Pat Metheny Group; First Circle;
1985; Bill Evans; The Alternative Man;
1986; Yellowjackets; Shades;
1986; Steps Ahead; Magnetic;
1986; Mike Stern; Upside Downside;
1986; John McLaughlin and Mahavishnu; Adventures In Radioland;
1986; Miles Davis; Tutu;
1986; Chick Corea Elektric Band; Chick Corea Elektric Band;
1987; Michael Brecker; Michael Brecker;

1987; David Sanborn; A Change Of Heart;
1987; Pat Metheny Group; Still Life (Talking);
1988; Yellowjackets; Politics;
1988; Michael Brecker; Don't Try This At Home;
1988; David Sanborn; Close Up;
1988; Chick Corea Elektric Band; Light Years;
1989; Yellowjackets; The Spin;
1989; Pat Metheny Group; Letter From Home;
1989; Miles Davis; Aura;
1990; The Mark Varney Project; Truth In Shredding;
1990; Nelson Rangell; Nelson Rangell;
1990; Dave Weckl Band; Master Plan;
1990; Chick Corea Elektric Band; Eye Of The Beholder;
1991; Chick Corea Elektric Band; Inside Out;
1992; Miles Davis; Black Devil;
1992; Yellowjackets; Live Wires;
1992; Michael Brecker; Now You See It (Now You Don't);
1992; The Brecker Brothers; Return Of The Brecker Brothers;
1992; Petite Blonde; Petite Blonde;
1992; The Zawinul Syndicate; Lost Tribes;
1992; Dave Weckl Band; Heads Up;
1992; Pat Metheny; Secret Story;
1992; Chick Corea Elektric Band; Beneath The Mask;
1993; Will Lee; Oh!;
1993; Charlie Parker; Charlie Parker On Dial: The Complete Sessions;
1993; Chick Corea Elektric Band II; Paint The World;
1994; The Brecker Brothers; Out Of The Loop;
1994; Bill Evans; Push;
1994; Herbie Hancock Trio; Live In New York;
1994; Yellowjackets; Run For Your Life;
1994; Herbie Hancock; Dis Is Da Drum;
1994; Jaco Pastorius; The Birthday Concert;
1994; Dave Weckl Band; Hard Wired;
1995; Quincy Jones; Q's Jook Joint;
1995; Miles Davis Quintet; Highlights from The Plugged Nickel;
1995; Yellowjackets; Dreamland;
1995; Wayne Shorter; High Life;
1995; Pat Metheny Group; We Live Here;
1996; Pat Metheny Group; We Live Here - Live In Japan [DVD];
1996; Bob Mintzer Big Band; Big Band Trane;
1996; Michael Brecker; Tales From The Hudson;
1996; Bill Evans; Escape;
1997; Tony Williams; Wilderness;
1997; Pat Metheny Group; Imaginary Day;
1998; Michael Brecker; Two Blocks from The Edge;
1998; John McLaughlin; The Heart Of Things Live In Paris;
1999; Jaco Pastorius Big Band; Twins I & II: Live In Japan 1982;
1999; Mike Stern; Play;
1999; Michael Brecker; Time Is Of The Essence;
1999; Mahavishnu Orchestra; The Lost Trident Sessions;

2000; Bob Berg, Randy Brecker, Dennis Chambers, Joey DeFrancesco; The JazzTimes Superband;
2000; Steely Dan; Two Against Nature;
2000; John Scofield; Bump;
2001; Miles Davis; At La Villette [DVD];
2001; Miles Davis; The Complete In A Silent Way Sessions;
2001; Yellowjackets; Mint Jam;
2001; Randy Brecker; Hangin' In The City;
2001; Mike Stern; Voices;
2001; Marcus Miller; M2;
2002; Herbie Hancock; Future 2 Future Live [DVD];
2002; Randy Brecker; 34th N Lex;
2002; Bill Evans; Big Fun;
2002; Wayne Shorter; Footprints Live;
2002; The Zawinul Syndicate; Faces & Places;
2002; John Scofield Band; Uberjam;
2003; Pat Metheny Group; Speaking Of Now Live [DVD];
2003; Yellowjackets; Time Squared;
2003; Jaco Pastorius Big Band; Word Of Mouth Revisited;
2003; Steely Dan; Everything Must Go;
2003; Dave Weckl Band; Live (and very plugged in);
2004; Miles Davis, John Coltrane; The Complete Columbia Recordings 1955-1961;
2004; Bill Evans, Randy Brecker; Soulbop Band Live;
2004; Wayne Shorter; Footprints: The Life And Music Of Wayne Shorter;
2005; Randy Brecker / Michael Brecker; Some Skunk Funk [DVD];
2005; Joe Zawinul; Joe Zawinul - A Musical Portrait;
2005; Miles Davis; The Cellar Door Sessions 1970;
2005; Yellowjackets; Altered State;
2005; Joshua Redman Elastic Band; Momentum;
2005; Carlos Santana, Wayne Shorter; Live At The 1988 Montreux Jazz Festival [DVD];
2005; Herbie Hancock; Possibilities;
2005; Pat Metheny Group; The Way Up;
2006; Tom Scott; Bebop United;
2006; Béla Fleck and the Flecktones; The Hidden Land;
2006; John McLaughlin; Industrial Zen;
2007; Stanley Clarke; The Toys Of Men;
2007; Michael Brecker; Pilgrimage;
2008; Yellowjackets featuring Mike Stern; Lifecycle;
2008; Pat Metheny, Christian McBride, Antonio Sanchez; Tokyo Day Trip;
2008; John McLaughlin; Floating Point;
2009; Joe Zawinul & The Zawinul Syndicate; 75th [DVD];
2009; Chick Corea and John McLaughlin; Five Peace Band;
2010; John McLaughlin and the 4th Dimension; To The One;
2010; Herbie Hancock; The Imagine Project;
2011; The Free Spirits; Live at the Scene Feburary 22nd 1967;
2011; Oz Noy; Fuzzy;
2011; Yellowjackets; Timeline;
2012; Snarky Puppy; groundUP;
2012; Snarky Puppy; Tell Your Friends;
2012; John McLaughlin and the 4th Dimension; Now Hear This;

2013; Exivious; Liminal;
2013; Yellowjackets; A Rise In The Road;
2013; Randy Brecker; The Brecker Brothers Band Reunion;
2014; John McLaughlin and the 4th Dimension; The Boston Record;
2014; Hedvig Mollestad Trio; Enfant Terrible;
2014; Snarky Puppy; We Like It Here;
2014; Animals As Leaders; The Joy Of Motion;
2015; Mörglbl; Tea Time For Punks;
2015; Snarky Puppy /w Metropole Orkest; Sylva;

# Glossary

| | |
|---|---|
| 2/4 | The time signature corresponding to two beats in a bar. Each beat corresponds to a quarter note or crotchet. Also called march time. Both beats are strong in march time. |
| 3/4 | The time signature corresponding to three beats in a bar. Each beat corresponds to a quarter note or crotchet. Also called waltz time. Only the first beat is strong in waltz time. |
| 4/4 | The time signature corresponding to four beats in a bar. Each beat corresponds to a quarter note or crotchet. The strong beats are usually the first and the third; second and fourth beats are weak. However, when strong beats are second and fourth – as they usually are in rock music - it is know as 'playing on the back beat'. 4/4 is also known as common time. |
| arpeggio | A rapid run of notes in series, either up or down a scale. Musicians often use arpeggios when practising their scales. |
| backbeat | A common rhythm used in rock music and jazz-rock. See 4/4 |
| backing | The music played by the other musicians in the band while a soloist or lead musician is playing. |
| bebop | The name given to the style of music that evolved in the early 1940s. It is characterised by very fast tempos and melodies that rise and fall sharply and contain variable intervals between the notes. |
| blues, bluesy | A style of jazz music based upon a scale having a flattened third and a flattened seventh, but strictly played so that the actual pitch is not obtainable from the notes on a piano. Bluesy: in the style of the blues. |
| bop | See bebop |
| bridge | A short section of music used to link two other sections such as two verses or a verse and a chorus. (A bridge is also the part on the body of a guitar to which the strings are attached.) |
| bum note | See glitch |
| busk | This word normally means to play for coins on street corners. However, in jazz it means to play unrehearsed. Jazzers are happy to do this when they play 'standards' because they know them. Clearly it is not normally possible to play unrehearsed pieces that you don't know, unless you are a good sight-reader. Unlike classical musicians, jazzers, when playing pieces they know, usually do not rely on written music. |
| chord | A chord is a combination of notes played at the same time. Chords are given the same names as the notes, with the added characteristic of being major, minor, dominant or diminished, |

depending on the particular combinations. Thus the chord of C major consists of the notes CEG, whilst the chord of C minor consists of CEbG. The chord of G major is comprised of GBD, whilst G minor is GBbD.

| | |
|---|---|
| chops | Originally the term applied to the condition of the lips and associated facial muscles that were necessary to play a wind instrument. Today any jazz musician who says his chops were good is saying that he played a solo particularly well, even if he used his fingers, rather than his mouth, to do it! |
| chorus | See verse. |
| coda | The final ending section of a piece. |
| cool | Relaxed, laid-back, undemanding, but also, by definition, very pleasant to listen to; delicious, hip. |
| crotchet | A quarter note. There are four crotchets or quarter notes in a bar of 4/4 music. |
| eighth note | A quaver. A half of a quarter note. Two eighth notes are played instead of a crotchet and there are eight of them in a bar of 4/4 music. |
| ensemble | The musicians playing as a band, rather than as individuals. |
| fill | A short section of music that fills a gap between two other sections. An instrumental fill is often used between two verses, for example. See bridge. |
| freebop | A term created in the 1960s to describe the mainstream jazz of the time. A clear play on the word bebop, it implied that freebop was a derivation of bebop but using elements of freer improvisation, less restricted by chord structures or musical forms. |
| funk, funky | A style of playing that developed from the 1960s on as jazz fused with soul and R&B music. It involves slow to moderately paced playing that is strongly rhythmic – even syncopated – and, with heavy bass lines, is quite percussive. |
| genre | A type of music. In this book, genres are jazz, rock, classical and ethnic/folk musics. Sub-genres are distinct styles within a given genre, e.g. bebop jazz, mainstream jazz or prog-rock. |
| gig | A live performance in front of an audience. (Sometimes, a job of employment.) |
| glissando | A slide from one note to another; there are no breaks in the execution of a series of notes. |
| glitch | A clear error in playing a note that results in either a different note from the one intended or an impure rasping sound on a wind instrument. Also a bum note, fluff, lemon… |
| groove | Instrumental music having a strong rhythmic character but is laid back and not necessarily highly charged. It aims to excite |

| | |
|---|---|
| | a listener such that he moves his body or, even better, starts to dance. |
| harmonic | An abnormal (usually high) note obtained on a guitar by causing the string to vibrate in an unusual way. On a wind instrument, harmonics are made by altering the pressure and tension of blowing on the mouthpiece. |
| hip | See cool. |
| improvisation | When a musician plays music during a piece that he creates spontaneously as he goes along. It is not written down on paper and is normally different each time he plays it. |
| interval | The difference in pitch between two notes. |
| intro (short for introduction) | The first or opening part of a piece of music before the commencement of the first main theme. |
| jam | When jazz musicians get together to play or improvise almost entirely unrehearsed. Thus jazz musicians jam and they do it at a jam session. |
| jazzer | Someone who plays (or just likes) jazz. |
| key | Most pieces of music are based in a key that is given the same name as one of the notes in a scale. The key of a piece of music has the added advantage of being either major or minor. In the western culture, major keys are generally associated with being happy and bright, whilst minor keys feel sad and dark. |
| lick | A line or phrase played on a solo instrument, often fast. |
| live | A piece of music played by musicians concurrently. Live music is most often associated with playing in front of an audience in an auditorium, but could equally well be done in a studio to tape. Unlike the trend in rock and pop recorded music, this has been popular in jazz for a number of years. Clearly music is not live when each musician makes his contribution on separately recorded tracks that are then assembled into the final recording during the process of mixing. |
| melody line | A group of musical notes constituting the minimum musical theme. It could be equivalent to a sentence or a paragraph in English. |
| meter | US preferred term for time signature. |
| middle-eight | A section of music, eight bars in length, found between verses or combinations of verses and choruses. In slang use, the length of the section could also be any other length, sixteen bars, for example. |
| mode | A way of playing jazz using a particular scale of notes. The modal style of playing jazz was developed by George Russell |

|   |   |
|---|---|
| | and taken up by Miles Davis and others. It does not necessarily involve the use of the familiar western diatonic scale but could use any of the many other kinds of scale, for example, Dorian, Lydian, Phrygian, Mixolydian etc. |
| modulation | When a piece moves from one key to another. |
| motif | A short group of notes; possibly equal to or shorter than a phrase. |
| number | See song. |
| ostinato | Repeated over and over. See vamp. |
| percussive | When applied to notes, similar to punctuated but playing the notes with some force, like a stabbing effect. |
| phrase | A short group of musical notes. Equivalent to a short sequence of words in English that is generally shorter than a sentence. |
| piece | Piece of music, song, tune or number. |
| punctuated | Playing notes (sometimes phrases) with deliberate gaps between them. See staccato. |
| quarter note | A crochet. There are four quarter notes in a bar of 4/4 music and three in a bar of 3/4 music. |
| rallantando or rall | A deceleration, or slowing down. Can occur anywhere in a piece of music, but is often used at the end. |
| register | The range of pitch on a wind instrument. Wind instruments generally have two full octaves available: the low register and the high register. Extra keys are also provided for the musician to extend his range; these vary according to the instrument. |
| scale | In the European system of music, a scale is a sequence of eight notes given the letters A-G. The scale can begin on any one of those letters and rise or fall stepwise until it returns to the note it started on: thus, CDEFGABC or GABCDEFG. |
| sixteenth note | A semi-quaver. A quarter of a quarter note. Four sixteenth notes are played instead of a crotchet and there are sixteen of them in a bar of 4/4 music. When music is played at fast speeds (tempos) only the very best musicians could play sixteenth notes at around 15-20 notes per second! |
| solo | When a musician takes the lead during a piece of music. Generally, in jazz, the music in a solo is improvised. |
| song | Slang in a jazz context: the piece of music, but not necessarily involving singing! Also a tune, or number. |
| soul | A fusion of R&B music with gospel that began in the late 1950s |
| staccato | Played with a sharp separation of notes. See also punctuated and percussive. |
| syncopated | Refers to the rhythm of a piece of music when it is played such that its strong beats do not coincide with the naturally strong |

| | |
|---|---|
| | beats in each bar associated with the time signature being used. |
| take | Each time a complete piece of music is recorded it is called a 'take'. A piece might be recorded several times, but only one take appears on the album. New editions of older 'classic' albums often have the alternate takes that were not included on the original. |
| tempo | The speed at which a piece of music is played. A metronome is a device that clicks according to a speed the musician sets on it, measured as beats per minute. A tempo of 60 beats per minute is obviously one beat per second. If 4/4 music is played at this tempo, then you are playing one quarter note or crotchet every second and this is on the slow side of a moderate tempo, which is about 100 beats per minute. |
| theme | A longer musical passage having a coherent musical thought. Equivalent to a paragraph in English. Themes generally come in groups of four bars. A theme could be made up of one or more melody lines, each made up of phrases. |
| tight | Generally used to describe a band. The high level of musicality that a band achieves when the musicians develop a deep level of understanding through extensive playing together. Also used to describe the tone of a saxophone that involves especially tight lip muscles. When drums are described as tight, the sound is that obtained from a tight skin on the snare drum, fashionable in the 1990s. |
| timbre | A measure of the sound quality of a note on a musical instrument. Notably different timbres are found in jazz compared to the traditional style of European music. |
| time signature | The number of beats in a bar. See 2/4, 3/4, 4/4. Also called meter. |
| tremolo | See vibrato. The tremolo arm creates vibrato on a guitar. |
| tune | See song. |
| vamp | Strictly a vamp is any repeated musical figure (phrase or motif, for example). When it describes a long repeated section of music over one chord it is similar to a groove, but to most ears is musically uninteresting. See also: ostinato |
| verse | A derivation from the time of the folk song when songs were divided into a number of verses and choruses. Jazz music is frequently divided in a similar fashion. Verses are different when there are words, but not necessarily when there are not. Choruses are generally similar if not identical. |
| vibe | A particular kind of feeling that the music aims to induce in a listener. A shortening of 'vibration', meaning a kind of |

| | |
|---|---|
| vibrato | resonance established between the band and the audience. Not to be confused with vibes, short for vibraphone.
When a note wobbles (vibrates) in such a way that its pitch varies slightly. This is a deliberate process in the European style of music because it is considered to enhance the beauty of the sound. Operatic singers, for example are well-known for their strong use of vibrato. Rock singers are not fussed about using it at all! Vibrato translates into tremolo when a guitarist does it. |
| voice, voicing | The sound of a musical instrument is sometimes called its voice. However, a voicing is a rather loose term to describe a way of producing a sound. Usually, on a given instrument, chords such as G major or A minor can be played in different ways. These are voicings. |
| walking bass | When a musician plays bass with strictly four beats to each bar and with quite small musical intervals between each note. |

## Jazz-Fusion timeline:

The following pages 251-256 are an approximate timeline showing the years when the main characters and bands described in this book were performing and recording. Pages are divided into decades, beginning at 1958 and continuing to the present day. This schematic is inevitably incomplete and intended only as an inspiration for further research.

## Timeline of Bands (1959–1968)

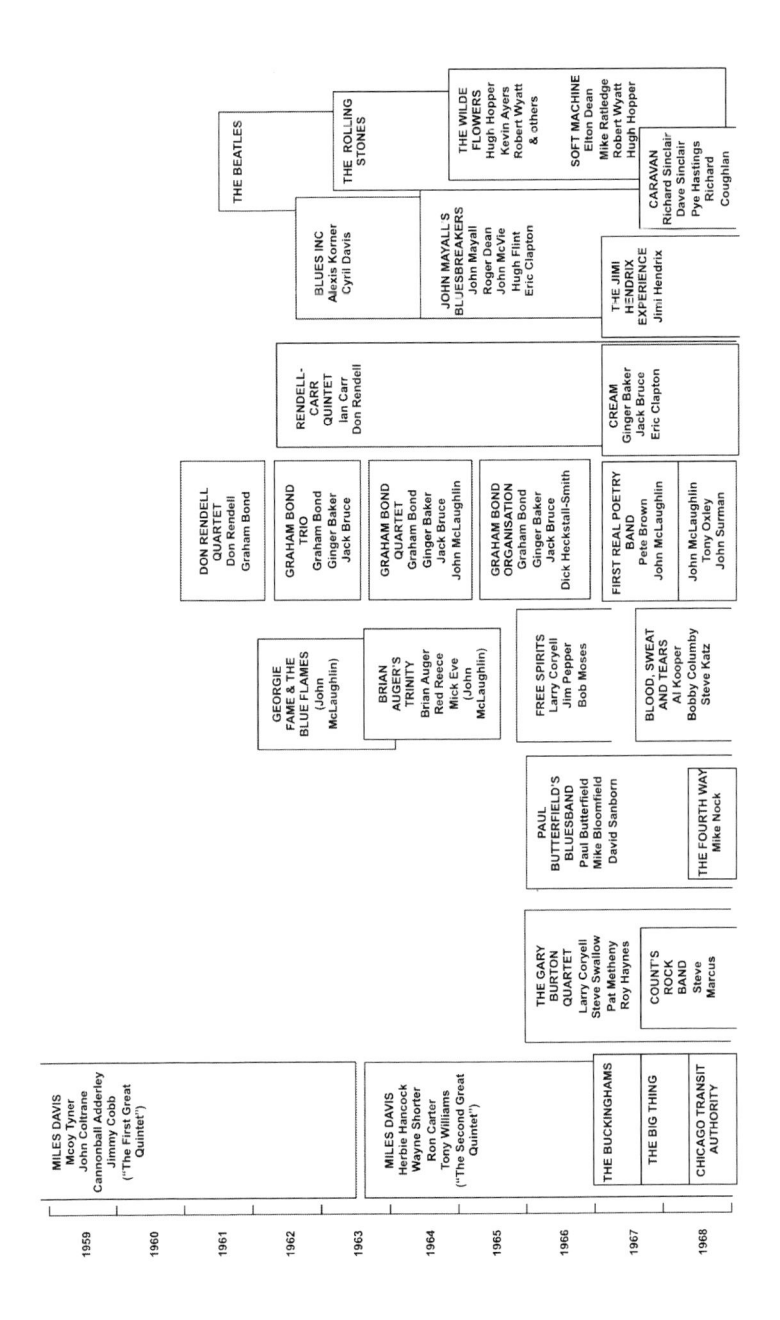

**THE BEATLES**

**THE ROLLING STONES**

**THE WILDE FLOWERS**
Hugh Hopper
Kevin Ayers
Robert Wyatt
& others

**SOFT MACHINE**
Elton Dean
Mike Ratledge
Robert Wyatt
Hugh Hopper

**CARAVAN**
Richard Sinclair
Dave Sinclair
Pye Hastings
Richard Coughlan

**BLUES INC**
Alexis Korner
Cyril Davis

**JOHN MAYALL'S BLUESBREAKERS**
John Mayall
Roger Dean
John McVie
Hugh Flint
Eric Clapton

**THE JIMI HENDRIX EXPERIENCE**
Jimi Hendrix

**RENDELL-CARR QUINTET**
Ian Carr
Don Rendell

**CREAM**
Ginger Baker
Jack Bruce
Eric Clapton

**DON RENDELL QUARTET**
Don Rendell
Graham Bond

**GRAHAM BOND TRIO**
Graham Bond
Ginger Baker
Jack Bruce

**GRAHAM BOND QUARTET**
Graham Bond
Ginger Baker
Jack Bruce
John McLaughlin

**GRAHAM BOND ORGANISATION**
Graham Bond
Ginger Baker
Jack Bruce
Dick Heckstall-Smith

**FIRST REAL POETRY BAND**
Pete Brown
John McLaughlin
Tony Oxley
John Surman

**GEORGIE FAME & THE BLUE FLAMES**
(John McLaughlin)

**BRIAN AUGER'S TRINITY**
Brian Auger
Red Reece
Mick Eve
(John McLaughlin)

**FREE SPIRITS**
Larry Coryell
Jim Pepper
Bob Moses

**BLOOD, SWEAT AND TEARS**
Al Kooper
Bobby Columby
Steve Katz

**PAUL BUTTERFIELD'S BLUESBAND**
Paul Butterfield
Mike Bloomfield
David Sanborn

**THE FOURTH WAY**
Mike Nock

**THE GARY BURTON QUARTET**
Larry Coryell
Steve Swallow
Pat Metheny
Roy Haynes

**COUNT'S ROCK BAND**
Steve Marcus

**MILES DAVIS**
McCoy Tyner
John Coltrane
Cannonball Adderley
Jimmy Cobb
("The First Great Quintet")

**MILES DAVIS**
Herbie Hancock
Wayne Shorter
Ron Carter
Tony Williams
("The Second Great Quintet")

**THE BUCKINGHAMS**

**THE BIG THING**

**CHICAGO TRANSIT AUTHORITY**

1959
1960
1961
1962
1963
1964
1965
1966
1967
1968

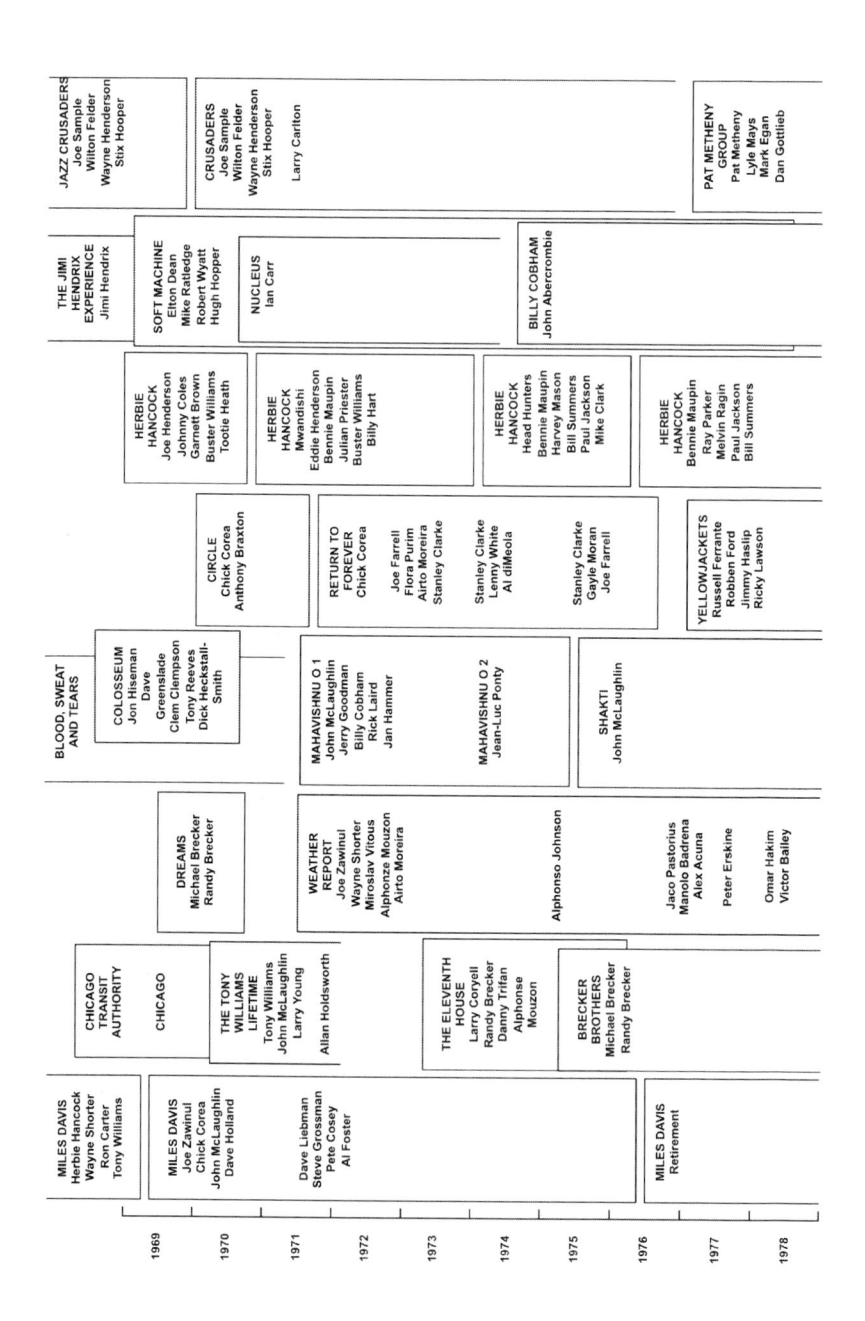

|  |  |
|---|---|
| **JAZZ CRUSADERS** (1969) | Joe Sample, Wilton Felder, Wayne Henderson, Stix Hooper |
| **CRUSADERS** | Joe Sample, Wilton Felder, Wayne Henderson, Stix Hooper, Larry Carlton |
| **PAT METHENY GROUP** (1977) | Pat Metheny, Lyle Mays, Mark Egan, Dan Gottlieb |
| **THE JIMI HENDRIX EXPERIENCE** | Jimi Hendrix |
| **SOFT MACHINE** | Elton Dean, Mike Ratledge, Robert Wyatt, Hugh Hopper |
| **NUCLEUS** | Ian Carr |
| **BILLY COBHAM** | John Abercrombie |
| **HERBIE HANCOCK** (1970) | Joe Henderson, Johnny Coles, Garnett Brown, Buster Williams, Tootie Heath |
| **HERBIE HANCOCK Mwandishi** | Eddie Henderson, Bennie Maupin, Julian Priester, Buster Williams, Billy Hart |
| **HERBIE HANCOCK Head Hunters** | Bennie Maupin, Harvey Mason, Bill Summers, Paul Jackson, Mike Clark |
| **HERBIE HANCOCK** | Bennie Maupin, Ray Parker, Melvin Ragin, Paul Jackson, Bill Summers |
| **CIRCLE** | Chick Corea, Anthony Braxton |
| **RETURN TO FOREVER** | Chick Corea, Joe Farrell, Flora Purim, Airto Moreira, Stanley Clarke |
| **RETURN TO FOREVER** | Stanley Clarke, Lenny White, Al diMeola |
| **RETURN TO FOREVER** | Stanley Clarke, Gayle Moran, Joe Farrell |
| **YELLOWJACKETS** | Russell Ferrante, Robben Ford, Jimmy Haslip, Ricky Lawson |
| **BLOOD, SWEAT AND TEARS** | |
| **COLOSSEUM** | Jon Hiseman, Dave Greenslade, Clem Clempson, Tony Reeves, Dick Heckstall-Smith |
| **MAHAVISHNU O 1** | John McLaughlin, Jerry Goodman, Billy Cobham, Rick Laird, Jan Hammer |
| **MAHAVISHNU O 2** | Jean-Luc Ponty |
| **SHAKTI** | John McLaughlin |
| **DREAMS** | Michael Brecker, Randy Brecker |
| **WEATHER REPORT** | Joe Zawinul, Wayne Shorter, Miroslav Vitous, Alphonze Mouzon, Airto Moreira |
| **WEATHER REPORT** | Alphonso Johnson |
| **WEATHER REPORT** | Jaco Pastorius, Manolo Badrena, Alex Acuna |
| **WEATHER REPORT** | Peter Erskine |
| **WEATHER REPORT** | Omar Hakim, Victor Bailey |
| **CHICAGO TRANSIT AUTHORITY** | |
| **CHICAGO** | |
| **THE TONY WILLIAMS LIFETIME** | Tony Williams, John McLaughlin, Larry Young, Allan Holdsworth |
| **THE ELEVENTH HOUSE** | Larry Coryell, Randy Brecker, Danny Trifan, Alphonse Mouzon |
| **BRECKER BROTHERS** | Michael Brecker, Randy Brecker |
| **MILES DAVIS** | Herbie Hancock, Wayne Shorter, Ron Carter, Tony Williams |
| **MILES DAVIS** (1970) | Joe Zawinul, Chick Corea, Dave Holland |
| **MILES DAVIS** | Dave Liebman, Steve Grossman, Pete Cosey, Al Foster |
| **MILES DAVIS Retirement** (1976) | |

Timeline: 1969 – 1978

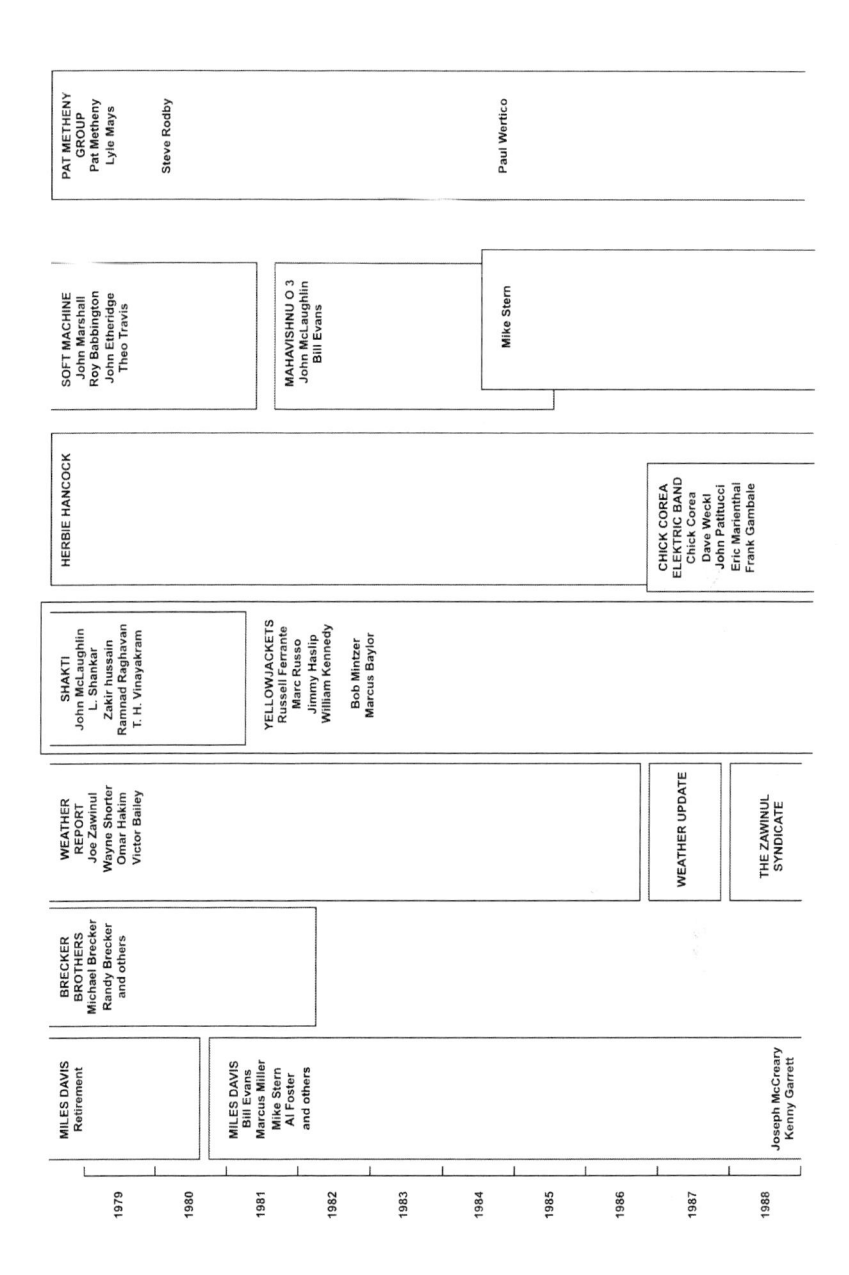

|  | | | | | | | | |
|---|---|---|---|---|---|---|---|---|
| 1979 | MILES DAVIS<br>Retirement | | | | | | | PAT METHENY GROUP<br>Pat Metheny<br>Lyle Mays |
| 1980 | | BRECKER BROTHERS<br>Michael Brecker<br>Randy Brecker<br>and others | WEATHER REPORT<br>Joe Zawinul<br>Wayne Shorter<br>Omar Hakim<br>Victor Bailey | SHAKTI<br>John McLaughlin<br>L. Shankar<br>Zakir hussain<br>Ramnad Raghavan<br>T. H. Vinayakram | HERBIE HANCOCK | SOFT MACHINE<br>John Marshall<br>Roy Babbington<br>John Etheridge<br>Theo Travis | Steve Rodby |
| 1981 | MILES DAVIS<br>Bill Evans<br>Marcus Miller<br>Mike Stern<br>Al Foster<br>and others | | | | | | |
| 1982 | | | | | | | |
| 1983 | | | | YELLOWJACKETS<br>Russell Ferrante<br>Marc Russo<br>Jimmy Haslip<br>William Kennedy | | MAHAVISHNU O 3<br>John McLaughlin<br>Bill Evans | |
| 1984 | | | | Bob Mintzer<br>Marcus Baylor | | | |
| 1985 | | | WEATHER UPDATE | | | | |
| 1986 | | | | | | Mike Stern | |
| 1987 | | | THE ZAWINUL SYNDICATE | | CHICK COREA ELEKTRIC BAND<br>Chick Corea<br>Dave Weckl<br>John Patitucci<br>Eric Marienthal<br>Frank Gambale | | Paul Wertico |
| 1988 | Joseph McCreary<br>Kenny Garrett | | | | | | |

## Timeline of Bands (1989–1998)

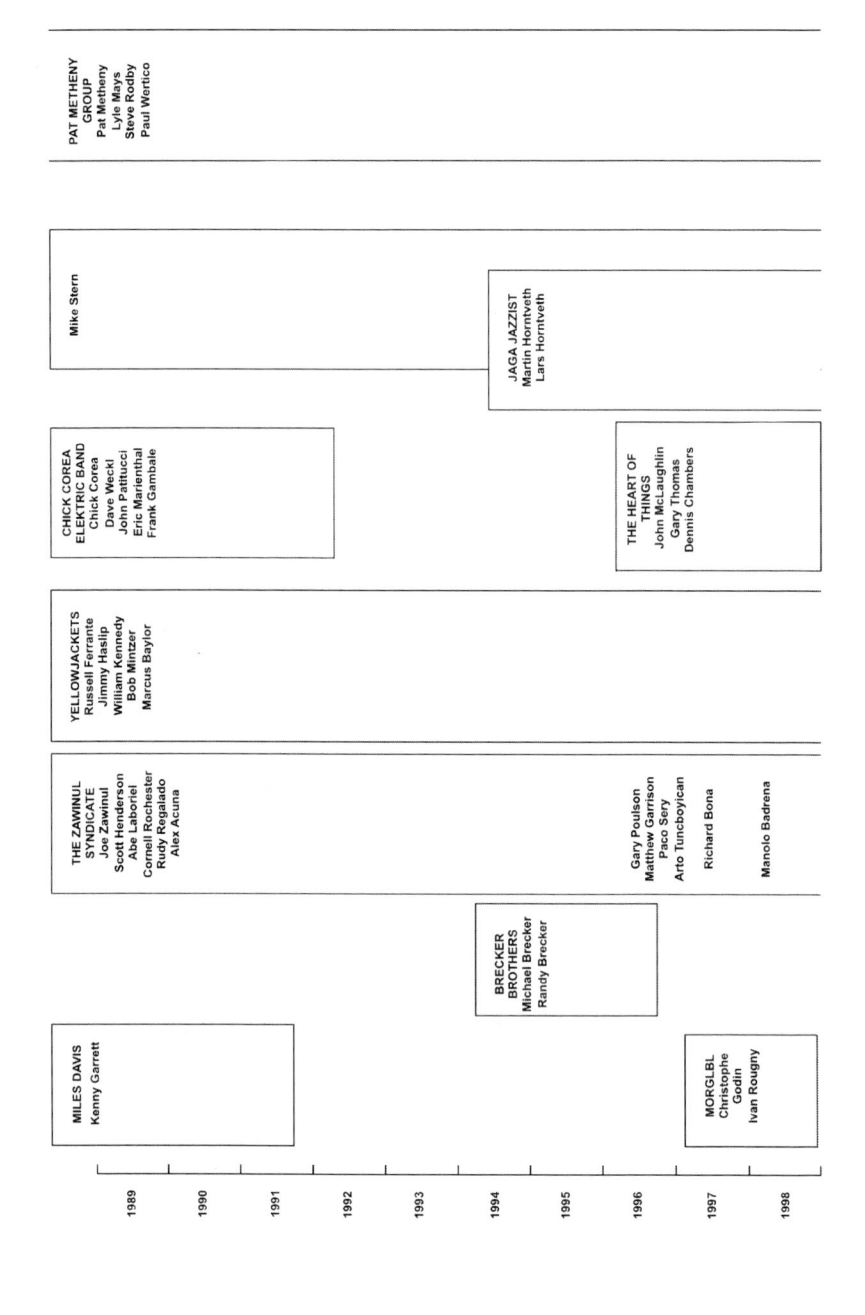

**PAT METHENY GROUP**
- Pat Metheny
- Lyle Mays
- Steve Rodby
- Paul Wertico

**Mike Stern**

**JAGA JAZZIST**
- Martin Horntveth
- Lars Horntveth

**CHICK COREA ELEKTRIC BAND**
- Chick Corea
- Dave Weckl
- John Patitucci
- Eric Marienthal
- Frank Gambale

**THE HEART OF THINGS**
- John McLaughlin
- Gary Thomas
- Dennis Chambers

**YELLOWJACKETS**
- Russell Ferrante
- Jimmy Haslip
- William Kennedy
- Bob Mintzer
- Marcus Baylor

**THE ZAWINUL SYNDICATE**
- Joe Zawinul
- Scott Henderson
- Abe Laboriel
- Cornell Rochester
- Rudy Regalado
- Alex Acuna
- Gary Poulson
- Matthew Garrison
- Paco Sery
- Arto Tuncboyician
- Richard Bona
- Manolo Badrena

**BRECKER BROTHERS**
- Michael Brecker
- Randy Brecker

**MILES DAVIS**
- Kenny Garrett

**MORGLBL**
- Christophe Godin
- Ivan Rougny

1989 — 1990 — 1991 — 1992 — 1993 — 1994 — 1995 — 1996 — 1997 — 1998

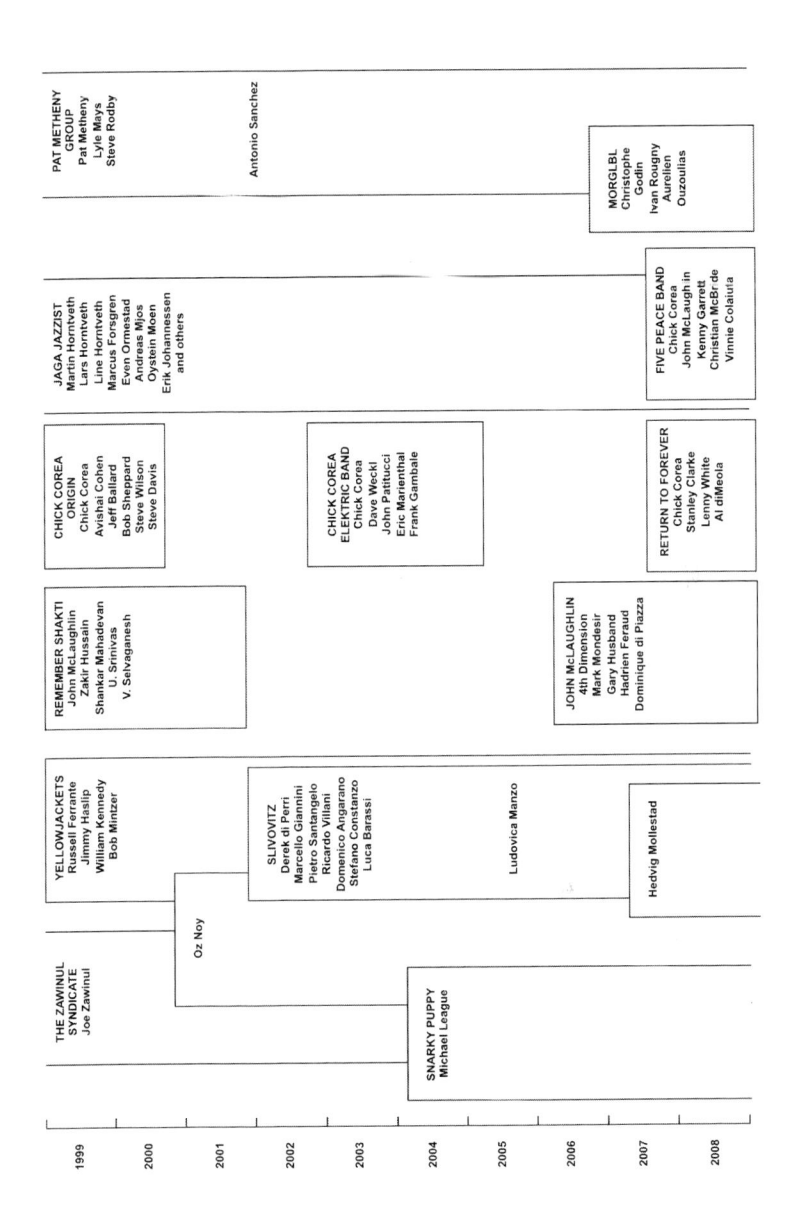

## PAT METHENY GROUP
Pat Metheny
Lyle Mays
Steve Rodby

Antonio Sanchez

## MORGLBL
Christophe Godin
Ivan Rougny
Aurélien Ouzoulias

## JAGA JAZZIST
Martin Horntveth
Lars Horntveth
Line Horntveth
Marcus Forsgren
Even Ormestad
Andreas Mjos
Oystein Moen
Erik Johannessen
and others

## FIVE PEACE BAND
Chick Corea
John McLaughlin
Kenny Garrett
Christian McBride
Vinnie Colaiuta

## CHICK COREA ORIGIN
Chick Corea
Avishai Cohen
Jeff Ballard
Bob Sheppard
Steve Wilson
Steve Davis

## CHICK COREA ELEKTRIC BAND
Chick Corea
Dave Weck
John Patitucci
Eric Marienthal
Frank Gambale

## RETURN TO FOREVER
Chick Corea
Stanley Clarke
Lenny White
Al diMeola

## REMEMBER SHAKTI
John McLaughlin
Zakir Hussain
Shankar Mahadevan
U. Srinivas
V. Selvaganesh

## JOHN McLAUGHLIN 4th Dimension
Mark Mondesir
Gary Husband
Hadrien Feraud
Dominique di Piazza

## YELLOWJACKETS
Russell Ferrante
Jimmy Haslip
William Kennedy
Bob Mintzer

Oz Noy

## SLIVOVITZ
Derek di Perri
Marcello Giannini
Pietro Santangelo
Ricardo Villani
Domenico Angarano
Stefano Constanzo
Luca Barassi

Ludovica Manzo

Hedvig Mollestad

## THE ZAWINUL SYNDICATE
Joe Zawinul

## SNARKY PUPPY
Michael League

1999
2000
2001
2002
2003
2004
2005
2006
2007
2008

255

## Timeline of Bands (2009–2018)

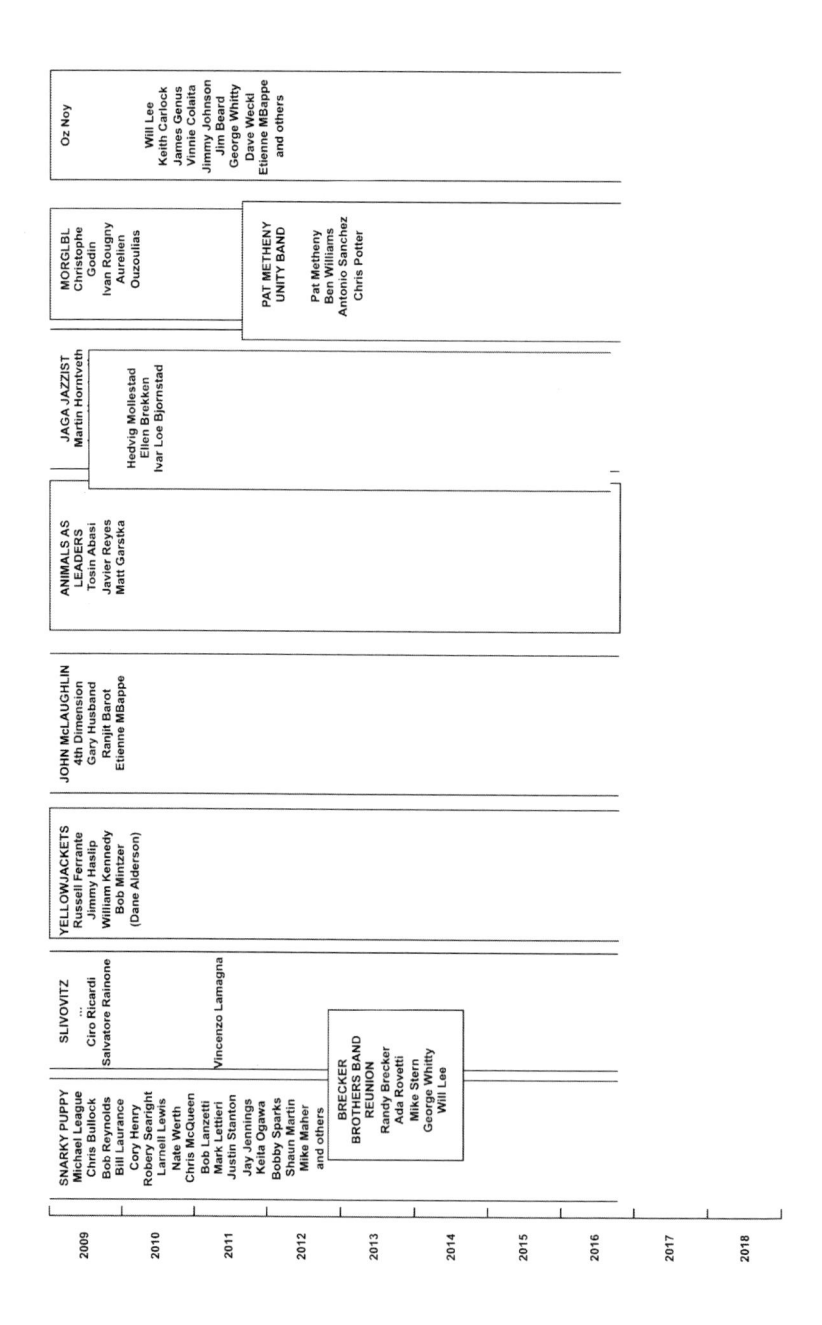

**SNARKY PUPPY**
Michael League
Chris Bullock
Bob Reynolds
Bill Laurance
Cory Henry
Robery Searight
Larnell Lewis
Nate Werth
Chris McQueen
Bob Lanzetti
Mark Lettieri
Jay Jennings
Keita Ogawa
Bobby Sparks
Shaun Martin
Mike Maher
and others

**SLIVOVITZ**
...
Ciro Ricardi
Salvatore Rainone
Vincenzo Lamagna

**BRECKER BROTHERS BAND REUNION**
Randy Brecker
Ada Rovetti
Mike Stern
George Whitty
Will Lee

**YELLOWJACKETS**
Russell Ferrante
Jimmy Haslip
William Kennedy
Bob Mintzer
(Dane Alderson)

**JOHN McLAUGHLIN**
4th Dimension
Gary Husband
Ranjit Barot
Etienne MBappe

**ANIMALS AS LEADERS**
Tosin Abasi
Javier Reyes
Matt Garstka

**JAGA JAZZIST**
Martin Horntveth
Hedvig Mollestad
Ellen Brekken
Ivar Loe Bjornstad

**MORGLBL**
Christophe Godin
Ivan Rougny
Aurelien Ouzoulias

**PAT METHENY UNITY BAND**
Pat Metheny
Ben Williams
Antonio Sanchez
Chris Potter

**Oz Noy**
Will Lee
Keith Carlock
James Genus
Vinnie Colaita
Jimmy Johnson
Jim Beard
George Whitty
Dave Weckl
Etienne MBappe
and others

2009 | 2010 | 2011 | 2012 | 2013 | 2014 | 2015 | 2016 | 2017 | 2018

# Index

## 1

100 Club, 104
125th Street Congress, 172
15 Miles to Provo, 113

## 3

34th N Lex, 209, 210, 213, 242

## 7

78-rpm disc, 31, 61
7th Ave South, 207

## 8

8.30, 173, 175,178,215
80/81, 204, 208

## A

A Change Of Heart, 208, 213, 219, 240
A Funky Thide of Sings, 200, 208, 209
A Go Go, 89
A Love Supreme, 106, 107
A Map of the World, 204
A Night In Tunisia, 176
A Prescription for the Blues, 210
A Song For You, 136
A Touch of Light, 221
A Tribute To Jack Johnson, 200
A Tribute to Miles, 198
A Whiter Shade Of Pale, 96
Abasi, Tosin, 146
Abercrombie, John, 113, 114, 200, 234
Acid Jazz, 8, 138, 139, 152
Across the Sky, 204
Adams, Greg, 137
Adderley, Julian Edwin, 40, 164, 175, 176, 220, 229
Adventures in Radioland, 221
Africa, 10, 27, 47, 160, 184
Africaine, 179
After All, 136, 138, 208
After The Rain, 191
Again and Again - Jo'berg Sessions, 195
Against All Odds, 232
Aguillera, Christina, 136
Air Force, 80
Aja, 178, 228, 231, 239
Akai (instrument manufacturer), 127
Ake, David, 151
Al Jarreau, 137, 186, 209
Albert Hall, 79
alcohol, 48, 82, 83, 85, 88, 173, 215
Alegria, 179, 242
Alias, Charles Don, 93, 230
Alias, Don, 93, 230

Alive in South Africa, 227
Alivemutherfoya, 201
Allen, David, 63, 83
Almeida, Laurindo, 157, 158, 160, 239
Alone But Never Alone, 231, 232
Alonso, Sydney, 123
Altered State, 234, 237
Amanda, 209
Amandla, 167, 169, 219
America, 21, 22, 25, 65, 66, 77, 80, 89, 129, 130, 131, 160
American Garage, 202, 204, 240
Amphetamines, 85
An Innocent Man, 208
And Beyond, 227
Anderson, Buddy, 35, 36
Anderson, Ian, 126
Angel Street, 198
Angela, 120
Angle, 209
Angle of Repose, 209
Anna, 205, 243
Another Hand, 213, 219
Another World, 209, 223
Anthology, 217
Apple Juice, 229
Apple/Macintosh computer, 122, 182
Appleton, Jon, 123
Arc, 195
Ardley, Neil, 97
Are You Experienced, 81
Armstrong, Louis, 17, 24, 25, 26, 27, 49, 50, 153
ARP, 122, 123
Arpeggio, 245
Art Blakey's Jazz Messengers, 177
Art of the Big Band, 210
As Falls Wichita, So Falls Wichita Falls, 204, 240
As We Speak, 212, 213, 219, 240
Ascenseur, 168
Asia, 10, 43
Aspects, 208
At Fillmore, 195
At Last!, 169
At the Lighthouse, 226
Atlantic, 21, 45, 63, 64, 92, 94, 100, 109, 112, 119, 197
Atlantis, 178, 201, 218
Auger, Brian, 69, 99, 112
Aura, 9, 167
Average White Band, 113, 133, 207, 208, 209
Ayers, Kevin, 83, 85
Ayler, Albert, 45, 106, 107

## B

Babbington, Roy, 104
Bach, J S, 158
Back to Back, 207, 208, 209, 212, 213
Backstreet, 212, 213, 219, 240
Bailey, Derek, 204
Bailey, Victor, 173, 201, 209
Baker, Chet, 170
Baker, Ginger, 70, 72, 77, 78, 79, 96, 117, 118, 119, 188
Baker, Peter (Ginger), 70, 72, 77, 78, 79, 188
Baldry, Long John, 85, 103
Ball and Chain, 107

257

Band of Gypsys, 81, 150
Band, HR-Big, 201
Baraka, 186
Bare Wires, 71
Bargeron, Dave, 93
Barker, Guy, 45, 50
Barot, Ranjit, 143, 190
Basie, William Allen (Count), 29, 31, 234
Bass, walking, 250
Bauza, Mario, 38
Baylor, Marcus, 236
BBC, 11, 50, 60, 64, 85, 149, 150
Beach Boys, 121
Beale Street, 62
Beard, James Arthur, 178, 209
Beat, 7, 62, 63, 65, 68, 75, 82, 116, 117, 124, 151, 176, 177, 189, 229
Beat It, 124
Beatles, 7, 64, 66, 67, 68, 69, 74, 76, 77, 78, 83, 86, 87, 96, 100, 105, 109, 116, 118, 121, 129, 135, 148, 149, 154, 159
Beatnik, 63, 67, 83
Beauty, 169, 191, 195, 238, 239
Bebop, 7, 17, 33, 40, 54, 112, 153, 207, 208, 209, 229, 239, 243, 245
Bebop United, 229
Bechet, Sidney, 29
Beck, Jeff, 71, 80, 135, 140
Beck, Joe, 45, 87
Becker, Walter Carl, 136, 137
Believe It, 198
Believer, 191
Bellevue, 48
Belo Horizonte, 125, 191
Beneath the Mask, 194, 196, 223
Bennett, Max, 228
Benny, 29, 30, 34, 35, 44, 107, 112, 177, 186
Benoit, David, 140
Benson, George, 45, 137, 139, 184, 186, 199, 223
Benton, Brook, 175
Berg, Bob, 210, 242
Berger, Karl, 190
Berklee Music College, 87, 143
Bernhardt, Warren, 89, 240
Berry, Chuck, 67, 74
Best of 82-96, 220
Best of the Jazz Crusaders, 226
Between Nothingness and Eternity, 188, 200
Between the Lines, 223
Beware The Ides of March, 96
Beyond, 4, 204, 221
Beyond the Missouri Sky (Short Stories), 204
Beyond Words, 221
Big band, 28, 37, 39, 233
Big Band, Bill Warfield, 210
Big Band, DR, 243
Big Band, HR, 201
Big Brother and the Holding Company, 77, 90, 107
Big Fun, 169, 175, 177, 184, 191, 195, 200, 222, 242
Big Girl, 213
Bill Evans, 8, 142, 164, 167, 189, 191, 210, 219, 220, 221, 222, 240, 241, 242
Billboard, 92, 94, 232
Billboard (magazine), 92
Billy Cobham, 113, 114
Birdland, 48, 171, 176, 177
Birds of Fire, 188, 200

Bitches Brew, 90, 109, 111, 166, 168, 169, 170, 171, 172, 175, 176, 177, 179, 188, 190, 191, 193, 195, 239
Black Beauty - Miles Davis at Fillmore West, 195
Black Light, 190, 192
Black Market, 173, 174, 175, 178, 214, 215, 239
Black Orpheus, 158, 159
Black Unity, 218
Black Water, 175
Blackhawk, 168
Blade, Brian, 179, 180, 186
Blakey, Arthur, 40, 45, 176, 177, 178, 179
Blanton, Jimmy, 30, 48
Bley, Carla, 87, 190, 204
Bley, Paul, 214
Blind Faith, 79
Blood Sweat & Tears, 7, 90, 91, 92, 93, 113, 135, 154, 206
Bloomfield, Mike, 211
Blow It Out, 228, 229
Blown Away, 221
Blue, 1, 4, 10, 42, 43, 49, 50, 69, 73, 112, 150, 151, 162, 164, 168, 171, 180, 183, 185, 186, 196, 199, 204, 208, 221, 229, 230, 232, 234, 237, 239, 240
Blue Asphalt, 204
Blue Flames, 69, 73, 112
Blue Hats, 234, 237
Blue Haze, 168
Blue Montreux, 240
Blue Note, 1, 4, 42, 43, 49, 185, 186, 196, 199, 221
Blue Note Records, 4
Blues, 24, 25, 50, 68, 70, 72, 73, 79, 87, 91, 116, 117, 118, 148, 150, 153, 169, 178, 185, 204, 210, 211, 213, 225, 227, 228, 231, 240
Blues for Pat, 204
Blues for Pat - Live in San Francisco, 204
Blues Incorporated, 70, 72, 73, 116, 117, 118
Bluesbreakers, 7, 70, 71, 72, 95
Bluestreak, 229
Bolin, Tommy, 200
Bollani, Stefano, 196
Bona, Richard, 204, 209
Bond, Graham, 7, 72, 73, 74, 77, 78, 80, 95, 96, 100, 117, 118, 119, 121, 150, 151, 154, 188, 190
Bonfa, Luiz, 159
Bono, 202
Boogie Woogie Waltz, 172
Born, 25, 29, 62, 210, 216, 229
Born Again, 210, 229
Boss DR-55, 122
Bossa, 159
Boston, 87
Both / And, 210
Both Sides Now, 179, 185, 230
Boyle, Gary, 104
Boys and Girls, 219
Braxton, Anthony, 193
Brazil, 159
Break N Da Rulz, 227
Bream, Julian, 159
Brecker Brothers, 4, 8, 20, 50, 86, 114, 132, 136, 142, 144, 150, 151, 154, 199, 206, 208, 209, 210, 212, 213, 219, 220, 239, 240, 241, 243
Brecker Brothers (band), 114
Brecker, Michael, 21, 136, 138, 152, 155, 185, 186, 204, 205, 208, 209, 210, 215, 217, 219, 230, 235, 240, 241, 242, 243
Brecker, Randal Edward, 15, 86, 91, 92, 100, 113, 118,

258

135, 150, 151, 199, 200, 206, 209, 210, 211, 213, 221, 222, 240, 241, 242, 243
Bridge, 25, 90, 122, 159, 245, 246
Bridge Over Troubled Water, 138
Bright Size Life, 204, 214, 215
Brooklyn NYC, 90, 145
Brooks, Clive, 102
Brothers, 26, 27, 28, 49, 50, 112, 133, 207, 208, 209, 210, 212, 213, 228, 239, 241
Brothers In Arms, 208
Brown Street, 176
Brown, Clifford, 48
Brown, James, 130, 132, 133, 154
Brown, Prince, 10, 135
Brubeck, Dave, 19
Bruce, Jack, 70, 72, 77, 78, 79, 117, 118, 119, 188, 190
Bruford, Bill, 103, 148, 151
BST, see Blood Sweat and Tears, 91, 93, 135
Bubana Be, Cubana Bop, 38
Buchla, 123
Buckinghams, 89, 90, 91
Bud Powell, 41, 42, 43, 196
Bullock, Hiram, 208, 211, 212
Burrell, Kenneth Earl, 183
Burton, Gary, 87, 116, 119, 195, 196, 202, 204, 205, 208, 209, 241
But Beautiful, 49
Butler, Jonathan, 185
Butterfield, Paul, 68, 153, 211, 213
By Design, 201
Byrd, Charles L., 45, 159
Byrd, Donald, 177, 183, 185

# C

Café Au Go-Go (jazz club), 92, 109
Cage, John, 75
Calderazzo, Joey, 209
California, 101, 151
Calloway, Cab, 29, 35, 36
Campbell, Mont, 102
Cannon Re-Loaded, 220, 229
Cannonball, 40, 164, 175, 176, 220, 229
Canoff, Rick, 91
Cantaloupe Island, 183, 197
Capitol Records, 81
Capri, 178, 185
Captain Marvel, 198, 216, 218
Caravaggio, 201
Caravan, 32, 83, 102, 177
Carey, Mariah, 136
Carla, 87, 190, 204
Carlos, Walter, 123
Carlton, Larry, 8, 136, 208, 217, 225, 228, 231, 232
Carnaval, 208
Carnegie Hall, 38
Carney, Harry, 30
Carpenters, 136
Carr, Ian, 65, 103, 104
Carter, Benny, 35, 44
Carter, Clifford, 136, 221
Carter, Ron, 47, 165, 178, 183, 184, 185, 186, 198, 201, 239
Casino Lights, 213, 219, 231
Castillo, Emilio, 137
CBS, 120, 131
Celebrating the Music of Weather Report, 209, 210, 213, 220
Celebration, 150, 153, 220, 229, 234, 237
Cellar Door, 191, 242
Cennamo, Louis, 98
Centipede Orchestra, 104
Central London Polytechnic, 79
Cetera, Peter, 89, 93, 97
Chain Reaction, 225, 226
Chalk Mark in a Rain Storm, 230
Chambers, Dennis, 210, 242
Chambers, Paul, 164
Chandler, Chas, 80, 84
Change of Heart, 212
Changes, 229
Chant, 183
Charig, Marc, 104
Charles, Teddy, 170
Cheap Thrills, 107
Cherokee, 39
Chicago, 7, 25, 28, 59, 89, 90, 91, 93, 94, 97, 98, 107, 112, 114, 153, 163, 186
Chicago Transit Authority, 90, 93, 94, 97
Chick Corea, 10, 56, 88, 110, 141, 142, 155, 165, 168, 173, 182, 190, 193, 194, 195, 196, 200, 203, 205, 208, 216, 217, 218, 223, 235
Chick Corea Akoustic Band, 196, 223
Chick Corea Compact Jazz, 196
Chick Corea Elektric Band, 5, 155, 194, 196, 222, 223, 240, 241
Child is Father to the Man, 206
Chile Con Soul, 226
Chitlin circuit, 106
Chops, 35, 99, 246
Chorus, 38, 245, 246
Chris, 3, 71, 80, 85, 88, 98, 103, 150
Christian, Charlie, 34, 35, 44
Christmas At My House, 232
Church music, 21
Circle, 125, 169, 175, 178, 184, 191, 195, 196, 198, 201, 203, 204
Circle 2 Gathering (Japan Only), 196
Circle in the Round, 195, 198, 201
Circus, 76
Cityscape, 208, 219
Civil Rights, 107, 130
Civilisation, 198
Clapton, Eric, 70, 71, 72, 77, 79, 81, 140, 150
Clapton, Eric Patrick, 70, 71, 72, 77, 79, 81, 140, 150
Clarke / Duke Project, 218
Clarke / Duke Project II, 218
Clarke / Duke Project III, 218
Clarke, Kenny, 33, 37, 78, 153
Clarke, Mark, 98, 99
Clarke, Stanley, 8, 178, 184, 191, 194, 195, 198, 200, 201, 216, 218, 220, 229, 232, 239, 243
Classical, 17
Claus Ogerman, 208, 219
Clayton-Thomas, David, 91, 92, 93
Clinton, George, 133, 134, 136
Close Up, 212, 213, 219
Closer, 213
Cloud Nine, 132
Clouds, 229, 230
Club Nocturne, 234, 237
Club, 100 Club, 104
Club, Cafe au Go-Go, 109
Club, Cotton Club, 29, 30

259

Club, Ealing, 70
Club, Fillmore East, 195
Club, Fillmore West, 79, 101
Club, Flamingo, 69, 71
Club, Hot Club de France, 44
Club, Little Theatre Club, 69
*Club, Marquee*, 68, 70, 71, 73
Club, Onyx, 38
Club, Spotlite, 36
Club, The Cavern, 68
Club, Village Gate, 103
Clyne, Jeff, 104
Clyne, Jeffrey, 104
Cobain, Kurt, 48
Cobb, Jimmy, 164
Cobham, Billy, 8, 47, 110, 113, 114, 142, 184, 186, 188, 199, 200, 201, 207, 208, 209, 210, 217, 229, 239
Cochran, Wayne, 214
Cocker, Joe, 225
Coda, 246
Cohen, Leonard, 229
Colaiuta, Vincent, 135, 136, 142, 185, 196, 220
Coleman, Nick, 58, 149
Coleman, Ornette, 40, 45, 47, 75, 79, 105, 153, 154
Collaboration, 157, 158
Collection, 152, 232, 234, 236, 237, 238
Collier, James Lincoln, 50
Colombier, Michel, 184
Colomby, Bobby, 92, 93
Colosseum, 7, 94, 95, 96, 97, 98, 154, 178, 184
Coltrane, John, 43, 45, 49, 75, 86, 87, 106, 111, 154, 163, 164, 168, 169, 170, 171, 183, 204, 207, 239, 241, 242
Columbia, 89, 90, 91, 92, 93, 163, 168, 176, 179, 180, 185, 186, 200, 239, 242
Columby, Bobby, 91, 92, 93
Come Morning, 219
Computer, 122, 123, 134, 182
Concerto, 175, 191, 195, 196
Concerto Retitled, 175
Concierto de Aranjuez, 158, 164
Connors, William, 216
Consequently, 46, 71, 120, 125, 214
Consortium, 201
Cook, Richard, 151
Cook, Will Marion, 30
Cooke, Sam, 80
Copeland, Stewart, 217
Copenhagen Live, 209
Copland, 210
Copland, Marc, 210
Corcovado, 159
Corea Hancock, 195
Corea, Chick, 5, 8, 10, 56, 88, 110, 141, 142, 155, 165, 168, 173, 182, 184, 186, 190, 192, 193, 194, 195, 196, 200, 203, 205, 208, 216, 217, 218, 222, 223, 235, 240, 241, 243
Corea/Hancock/Jarrett/Tyner, 195
Cornbread, 183
Coryell, Larry, 86, 87, 100, 110, 116, 118, 149, 150, 178, 190, 191, 195, 200, 201, 207, 208, 209
Cosby, Bill, 184
Cotton Club, 29, 30, 153
Cotton Tail, 32
Coughlan, Richard, 83, 102
Counterpoint, 204
Country Preacher, 175
Court and Spark, 228, 229, 230

Coventry UK, 75
Cox, Billy, 81
Crawford, Randy, 225
Cream, 7, 77, 78, 79, 81, 101, 118, 154
Crech, Ric, 79
Creole, 22, 23, 24, 25, 31, 32, 56
Crochet, 245, 246, 248, 249
Crosby, David, 229
Crosswinds, 200, 208, 209
Crusaders I, 225, 226, 231
Crystal Silence, 195, 196
CTS Studios, 20
Cuban, 38, 56, 128

# D

Dada Was Here, 85
Dalto, Jorge, 213
Dangerous, 137
Dankworth, John, 65
Dark Side of the Moon, 122
Dartmouth College, 123
David Clayton-Thomas, 93
Davies, Cyril, 70, 72, 116, 117
Davis, Clive, 90, 91, 131
Davis, Clive (Columbia executive), 90
Davis, Michael, 151
Davis, Miles, 4, 7, 8, 9, 10, 12, 14, 21, 38, 40, 43, 45, 46, 47, 54, 58, 68, 81, 83, 90, 94, 101, 106, 108, 109, 110, 119, 131, 136, 141, 142, 149, 150, 153, 154, 155, 158, 160, 162, 163, 164, 166, 167, 168, 169, 170, 171, 175, 176, 177, 178, 179, 180, 181, 183, 184, 185, 186, 188, 189, 190, 191, 192, 193, 195, 197, 198, 199, 200, 201, 219, 221, 239, 240, 241, 242, 247
Dawn, 214
Day Trip, 205, 243
De Lucia, Paco, 189, 191
De Moraes, Vinicius, 159
Deacon Blue, 137
Deacon Blues, 137
Dean, Elton, 85, 103, 104
Dean, Roger, 70, 71
Decoy, 167, 169, 221
Dedicated To You, 85, 104
Deep Into It, 232
DeFrancesco, Joey, 210
Delaney and Bonnie, 80
Delphi 1, 195
Delphi 2 and 3, 195
Derek and the Dominoes, 80
Desire, 229
Détente, 207, 208, 209, 219
Detroit, 186
Devil Lady, 113
Devotion, 190, 191, 200
Di Meola, Al, 86, 189, 191, 194, 195, 214, 215, 217, 218
Diagram, Venn, 53, 54, 55, 56, 57, 115
Different Trains/Electric Counterpoint, 204
Dig, 168
Directions, 169, 170, 186, 209, 242
Directions I, 186, 242
Directions in Music, 209
Disc, compact, 146
Disc, vinyl, 61, 113, 129, 146, 155
Disco, 134
Discovery, 231, 232

260

Dixie Jass Band One Step, 28
Django, 44, 88
DNA, 144
Dog Eat Dog, 230
Dolphin Dance, 108
Dolphy, Eric Allan, 45, 183, 186
Domino, 173, 175, 178
Domino Theory, 173, 175, 178
Don Juan's Reckless Daughter, 215, 230, 231
Don t Stop the Music, 208, 209
Donaldson, Lou, 177
Donnegan, Lonnie, 63, 153
Doom, 192, 198, 215
Dorian, 247
Dorsey, Jimmy, 29
Double Image, 169, 178
Double Vision, 212, 213, 219
Dream, 113, 123
Dream Suite
　Asset Stop / Jane / Crunchy Grenola, 113
Dreamland, 234, 236, 241
Dreams, 7, 113, 114, 118, 183, 191, 199, 200, 204, 206, 208, 209, 210, 212, 213
Dreams So Real, 204
　Music of Carla Bley, 204
Dreyfus Night in Paris, 220
Drugs, 42, 43, 48, 75, 88, 101, 105, 106, 107, 153, 163, 173
Drum 'n' Voice 2, 201
Drum machine, 121
Drumming, backbeat, 78
Drumming, polyrhythmic, 78
Duet, 195, 196
Duke, George, 178, 200, 217, 218
Dulfer, Candy, 213
Dunbar, Aynsley, 72
Dunn, Larry, 134, 152
Duran, 124
Duran Duran, 124
Duster, 87, 150
Dyer, Geoff, 12, 40, 42, 48, 49, 50, 106, 107, 108, 125, 141, 151, 152
Dylan, Bob, 8, 64, 105, 127, 135, 137, 149, 152, 154, 229

# E

E.S.P., 169, 177, 183, 197, 239
Eager, Vince, 64
Ealing Club, 70
East River, 209, 210, 217, 218
East River Drive, 217, 218
East St Louis Toodle-oo, 31
East, Nathan, 136, 237
Echoes, 195, 217, 218
Echoes Of An Era, 195, 218
Echoes Of An Era 2, 195
Eckstine, Billy, 38
Economu, Nicolas, 195
Egan, Mark, 221, 222, 242
Egg, 102
Ego, 198
Eight Miles High, 107
Eight Times Up, 231
Elastic Rock, 103
Eldridge, Roy, 33, 34, 35, 39, 40
Electric Dreams, 212, 213
Electric keyboard, 165, 174, 229

Electric piano, 89, 120, 131, 193
Electric Red, 4, 151
Electronic instruments, 9, 60, 104, 121, 122, 123, 125, 140
Electronic instruments, Boss DR-55, 122
Electronic instruments, drum machine, 121
Electronic instruments, electric piano, 120, 131, 193
Electronic instruments, EWI Electronic Wind Instrument, 155, 207, 234, 235
Electronic instruments, Fender-Rhodes piano, 120
Electronic instruments, guitar synthesiser, 124, 125, 151, 189
Electronic instruments, Hammond organ, 72
Electronic instruments, Linn LM-1, 122
Electronic instruments, Mellotron, 74, 121, 122
Electronic instruments, Midi, 123
Electronic instruments, monophonic synthesiser, 121
Electronic instruments, Moog, 122, 123
Electronic instruments, Oberheim, 122
Electronic instruments, organ, 74, 123, 131, 132, 135, 188
Electronic instruments, polyphonic synthesiser, 122
Electronic instruments, Rhythm Ace drum machine, 121
Electronic instruments, Roland CR-78, 122
Electronic instruments, Roland GR300, 125
Electronic instruments, Synclavier, 125, 152
Electronic Wind Instrument (EWI), 126, 127
Elements, 191, 204, 221, 239
Eleventh House, 88, 207, 208, 209
Elias, Eliane, 209
Ellington, Duke, 7, 28, 29, 31, 32, 37, 153
Ellington, Edward, 7, 28, 29, 31, 32, 37, 153
Ellington, Edward (Duke), 28, 29, 31, 32
Elliot, Richard, 137
Elliott, Dennis, 112
Ellis, Herb, 158
Emergency, 109, 190, 197, 198
EMI, 73
Empyrean Isles, 197
Enchantment, 196
Endangered Species, 227
Ensemble, 25, 246
Ensemble New Hope Street, 201
Ensemble, Absolute, 176, 243
Epstein, Brian, 66
Equinox, 149
Equipment Manufacturer, ARP, 122, 123
Equipment Manufacturer, Buchla, 123
Equipment Manufacturer, Emu, 123
Equipment Manufacturer, Linn Company, 122
Equipment Manufacturer, New England Digital Company, 124
Equipment Manufacturer, Sequential Circuits, 122, 125
Equipment Manufacturer, Yamaha, 122
Errico, Gregg, 131
Erskine, Peter, 173, 208, 209, 215, 234, 240
Escalator Over The Hill, 190
Escape, 208, 220, 221, 241
Ethnic, 17
Europe, 10, 21, 37, 43, 59, 80, 96, 98, 103, 105, 113, 121, 143, 169, 170, 171, 175, 176, 179, 180, 183, 186, 196, 197, 199, 200, 221
European, 18, 19, 20, 21, 22, 23, 28, 30, 32, 40, 42, 43, 47, 56, 59, 64, 105, 143, 170, 172, 174, 194, 203, 248, 249, 250
Evans, Bill (piano), 164
Evans, Bill (sax), 167, 221

Evans, Gil, 153, 163, 177, 179
Evans, Nick, 85, 104
Everything Must Go, 137, 242
EVI (Electronic Valve Instrument), 126, 127
EWI (Electronic Wind Instrument), 126, 127, 152
Expressions (Solo Piano), 196
Extrapolation, 188, 190, 239
Eye of the Beholder, 194, 196, 223
Ezz-Thetic, 170

## F

Fables of Faubus, 128
Fagen, Donald, 14, 136, 137, 208, 209, 210, 219, 231
Fairlight CMI, 124
Fame, Georgie, 69, 73, 99, 112
Family, 10, 131, 132, 134, 136, 145, 149
Family Stone, 131, 132, 134, 136
Farlowe, Chris, 98
Farrell, Joe, 184, 194, 216, 218
Fat Albert Rotunda, 183
Fat Time, 170
Felder, Wilton, 8, 224, 226, 229
Fender Stratocaster, 77, 127
Fender, Leo, 120
Fender-Rhodes piano, 120
Ferrante, Russell, 232, 233, 235
Ferrell, Rachelle, 178
Ferry, Bryan, 219
Festival, 5, 30, 32, 79, 97, 103, 128, 162, 163, 169, 170, 179, 186, 191, 192, 193, 210, 211, 215, 222, 226, 241, 242
Festival, Montreux Jazz, 103
Festival, Newport Folk, 128
Festival, Newport Jazz, 30, 103, 163
Fielder, Jim, 92
fill, 9, 13, 40, 246
Filles de Kilimanjaro, 108, 110, 169, 177, 183, 195, 197, 239
Fillmore, 79, 97, 101, 169, 170, 179, 195, 239
Fillmore East, 169, 170, 179, 195
Fillmore West, 79, 97, 101, 169, 195, 239
Finest Hour, 227
Fingerprints, 232
Fire Engine Passing With Bells Clanging, 85
Fire Wire, 232
First Circle, 125, 203, 204, 240
First Great Quintet, 164
First Light, 183
Five Peace Band, 15, 142, 190, 192, 194, 196, 243
Flack, Roberta, 219
Flamenco, 196
Flamingo, 69, 71, 116
Flashpoint, 229
Fleck, Béla, 196, 221, 243
Fleetwood Mac, 72
Flight, 201
Flight, Graham, 83
Flint, Hugh, 72
Floating Point, 15, 143, 189
Florida, 214, 240
Foday Musa Suso, 184
Foi A Saudade, 158
Folk, 17, 21, 129
Footprints, 58, 179, 242
For the Roses, 228, 229, 230
For Your Love, 71

Ford, Robben, 136, 214, 228, 230, 232
Forecast Tomorrow, 215
Foreign Intrigue, 198
Foreigner, 113
Forever & Beyond (5-Cd Boxed Set), 196
Forrest, Jimmy, 170
Forward Motion, 221
Four Corners, 233, 236
Fourth Way, 117
France, 59, 84, 103
Francisco, 63, 79, 97, 101, 117, 131, 168, 191, 204, 228
Franklin, Aretha, 175
Free As the Wind, 227, 231
Free For All, 177
Free Form, 177, 183
Free Jazz, 7, 17, 45, 46, 105, 153, 154
Free Spirits, 86, 191
Freebop, 142, 246
Freedom Sound, 225, 226, 238
Freedom Suite, 128
Freedom Town, 222
Freetime, 208
Fresh Cream, 79
Friends, 195, 196, 208, 232, 243
Fripp, Robert, 99, 104
From All Sides, 208
From Nothing - Chick Corea Solo Piano (Japan Only), 196
Fugue in A Minor, 158
Fuller, Gil, 37
Fuller, Walter Gilbert, 37
Fuller, Walter Gilbert (Gil), 37
Funk, 8, 17, 130, 152, 186, 209, 210
Funkadelic, 133, 134, 136
Fury, Billy, 64, 73
Fusion, 7, 8, 52, 58, 72, 86, 99, 115, 127, 149, 176, 179, 201
Fusion (music genre), 92
Futterman, Lew, 112
Future 2 Future, 198
Future Shock, 182, 184

## G

G, Kenny, 140, 142, 155, 167, 204, 241
Gadd, Steve, 136, 138, 207, 212
Galper, Hal, 239
Gambale, Frank, 5, 142
Garfunkel, Art, 138
Garner, Errol, 41
Garrett, Kenny, 142, 167, 204, 241
Gaucho, 208, 213, 229, 232, 240
Gay, Marvin, 74
Gemini, 170, 179
Generation, Beat, 62, 63
Genesis, 122, 124
Genre, African, 9, 21, 23, 56, 166
Genre, blues, 17, 18, 22, 23, 35, 40, 43, 44, 56, 57, 61, 62, 68, 70, 71, 72, 73, 79, 80, 87, 108, 164, 172, 203, 211, 212, 214, 224, 225, 226, 232, 245
Genre, church music, 22
Genre, classical, 9, 10, 20, 40, 41, 42, 43, 44, 52, 54, 55, 56, 59, 129, 153, 154, 157, 158, 159, 172, 182, 188, 194, 245
Genre, Cuban, 38, 56, 128
Genre, ethnic, 24, 52, 54, 55, 56, 57, 160, 164, 172, 174, 188, 194

262

Genre, European, 18, 19, 20, 21, 22, 23, 28, 30, 40, 42, 43, 47, 56, 64, 105, 172, 174, 194, 203, 248, 249, 250
Genre, folk, 9, 10, 18, 22, 52, 54, 56, 59, 127, 129, 154, 160, 174, 188, 194, 202, 203, 229, 230, 249
Genre, hip hop, 147, 155
Genre, Latin, 38, 45, 56, 160, 194, 199, 203, 216
Genre, skiffle, 63, 140
Genres
    Fusion, 92
    Jazz-fusion, 113, 114
    Rock, 90, 91
Germany, 170, 176, 179
Gerrits, Louis (discographer), 152
Gershwin, George, 27
Get Up With It, 200
Getz, Stan, 87, 158, 159, 160, 198, 216, 218
Getz/Gilberto, 159
Getz/Gilberto #2, 160
Ghetto Blaster, 227
Gibbs, Michael, 29, 239
Gibson, 44, 124
Gibson 150, 44
Gibson ES 335, 44
Gibson Les Paul, 124
Giddins, Gary, 50
Gilberto, Astrud, 159
Gilberto, Joao, 45, 159
Gillespie, John Birks 'Dizzy', 30, 36, 37, 38, 39, 40, 42, 44, 49, 58, 153
Ginsberg, Allen, 62
Give and Take, 209, 213
Give It What U Got, 208
Give Peace A Chance, 226
Glickstein, Fred, 91
Glissando, 246
Glitch, 245, 246
Global Warning - Jazz in the Hip Hop Generation, 227
Gogh, Vincent Van, 105
Go-Go, 92
Going Down, 143
Goins, Herbie, 117
Goldstein, Gil, 241
Golson, Benny, 112, 177
Gomelsky, Giorgio, 104
Gomez, Eddie, 89
Gong, 84, 103
Gonsalves, Paul, 30
Good Vibes, 88
Good Vibrations, 121
Goodman, Benjamin (Benny), 29, 30, 34, 44
Goodman, Jerry, 91, 188
Gordon, Dexter, 178, 184, 191
Gorelick, Kenneth, 140, 142, 155, 167, 204, 241
Gottlieb, Danny, 221
Graceland, 138
Graham, Bill, 79, 101
Graham, Larry, 131, 132
Grammy, 138, 145, 182, 189, 212, 230, 231, 233, 234
Grammy Awards, 138, 182, 189, 212, 230, 231, 233, 234
Grand Piano Canyon, 209
Grant, Gary, 137
Granz, Norman, 41, 42
Grateful Dead, 101
Great Scott, 228
Greek Theater, 169
Green, Grant, 87
Green, Peter, 72, 80

Greenhouse, 233, 236
Greenslade, Dave, 95, 98
Greenwich Village, 80
Griffith Park Collection, 195, 217, 218
Groban, Joshua, 186
Grolnick, Don, 114, 127, 207, 209, 210, 212, 219, 240
Groove, 20, 139, 152, 168, 227, 246, 249
Groove Crusade, 227
Grossman, Steve, 166, 200
GRP, 29, 139, 155, 196, 228, 233, 234, 236, 241
GRP All-Star Big Band, 29
GRP Super Live In Concert, 196
Gruppen, 106
Grusin, Dave, 29, 139
Grusin, David, 29, 139
Guerico, Jim, 89, 93
Guillery, Adrian, 89
Guitar synthesiser, 124, 155
Guitar, cithara, 43
Guitar, Gibson, 44, 124
Guitar, Gibson 150, 44
Guitar, Gibson ES 335, 44
Guitar, Gibson Les Paul, 124
Gulda, Friedrich, 195
Gurley, James, 107

# H

Haden, Charlie, 47, 125, 204
Haines, Paul, 191
Hair to Jazz, 228
Haley, Bill, 62
Hall, Albert, 79
Hall, Jim, 44, 158, 178, 203, 204
Halligan, Dick, 92
Hammer, Jan, 188
Hammond organ, 69, 72, 91
Hampton, Lionel, 34, 44
Hancock, Herbie, 4, 8, 10, 47, 90, 93, 107, 110, 111, 122, 123, 131, 141, 142, 151, 155, 160, 162, 165, 168, 173, 174, 177, 178, 179, 180, 181, 182, 183, 184, 185, 186, 191, 195, 197, 198, 200, 201, 203, 207, 208, 209, 215, 216, 217, 220, 237, 239, 240, 241, 242, 243
Hangin in the City, 209, 210
Hanover New Hampshire, 123
Happy Again, 227, 232
Happy Anniversary Charlie Brown, 196
Harbor Lights, 204
Hard bop, 40
Hard Wired, 223
Harlem, 29, 32
Harmonic, 18, 38, 41, 45, 46, 104, 106, 144, 213, 247
Harriott, Joe, 65
Harrison, George, 228
Hart, Clyde, 34, 35
Haslip, Jimmy, 232, 236
Hastings, Pye, 83, 102
Hathaway, Lalah, 145
Hawkins, Coleman, 44
Hawkins, Collier, 17, 21, 22, 24, 30, 31, 41, 42, 43, 50
Hayes, Edgar, 35
Hayes, Isaac, 133
Hayes, Tubby, 65
Hayes, Vangelis, 122
Haynes, Roy, 87, 204
Head Hunters, 123, 141, 173, 182

263

Headhunters, 185, 186, 242
Heads Up, 210, 223, 234, 241
Healing the Wounds, 219, 226, 227
Heart To Heart, 208, 209, 213
Hearts and Numbers, 210, 219, 240
Heat Wave, 226
Heath, Percy, 37
Heath, Ted, 65
Heavy Metal, 207, 208, 209, 239
Heavy Metal Bebop, 207, 208, 209
Heavy Weather, 173, 174, 214, 215
Heckstall-Smith, Richard Malden, 63, 70, 71, 72, 73, 74, 95, 98, 99, 117, 118, 148, 150
Hejira, 215, 228, 230, 231
Hello Big Man, 219
Henderson, Joseph, 217
Henderson, Wayne, 8, 224, 225, 226, 238
Hendrix, Jimi, 7, 77, 79, 80, 81, 84, 138, 140, 150
Henry Cow, 102
Herbie Hancock Quartet, 198
Herbie Hancock Trio (1981), 198
Herbs, 177
Here To Stay, 177
Herman, Woody, 31
Heroes, 226
Hey Joe, 80, 81
Hey, Jerry, 137
Hideaway, 184, 213, 218, 219
High Life, 179, 220, 241
Hill, Teddy, 29, 33, 35
Hillage, Steve, 102, 103
Hines, Earl, 29, 42
Hinton, Milton, 34
Hip Hop, 182, 227
Hiseman, Jon, 7, 71, 78, 94, 95, 148, 151
Hodges, Johnny, 30
Holdsworth, Allan, 99, 103
Holiday For Pans, 179
Holland, Dave, 108, 165, 179, 186, 190
Holli Be Home, 113
Holly, Buddy, 62, 64, 76, 153
Hollywood, 31, 64, 226, 228
Hollywood Bowl, 171
Homage, 242
Home, 113, 152, 178, 183, 184, 203, 204, 208, 227, 230, 240
Honeysuckle Breeze, 228
Hooper, Nesbert, 224
Hopper, Brian, 83, 84
Hopper, Hugh, 63, 83, 85, 86, 103
Hornsby, Bruce, 204, 236
Hornveth, Lars, 143, 144
Horta, Toninho, 178
Hot Club de France, 44
Hot House, 196, 204
Hot Mallets, 34
Houston, Witney, 136
Howard, Phil, 104
Hubbard, Freddie, 217
Hubbard, Frederick Dewayne, 177, 183, 217
Hub-Tones, 183
Human League, 122, 141
Human Nature, 170
Husband, Gary, 143, 187, 190
Hush, 143
Hussain, Zakir, 191
Hutchcroft, Kim, 137
Hutcherson, Bobby, 183, 213
Hymn of the Seventh Galaxy, 194, 195, 218

# I

I Ain't Got Nobody, 131
I Can See Your House From Here, 204
I Do It For Your Love, 138
I Feel Free, 79
I Love You, 92
I Sing the Body Electric, 172
I Wanna Play For You, 218, 229
I Wonder, 235
Idiot Savant (band), 127
Idol, Billy, 219
If I Could, 102
If This Bass Could Only Talk, 178, 218
Illinois, 89, 90, 183
Illinois Speed Press, 89
Imaginary Day, 203, 204, 242
Imaginary Day Live, 204
Imagine My Surprise, 114, 200, 206, 208, 209
Improvisation, 17, 46, 81, 82, 83, 96, 106, 107, 140, 158, 172, 181, 202, 246, 247
Improvise, 19, 20, 21, 22, 23, 24, 41, 108, 247
In A Sentimental Mood, 32
In A Silent Way, 90, 94, 110, 151, 152, 165, 166, 168, 169, 172, 175, 176, 177, 179, 181, 183, 185, 188, 190, 191, 193, 195, 198, 239
In Pursuit of the 27th Man, 208, 209
In the Court of the Crimson King, 121
In the Idiom, 210
In The Public Interest, 208, 209
Incoming, 201
India, 43, 107
Indigo, 17, 31, 32, 179, 230
Indo-Jazz, 57, 189
Industrial Zen, 15, 143, 189, 222
Infinite Search, 183, 190
Inner Conflicts, 201, 208
Inner Space, 195
Inside, 194, 196, 209, 213, 220, 223
Inside Out, 194, 196, 223, 241
Instrumental, 212, 231, 246
Intimate Strangers, 229
Into the Sun, 210, 213
Invitation, 209, 215, 240
Irish, 18
Is What It Is, 209
Iska, 177
Islands, 104
Isley Brothers, 80, 132
Israel, 186

# J

Jack Johnson, 169, 184, 190, 191, 200
Jackson Jr, Paul M., 136
Jackson, Alan, 104
Jackson, Anthony, 136
Jackson, Michael, 124, 136, 182, 231
Jackson, Milt, 37, 157, 168
Jaco, 8, 81, 91, 93, 155, 173, 174, 178, 179, 184, 185, 192, 198, 204, 208, 209, 213, 214, 215, 216, 220, 229, 230, 236, 239, 240, 241, 242
Jaco Pastorius, 81, 91, 93, 155, 173, 174, 198, 208, 209, 213, 214, 215, 216, 220, 229, 230

Jaco Pastorius in New York, 215
Jagger, Mick, 70
Jam, 20, 35, 36, 82, 88, 247
James, Robert McElhiney, 120, 138, 140, 208, 209, 212, 213, 219
Japan, 169, 175, 178, 186, 196, 204, 215, 223, 227, 231, 241, 242
Jarreau, Al, 137, 186, 209
Jarrett, Keith, 87, 168, 171
Jazz club
   Café Au Go-Go, 92
   Village Gate, 114
Jazz Door, 169, 170, 178
Jazz FM radio, 139, 155
Jazz Samba, 159
Jazz, acid-jazz, 139
Jazz, avant-garde, 47, 69, 122
Jazz, free jazz, 46, 48, 69, 79, 86, 87, 106, 107, 108, 109, 111, 166, 168, 172, 181, 193, 203, 216
Jazz, hard bop, 40, 153
Jazz, Indo-Jazz, 57, 189
Jazz, jazz-fusion, 9, 10, 14, 15, 29, 43, 45, 46, 47, 48, 49, 52, 55, 56, 57, 58, 71, 73, 74, 81, 82, 85, 86, 88, 103, 105, 106, 108, 110, 123, 125, 134, 136, 138, 139, 140, 141, 142, 154, 155, 157, 158, 159, 160, 164, 165, 166, 167, 168, 172, 173, 174, 181, 187, 188, 189, 194, 197, 199, 200, 202, 203, 206, 207, 211, 212, 214, 216, 217, 218, 221, 223, 224, 225, 226, 228, 229, 231, 232, 234, 235, 236
Jazz, jazz-rock, 9, 45, 54, 55, 56, 57, 71, 87, 88, 98, 103, 104, 115, 117, 139, 140, 167, 168, 172, 173, 188, 189, 193, 197, 216, 217, 234, 235
Jazz, mainstream jazz, 33, 45, 64, 77, 88, 129, 132, 142, 158, 164, 168, 174, 182, 203, 211, 216, 226, 234, 246
Jazz, modal, 38, 139, 235, 247
Jazz, R&B, 67, 69, 70, 73, 139, 149, 212, 224, 233
Jazz, ragtime, 23, 24
Jazz, smooth jazz, 58, 139, 155, 211, 234
Jazz, stride, 41
Jazz, swing, 30, 35, 40, 41, 43, 44, 70, 88, 158
Jazz, the Cool, 153
Jazz, third stream, 40, 154
Jazz, Traditional (Dixieland) Jazz, 17, 33, 105, 157, 164
Jazz, world music, 14, 56, 154
Jazz-fusion, 7, 9, 48, 58, 97, 146, 155
Jazz-fusion (music genre), 113, 114
Jazz-rock, 8, 116, 137, 154, 160
Jefferson Airplane, 101
Jenkins, Karl, 86, 104
Jeremy and the Satyrs, 88
Jigsaw, 209
Jim Hall and Pat Metheny, 204
Jimi Hendrix Experience, 80, 81, 84
Jobim, Antonio Carlos, 158, 185
Joel, Billy, 90, 136, 138, 208
John McLaughlin, 4, 8, 10, 15, 20, 45, 47, 57, 63, 69, 73, 79, 80, 88, 91, 99, 100, 107, 109, 110, 112, 118, 119, 125, 135, 142, 152, 155, 165, 168, 172, 187, 190, 191, 192, 194, 195, 196, 197, 198, 200, 201, 203, 209, 212, 213, 215, 218, 221, 222, 239, 240, 241, 242, 243
John Patitucci, 142, 196, 208, 209, 223, 234
John Scofield, 167, 204
John, Elton, 85, 90, 103, 137
Johnny Burch Octet, 72
Johnny McLaughlin - Electric Guitarist, 195, 198, 201, 213, 218

Johnson, Alphonso, 172
Johnson, Deron, 217
Johnson, Marc, 204
Jones, Brian, 70
Jones, Cameron, 123
Jones, Chris, 85, 150
Jones, John Paul, 69
Jones, Quincy, 137, 149, 154, 175, 182, 184, 185, 241
Jones, Ronnie, 72
Jones, Thad, 233
Joni, 8, 58, 72, 154, 173, 178, 179, 182, 184, 185, 186, 204, 207, 208, 214, 215, 228, 229, 230, 231, 240, 243
Jopek, Anna Maria, 205, 243
Joplin, Janis, 77, 90
Joplin, Scott, 23
Joshua Redman, 204
Jost, Ekkehard, 50
Journey To Love, 191, 195, 218
Joy Of A Toy, 85
Joy Ryder, 178, 185
Juju, 177, 239
Jump For Joy, 32
Junior, Sammy Davis, 28
Just the Way You Are, 136, 138

# K

Kamakyriad, 210
Kansas City, 35
Karma, 107
Karpman, Ron, 91
Kath, Terry, 93, 94
Katia, 125, 186
Katy Lied, 231
Katz, Steve, 91, 92
Keats, 48
Keep This Love Alive, 229
Kelly, Wynton, 176
Kent, Jeff, 113, 114
Kermode, Mark, 11
Kerouac, Jack, 62, 145
Kessel, Barney, 44, 203
Key, 9, 18, 20, 27, 36, 37, 61, 66, 81, 110, 116, 120, 127, 194, 247, 248
Khan, Chaka, 184
Kick the Jazz, 227
Kid Charlemagne, 231
Kid Gloves, 232
Kin (<-->), 142, 205
Kind of Blue, 162, 164
King Crimson, 57, 97, 104, 121, 148, 151
King, B. B., 62
Kirk, Rahsaan Roland, 75, 81
Klein, Larry, 183
Knopfler, Mark, 97
Konitz, Lee, 170
Kontrapunkte, 106
Kooper, Al, 91, 135, 149, 151, 152, 224, 238
Korner, Alexis, 7, 68, 70, 71, 72, 116, 117, 118, 153
Kraftwerk, 121
Kramer, Eddie, 81
Kujula, Steve, 195
Kyoto, 177

# L

LA Express, 228, 229, 232

La Villette, 170, 176, 179, 185, 191, 242
Labeque, Katia, 125, 186
Ladies of the Canyon, 229, 230
LaFaro, Scott, 88
Laine, Denny, 80
Laird, Rick, 188
Lamm, Robert, 93
Lanchester Arts Festival, 97
Land of the Midnight Sun, 195, 214, 215, 218
Larry & Lee, 232
Larry Carlton, 136, 208, 217, 225, 228, 231, 232
Last Nite, 232
Laswell, Bill, 182
Latin, 38, 45, 56, 160, 194, 199, 203, 216
Laurel Canyon, 71
Lawson, Ricky, 232, 233, 236
Led Zeppelin, 71, 79
Lee, Albert, 80
Lee, Will, 114, 207
Left Alone, 186
Legrand, Michel, 169, 170
Lennon and McCartney, 67, 128
Lennon, John, 63, 66, 67, 100, 128, 137
Let Me Know You, 217, 218
Let the Juice Loose, 221
Let the Juice Loose - Live at the Blue Note Tokyo, 221
Letter From Home, 203, 204, 240
Levin, Tony, 138
Lewis, Furry, 62
Lewis, Huey, 137
Lewis, John, 37, 158
Lewis, Mel, 233
Liberal Arts, 221
Liberation, 47
Lick, 247
Liebman, Dave, 204
Life and Times, 200
Life Colors, 209
Life In The Modern World, 227
Lifecycle, 234, 237
Lifetime, 47, 56, 99, 109, 141, 146, 165, 183, 188, 197, 198
Light As A Feather, 195, 218, 239
Light Years, 194, 196, 223, 240
Lightfoot, Gordon, 229
Lighthouse, 69, 169, 170, 181, 202, 225, 226
Like a River, 236
Like A Rolling Stone, 135
Like Minds, 196, 204
Like Someone In Love, 176
Lily, 102
Linn LM-1, 122
Lion, Alfred, 43
Lipsius, Fred, 92, 93, 135
Litherland, James, 95, 97
Lithuania, 143
Little Help From My Friends, 231
Little Theatre, 69
Live, 29, 68, 72, 135, 172, 189, 193, 195, 196, 198, 200, 201, 208, 210, 215, 217, 218, 219, 220, 221, 223, 226, 227, 232, 234, 236, 247
   Flight Time, 201
Live (and very plugged in), 223
Live Aid, 135
Live and More, 220
Live and Unreleased, 215
Live at Montreux 2003, 227
Live at Sweet Basil, 210
Live At The Greek, 201, 218, 232
Live at the Lighthouse 66, 226
Live Evil, 68, 193, 195, 200
Live From Elario's (First Gig) Chick Corea Elektri, 196, 223
Live From The Blue Note Tokyo (Japan Only), 196, 223
Live From The Country Club (Japan Only), 196
Live in Europe, 221
Live in Japan 1993, 227
Live in Japan 2003, 227
Live In Montreux, 195
Live in Tokyo, 172, 208, 232
Live on Tour in Europe, 200
Live Sides, 226
Live Under the Sky, 198
Live Wires, 234, 236
Liverpool, 66, 67, 68, 77, 89, 116
Livery Stable Blues, 28
Living in the Crest of a Wave, 221
Lizard, 104
Lloyd, Charles, 87, 175
Loeb, Chuck, 209
London, 30, 54, 68, 70, 71, 77, 78, 79, 80, 81, 82, 85, 104, 105, 108, 135, 149, 150, 187, 196
London House, 107
Lonely Planet Guide, 12
Long John, 85, 103
Los Angeles, 224, 225, 230
Lost Tribes, 176, 241
Louecke, Lionel, 186
Loughnane, Lee, 93
Louisiana, 17, 22, 56, 227
Louisiana Hot Sauce, 227
Loussier, Jacques, 157
Love Devotion Surrender, 200
Love Me Do, 66, 154
Love Play, 208
Love Song, 213, 219
Love Songs, 213, 219
Lowther, Henry, 71
LP-record, 61
Lubahn, Doug, 113, 114
Lucky Seven, 208
Lukather, Steve, 232
Lush Life, 177
Lydian, 247
Lyle Mays, 125, 204, 210, 230
Lyric Suite For Sextet, 195
Lyttelton, Humphrey, 65

# M

M2, 220
Mabry, Betty, 165
MacDonald, Donald, 89
MacDonald, Ralph, 138, 207
Macero, Teo, 166
Machine Gun, 81
Made For Radio, 143
Magazine, Downbeat, 117
Magazine, Melody Maker, 73, 74
Magazine, Metronome, 38
Magic Windows, 208
Magnetic, 207, 208
Mahavishnu, 45, 47, 125, 141, 152, 154, 155, 172, 173, 188, 189, 194, 197, 200, 201, 216, 221, 238

Mahavishnu Orchestra, 45, 47, 91, 141, 146, 154, 155, 172, 173, 188, 189, 190, 191, 194, 197, 200, 201, 216, 221, 238, 239, 240, 242
Maiden Voyage, 93, 183, 197, 239
Mainieri, Michael, 88, 207, 208, 240
Making Music, 191
Manchester, 70, 116, 170, 186
Manfred Mann, 70, 74
Manhattan, 178
Mann, Bob, 114
Many Years BC, 201
Marbles, 190
Marcelli, Andrea, 178
Marcus Miller, 47, 142, 167, 198, 212, 213, 217, 218, 219, 220
Marcus, Steve, 87, 100, 116, 117
Mariah Carey, 136
Marienthal, Eric, 5, 142, 223, 241
Marquee, 68, 69, 70, 71, 73, 112, 116
Marsalis, Branford, 135
Marshall, Edwin, 117
Marshall, John, 86, 103, 104
Marshall, John Stanley, 104
Martin, 44, 66, 87, 127, 143, 152
Martin, George, 66
Martin, Stuart, 87, 190
Martini, Jerry, 131
Marvin, Hank Brian, 76
Master Plan, 196, 209, 223, 241
Matching Mole, 103
Matsumoto, Takahiro, 232
Maupin, Bennie, 199, 200
Mayall, John, 7, 68, 70, 71, 72, 95, 150, 153
Mayer, John, 189
Mays, Lyle, 125, 204, 210, 230, 240
McBride, Christian, 142, 205, 243
McCartney, Paul, 66, 136, 137, 149
McClure, Ron, 93
McCracken, Hugh, 138
McCreary, Mary, 131
McDuff, Jack, 106, 112
McFerrin, Bobby, 178, 186, 196
McGuinn, Roger, 107
McLaughlin, John, 4, 8, 10, 15, 20, 45, 47, 57, 63, 69, 73, 79, 80, 88, 91, 99, 100, 107, 109, 110, 112, 118, 119, 125, 135, 142, 152, 155, 165, 168, 172, 187, 190, 191, 192, 194, 195, 196, 197, 198, 200, 201, 203, 209, 212, 213, 215, 218, 221, 222, 239, 240, 241, 242, 243
McLean, Jackie, 183
McLure, Ron, 87, 117
McShann, Jay, 36
McVie, John, 70, 72
Me, Myself, An Eye, 208
Mealing, John, 112
Measure of a Man, 234
Medianoche, 209
Meeting of the Spirits, 201
Mehldau, Brad, 205, 243
Mellotron, 74, 118, 121, 122
Melody Maker, 73, 74, 112, 150
Members Only, 208
Memoirs, 149, 238
Memories, 62
Memphis, 61, 80
Men Without Hats, 122
Mental breakdown, 48, 215

Mercer, Chris, 71
Mercy, Mercy, Mercy, 175
Merseyside, 45, 116
Meter, 19, 20, 247, 249
Metheny Mehldau, 205
Metheny Mehldau Quartet, 205
Metheny, Pat, 4, 8, 10, 15, 20, 47, 50, 80, 111, 125, 141, 142, 144, 145, 154, 155, 160, 189, 202, 203, 204, 205, 207, 208, 209, 214, 215, 217, 221, 230, 233, 240, 241, 242, 243
Metronome, 38
Michael Brecker, 136, 138, 152, 155, 204, 205, 208, 209, 210, 215, 217, 219, 230, 235
Mikkelborg, Palle, 167
Miles Ahead, 164, 168, 239
Miles Away, 175
Miles Davis, 4, 7, 8, 9, 10, 12, 14, 21, 38, 40, 43, 45, 46, 47, 54, 58, 68, 81, 83, 90, 94, 101, 106, 108, 109, 110, 119, 131, 136, 141, 142, 149, 150, 153, 154, 155, 158, 160, 162, 163, 164, 166, 167, 168, 169, 170, 171, 175, 176, 177, 178, 179, 180, 181, 183, 184, 185, 186, 188, 189, 190, 191, 192, 193, 195, 197, 198, 199, 200, 201, 219, 221, 239, 240, 241, 242, 247
Miles Davis All Stars, 168
Miles Davis in Europe, 197
Miles in the Sky, 198
Miles in Tokyo, 197
Miles of Aisles, 228, 230
Miles Smiles, 197
Miles, Barry, 149
Miles, Buddy, 81
Milestones, 164, 168, 171, 239
Miley, James, 29
Milkowski, Bill, 58, 109, 125, 149, 151
Millenium, 232, 238, 243
Miller, Glen, 29
Miller, Harry, 104
Miller, Marcus, 8, 47, 142, 167, 169, 179, 185, 198, 212, 213, 217, 218, 219, 220, 242
Million Dollar Legs, 198
Mills, Irving, 29
Mingus, Charles, 45, 47, 108, 207, 208
Minnelli, Liza, 185
Mint Jam, 234, 237
Mintzer, Bob, 29, 207, 208, 209, 210, 215, 233, 235, 240, 241, 242
Mirage, 233, 236
Mirage a Trois, 236
Mississippi Nights Live, 201
Missouri, 203, 204
Mistura Fina, 223
Mitchell, Joni, 8, 58, 72, 154, 173, 178, 179, 182, 184, 185, 186, 204, 207, 208, 214, 215, 228, 229, 230, 231, 240
Mitchell, Mitch, 80, 81
Mitchell, Richard 'Blue', 183
Mixolydian, 247
Mobley, Hank, 183
Modern Jazz Quartet, 37, 157, 158, 170, 239
Modern Jazz Sextet, 225
Modern Man, 217, 218
Modern Times, 208
Modulation, 248
Moncur, Grachan, 177, 183
Mondesir, Mark, 190
Money In The Pocket, 175

267

Money, Zoot, 104
Monk, Thelonius, 33, 41, 42, 153, 170
Monophonic synthesiser, 121
Monteca, 38
Monterey Jazz, 170, 186
Montgomery, John Leslie (Wes), 44, 158, 203
Montgomery, Wes, 44, 158, 203
Montreux Jazz, 97, 103, 179, 192, 242
Mood, 31, 32
Moog, 122, 123
Moog, Robert, 123
Moon Germs, 184, 216, 218
Moorish, 43, 44
More Than Ever, 93
Moreira, Airto, 178, 184, 194, 216
Morgan, Lee, 176, 177, 183, 185
Morning, 184, 208, 209, 219
Morning Dance, 208, 209
Morrissey, Dick, 112
Morton, Jelly Roll, 24, 153
Mosaic, 177
Motif, 107, 144, 248, 249
Motion, 145, 209, 221, 223, 240
Motion Poet, 209
Moto Grosso Feio, 177, 190, 195
Motown, 130, 132
Mouton, Elva, 131
Mozart Double Piano Concerto Fantasy For Two Piano, 195
Mr 335 - Live in Japan, 231
Mr. Funk, 185
Mr. Go, 173, 175, 178, 239
Mr. Gone, 173, 175, 178, 239
Mr. Hands, 198, 215
Mullen, Jim, 113
Mulligan, Gerry, 153
Multiplicity, 223
Music From Siesta, 219
Musicmagic, 218
Mwandishi, 47, 107, 181, 183, 185
My Funny Valentine, 169, 183, 197, 239
My Goal's Beyond, 200
My Point of View, 197
My Spanish Heart, 195, 216, 218
Mysterious Traveller, 172, 175, 177, 239

## N

Nascimento, Milton, 178, 184
Nash, Larry, 228
Native Dancer, 177, 184
Native Heart, 198
Native Sense, 196
Native Sense - The New Duets, 196
Navarro, Fats, 40
Nearness of You
 The Ballad Book, 204, 209
Neesh, 213
Nefertiti, 169, 177, 183, 197, 239
Negro Philharmonic Society, 22
Nelson Rangell, 155, 208
Netherlands, 146
Neu!, 121
Never Alone, 231, 232
Never Too Much, 219
New Blood, 93
New Chautauqua, 204

New Orleans, 17, 22, 23, 24
New Shoes, 226
New York, 28, 29, 33, 36, 42, 43, 48, 49, 59, 62, 78, 79, 86, 89, 90, 93, 100, 101, 108, 113, 117, 118, 150, 153, 163, 175, 182, 185, 188, 196, 199, 206, 215, 219, 224, 228, 241
New York Connection, 228
Newcastle UK, 127
Newfound Freedom, 229
Newport Folk, 128
Newport Jazz, 30, 32, 103, 163
Nicholson, Stuart, 50, 148, 149, 197, 238
Night Creatures, 229
Night Dreamer, 177, 239
Night In Calisia, 210
Night Passage, 173, 175, 178, 215, 240
Night Ride Home, 230
Nightwind, 185
Nite Hawks, 225
No Filters, 201
No Mystery, 194, 195, 218
No Substitutions - Live in Osaka, 232
Nock, Mike, 117
Nocturne, 204, 234, 237
Nordic, 201
North, 17, 21, 42, 49, 56, 145, 174, 201, 210, 228, 238
North Africa, 56, 174
North By Northwest, 201
North Carolina, 42, 238
Nostalgic Journey, 210, 243
Note, eighth, 246
Note, quarter, 245, 246, 248, 249
Note, sixteenth, 248
November, 92
Now He Sings, Now He Sobs, 195
Now You See It (Now You Don't), 209
Nucleus, 103, 239
Nutcracker Suite, 61

## O

Oberheim, 122
Observations and Reflections, 201
Observatory, 201
Obsession, 208
Ode, 228
Odeon, 61, 170
Odyssey, 177, 178
Off the Wall, 137, 231
Offramp, 203, 204, 240
Ogerman, Claus, 208, 219
Old Socks New Shoes, New Socks Old Shoes, 226
Oldfield, Mike, 123
Oliver, Jay, 223
Oliver, King, 17, 25, 26, 50, 153
Omartian, Michael, 136
On Solid Ground, 231, 232
On The Corner, 195, 196, 209, 223
On Two Pianos, 195
One More Angel, 209
One Music, 233
One Night, One Day, 229
One Note Samba, 157, 159
One Quiet Night, 205, 242
Onyx, 38
Orchestrion, 205
Origin Live at the Blue Note, 196

Orion, 149
Oslo, 143, 169
Oslo Skyline, 143
Ostinato, 248, 249
Out of the Loop, 208, 209, 210
Out Of This World, 183
Ozone, Makoto, 196

## P

Page, Jimmy, 71, 79, 80, 140
Paint The World, 196, 241
Paint Your Wagon, 228
Panama, 201
Pankow, James, 93
Papa Lips, 29, 208, 209, 240
Paradiso, 204
Paradox, 201, 208
Parallel Realities Live, 204
Paraphernalia, 178
Parazaider, Walter, 93
Parker, Charlie, 14, 30, 33, 35, 37, 40, 42, 55, 58, 83, 107, 109, 138, 153, 163
Parker, Johnny, 70, 72
Parliament/Funkadelic, 136
Parlophone, 66, 154
Parnes, Larry, 64
Pass the Plate, 226
Passage, 173, 215
Passagio per il Paradiso, 204
Passengers, 204
Passion, 191, 238
Past Present & Futures, 196
Pastorius, Felix, 236
Pastorius, Jaco, 8, 81, 91, 93, 155, 173, 174, 178, 179, 184, 185, 192, 198, 208, 209, 213, 214, 215, 216, 220, 229, 230, 239, 240, 241, 242
Pat Metheny Group, 10, 15, 142, 154, 155, 202, 203, 204, 205, 221
Patitucci, John, 5, 142, 180, 196, 208, 209, 223, 234
Patto, Mike, 104
Paul, Les, 124
Pawlik, Wlodek, 210
Peace Round - A Christmas Celebration, 234, 237
Pearls, 213, 219
Peg, 126
Penny Lane, 135
Perdido, 32
Perez, Danilo, 180
Perfect Machine, 185
Perfect Way, 170
Perpetual Motion, 223
Peskin, Joel C. (writer), 152
Pet Sounds, 121
Peter Erskine, 173, 208, 209, 215, 234
Peterson, Oscar, 41
Petite Blonde, 221
Petridis, Alexis, 78, 150
Phantom Navigator, 196
Philadelphia, 216
Phillips, 62, 112
Phillips, Sam, 62
Phrase, 14, 21, 40, 47, 57, 62, 105, 144, 247, 248, 249
Phrygian, 247
Piano Improvisations Vol. 1, 195
Piano Improvisations Vol. 2, 195
Picture This, 201, 229

Pilgrimage, 186, 205, 209, 243
Pine, Courtney, 20, 50
Pink Floyd, 75, 84, 90, 122
Pisces, 177
Pitch, 18, 22, 121, 124, 245, 247, 248, 250
Play Bach Trio, 157
Plugged Nickel, 178, 179, 185, 241
Plumeri, Terry, 183
Point Of View, 183
Police, 81
Politics, 233, 236
Polydor, 150
Polyphonic synthesiser, 123
Ponty, Jean-Luc, 217, 218
Porcaro, Jeff, 136
Porgy and Bess, 164
Porter, Lewis, 49
Portrait, 152
Posa, Frank, 91
Powell, Bud, 41, 42, 43, 196
Powell, Rudy, 34
Power of our Music - The Endangered Species, 227
Power Play, 201
Power, Duffy, 191
Powerhouse, 226
Pozo, Chano, 38
Praise, 204
Prelude, 32
Presley, Elvis, 55, 61, 62, 153
Prestige, 43, 163, 168
Prince, 4, 10, 134, 135
Procession, 173, 175, 178, 240
Procope, Russell, 30
Prog-rock, 101
Promise Me, 213
Promise Me the Moon, 213
Purim, Flora, 184, 194, 216
Purple, 1, 4, 80, 98, 175, 190, 200
Purple Haze, 1, 80
Pursuance, 204, 241
Push, 219, 221, 241

## Q

Quarrymen, 64
Quartet, 49, 73, 74, 196, 198, 204, 205
quaver, 246
Question and Answer, 204
Quincy, David, 112

## R

R&B, 66, 67, 68, 69, 70, 73, 83, 100, 115, 116, 117, 118, 119, 130, 132, 139, 145, 149, 212, 224, 233, 246, 248
Ra, Sun, 45
Radio, 50, 64, 143, 175
Ragtime, 23, 24
Rain, 178, 220, 230
Rallantando, 248
Ramones, 141
Randy in Brasil, 210
Raney, Jimmy, 170
Rangell, Nelson, 155, 208, 241
Ratledge, Michael Roland, 83, 84, 86
Ready Steady Go!, 74
Record label, Apple, 122, 182, 207, 224, 229
Record label, Blue Note, 1, 4, 42, 43, 199

Record label, Columbia, 90, 92
Record label, GRP, 29, 139, 155, 196, 228, 233, 234, 236
Record label, Motown, 132
Record label, Odeon, 61
Record label, Parlophone, 66, 154
Record label, Prestige, 43, 163
Record label, RCA, 61, 104
Record label, Verve, 42, 159
Red, 4, 10, 69, 183
Red Clay, 183
Redding, Noel, 80, 81
Redman, Joshua, 204, 242
Reece, Red, 69
Reed My Lips, 229
Reeves, Tony, 71, 95, 97
Reflections, 201
Refugee From Yuhupitz, 92
Register, 37, 40, 74, 248
Reich, Steve, 204
Reichenbach, Bill, 137
Rejoicing, 204
Remember Shakti, 189
Remembering Bud Powell, 196
Rendell, Don, 65, 72
Rendezvous, 196, 213
Rendezvous In New York, 196
Rendezvous In New York (10-DVD Boxed Set), 196
Renegade Gentleman, 232
Renewal, 226, 227
Return of the Brecker Brothers, 208, 209, 210, 213
Return to Forever, 47, 90, 141, 142, 146, 154, 173, 189, 193, 194, 195, 196, 216, 217, 218, 239
Reunion, 204, 210, 241, 243
Reverence, 204, 209
Revolution, 148, 149
Revolver, 121
Rhapsody and Blues, 225, 227
Rheinhardt, Django, 44, 88
Rhodes, Harold, 120
Rhumba Flamenco, 196
Rhythm & Blues, 7, 68, 109
Rhythm of the Soul, 223
Rhythm, tempo, 249
Rich, Buddy, 233
Richard, Cliff, 64, 77, 153
Richard, Little, 80
Richards, Keith, 70, 149
Richardson, James, 112
Riot, 185
Rippingtons, 140, 155
Rise And Fall, 175
Rite of Strings, 217
Ritenour, Lee, 140, 232
River, 179, 186, 209, 210, 213, 217, 218, 221, 234, 236, 243
Roach, Max, 36, 40
Roberta, 219, 229
Robinson, Cynthia, 131, 132
Rock, 7, 10, 17, 54, 61, 62, 63, 76, 101, 103, 117, 123, 148, 149, 153, 154, 183, 217, 238, 250
Rock (music genre), 90, 91
Rock Island Line, 63
Rock, baroque-rock, 101
Rock, blues-rock, 101
Rock, prog-rock, 57, 101, 104
Rock, punk, 140
Rock, raga-rock, 101

Rock, rock 'n' roll, 62, 64, 76, 77
Rock, rock-fusion, 78, 137
Rock, rock-jazz, 56, 57, 78, 79, 82, 85, 94, 98, 100, 135, 137, 140
Rock, shock-rock, 101
Rockit, 182, 186
Rocks, 218
Rocks, Pebbles And Sand, 218
Rodrigo, 158, 164
Rodrigo,, 158, 164
Rogers, Barry, 113
Roland CR-78, 122
Roland GR300, 125
Rolling Stones, 7, 67, 68, 70, 73, 105, 191
Rollins, Sonny, 126, 168
Romantic Warrior, 194, 195, 218
Roney, Wallace, 178, 185
Rosemary, 131
Rosen, Larry, 139
Ross, Diana, 132
Round About Midnight, 163
Round Midnight, 178, 184, 186, 191
Round Trip, 223
Royal Jam, 227
RTF Live (4-Record Set), 218
Run For Your Life, 234, 236, 241
Rural Renewal, 226, 227
Rural Still Life, 228
Russell, George, 38, 247
Russo, Marc, 233
Rustichelli, Paolo, 178, 185

# S

Salle Pleyel, 176
Sample, Joseph Leslie, 8, 120, 224, 226, 228, 229
Samurai Samba, 233, 236
San Francisco, 79, 101, 117, 131
Sanborn, David William, 8, 138, 155, 207, 208, 209, 210, 211, 212, 213, 219, 220, 229, 233, 240
Sanchez, Antonio, 202, 205, 243
Sanctuary, 151, 152
Sanders, Pharoah, 106, 218
Santamaria, Mongo, 181
Santana, Carlos, 107, 178, 179, 184, 191, 200, 242
Sapphire Blue, 232
Satoh, Masahiko, 178
Saturday Night, 168, 191, 219
Scaggs, Boz, 90, 228
Scenes From My Life, 209
Schiller, David, 76, 150
Schizophrenia, 177, 183
School Days, 191, 200, 216, 217, 218, 239
Scofield, John, 167, 179, 204, 242
Score, 133, 209, 210
Scott, Tom, 8, 126, 136, 155, 207, 210, 228, 229, 231, 232, 243
Scottish, 18
Scratch, 225, 226, 231
Seamen, Phillip William, 112
Search For The New Land, 177, 183
Seattle, 80, 86
Second Genesis, 177
Second Great Quintet, 165, 172, 197
Secret Agent, 195
Secret Story, 204
Seeger, Pete, 128

270

Segovia, Andres, 43
Selected Recordings, 205, 209, 215
Selim, 68
Septet, 195
Septober Energy, 104
Sequential Circuits, 122, 125
Seraphine, Daniel, 93
Sergeant Pepper's Lonely Hearts Club Band, 121
Seven Steps To Heaven, 169, 183, 197
Sex Pistols, 141, 154
Shabazz, 200, 208
Shades, 233, 236, 240
Shadows, 64, 77, 153, 204, 207, 208, 215, 225, 227, 230, 240
Shadows and Light, 204, 207, 208, 215, 230
Shakti, 188, 189, 191, 239
Shaw, Arnold, 84, 150
Shaw, Arthur (Artie), 31
Shaw, Billy, 36
Shea Stadium, 78
Shearing, George, 41, 87
Shepp, Archie, 45, 75, 105, 154
Shine, 230
Shorter, Wayne, 8, 10, 58, 110, 160, 165, 166, 168, 172, 174, 176, 177, 178, 179, 180, 183, 184, 185, 186, 190, 195, 196, 197, 203, 220, 230, 239, 241, 242
Signature, time, 19, 53, 54, 78, 245, 247, 248, 249
Silence, 125, 195, 204
Silhouette, 140
Silk Degrees, 228
Silver, 40, 93, 158, 199, 208, 209, 210, 220
Silver Rain, 220
Silver, Horace, 40, 92, 199, 208, 209, 210
Simon, Carly, 219
Simon, Paul, 136, 137, 138, 154, 208
Simplicity of Expression
  Depth of Thought, 201
Sinatra, Frank, 28
Sinclair, Richard, 83, 102
Sinfonia, Britten, 143
Sing Me Softly of the Blues, 87
Singing / Playing, 231
Sivad, 68
Sketchbook, 209
Sketches, 158, 164, 168
Sketches of Spain, 158, 164
Skidmore, Alan, 104
Skiffle, 63, 153
Sklar, Lee, 200
Slang, 248
Sleepwalk, 231
Sly, 131, 132, 134, 136, 154, 182
Smile, 138, 219
Smith, Jerry, 91
Smith, Jimmy, 106
Smith, Terry, 112
Smooth jazz, 139, 155
So What, 170
Soft Machine, 7, 57, 82, 83, 84, 85, 86, 102, 103, 105, 150, 154
Solitude, 32
Solo Piano - Originals, 196
Solo Piano - Standards, 196
Soloff, Lew, 93
Some Skunk Funk, 144, 209, 210, 242, 243
Someday My Prince Will Come, 168
Something Else, 150

Something Like a Bird, 208
Something More, 178, 185
Something To Remind You, 144
Song of the Sun, 209
Song to a Seagull, 229, 230
Song X, 205
Songs From The Night Before, 210, 213
Sonny, 126, 168, 169, 170, 241
Soon, 24, 38, 67, 90, 109, 127, 133, 139, 165, 202
Sophisticated Lady, 32
Sorcerer, 169, 177, 183, 197
Sorcery, 170, 179, 185
Soul, 17, 112, 130, 175, 177, 183, 210, 221, 222, 223, 225, 226, 227
Soul Axess, 227
Soul Bop, 210, 221, 222, 242
Soul Bop Band Live, 210, 222
Soul Grass, 221, 222
Soul Insider, 222
Soul Shadows, 225, 227
Soulmates, 175
Sound System, 178, 184
South Africa, 138, 227
South, Harry, 112
Southern Comfort, 225, 226, 231
Spaces, 88, 150, 195, 200, 201
Spaces (Infinite), 88
Spaces Revisited, 200, 201
Spain, 43, 158, 164, 168
Speak Like A Child, 108, 183
Speak No Evil, 177, 183, 239
Speaking of Now, 203, 204
Spectrum, 200, 201
Spin, 233, 236
Spirit, 221
Spirit River, 221
Spirits, 201
Spontaneous Music Ensemble, 69
Spotlite, 36
Spring, 197
Spring, Bryan, 104
Springsteen, Bruce, 90
Spyro Gyra, 140, 155, 208, 209
Staccato, 248
Standards and Other Songs, 210
Standing Tall, 219, 225, 227, 231, 240
Stanger, Nigel, 71
Stanley Clarke, 194, 195, 198, 200, 201, 216, 218, 220, 229, 232
Star People, 167, 169, 219, 221
Starfish and the Moon, 222
Steele, Tommy, 64
Steely Dan, 58, 126, 136, 137, 138, 154, 178, 179, 207, 208, 213, 228, 229, 231, 232, 239, 240, 242
Steig, Jeremy, 88, 100, 116
Stein, John, 28
Steiner, Nyle (inventor), 126, 127
Stella by Starlight, 239
Step By Step, 208
Step Lightly, 183
Stephens, John, 69
Steps Ahead, 88, 155, 207, 208, 209
Stern, Leni, 191
Stern, Mike, 93, 142, 167, 208, 209, 210, 213, 215, 223, 234, 237, 240, 242, 243
Stewart, David, 102
Stewart, Sylvester, 131

271

Still Crazy After All These Years, 136, 138, 208
Still Life (Talking), 203, 204
Sting, 80, 135, 136, 166, 238
Stitt, Sonny, 169, 170, 241
Stockhausen, Karlheinz, 75, 106
Stone, Freddie, 132
Stone, Sly, 131, 154, 182
Straight Life, 183
Straight To The Heart, 208, 213, 219, 240
Stranger, 138
Stratus, 201
Strawberry Fields Forever, 74, 121
Strayhorn, Billy, 31
Streamlines, 229
Street Beat, 229
Street Dance, 241
Street Dreams, 210
Street Life, 225, 227, 240
Strikes Twice, 231
Strokin, 208
Stuff Like That, 184
Stump, Paul, 67, 148, 149
Summer, 104, 185, 204, 230
Summer Running, 204
Summers, Andy, 186
Summertime, 221
Summit, 210
Sundance, 195
Sunday, 149
Sunlight, 184, 198, 215
Super Nova, 177, 190
Supergroup, 77, 78, 79, 134, 217, 234
Supernova, 195
Superstition, 133
Surman, John, 190
Suso, Foday Musa, 184
Sutch, Screaming Lord, 80
Swallow, Steve, 87, 205
Sweet Slumber, 177
Sweetnighter, 172
Swing, 7, 17, 28, 31, 32, 153, 178, 184
Swingsters, 224
Switched On Bach, 123
Switzerland, 170
Sydney, 123
Sylvester, 131
Synclavier guitar synthesiser, 125
Syncopated, 144, 246, 248
Synergy, 223
Synthesiser, 118, 121, 122, 123, 124, 125, 126, 127, 154, 174, 182, 189, 235

## T

Take Five, 19
Taking Off, 138, 208, 209, 213
Tale Spinnin, 173
Tales, 201, 204, 209, 219, 241
Tales From the Hudson, 204, 209
Talk That Talk, 226
Talking Book, 122, 135, 212, 213
Taming the Tiger, 230
Tangerine Dream, 123
Tanglewood, 29, 239
Tap Step, 195, 216, 218
Tape, magnetic, 60
Tatum, Arthur, 35, 41, 42, 43

Tauhid, 107
Taylor, Cecil, 45, 75, 84, 105, 154
Taylor, Mick, 71, 72
Tchaikovsky, 61
Te Vous / Praise, 204
Tee, Richard, 138, 208
Temperton, Rod, 182
Tempest, 99, 178, 184
Tenderness, 209
Teo Macero, 166
Texas, 62, 145, 224
The 2nd Crusade, 226, 231
The All Seeing Eye, 177, 183
The Alternative Man, 191, 219, 221, 240
The Answer is Blowing in the Wind, 128
The Anthology, 194, 196, 218
The Art of Five, 201
The Art of Three, 201
The Beginning, 196
The Best of David Sanborn, 213
The Best of Mr 335, 232
The Best Of Return To Forever, 218
The Best of Yellowjackets, 237
The Birthday Concert, 209, 215
The Blue Note Tokyo, 196, 223
The Blues, 239
The Brecker Brothers, 114, 206, 207, 208, 209, 210, 212, 213, 219, 220
The Byrds, 107
The Clash, 154
The Complete Concert 1964, 197
The Crusaders At Their Best, 227
The Crusaders Best, 227
The Dark Side, 122
The Dude, 184
The Elements - Water, 204
The Eleventh House, 209
The Enchantment, 196
The Essence, 242
The Essentials, 213
The Falcon, 204
The Falcon and the Snowman, 204
The Festival Album, 226
The Freedom Rider, 177
The Gambler, 221
The Gambler - Live at the Blue Note Tokyo 2, 221
The Genie, 208
The Gift, 232
The Gigolo, 177
The Golden Years, 227
The Good And Bad Times, 227, 232
The Graduate, 138
The Grass Is Greener, 97
The Greatest Crusade, 227
The Heart of Things, 189
The Herbie Hancock Trio (1977), 198
The Hissing of Summer Lawns, 230
The Inner Mounting Flame, 200
The Inside Story, 232
The Isley Brothers, 90, 132
The JazzTimes Superband, 210
The Joy of Flying, 198, 207, 208
The Larry Carlton Collection Vol 2, 232
The Leprechaun, 195
The London Concert, 209, 210
The Lost Trident Sessions, 201
The Mad Hatter, 195

The Man With The Horn, 169, 221
The Maryanne, 113
The Mask, 241
The Meeting, 195
The Music Inside, 209
The New Crystal Silence, 196
The New Standard, 209
The Night, 208, 209, 210, 213, 219, 231
The Nightfly, 208, 209, 219, 231
The Old Bums Rush, 198
The Other Side of Something, 210, 221, 222
The Ozell Tapes, 220
The Pacific Jazz Quintet Studio Sessions, 227
The Paul Butterfield Blues Band, 213
The Prisoner, 183
The Procrastinator, 177, 183
The Promise, 209, 213
The Quintet, 198
The Rain, 191
The Real Great Escape, 208
The Resurrection of Pigboy Crabshaw, 213
The Rite of Strings, 218
The River, 183
The Road To You, 204, 241
The Royal Scam, 231
The Scene, 92
The Shape of Jazz to Come, 45
The Sign of 4, 204
The Six, 123
The Sky, 76, 169, 177, 178, 183, 184, 240, 241
The Song is You, 196, 205
The Song Of Singing, 195
The Soothsayer, 177, 197
The Sound of 65, 74
The Sound of Summer Running, 204
The Spin, 233, 236, 240
The Spook Who Sat By The Door, 184
The Stix, 143
The Story of Neptune, 198
The Streets of San Francisco, 228
The Sun Don't Lie, 179, 198, 213, 219
The Temptations, 132
The Thing, 226
The Toys of Men, 217, 218
The Traveler, 201
The Turnaround, 183
The Turning Point, 71
The Ultimate Adventure, 196
The Ultimate Compilation, 227
The Very Best of, 209, 210, 213, 220, 229, 232
The Very Best of Larry Carlton, 232
The Very Best of Tom Scott, 229
The Vocal Album, 227
The Way Up, 4, 10, 15, 203, 205
The Way Up Live, 205
The Who, 58, 77
The Witch Doctor, 177
The Word is Out, 215
The Zone, 223
Them Changes, 229
Then And Now, 186
There Goes Rhymin' Simon, 138
Thielemans, Toots, 138
Things We Like, 190
Third Plane, 184, 198, 239
This Here, 175
This is This, 173

Thomas, Gary, 204
Thompson, Barbara, 95, 97
Thornburg, Lee, 137
Those Southern Nights, 226, 231
Those Who Are About to Die Salute You, 95
Three Blind Mice, 177
Three Quartets, 195, 208
Thriller, 124, 137, 182
Thunder, 217, 218, 220
Tight, 37, 132, 136, 249
Till We Have Faces, 204
Timbre, 18, 24, 46, 121, 249
Time After Time, 170, 171
Time Exposure, 218
Time In Place, 208
Time is of the Essence, 204, 209
Time Out, 19
Time Remembered, 191
Time Squared, 234, 237, 242
Time Warp, 196
Timeagain, 210, 213
Timeline, 51, 153, 237, 243
Times Like These, 208
Timmons, Bobby, 177
Tippett, Keith, 85, 103
To The One, 15, 143, 190, 192, 243
To the Stars, 194, 196, 223
Today and Tomorrow, 232
Toe to Toe, 209, 210
Tokyo Day Trip, 205
Tokyo Live, 198
Tom Cat, 228
Tom Scott and LA Express, 228
Tones For Joan's Bones, 195
Tony Williams, 8, 47, 56, 79, 99, 109, 141, 165, 177,
    178, 183, 184, 185, 188, 190, 192, 197, 198, 204,
    207, 208, 209, 215, 216, 217, 218, 239, 242
Tony Williams Lifetime, 47, 184, 190, 198
Total Eclipse, 200, 208, 209, 239
Touch, 221, 222
Touchstone, 185, 195, 216, 218
Tough Talk, 226
Tough Talk , 226
Tower of Power, 137
Towns, Colin, 29, 201
Townsend, Pete, 149
Toys, 217, 218, 243
Tracks, 186, 235
Traditional (Dixieland) Jazz, 33
Trains, 204
Transition, 223
Travelogue, 230
Travels, 204, 240
Tremolo, 18, 249, 250
Trethewey, Ken, 1, 2, 4, 5, 50, 75, 150, 151, 180, 181,
    193, 199, 202, 205, 211, 220, 222, 224, 227, 237
Tribute, 169, 178, 184, 185, 190, 198, 200
Trieste, 158
Trifan, Danny, 93
Trinity, 69, 112
Trio 99-00, 204
Trio Live, 204
Trio Music, 195, 196
Trio Music Live In Europe, 196
Trio of Doom, 195, 215
Tubular Bells, 123
Turbulent Indigo, 230

Turn It Over, 198
Turrentine, Stanley, 183
Tutu, 167, 169, 219, 220, 240
Twentieth Century Masters - The Millenium Collection, 232
Twenty Five, 234, 237
Twins, 242
Two Against Nature, 242
Two Blocks from the Edge, 209
Two T's, 209
Tyner, McCoy, 177, 217, 219

## U

Uberjam, 242
Uehara, Hiromi, 196
Ugetsu, 177
Uh Huh, 226
Ulanov, Barry, 38
Underground, 78
United, 2, 14, 22, 54, 101, 103, 116, 199, 203, 229, 243
Unity, 142, 205, 218
Universal, 191, 230, 238
Unsung Heroes, 226
Upfront, 210, 213, 219
Upojenie, 205
Upside Downside, 213, 215, 223, 240
Uptown Conversation, 183
Urbaniak, Michal, 185
Uriel, 102

## V

V.S.O.P., 178, 184, 198, 240
Valeria, 158
Vamp, 168, 248, 249
Vandross, Luther, 219
VanGelder, Rudy, 199
Vangelis, 122
Vangelis,, 122
Vanoni, Ornella, 184
Vans Joint, 222
Vaughan, Sarah, 38
Venn diagram, 53, 54, 55, 56, 57, 115, 160, 162, 182
Vertigo, 85, 104, 183
Verve, 42, 159
Very Best of the Crusaders, 227
Vibe, 249
Vibrafinger, 88
Vibrato, 18, 24, 124, 127, 249, 250
Vicious, Sid, 48
Vietnam War, 105
Village Gate (jazz club), 103, 114
Vinnie Colaiuta, 135, 136, 142, 196
Vinyl disc, 61, 129, 146, 155
Virgin Forest, 186
Vitous, Miroslav, 88, 172, 175, 183, 190, 191
Vocoder, 182
Vodry, Will, 30
Voices, 209
Voicing, 250
Voyage, 93, 195, 197
Voyeur, 212, 213, 219, 229

## W

Wakeman, Rick, 122

Walden, Narada Michael, 178
Walker, David T., 232
Walking In The Park, 96
Wanderlust, 208
Warfield, Bill, 210
Warner Bros., 185, 231, 232, 234
Washington Jr, Grover, 219
Washington, Dinah, 175
Water, 138, 169, 178, 184, 195, 198, 204
Water Babies, 169, 178, 184, 195, 198
Watercolors, 204
Waterfall, 113
Watermelon Man, 181, 186
Watson, Bernie, 80
Watts, Charlie, 70
Way Back Home, 227
Wayning Moments, 177
We Live Here, 144, 203, 204, 241
We Live Here - Live in Japan, 204
We Want Miles, 219, 221
Weather Report, 4, 8, 10, 47, 58, 93, 108, 141, 146, 151, 154, 172, 173, 174, 175, 176, 177, 178, 179, 180, 181, 198, 209, 210, 213, 214, 215, 220, 239, 240, 242, 243
Weather Report (band), 4
Weather Report 2, 173, 215
Webb, Tom, 91
Weber, Eberhard, 204
Webster, Ben, 30, 44, 175
Webster, Freddie, 37
Weckl, Dave, 8, 142, 196, 209, 210, 222, 223, 241, 242
Weiss, Jerry, 92
Welch, Bruce, 64
Wertico, Paul, 204
West Coast, 117, 224, 228, 231
What It Is, 209
Where Fortune Smiles, 190
Where Have I Known You Before, 194, 195
Whiplash Smile, 219
White, 4, 10, 117, 194, 195, 196, 202, 207, 208, 216, 217, 218, 220
White Elephant, 207, 208
White, Lenny, 194, 216, 217
White, Michael, 117
Whitehead, Neville, 104
Whitfield, Norman, 132
Who Let the Cats Out?, 223
Wichita, 204
Wide Angles, 209
Wikipedia, 50, 52, 53, 57, 87, 116, 119, 139, 149, 150, 151, 152
Wilburn, Vincent, 167
Wild Things Run Fast, 230, 231
Wilde Flowers, 83, 102
Wilderness, 197, 198, 204, 209, 217, 218
Wilen, Barney, 170
Williams, Anthony, 8, 47, 56, 79, 99, 109, 141, 165, 177, 178, 183, 184, 185, 188, 190, 192, 197, 198, 204, 207, 208, 209, 215, 216, 217, 218, 239, 242
Williams, Cootie, 30, 42
Williams, John, 43, 158, 759
Williams, Larry, 137
Williams, Lawrence Lowell, 137
Williams, Paul, 99
Wilson, Nancy, 175
Wind Cries Mary, 80
Windows, 168, 184, 208

Winelight, 219
Winwood, Stevie, 79
With A Little Help From My Friends, 231
Withers, Bill, 225
Wonder, Stevie, 122, 132, 135, 154, 184, 212, 213
Wood, Chris, 80
Woods, Phil, 136, 138
Wooten, Victor, 217, 218, 220, 236
Word of Mouth, 208, 215, 220, 229
Works, 195, 204, 208, 215
Works II, 204, 208, 215
World music, 47, 174
Wright, Elmon, 37
Wrong is Right, 88
Wyatt, Robert, 63, 82, 83, 84, 86, 103, 104, 150
Wyman, Bill, 70

# Y

Yamaha (instrument manufacturer), 127
Yardbirds, 70, 71, 79
Yellow Submarine, 135
Yellowjackets, 8, 20, 140, 155, 232, 233, 234, 236, 237, 238, 240, 241, 242, 243
Yes, Then Yes, 241
Yesterday, 89
You Gotta Take a Little Love, 199
Young at Heart, 198
Young Rabbits, 226
Young, Jesse Colin, 135, 154
Young, Lester, 36, 170
Young, Lester Willis, 36, 170
Young, Neil, 229
Young, Reggie, 80

# Z

Zakir, 191
Zappa, Frank, 72, 124, 217
Zawinul, 46, 172, 173, 174, 215
Zawinul, Josef, 8, 10, 47, 108, 110, 141, 142, 144, 151, 152, 155, 160, 165, 168, 172, 174, 175, 176, 177, 179, 183, 190, 214, 241, 242, 243
Zero Tolerance for Silence, 204